CITIZENSHIP AND
NATIONAL IDENTITY IN
TWENTIETH-CENTURY GERMANY

Citizenship and National Identity in Twentieth-Century Germany

Edited by GEOFF ELEY and JAN PALMOWSKI

STANFORD UNIVERSITY PRESS

STANFORD, CALIFORNIA

2008

Stanford University Press
Stanford, California

Printed in the United States of America on acid-free, archival-quality paper

Library of Congress Cataloging-in-Publication Data
Citizenship and national identity in twentieth-century Germany / edited by
Geoff Eley and Jan Palmowski.
    p. cm.
    "This book is based on papers delivered at a conference on 'Citizenship and
National Identity in Twentieth-Century Germany'"—Acknowledgments.
    Includes bibliographical references and index.
    ISBN 978-0-8047-5204-6 (cloth : alk. paper)—ISBN 978-0-8047-5205-3 (pbk. : alk.
paper)
    1. Germany—History—20th century.   2. Citizenship—Germany—History—
20th century.   3. Nationalism—Germany—History—20th century.   I. Eley,
Geoff, 1949–   II. Palmowski, Jan.
DD232.c58 2008
323.60943'0904—dc22   2007029132

Typeset by Newgen–Austin in 10/12.5 Palatino

Contents

Contributors

Peter C. Caldwell is Professor of History at Rice University in Houston, Texas. He is the author of *Popular Sovereignty and the Crisis of German Constitutional Law* (University of North Carolina Press, 1997) and *Dictatorship, State Planning, and Social Theory in the German Democratic Republic* (Cambridge University Press, 2003). He is currently at work on problems of love, death, and revolution in mid-nineteenth-century Germany.

Kathleen Canning is Professor of History and Women's Studies at the University of Michigan. She is the author of *Languages of Labor and Gender: Female Factory Work in Germany, 1850–1914* (Cornell University Press, 1996; University of Michigan Press, 2002) and *Gender History in Practice: Historical Perspectives on Bodies, Class and Citizenship* (Cornell University Press, 2006). She is also the coeditor with Kerstin Barndt and Kristin McGuire of the essay collection *Weimar Publics/Weimar Subjects* (Berghahn, 2006). Her current book project is entitled *Embodied Citizenships: Gender and the Crisis of Nation in Germany, 1918–1930*.

Geoff Eley is the Karl Pohrt Distinguished University Professor of Contemporary History, Professor of History and German Studies, at the University of Michigan, Ann Arbor. His recent publications include *Forging Democracy: The History of the Left in Europe, 1850–2000* (Oxford University Press, 2002), and *A Crooked Line: From Cultural History to the History of Society* (University of Michigan Press, 2005). He is currently working on *The Twentieth Century, 1914–2000*, Volume V of the new *Cambridge History of Europe*. He is also completing a book titled *Liberalism, the National State, and Popular Politics in Germany, 1860–1900*.

Dieter Gosewinkel is director of the research project on Civil Society, Citizenship and Political Mobilization in Europe at the Social Science Research Center Berlin (Wissenschaftszentrum Berlin für Sozialforschung). His published work on the history of citizenship in Germany includes *Einbürgern und Ausschließen: Die Nationalisierung der Staatsangehörigkeit vom Deutschen Bund bis zur Bundesrepublik Deutschland* (Vandenhoeck und Ruprecht, 2001).

Pascal Grosse is a historian and neurologist at Humboldt University, Berlin. He has published *Kolonialismus und bürgerliche Gesellschaft in Deutschland, 1850–1918* (Campus, 2000). He currently is working on a project titled "The Gendered Brain: Neurobiology, Sexuality, and Bourgeois Order, 1750–1900" while also conducting research on cerebral citizenship.

Jennifer Jenkins is Associate Professor of History and Canada Research Chair in Modern German History at the University of Toronto. She has published on modernism and politics, including *Provincial Modernity: Local Culture and Liberal Politics in Fin-de-Siècle Hamburg* (Cornell University Press, 2003). Her current projects include a study of architecture and national memory in twentieth-century Germany and a book-length project on Germany and Iran from 1906 to 1979.

Thomas Lindenberger is project director at the Zentrum für Zeithistorische Forschung Potsdam and teaches at Potsdam University. He has published on German *Alltagsgeschichte* and politics, including *Straßenpolitik: Zur Sozialgeschichte der öffentlichen Ordnung, 1900–1914* (Dietz, 1995) and *Volkspolizei: Herrschaftspraxis und öffentliche Ordnung im SED-Staat, 1952–1968* (Böhlau, 2003). He is currently completing an edited volume on mass media in the Cold War.

Jan Palmowski is Senior Lecturer and Head of the School of Humanities, King's College London. He has published on nineteenth- and twentieth-century politics and culture, including *Urban Liberalism in Imperial Germany: Frankfurt am Main, 1866–1914* (Oxford University Press, 1999). He has worked on the construction of local identity in the GDR, and is completing a book on *Socialist Patriotism in Everyday Life: Power and Identity in the GDR, 1945–1990*.

Annemarie Sammartino is Assistant Professor of History at Oberlin College. She is currently completing a book entitled *Utopia, Exile, and Crisis: Migration in Germany, 1914–1922*.

Toby Thacker is a Lecturer at Cardiff University. He has published several articles about music and politics in Germany, and is the author of *Music after Hitler, 1945–1955* (Ashgate, 2007). He is also working on the formation of new social elites in post-Nazi Germany.

Cornelie Usborne is the author of *The Politics of the Body: Women's Reproductive Rights and Duties* (University of Michigan Press, 1992), and she has coedited a book on *Cultural Approaches to the History of Medicine: Mediating Medicine in Early Modern and Modern Europe* (Palgrave, 2004). A Reader at Roehampton University, she is completing two books, *Women and Nazism: Agents and Victims* and *Cultures of Abortion in Weimar Germany*.

Adelheid von Saldern was Professor for Modern History at the University of Hanover before she retired in 2004. She has published on nineteenth- and twentieth-century social, urban, and cultural history, including the media. A collection of her articles appeared as *The Challenge of Modernity: German Social and Cultural Studies, 1890–1960* (Michigan University Press, 2002). Most recently, she edited two volumes on city representations, one on GDR cities (*Inszenierte Einigkeit*, Steiner, 2003) and the other on cities in three German societies (*Inszenierter Stolz 1935–1975*, Steiner, 2003).

S. Jonathan Wiesen is Associate Professor of History at Southern Illinois University Carbondale. He has published on West German business, transatlantic relations, and historical memory after World War II, including *West German Industry and the Challenge of the Nazi Past, 1945–1955* (University of North Carolina Press, 2001). He is currently working on a book about business leaders, consumer culture, and debates about "mass society" during the Third Reich.

Acknowledgments

THIS BOOK IS BASED ON papers delivered at the conference "Citizenship and National Identity in Twentieth-Century Germany," held at Lady Margaret Hall, Oxford, UK, on September 10–12, 2004. We wish to acknowledge our gratitude to those bodies and institutions that made this project possible through their generous funding. First and foremost, the Arts and Humanities Research Council (AHRC) sponsored a research project on constitutional evolution and national identity in twentieth-century Germany at King's College London, and this conference presented some of the project's major conclusions. The Gerda-Henkel Foundation provided crucial additional funding, without which this conference could not have allowed the genuine transatlantic dialogue that we wanted to facilitate. Finally, we are grateful to the Department of History at the University of Michigan (Ann Arbor) and the Department of German at King's College London, as both of these institutions provided further valuable funds for the conference. We would like to thank Alexander Heinz (King's College London) for his professional and efficient help with the conference organization. Furthermore, Alexander Heinz and Mary O'Reilly (University of Michigan) helped in the preparation of the manuscript, and we are grateful to both for their reliable and perceptive help. Finally, Jan Palmowski would like to express his appreciation to his codirector in the AHRC-funded project, Chris Thornhill, for his collegiality and support throughout, and to Martin Jones who, as head of department, provided generous advice and guidance throughout the project.

CITIZENSHIP AND

NATIONAL IDENTITY IN

TWENTIETH-CENTURY GERMANY

Introduction

Citizenship and National Identity in Twentieth-Century Germany

GEOFF ELEY AND JAN PALMOWSKI

HISTORIANS HAVE HAD A DIFFICULT RELATIONSHIP with notions of citizenship and identity, each of which recently has enjoyed widespread attention in sociology, anthropology, and the political sciences. For example, political scientists began returning in the 1980s to T. H. Marshall's influential model of citizenship, somewhat to the surprise of social historians, who had subjected such ideas to extensive critique during the preceding decades.[1] Writing in 1949, Marshall observed a close relationship among civic, political, and social rights. Citizenship denoted to Marshall "full membership of the human community"; whereas civic and class equality moved in opposite directions during the early development of capitalism, an expansion of rights during the twentieth century led to an equalization of opportunity that affected social as much as civic and political rights.[2] Marshall's contention that social welfare was conducive to citizenship was challenged under the transformed political and economic environment of the Reagan and Thatcher eras. A number of scholars from the "New Right" argued that social rights dampened individual initiative for the community.[3] Marshall's explanation that citizenship rights had developed as an interdependent corollary to modern capitalism also came under attack. Critics raised the question of agency, because it was clear neither how this apparently automatic relationship came about nor which individuals or groups were at the forefront of this expanded notion of citizenship.

A further influential concept of citizenship, that developed by Jürgen Habermas, has been challenged over the past two decades. Like Marshall, Habermas noted a close relationship between citizenship and social welfare. However, Habermas argued that the growing state intervention that social welfare entailed made individuals unable, as citizens, to stand at a critical distance to the state. What was lacking, from his perspective, was the distinct public sphere that had existed during the seventeenth and eighteenth centuries, when citizens debated, and thus identified with and took responsibility for, the common weal. At that time, private interests were contested in the public sphere, and this formed the basis of state action. By contrast, in modern states, and particularly in the welfare democracy of the Federal Republic of Germany, the bureaucratic state directly interfered in the private sphere. The public sphere thus encouraged individuals into passivity, a passivity that was reinforced by the emergence of new discursive contexts, notably the mass media.[4] Habermas's ideal of the seventeenth- and eighteenth-century public sphere later was challenged by a range of studies that demonstrated the exclusivity of this civil society, which was predicated on the inequality of Jews and women, to name but two disadvantaged groups.[5] The public sphere that Habermas had idealized was, in fact, heavily contested among different groups that sought to appropriate the ideal of the public sphere to register their own claims for social and political domination.[6]

The end of the Cold War provided a further and decisive catalyst in debates in the social sciences about citizenship. New states emerged, often violently, as nationalism revived in many parts of the world. At the same time, globalization and enhanced communications enabled and promoted the articulation of multiple identities across borders. The consequent ascendancy of "multiculturalism" greatly complicated any understanding of entitlements, and rendered all the more necessary clear concepts of universal as well as equal rights.[7] Citizenship not only allowed a better understanding of questions of inclusion and exclusion or of the actual acquisition of rights and duties as it pertained to each group; its evaluation also provided a common denominator for comparing the rights and entitlements of different groups in relation to each other.

In response to the end of the Cold War, scholars began to reconsider the significance of formal citizenship. As political scientist Rogers Brubaker has pointed out, neither state institutions nor national borders could be taken for granted in the history of continental Europe; hence, the evolving nature of formal citizenship required further investigation.[8] Only citizens enjoyed a full set of privileges. The evolution and the nature of formal citizenship rights thus were crucial, especially for those to whom they were denied, notably immigrants.[9] Indeed, the concept of formal citizenship underwent dramatic change. The inception of a European Union citizenship that was both distinct and yet conditional on citizenship of an EU member state introduced the prospect of multiple types of citizenship, even in a formal sense.[10]

Following an increasingly wide application of the citizenship concept, most social scientists have observed a distinction between "thin" and "thick" conceptions of citizenship. Scholars interested in the former have been concerned with the development and contestation of citizenship as legal status; that is, how different groups vie for recognition before the law for their ability to exercise legal and formal citizenship rights in theory and in practice. Such perspectives have been complemented by investigations into "thick" conceptions of citizenship, or what Charles Tilly has described as "citizenship as role."[11] The focus here has been on the constructedness of citizenship through cultural artifacts, action, and communication. Although the political, legal, and institutional agendas of individual groups have remained in focus, scholars in this area have been interested in how social groups relate to each other in the attainment of these goals and how they construct their own self-understandings and mutual ties.[12]

Citizenship has come to address questions that are central to the social sciences. The concept has been used as a framework to determine how different groups define and contest their identities in relation to each other and to the state. Citizenship has also been seen as a concept through which the changing functions of the state could be understood; for example, how the transformation of the welfare system affected the relationship between state and citizen. A further important theme in this context has been the basis that citizenship has provided for the allocation of resources and participation rights to immigrants, an issue of particular note to scholars concerned with the legitimacy of political systems and the ethical basis of political membership.[13] Indeed, the political debates surrounding citizenship rights and immigration could present major challenges to the stability of political systems, for instance, by invigorating populist right-wing parties.[14]

The concern with citizenship has brought about some cross-disciplinary work between social scientists and historians. After all, both Habermas and Marshall founded their citizenship concepts upon a model of historical evolution that turned out to be assumed rather than proven.[15] The multiplication of citizenship rights between the nation-state and the EU, for instance, has important and enlightening parallels in the past that could contribute to an understanding of citizenship in its current dimensions.[16] History is significant not just for understanding citizenship but for the construction of citizenship itself, because history and historical memory have an important impact on the formation of group identities relative to the state and to each other.[17]

In turn, the proliferation of debates about citizenship in the social sciences has impacted upon historical debate, and this has affected German historiography. In 1992, Rogers Brubaker published his influential contention that German and French citizenship laws were effectively created in the early nineteenth century, and that both represented diametrically opposite definitions of identity, one based on ethnicity (*ius sanguinis*), the other on culture and territorial belonging (*ius soli*). This spurred a number of important historical investigations, all of which demonstrated that Brubaker's historical trajectory failed to stand up to closer historical scrutiny. Andreas Fahrmeir was the first to provide a sustained historical investigation in this regard. He noted that individual German states defined citizenship until well into the nineteenth century. Indeed, a German citizenship law did not come into effect until 1913, and even after that date individual states retained important rights to interpret and execute the law's provisions, as Annemarie Sammartino shows in her contribution to this book. Fahrmeir argued that for much of the nineteenth century neither ethnicity nor cultural attributes were particularly important in the granting of citizenship in Germany, and that Germany was not particularly distinctive in this regard.[18]

The debate about Brubaker's work was continued by further examinations of Germany and France. Patrick Weil has shown that the influential Prussian citizenship law of 1842 was inspired significantly by the French Civil Code of 1803. The French changed their definition of citizenship to elevate the significance of birth in 1889, and not until 1927 did French citizenship law become relatively open to the naturalization of foreigners.[19] In his magisterial study of the evolution of German citizenship law during the nineteenth and twentieth centuries, Dieter Gosewinkel has underlined that ethnicity was not the sole criterion for the attribution of citizenship until 1933. The importance of ethnicity in the Federal Republic of Germany was constructed (pace Brubaker) not in continuation of, but as an atonement for, the uncharacteristic use of race as the sole criterion of citizenship during the Third Reich.[20] Gosewinkel's rich findings have been supported by more recent work that confirms the ambiguity of German citizenship laws before 1933.[21]

If citizenship was a historical reflection of German and French identity constructions, then this identity of the national community and of how it related to outsiders was clearly much more complex than Brubaker suggested.

In addition to considering in detail the history of citizenship in its "thin" conceptions as legal status, historians have begun to examine the "thick" dimensions of citizenship in German history. As scholars explored the fluidity and complexity of concepts like class, gender, and ethnicity, citizenship became an important category through which the meanings of these constructions could be reconfigured.[22] On this basis, Kathleen Canning has suggested that we can arrive at a more complex understanding of both citizenship and gender if we focus on the subjectivities of contemporary discourses and constructions of inclusion and exclusion.[23] Taking up this argument, Geoff Eley has argued that the perspective of citizenship, understood as the "set of practices—juridical, political, economic, and cultural—which define a person or through which persons define themselves as competent members of society" could provide a new paradigm for understanding the history of Wilhelmine Germany.[24] Such a perspective could encompass notions that otherwise seem contradictory, such as the continued, and in many respects increasing, importance both of the locality and the nation; the evolving relationship between the private and the public spheres; and the coexistence of stasis and change.[25]

In addition to the debates concentrating on the specific dimensions of citizenship, there has been a proliferation of studies that relate closely to the citizenship concept. One is the fruitful use that scholars have made of the notion of the public sphere—or rather of a framework that emphasizes the contestation of distinct but interrelated public spheres—as a space in which cultural, denominational, and social constructions interact to produce political outcomes and enable political claims to be made. Kate Lacey has shown how German public broadcasting in its first two decades reconfigured and invigorated contestations of the public sphere and created new boundaries of exclusion between the public and the private, boundaries that responded to, and in turn helped reconstruct, gender divides.[26] Moreover, Madeleine Hurd has explored some of the links between cultural contestations of the public sphere and political outcomes. Her pioneering book demonstrates the pervasive influence of bourgeois cultural, behavioral, and moral norms on gender roles in Hamburg and Stockholm, as well as on the politics and culture of the working classes.[27] As other work has confirmed, the public sphere can be a useful tool for reconceptualizing rivalrous political debates in relation to each other.[28] Analyzing political contestation in the public sphere can present a new—and, at present, surprisingly lacking—understanding of how political parties construct their actions and arguments relative to each other.[29]

Another intimately related area is the growing interest in migration and the integration of foreigners. Migration and immigration were central to the political, cultural, and economic dynamic of the Federal Republic of Germany. Indeed, recent work on migration has been so important precisely because it analyzes how public and political debates about citizenship are linked to the cultural reception of immigrants and their successor generations in Germany. Scholars have shown how an analysis of state policies concerned with groups "at the margin" offers important insights not just on citizenship as such but also on the nature of the state more generally.[30] For instance, Karin Schönwälder has demonstrated that the West German reception of foreign "guest workers" from the 1960s up until 1973 cannot be considered in isolation but was integrally linked to cultural constructions of the "economic miracle" and to the political goals of Western integration.[31] In terms of the German Democratic Republic, analyses of how the state attempted to micromanage relations between citizens and foreigners have been highly instructive in examining its understanding of citizenship and the nature of the state more generally. Relatively few foreigners were resident in East Germany, and the state did its best to keep them residentially and even culturally separate from its citizens. However, this clearly demarcated "otherness" added to the allure that many of these foreigners were considered to have by the population.[32] The attempted exclusion of foreigners thus offers important insight into the ambiguities that characterized the relationship between the state and its citizens. For both East and West Germany after 1945, this work about immigration and the (lack of) integration of foreigners suggests that an exploration of the interrelationship between "thick" and "thin" conceptions of citizenship can provide a much richer and fuller understanding of the complexities of modern German history.

*   *   *

There are good grounds for considering in broader terms whether, and how, citizenship can provide a framework for an understanding of modern German history, and how historians might consider citizenship in relation to the state and to the nation. This book takes up this challenge, as its contributors explore a variety of major themes of twentieth-century German history through the lens of citizenship. The contributions can be roughly divided into three broad categories. The first takes as its starting point the historical evolution, construction, and application of the political-legal concept of citizenship, of *Staatsangehörigkeit* or *Staatsbürgerschaft*. The second begins its line of inquiry in scientific, cultural, political, and economic debates and asks how they impacted on, and were defined by, citizenship. What unites these chapters is a common concern to explore the interrelationship between political-legal and cultural constructions of citizenship. Finally, if the first two sections of this book attempt to complicate our understanding of citizenship in relation to the state and to the nation, the authors in the third section seek to place the concept of citizenship more generally in the study of modern German history. The authors draw on the work presented in the first two sections but go beyond it by reflecting on the possibilities and the limits of the concept in relation to how individuals seek to identify themselves and how the German nation tends to be constructed.

Dieter Gosewinkel opens the first part of this book by investigating more closely the interplay among cultural, social, and national debates as important factors in determining the outcome of political-legal definitions of citizenship. Through a comparison with France, which introduces the work of Patrick Weil to an English-language readership, Gosewinkel confirms that official conceptions of citizenship among German state personnel were very close to those of French bureaucrats for much of the nineteenth century. If from the late nineteenth century the two countries began to diverge in their definitions of citizenship and practices of naturalization, this was in response to different challenges of immigration and different political conditions. As Gosewinkel argues, it was the weakness of the German state, rather than any aggressive notion of ethnicity, that prompted officials to define the national community increasingly through culture rather than place of birth.

Peter C. Caldwell focuses more specifically on the constructions and challenges of citizenship in the Weimar Republic. His chapter explores the mutually reinforcing tensions between different theoretical conceptions of citizenship and the social and cultural contestations of citizenship claims to which they gave rise. Caldwell shows that definitions of citizenship, the relationship between individuals and the state, were constantly renegotiated and that this was directly reflected in the political theory of the Weimar Republic. He demonstrates that citizenship is not an ahistorical construct borrowed from the social sciences but that contestations of identities and individual groups both against each other and in relation to the state were integrally linked to the survival of the Weimar Republic.

Annemarie Sammartino complements Peter Caldwell's analysis of the Weimar Republic and Dieter Gosewinkel's exploration of the genesis of the German citizenship law by concentrating on the citizenship debates triggered by disputed cases of naturalization. These cases represent the juncture at which citizenship was contested directly and concretely among political leaders, administrators, the individuals concerned, and their community environment. Sammartino's rich tapestry of the motivations and interests that determined the final outcomes does more than demonstrate the fluidity and openness of citizenship constructions during the Weimar Republic. It also determines more clearly which attributes of citizenship were contested and which were universally accepted among those who sought belonging through citizenship. Her chapter points in tangible ways to the importance of regional bias in terms of how citizenship was contested in Germany, at least until 1934.

Jan Palmowski considers the interface between the ideal of citizenship of state and party, and the impact of such constructions on popular practice at the local level for a very different political context, the German Democratic Republic. Citizenship became a crucial category in the self-representation of the GDR because it brought together individual belonging to the state and the ideological goal of a socialist community. At the same time, the party was fully aware that the ideal of the socialist citizen could only be realized at the grassroots, in the daily encounters of the individual with the local community and the administration. For this reason, the state instituted a variety of procedures for "socialist" conflict resolution, which were primarily local in nature. There is no evidence, however, that these procedures managed to reconcile the individual citizen and the state. In practice, Palmowski contends, socialist citizenship did promote a feeling of local togetherness and belonging but not, on the whole, in ways that solidified feelings of identification between citizens and the state.

The contributions to the first part of this book demonstrate that political-legal definitions of citizenship formed a critical arena in which attributes of belonging were contested. At the same time, they show in different yet complementary forms that such contestations cannot be grasped without considering the cultural, social, and political identifications and representations to which they referred. The chapters that follow explore political and cultural contestations more directly and consider how these related to perceptions of citizenship. They examine how communities of citizens were constructed, who was to be included in them, and what rights and duties such membership would entail.

Jennifer Jenkins considers the relationship between citizenship and culture by exploring how cultural constructions of citizenship could be mediated and popularized. At the beginning of the twentieth century, influential members of the *Werkbund* sought to "thicken" the meanings of citizenship through taste, developing an interior style that was to define culturally the meaning of citizenship and belonging. Interestingly, this perception of cultural citizenship also had an important pedagogic dimension and entailed a strong commitment to the contestation and transformation of contemporary popular tastes.

Thomas Lindenberger turns the analytical focus back to the relationship between citizenship and the state. He is less concerned about the politics of citizenship as such than about the relationship between citizenship and the law, notably its application. Understanding police action, he contends, remains superficial and one-dimensional if it is considered merely in statistical, quantitative ways. The enforcement of the law responds to cultural codes both in the police force and in the public sphere. The protection and enforcement of citizenship rights thus is decisively if subtly impacted by a dialectic between evolving codes of camaraderie within the police force (which continues to limit the application of legal norms) and developing public expectations about the inviolability of the human body.

Cornelie Usborne's work similarly demonstrates the interdependence between contested cultural norms and political-legal definitions of citizenship rights. She focuses on gendered contestations around political rights, an issue integral to any notion of citizenship. More specifically, Usborne explores the campaigns to decriminalize abortion from the late Empire to the Weimar Republic. These debates are highly revelatory of contemporary perceptions of the body politic and especially of women's ability to impact political decisions. By discussing the political and legal debates leading up to and surrounding the abortion laws that were eventually instituted in 1927, Usborne not only throws a remarkably positive light on the implications of the new law enshrined in §218 of the Criminal Code but also shows how the debates reflected, and in turn helped shape, attitudes about sexuality, the body, and ultimately the place of female belonging to the body politic, the German community in state and nation. Delineating important continuities emerging from Imperial Germany, her focus on evolving definitions of the female body in relation to the body politic allows Usborne to reconsider the relationship between continuity and rupture before and after World War I.

S. Jonathan Wiesen broadens the perspective of how the community of citizens could be defined and contested, focusing on company public relations during the Third Reich, when both consumption and citizenship rights were severely constrained. Wiesen embeds his detailed account of the Henkel company in a broader history of business practices to show how companies helped translate Nazi racial ideals into practice through their public relations and, in doing so, reinforced them. At the same time, companies pursued their own agendas of promoting private consumption and personal fulfillment against Nazi ideals of individuals putting the community, the *Volk*, above all else. Such individual spaces helped stabilize the regime by suggesting a sense of normality, even though, as Wiesen notes, they provided poor substitutes for political rights and legal protection.

Finally in this section, Toby Thacker expands our horizon beyond political-legal considerations of citizenship back to the cultural domain, perhaps an arena that is particularly suited to comparative perspectives on different political systems. Thacker argues that music had an important role in constructing citizenship through determining who was to be accepted into the national community. In the GDR, he shows, active and passive musical appreciation became an integral part of the socialist citizenship ideal. Culture—in this case, music—thus became an essential determinant of inclusion. Conversely, music could also provide an important context for strategies of exclusion. As the Third Reich showed with particular clarity, music added meanings and attributes to a concept that constituted the legal and cultural basis of citizenship under National Socialism, the *Volk*.

This book's first section seeks to demonstrate the fruitfulness of going beyond the straightforward relationship between the political-legal evolution of citizenship and national identity suggested so forcefully by Brubaker. Only by looking more closely at how citizenship came to be contested in political debate and at the local level can we uncover the self-identifications of Germans in relation to citizenship that Brubaker was apparently more inclined to take for granted. The book's second section builds on these findings by broadening the scope of the analysis. Identifications of Germany as a community of citizens existed even where languages of citizenship might not have prevailed, such as in the political debates of the Weimar Republic or in the cultural constructions of what it meant to be a citizen living in the GDR. Once we begin exploring the impact of citizenship upon gendered, social, cultural, and local self-identifications, we can begin to see how it might extend beyond the narrower institutional understandings of the German nation in the latter's more familiar political and legal definitions. This has profound implications for our understanding of the relationship between citizenship and nationhood. Acknowledging the importance of that relationship, the authors contributing to the final section of this book also explore ways in which citizenship may depart from, complicate, or disobey the forms of identification that nationhood seems to require or ascribe. Understandings of citizenship may fall outside the terms of the especially powerful social, political, and cultural imaginary that the idea of the nation entails. Forms of citizenship and national belonging do not always map straightforwardly or comfortably onto one another.

Pascal Grosse takes a radically different approach to citizenship by analyzing how ideals of citizenship and agency were framed through biopolitical assumptions. Grosse shows how, from the eighteenth century, the brain was regarded as the core of the human being. It determined volition and self-control, notions that underwrote nineteenth-century bourgeois perceptions of the citizenship ideal. The brain also became central to the contentious interplay of race, gender, and sexuality, issues that became central to constructions and challenges of citizenship. Exploring citizenship from this biopolitical vantage point provides a broad and complex perspective through which constructions of state, entitlement, and public spheres can be analyzed and understood beyond the nation-state, a finding of crucial relevance for our grasp of how citizenship might be related to the Third Reich.

Adelheid von Saldern reflects on the conference debates preceding these articles, as well as on the articles themselves, in order to present her own evaluation of the relationship between citizenship and German history. She underlines that the analytical value of citizenship is relational, and this allows citizenship to provide a common vocabulary for conceptualizing the relationship of different kinds of agents, different geographical spheres, and different historical fields. This is a point that has often been made in the political sciences but that historians have scarcely begun to address. Von Saldern reinforces a central argument of this book: citizenship provides a common denominator that complicates our understanding of the interdependent relationship between politics and culture while enabling a transcendence of hitherto distinct historical fields and perspectives.

Kathleen Canning's commentary reaffirms a central thesis of her own work on citizenship—although long assumed to coincide with each other or possess an equivalence, national identity and participatory citizenship need to be uncoupled and clearly distinguished. Examinations of citizenship in its meanings across political, legal, institutional, and cultural spheres, she suggests, invite us to reconsider citizenship as a relational category, whose effectivities and consequences require a range of differing analytical approaches. Beyond its more familiar relationship to national identity and the nation, citizenship makes possible a much more complex understanding of the "disparate spaces and sites of citizenship, but also its temporal framing."

In his concluding contribution, Geoff Eley seeks to move the debate about citizenship beyond the terms established by Brubaker to yet a further perspective, by challenging the analytical value of considering "thick" and "thin" conceptions of citizenship side by side. One of the central problems of Brubaker's argument was not his lack of awareness of the cultural tenets of citizenship but his failure to analyze closely the cultural contestations of community on which legal definitions were based. Noting the essential interconnectedness between political-legal debates and the indeterminacy and constructedness of the social, cultural, and political context to which they referred, Eley proposes that citizenship can inform a new understanding of German history. By exploring how citizenship was continuously constructed and challenged, he suggests, we can obtain a new understanding of the meanings of continuity and rupture in the German past. Citizenship provides a lens through which we might sharpen our attentiveness to the elements of indeterminacy and contestedness in German history while recovering our appreciation of the complexities of the processes by which inclusion in the nation was competed for and claimed.

*   *   *

This book offers a new perspective on twentieth-century Germany history, as its different investigations seek to break down what tend to be still relatively fixed dividing lines among cultural, political, social, and legal history. The articles presented here collectively provide new perspectives on how and by whom citizenship was defined, and how citizenship impacted upon individuals and groups. They point to the complexity of the relationship between citizenship and the nation, precisely because citizenship gives rise to such very complex identifications. Indeed, these identifications can even set themselves apart from or against the nation. The contributors also suggest a new perspective for thinking about the continuities and ruptures of German history. Many contributors present an analysis that cuts across or runs counter to the traditionally conceived turning points of 1914, 1918, and 1945. Citizenship, it turns out, provides a particular framework through which the German dictatorships, the Third Reich, and the GDR can be compared against each other and against other periods and political contexts.

This book's major ambition is not to present hard-and-fast conclusions but to complicate and open up lines of investigation. Collectively, the essays presented here not only demonstrate the fruitfulness of analyzing German history through the lens of citizenship but also enable a response to four major issues that arise from considering the scholarly literature on citizenship, which were also raised and discussed at the conference on which this book is based.[33]

At a methodological level, it should be noted that the relevance of citizenship as a formal category in the context of German history is less than immediately clear. Germans have used terms such as *Staatsbürgerschaft* and *Staatsangehörigkeit* to denote citizenship, but neither term captures the full legal and cultural richness of the Anglo-American *citizen* or the French *citoyen*. Indeed, the very absence in Germany of a U.S.-type citizen who could be spurred into action by an identification and contestation with the constitution was at the heart of Habermas's critiques of the West German polity before 1989. This quickly raises the question, familiar to German historians, of how far the concept of citizenship legitimately can be used for periods and contexts in which the term may have been barely developed.

As an ideal of the active, involved individual with a share in the state in the French sense, the idea of citizenship was very weakly developed in Germany until the twentieth century. It might be concluded on that basis that, for Germany, citizenship should only be used as a meaningful analytical category from 1918.[34] Yet the relationships among the individual, the state, and the wider community of German states and the question of how these relationships might be encoded can be shown to have played an important part in the governing of populations over many centuries of German history. Indeed, since the Reformation, individual territories were not just defined by attributes like sovereign power and the law;[35] they also obtained a crucial religious, cultural definition that tangibly impacted everyday life. Moreover, from the early nineteenth century at the very latest, such cultural expressions of territorial belonging became important issues at the level of the everyday, as manifested in public debates, festivals, public representations, and even individual dress codes.[36] Questions about citizenship, notably the interaction among individuals, groups, and the state, and the ways in which groups define inclusion and exclusion in relation to territorial belonging, have been crucial questions of German history. Such concerns do not necessitate the use of *citizenship* as a formal term of analysis and might just as easily be discussed in nineteenth-century terms such as *individuality* and *community*.[37] However, by providing a common framework of reference across periods and between states, the citizenship concept can clearly facilitate comparative debate. This book focuses on citizenship in twentieth-century Germany, yet some of its contributions demonstrate the usefulness of applying the analytical category of citizenship to debates going back to the nineteenth and even to the eighteenth century, as most notably in the chapters from Dieter Gosewinkel and Pascal Grosse.

The importance of T. H. Marshall's work remains undeniable, but for German historians his categorization seems unhelpful at best, and misleading at worst. Marshall delivered his lecture on citizenship and social class as a statement at a particular moment in British history (in 1949, just after the inauguration of the welfare state). He did so with exclusive reference to British history, even while articulating many of his inferences in quite general ways. It is not at all clear how any sequencing between these types of citizenship could work for Germany. As Kathleen Canning has pointed out, Bismarck's social insurance laws alone make it difficult to distinguish between social and political dimensions of German citizenship.[38] Furthermore, Marshall's categories speak not at all to our contemporary understandings of "cultural citizenship"; indeed, they remain innocent of everything we now associate with the "new cultural history" and with the broader "cultural turn" in the human sciences. As this book documents in all its contributions, citizenship can no longer be understood apart from its cultural contexts, which are of vital use in determining its meanings. Contentions about social, civic, or political entitlement have been closely related to how groups and individuals have seen themselves—and have been defined from the outside—in relation to music, entertainment, consumer behavior, and taste. The question, then, is not so much *whether* culture possesses significance for a consideration of citizenship, but *how*. From a vantage point of citizenship, what forms exactly did that relationship between culture and politics take?

Historians fortunately remain free from reliance on the formal models whose prescriptions political scientists are more constrained to observe. By using the category of citizenship to investigate the inter-relationships among cultural, social, political, and legal factors, historians may explore how those interrelations evolved with unevenness and complexity across different junctures and periods. For instance, by examining the ways in which the law and its disputation in colonial societies related to collective identifications and individual subjectivities, we can see how our analysis breaks up and reconfigures notions of race.[39] By exploring how women sought to contest received understandings of rights and duties and how the resulting histories impacted upon their subjectivities, we can break up and reconfigure notions of gender.[40] And, by examining ways in which political and legal rights were defined in relation to the individual, we can develop new categories for understanding how membership in the political and legal community came to be defined. For instance, Pascal Grosse's highly original argument in this book about the cerebral nature of citizenship raises issues about the relationship between the brain and the body, whose importance to the contestation of rights and self-representation is further underlined by Cornelie Usborne's contribution. Citizenship, therefore, can open up new understandings and connections in German history inasmuch as it allows the complexity and interconnectedness of personal, public, and official relationships to be freshly addressed. Put differently, rather than beginning with a set of already finished categories whose purpose is to fix the definition of citizenship in history, we favor the use of citizenship as an analytical tool that certainly determines the lines of inquiry, but whose meanings and expressions may shift and evolve over time and for any given situation. Our purposes are avowedly exploratory in that sense.

In considering the idea of citizenship for German history, a second problem emerges. If citizenship is intimately—though, as this volume argues, not exclusively—related to the state and the nation, this raises the question of precisely how this relationship works in a federal state like Germany (and, by implication, in countries further to the south and east, such as Poland) whose borders have frequently been revised and where a central state has existed for only a relatively short time. As Andreas Fahrmeir has shown, if at a formal level the rights and meanings attaching to citizenship were indeed weakly developed in Germany before the middle of the nineteenth century, then this was equally true for Britain, a state with particularly clear external borders.[41] Thus the relationships among citizenship, the state, and the nation should not be assumed to be given. Citizenship can be used instead to examine anew how individual and collective identifications with state and nation became constructed.

Indeed, citizenship becomes a particularly important category for unpacking the meanings of cultural and legal constructions of community and the setting of internal and external boundaries. We argue that it can be helpful in exploring how such boundaries became constructed and reconstructed, contested and fixed. More concretely, in areas that were forced to adopt new legal systems and accept different political rulers, there was likely to be a much higher level of public and individual contestation related to these issues.[42] Precisely because political boundaries were constantly shifting, it becomes relevant and important to ask how individuals positioned themselves vis-à-vis the community where they lived, and to ask which coordinates determined individual formulations of rights and belonging. Once we use citizenship to determine our lines of inquiry, without setting its reference points in stone, we can discover how individuals saw themselves in relation to the locality, the region, the state, and the nation.

Conversely, as James Retallack has pointed out, the local and regional levels contribute to a much better and more focused understanding of the meanings of citizenship.[43] Annemarie Sammartino and Jan Palmowski show from very different vantage points how the local context shaped and was informed by individual experiences of citizenship. As Adelheid von Saldern summarizes in this volume, the more we want to find out about the meanings of citizenship for the individual, the more important the local context becomes in our analysis.

A third difficulty is that in history, as in the social sciences, the more widely we seek to apply the concept of citizenship as an analytical category and the more loosely we thus define it, the more difficult finding a distinctive meaning becomes. At the conference on which this book is based, this issue was easily the most contentious. If, at one extreme, citizenship were simply and solely defined as a cultural construct, then it would not be clear why one would call one's object of observation "citizenship" (as opposed to, say, "national identity"). If one pleaded, as we do, for a concept of citizenship without fixed and predetermined meanings in any given period, might this tend to divest citizenship of any distinctive meaning at all?

The potential meanings of citizenship (and their limits) are not subject to general agreement. In their contributions, Peter C. Caldwell and Kathleen Canning agree on three definitions. Citizenship first denotes the individual's formal belonging to a state. Second, it refers to the objective rights and duties enjoyed by the citizen; and, third, citizenship denotes the subjective use of those rights, the "meanings" ascribed by individuals to the rights that they enjoy as citizens. These three definitions describe a use of the citizenship concept with which all historians might well agree. Caldwell then makes a further point that is perhaps a little more contentious, namely, that citizenship refers to the collective experience of the state, which he describes as a "category of identity." What may be debated are the implications of these categories as we encounter them in twentieth-century German history. If citizenship is about rights that individuals enjoy as citizens, how did the possession and contestation of these rights affect the larger communities of citizens and notions of belonging? In turn, what is the relationship between contestations of citizenship between historical actors and individual subjectivities? What remains subject to intense debate is the question of how far the citizenship concept can help us in analyzing modern German history beyond the relatively clearly defined boundaries of legal and political contestations. In other words, exactly what more do we gain by exploring aspects of modern German political and legal history as well as cultural, social, and institutional history through the lens of citizenship?

It may be useful at this point to recall one of the principal aims of citizenship debates in the political sciences. What citizenship helps determine for political scientists is how borders are constructed and how those borders then determine the relationship between inclusion and exclusion.[44] Such borders are constantly shifting, not least because of the perennial gap between the legal constructions of citizenship and its practices. Of course, this returns us again to the broader arguments about citizenship's indeterminacies. The analytical problem that arises is that very often citizenship is contested without direct reference to the law or the state, even if the terms of political and legal citizenship emerge as being ultimately at stake. In Frankfurt am Main at the turn of the nineteenth century, for instance, citizens contested the nature of the local educational system from primary school to university. The liberal majority among the enfranchised citizens pursued, through the local secondary schools as well as the university, an ideal of the individual who was educated (*gebildet*), rational, and equipped to embrace modernity and change. All students, including those at primary schools, were to develop a strong sense of belonging to the locality (the *Heimat*), as well as a religious tolerance. A majority of Frankfurt liberals thus crafted an educational system that would shape the ideal Frankfurt citizen, a model for the city as well as for the fatherland. At issue, in other words, was a fundamental vision of what constituted a "good" citizen based on religious toleration, a vision linking the local and the national levels.[45] This was not a debate about legal codes, about codified rights and duties; it was about contesting visions of citizenship, about how the ideal of equality before the law could be realized on the ground, and how it could become an underlying principle for social, economic, and cultural action. This reminds us once more of how important it is to bring a generously multifaceted understanding of citizenship to our work.[46]

But if citizenship refers to more than contestations of nationality and the law, where do we draw the line? What kinds of debates pertain to citizenship, and where are the limits of applying the citizenship concept? We do not claim that citizenship is a new catch-all concept that solves every problem. This book shows that many of the issues that can be considered from the point of view of citizenship also can be investigated with other questions in mind. S. Jonathan Wiesen's contribution, for instance, is as significant for our understanding of consumerism and corporate history as of citizenship itself. Toby Thacker's findings on music are explored through the concept of citizenship, even though they say as much (if not more) about cultural representations of Germanness.

What links these papers is not just that they deal with debates about collective identifications and individual subjectivities but that they also address the manifestations of those debates in practice. Citizenship, in other words, offers a framework of analysis that asks not how a community is defined per se, but how individuals, different collectivities, or the state seeks to realize a self-identification and a vision of community in practice. Especially in the German context, the community in question can be the local community, the region, the federal state, or the national state. Or, as Pascal Grosse argues here and as Kathleen Canning has argued elsewhere, this community can be defined through individual subjectivities such as race or gender. And as German historians know only too well, the Third Reich sought to concentrate all these lines of affiliation into a single totalizing, unmediated, and exclusionary version of the national community in the form of the coercively unitary *Volksgemeinschaft*. In each case, studies of citizenship ask how individuals relate to these entities, either directly or in relation to each other. What is at stake are concrete negotiations and contestations about the limits of this community, how its borders can be defined, what the basis for inclusion and exclusion should be, and ultimately how these practical contestations relate to the political-legal definitions of citizenship through constitutions and the law.

A fourth issue concerns the relationship between citizenship and identity. Both often are integrally linked in the political sciences. Charles Tilly, for instance, posits that identities consist of shared understandings among actors that are constantly subject to contestation. Identities refer to individuals in their relationship to each other, but they are also constructed through the multitude of actions and relations that emerge out of the individual's relation to the state.[47] "Citizenship," writes William A. Barbieri, "serves as a primary basis of identity," because it forms the basis of interpersonal relationships, social and economic group relations, and political participation. In the case of Germany, citizenship sought to express a sense of ethnic and cultural "national" identity that had predated it.[48] From this perspective, identities have been constructed through cultural boundaries, boundaries that determine the public sphere linking the individual and the state that is so crucial to citizenship.[49]

Yet the prevalence of *identity* as an analytical term has vehement critics. In the social sciences, Rogers Brubaker and Frederick Cooper have argued that the concept of identity is either too rigid or, if it takes into account the shifting and complex self-definitions of individuals, too ill-defined to be helpful.[50] Among historians, Lutz Niethammer has warned against the use of *identity* as an analytical term, arguing that it overshadows the complex differences among individuals. From a historical perspective, he argues, the identity concept has been most commonly used to cover up the absence of real identifications, notably the identity of the *Volk* (and its Führer) during the Third Reich.[51]

Niethammer's point, however, does make it legitimate to talk about identity in certain contexts. As Caldwell, Wiesen, and Palmowski show in this volume, citizenship was closely related to formulations of identity in political thought, whether under the Third Reich or in the GDR. If state and party in the GDR postulated the identity between state and citizen, then the term can hardly be avoided in any analysis of the citizenship ideal and its reality in that context. In fact, citizenship is closely related to the concept of identity, even if we accept Brubaker and Cooper's claim that it may be possible, and desirable, to replace the notion of identity with more precise categories. For if citizenship is about the manifestation of community and about the negotiations concerning rights, duties, and other citizenship attributes, then it is integrally linked to many components of identity, such as self-representation and individual identification with the community and the state.

There is one remaining difficulty we would like to flag. Discussions of citizenship, not least in the ascendant liberal democratic contexts of the 1990s under which those scholarly and political discussions have been so vigorously and elaborately revived, possess or entail a normative dimension. Accordingly, we need to consider very carefully whether there might be contexts and times when the category of citizenship becomes inoperative. Among our contributors, S. Jonathan Wiesen considers cultural and commercial constructions of citizenship under the Third Reich, while Pascal Grosse's discussion of citizenship as a bio-political category clearly has important implications for the ways in which citizenship was "racialized" during the same period. These insights should not preclude a wider debate about the concrete possibility that during the Nazi period citizenship as a category lost much, if not all, of its core meanings, as its contexts of rights, entitlements, validations, and claims become voided, negated, or in important degrees compromised and hollowed out. In other words, are there types of polity or political conjuncture—like the Third Reich, for example—for which terms like *citizenship, civil society,* and *public sphere,* loaded as they are with priorities and values of an avowedly liberal or democratic kind, simply become inappropriate? Of course, the GDR was an authoritarian polity, whose centralist and bureaucratic machineries of policing and administrative power specifically subordinated the population, severely constrained their possibilities of self-assertion and self-recognition, both individually and collectively, and disallowed all sorts of ideas and activities. Yet in the forms of its coercive power, the overtness and extremes of its violence, and the recourse to killing, mass murder, and genocide, the Nazi state remains vitally different.[52] Among all the recent turning by historians to the study of popular consent under the Third Reich, these distinctions must never be effaced.

If we have not yet established a commonly accepted definition of *citizenship* for analytical purposes, we would stop short of the verdict of one of our contributors, who sees it as one "of the most porous concepts in contemporary academic parlance."[53] We find it a concept particularly well-suited to link the cultural and the political and to provide a basis for bringing together an increasingly disparate historical field in the pursuit of a common range of questions. If some historians prefer to pursue the concept in its more political-legal sense, this is all to be welcomed, as we still know very little about how citizenship was experienced and negotiated on the ground. If others instead choose to investigate the cultural constructions to which perceptions and entitlements of citizenship gave rise, this allows us to reconfigure our thinking about German history. It might then be possible to relate these sets of findings to each other, as we have tried to do in this book. We might further consider how the diversity of meanings pertaining to citizenship could travel across different spheres and different periods of the German past. Citizenship, we would argue, provides a concreteness to the fields of interaction among individuals, their public relationships, and their communities, which notably eludes notions like identity or even national identity. Citizenship gives a specificity to communal relations vis-à-vis the state and the individual because it involves hard choices, the setting of boundaries, and, even if implicitly, the allocation of rights and resources.

PART ONE

Citizenship, State, and Nation

Citizenship in Germany and France at the Turn of the Twentieth Century: Some New Observations on an Old Comparison

DIETER GOSEWINKEL

CITIZENSHIP IN NATION-STATES is a construction of their national elites. At the same time, it is a legal institution that, although long considered the preserve of experts in constitutional law, historically has exercised a profound influence on the everyday lives of state citizens. Government members, parliamentarians, and organizations shaped and influenced the legal regulations concerning citizenship, while jurists and civil servants commented upon and applied them. Decisions about citizenship distinguished one nation-state from another and determined individuals' personal "worthiness" for acceptance into citizen status. They assigned rights and duties that distinguished citizens from foreigners and helped determine their material life chances. In the age of nation-states, regulations that determined who would be included in or excluded from the national community of citizens were a constitutive component of the national discourse. They were politically contested and symbolically charged. The dominant conception of the nation was reflected in the concept of citizenship. National differences between systems of citizenship thus represent differences between concepts of the nation.

Over the past decade, these connections have penetrated the consciousness of the political and scholarly publics. Political conflicts over the reshaping of citizenship law are also struggles over the definition of the nation-state tradition. This tradition, in turn, only emerges from a retrospective historical view, which compares it to other national traditions of citizenship. The interpretation of the history of citizenship thus becomes highly significant for the conception of the nation-state in the present. Rogers Brubaker's work offers an example of such an interpretation. His comparative historical study of citizenship in Germany and France has already become part of the national construction of history in the two countries he treats.[1] The difference between the German and French paths of development, it seems, is obvious. Brubaker shows how two contrary political and cultural models of citizenship arose historically from opposite concepts of the nation. In Germany, the inception of the idea of the nation before the state remained decisive. In this way, an *ethnocultural* model emerged that was oriented toward the pre-state concept of the people (*Volk*). It existed in tension with the state, and promoted restrictive, objective criteria that restricted naturalization. This restrictive basic character was embodied in the dominant principle of descent (*ius sanguinis*), which was enshrined in the imperial citizenship law of 1913. In France, in contrast, a model developed that referred to both the nation *and* the state. This *nation-state* concept of citizenship was associated with the political form of the republic. It relied on assimilation and facilitated naturalization. It was embodied in a broadly conceived territorial principle (*ius soli*) that was enforced in the republican law of 1889.

Thus arose two polar opposite models, which have continued to shape naturalization practice down to the present day: a relatively closed, ethnically oriented model in Germany, and an open, state-oriented model based on assimilation in France.

This contribution provides a different interpretation of the history of German and French citizenship. My focus will not be on national differences as such. Rather, I will dispense with an "essentialist" reading of two polarized ideal types of citizenship law and look instead at the historical process of *nationalization* that citizenship law underwent both in France and Germany during the last third of the nineteenth century. Thus, I will focus on three questions:

1. What were the changing historical conditions under which the national differences in citizenship law emerged?
2. How did the perception of the other nation affect the shaping of citizenship law in France and Germany? To what degree was this a process of transnational development, which would imply mutual observation resulting in national polarization?
3. Did citizenship law and its two principles of *ius soli* and *ius sanguinis* also reflect—from the initial confrontation between the two nation-states in 1871 onward—the confrontation of two polar

concepts of nation (and nationhood), or was this rather a gradual process of interpreting and enforcing two juridical principles according to conflicting national concepts and interests?

Through Rogers Brubaker's work, the familiar juxtaposition of the French and German concepts of the nation—that is, the nation-state versus the cultural nation—has acquired a new, more profound explanation. By showing, through the example of citizenship, the effect of a central institution of the nation-state in its contrary historical consequences, he presents us with the very nature and essence of the different concepts of the nation. We see before us, in ideal-typical clarity, two models that explain in historical terms the national differences in citizenship policy. These are not "iron-clad casings" but rather stable, culturally determined structures that place limits on the changes in material interests. It is the recourse to cultural explanation, as Geoff Eley points out, that gives to the analysis of divergent juridical systems of citizenship the explanatory depth of divergent cultural formations separating the two national histories across a period of two centuries.[2]

But how stable are the underlying concepts of the nation? Aren't they themselves epoch-specific constructions shaped by political interests? And if this is the case, what specific historical conditions are responsible for the stability of national "cultural idioms" and thus also for their transformation? These questions aim at the historicization of national differences presumably shaped by deeply rooted national cultures. We must go back to the contingency of political and economic changes, to breaks and conjunctures as much as to the long-term continuities. In accordance with Geoff Eley, this article starts from the thesis that the extreme "indeterminacy" of Germany as a political term and a territorial-political entity helps to explain the (radical) changes in German citizenship policy and its difference from France.[3] This interpretation is confirmed by Eli Nathan's recent reconstruction of the politics of citizenship in Germany. In fact, as Nathan says, "German history is not a teleology, with one internal logic and one predestined outcome."[4]

In what follows, I will critically examine Rogers Brubaker's ideal-typical construction and its temporal dependency from two perspectives. I will begin by addressing the concepts of the nation and citizenship as the constructs of opposing political interests. I will then trace the key breaks in the development of citizenship laws in Germany and France from the background of mutual perceptions and national reactions, before turning to the analysis of differing political frameworks as a means of explanation for different citizenship laws.

In conclusion, I will offer some remarks on the relationship between national concepts and national citizenship laws.

I. Concepts of the Nation as Political Constructs

It is well-known and should be emphasized again here: from the very beginning, the German and French concepts of the nation emerged in historical competition and did not merely refer to, but were directed against, each other. The transcendental German Romantic idea of the nation, which was based on inwardness and cultural cohesion, only gained political and mass appeal during the war against occupation by Napoleonic France in the early nineteenth century. The primacy of culture, aestheticization, and the claim to uniqueness as the core of this national self-definition were directed against the hegemonic claims of the French nation.[5] The French nation defined itself largely as political, universalistic, and expansive, to be sure. This self-image was only rendered absolute in the negative perceptions of the German side, which in turn lent sharper contours to the German counterimage.

This process of national definition by negative example continued under wholly altered political circumstances with the founding of the German nation-state in 1871.[6] In the dispute over the annexation of Alsace-Lorraine, a debate ensued among leading German and French scholars of the day over whom Alsace belonged to, which was used as the occasion to exaggerate their respective concepts of the nation into systematic opposites. Numa Denis Fustel de Coulanges and Ernest Renan supported the subjective, voluntarist—French—concept of the nation, while Theodor Mommsen and David Strauss favored the linguistic-ethnic—German—counteridiom. At the turn of the century, this contrast was virtually enshrined in Friedrich Meinecke's ideal-typical categories of the *Staatsnation* and the *Kulturnation*.[7]

I do not intend to question here in any way the existence of contrary concepts of the nation or their powerful influence on concepts of citizenship in the two countries. However, I would like to open our eyes to a basic circumstance that Dominique Schnapper has formulated as follows:

Since the French Revolution, the idea of the nation, which has accompanied the birth and development of European nations, has always been indissolubly normative and descriptive, to the extent that the idea itself forms part of objective reality or translates and reinforces implicit values. . . .[8]

Thus insofar as the at once temporally dependent and polemical character of traditional concepts of the nation becomes apparent, their analytical value becomes dubious. The analysis needs to uncover the ambivalence of motivations and potentials for political development behind the suggestive political explicitness of the concept.

What did the constructive and polar character of *national concepts* mean to the construction of citizenship law in the two nation-states? Was it reflected by two polarized systems of *citizenship law*?

As a point of departure, it is perhaps useful to examine the two regimes of citizenship law in Germany and France *before* 1871, when the Franco-German war and the unification of the German Reich led to a confrontation between the two nation-states. The law of the North German Confederation from 1870, which was then adopted by the German Reich, regulated citizenship in the German states in a federal manner. Citizenship was issued by the federal states (Prussia, Bavaria, Saxony, etc.) through the respective state authorities. Only with a passport from one of those states did one also become "German," that is, a citizen of the North German Confederation or of the German Reich. This law was based on the model of the Prussian "subjects law" from 1842, which stated that, except through later naturalization, citizenship could only be attained by descent from a Prussian (i.e., from a Prussian father or, in the case of an illegitimate birth, from a Prussian mother).[9] In 1842, this *ius sanguinis* was not understood in the sense of an ethnic community, and even less in terms of a national community. And this did not change fundamentally with the passing of the Federal Law in 1870. Although there were voices in the legislative assembly that wanted to see German citizenship raised to a "national" symbol, the territorial idea of a "statute of limitations" for German citizenship was ultimately also established in the law of the Reich: those who lived for more than ten years outside of Germany lost their German citizenship if they did not take special measures to retain it.

Nor did, up until the 1870s, the principle of descent in citizenship law outside of Germany imply a specific understanding of the nation. This is clearly demonstrated by the importance of the principle of descent in French citizenship law, whose conception of the nation was increasingly opposed to that of Germany's citizenship law. Patrick Weil,[10] whose remarks I follow here, has pointed out that the French Civil Code of 1804 was supposed to break with the ruling feudal territorial principle and that the dominant principle of descent in French law influenced citizenship law in Europe, including in Prussia, throughout the entire nineteenth century. The awareness of having influenced legal codification in almost all of Europe through a "modern," antifeudal law actually gave rise to a conservative, national tendency that was opposed to an alteration of the *ius sanguinis*. In addition, there were legal concerns about the international complications that could arise through a unilateral change in French citizenship law, injurious to the principle of reciprocity, through which foreign citizens would become French. Defenders were able to assert this position against political supporters who demanded, with increasing pressure, equality in regards to military service and military security. The latter argued that those foreigners who, from the perspective of assimilation and acculturation, could be regarded as "French" in sociological terms—a group rapidly increasing both in absolute numbers and in percentage of the population[11]—should also be legally naturalized. With the law of 1851—the introduction of "double *ius soli*" [12]—this side was able to attain a victory. However, the measure was insufficient for the central military-political concern at stake here, as the children of immigrants who became French in this way could reject French citizenship when they attained maturity and thereby avoid military service. The political intensification of the subjective, political concept of the nation resulting from the annexation of Alsace-Lorraine by the German Reich in 1870–71 did not—initially—affect citizenship law.

In view of this history, the law of 1889 reforming French citizenship can no longer be interpreted as the inevitable breakthrough of a "revolutionary," long-existent republican principle of the nation. On the contrary, the "French" principle of citizenship was, from its beginning up into the 1870s, *ius sanguinis*.

However, the introduction of an unrestricted *ius soli* for second-generation immigrants in 1889 continues to mark French citizenship law today. A century after the Revolution, it was considered a typical symbol of the political, subjective idea of the nation, which is characterized by the voluntary declaration of the individual and the willingness of the French state to assimilate new citizens. It has commonly been held to reflect the victory of universal Republicanism over the countermovement of particularist Boulangism.[13]

More recent scholarship paints a different picture. The 1889 law is the endpoint of a development away from free choice and toward a co-optation of the individual by the state on the grounds that he or she was socialized on French soil. The territorial principle also was not an invention of the French Republic, but took up where ancien régime legal constructions had left off. The republican value of equality asserted itself because, in the situation of 1889, it coincided with the French state's economic and military interests. The extension of French citizenship to the children of Italians in the border provinces of Savoy and Nice as well as in Algeria was intended to combat Italian irredentism. Although the actual increase of males subject to military service was relatively low,[14] the expansion of military capacities did play an important role in the perceptions of contemporaries. Finally, it was also in the interest of industrial entrepreneurs to create a larger pool of potential laborers. The opponents of the reform who wished to retain the *ius sanguinis* appeared, in contrast, not merely as supporters of the aristocratic party and as antimodernists but virtually as the enemies of national interests.[15] At the same time, the "reinvention" of the *ius soli* had unrestricted validity only in the mother country itself. In Algeria, which was after all part of metropolitan France, *ius soli* was ethnically coded: only "Europeans" were granted full French citizenship; indigenous Muslims did not become *citoyens français* but rather remained *sujets français*.[16]

In light of this mixture of political and pragmatic motives, the "republican" interpretation of the 1889 law appears as part of a republican founding myth. It obscures a fundamental fact: in the history of both nation-states, in both Germany and France, ethnocultural *as well as* nation-state elements existed side by side from the beginning.[17] This, however, has been veiled by the fact that the law of 1899 was raised to the *lieu de mémoire*[18] of French republicanism.

II. Citizenship Laws as a Result of Mutual Perception and National Reaction

Principles of citizenship thus contained a fundamental ambivalence. What counted, however, was which element managed to prevail in which historical situation.

The solidification and autonomization of a cultural idiom of ethnoculturality or state nationality was *one* important explanation for this. But it is not—and this takes us to my central thesis—a sufficient or the decisive explanation. Far more important was the basic political, social, and institutional constellation that enforced and supported a (cultural) model in the first place and allowed it to fade when the structures themselves changed.

What do we mean by "the basic political and social constellation"? I will attempt to explain this through an example, one that takes us back to the inception of the French law of 1889 and demonstrates again how closely developments in the two states referred to each other in their concepts not only of the nation but also of citizenship. New legislation on citizenship in France was followed with interest in Germany for many years, particularly with reference to the implications for military and population policy. When as a result of the 1889 law the number of naturalizations in France skyrocketed, the German imperial governor in Alsace-Lorraine took the occasion to recommend a change in German citizenship legislation. The principle of descent should be supplemented by the territorial principle, particularly in order to prevent the formation of "French colonies" in Alsace-Lorraine and to be able to draft members of these groups into the German army. Very similar arguments had been invoked in favor of the new French law—a striking parallel. In contrast, however, the introduction of the territorial principle failed in Germany because of the opposition of the administrative heads of the eastern provinces of the empire. They rejected the naturalization of descendants of "Polish, Russian, and Jewish" families because they were allegedly "difficult to assimilate." [19]

One could conclude that this is evidence of the primacy of an ethnocultural concept of citizenship, and that it was anti-Slavic and anti-Jewish defensive attitudes that prevented the liberalization of German citizenship law. The explanation is more complicated, however. First of all, immigrants from Eastern Europe were relatively poor compared to the labor migrants in the western regions of Germany, particularly compared to those who came from Holland and Belgium. Further, from the beginning it was assumed that—like the Danes—foreign Poles and their descendants were not prepared to assimilate within the German state structure. "The Pole . . . [clings] . . . stubbornly to his national character. Up until now he has successfully resisted incessant efforts at Germanization," noted the Lord Lieutenant (*Oberpräsident*) of Silesia in 1893.[20] In contrast, integration of Dutch and Belgian migrants as citizens was welcomed because, as the authorities saw it, they adapted linguistically and willingly participated in all public institutions.

These arguments point to the fundamental—demographic and socioeconomic—preconditions for any citizenship law. During the very period when reforms were being considered, the mid-1890s, imperial Germany was becoming a country of immigration, or more precisely an importer of labor power. After a century of out-migration, the booming industrial state had begun to recruit laborers from abroad, most of them Eastern Europeans, especially from the Polish regions of the Russian and Habsburg empires. They were intended to replace agricultural workers in the eastern regions of the German empire who had migrated to the western industrial centers. France was also an importer of labor at this period, to a far greater extent than Germany. In contrast to its eastern neighbor, however, France had a much lower rate of population growth. This discrepancy worried French public opinion at the end of the nineteenth century and was a significant motive for the inclusive citizenship legislation. France was—and regarded itself as—more strongly dependent upon constant and stable immigration than Germany, which thus could choose more carefully among immigrant groups and candidates for naturalization.

To that extent, the selection criteria of a capacity and willingness to assimilate played a greater role in Germany than in France. This applied all the more because the immigrant groups in the two countries were perceived as variously assimilable according to their linguistic-cultural and national origins.[21] In France, between the censuses of 1851 and 1921, the Italians,[22] Belgians, and Spanish, that is, people from "Latin" and Catholic nations, represented the three largest groups of foreigners and comprised up to three-quarters of total immigrants.[23]

In Germany, the proportion of foreigners with a Slavic mother tongue, mainly ethnic Poles from Russia and the Austro-Hungarian Empire, rose from the turn of the century onward.[24] Intensifying this was the fact that the immigrants were mainly Catholic and Jewish in a Protestant-dominated host society, presenting more objective obstacles to assimilation than Latin-Catholic immigration to France. Even the Danes, who were a significant group before World War I, could not simply be annexed to the "Germanic" linguistic family, although they were considered to have relatively few problems in assimilating. Conflicts among different nationalities existed in Germany that were unknown in France. So-called Poles and Danes—German citizens of Danish and Polish nationality—represented strong, organized minority groups within Germany who since the late nineteenth century had increasingly resisted and cut themselves off from the German majority culture. The naturalization of foreigners of Polish or Danish nationality strengthened a national potential for resistance, threatening the cohesion of the state from within. That, at least, was how the German government viewed matters. The Prussian minister of the interior noted what he considered an essential difference between Germany and France: in

France, the population declined from year to year. The French state had an interest in increasing the population and in drawing in foreigners born in France, "most of whom, by virtue of the Frenchmen's capacity to act in an assimilatory manner on their environment, have accepted the French essence after a brief period of time,"[25] in as much as it was not already instilled in them by their own parents.

The lack of faith in the assimilatory powers of the German state in comparison to those of the French state at the end of the nineteenth century rested largely on the experiences of reciprocally aggravating nationalization processes. On the one hand, the state's expectations regarding assimilation had been discredited in the eyes of national minorities by an extreme policy of Germanization. On the other hand, the conflict was exacerbated by the latent, growing threat of separatism. The Danish nationalist movement in northern Schleswig aimed at a return to Denmark, while the Polish movement sought in the long term to reestablish a Polish nation-state. The French minority in Alsace-Lorraine worked toward a revision of the annexation.

At the height of nationalization in Europe in the late nineteenth century, therefore, any attempt in Germany at introducing assimilatory and inclusive citizenship policy faced resistance from organized and increasingly secessionist national movements or found its integrative intentions undermined. This distinguished Germany from France, which did not face any real separatist challenge during the nineteenth century.[26] I do not mean to downplay the political significance of the strong Italian minority in or immigration to France, for France was repeatedly visited by fears of Italian irredentism in light of its 1860 incorporation of the Italian-dominated border provinces of Savoy and Nice. Broadly speaking, however, there was no nationalist movement among the Italian population of the border regions[27] comparable in size, organizational strength, or political determination to the Polish movement in Germany.

The national codifications of citizenship that dominated the entire twentieth century were formed during the late nineteenth century in both France and Germany and referred to each other. In both nation-states, the motive of state assimilation and integration represented the starting point for policy. The fact that, in its imperial citizenship law of 1913, Germany ultimately and definitively rejected the territorial principle is not sufficiently explained by the persistence of an ethnocultural model. More decisive were the differing sets of demographic, economic, and nationality policy conditions that narrowed and ultimately determined the choice between the principles of citizenship.

III. Differing Political Frameworks—
Different National Models of Citizenship

From this finding for the transition period of national citizenship legislation, one can extend the question to a comparison for the nineteenth and the beginning of the twentieth century as a whole: which differing political frameworks were at the root of the enforcement of divergent national models of citizenship?

One significant difference was that citizenship developed within a centralized state in France and within a federal state in Germany. The first French codification of citizenship in the Revolutionary Constitution of 1791, which introduced the (general and equal) status of *citoyen*, created not just the French state but also the nation. The simultaneous emergence of the state and the nation and their legal codification lent French citizenship greater institutional stability than German citizenship from its very inception. The revolutionary nation-state also took up the legacy of the centralizing absolutist state to the extent that from the beginning it regulated citizenship centrally and uniformly as an affair of the nation. When, in 1889, the citizenship law of the French nation-state was devised in the form it would retain throughout the twentieth century, it had already been preceded by a century of codification. During this period, basic principles of both descent and territory had been tested in changing political systems. Only after a century, then, was the primacy of the *ius sanguinis* abandoned for the *ius soli*, because the majority of the French regarded it as a better guarantee of the internal homogeneity and external integrity of their nation-state.

In Germany, in contrast, citizenship emerged in the early nineteenth century as an instrument of the territorial and political reordering of generally regional political entities, which had treated one another as foreign countries until 1871.[28] Even within the German nation-state, there was no central and uniform citizenship. One only became a German indirectly, by incorporation into one of the federal states, a situation that persisted until 1934 when the absolutism of National Socialist rule introduced uniform national citizenship. This institutional non-uniformity is evident in the uncertainty of the constitutional terminology. The Basic Law of 1949 was the first German constitution—a century and a half after the French Revolution—to define the concept of "the German."

Differing interpretations regarding the political role of one's own nation-state played a significant part in the codification of national citizenship law that began in both states in the 1880s. In France, citizenship policy rested on the experience of an institutionally established state, particularly its territorial stability. The spatial notion of France's "natural borders" and the invention of the "hexagon"[29] helped constitute the political conception of the nation. This "mental map" of the French nation was further intensified after 1871 by the loss of Alsace-Lorraine.

The familiar assertion that Germany was a late nation-state, a "delayed nation," also affected the concept of citizenship. Germany's idea of a fixed national territory could only develop after 1871 and was at first limited to the politics of "saturation." As a late colonial power, Germany ranked far behind England and France in the race for colonies. So-called overseas Germans (*Auslandsdeutsche*) living in distant foreign states and colonies thus became the point of reference for an ethnic-national sentiment because the relatively small German colonies offered only a weak territorial link. The majority in the Reichstag, which strengthened the right of overseas Germans to retain their German citizenship in the law of 1913,[30] sought in so doing to close the gap between Germany and the nationally conscious legal traditions of the colonial powers of England and France.[31]

Ethnocultural ideas of the nation were thus quite clearly viewed and deployed as a means of compensating for the political weakness of the state. This relationship became apparent in the imperial period, and obvious and dominant after 1918—a development that lies beyond the scope of this contribution and can only be mentioned briefly. The radical ethnicization that led to the *völkish* conception of citizenship in Germany following World War I occurred in the context of a crushing military defeat that brought about the separation of large territories with former German citizens. It was only during this phase, in which the German *Reich* as a nation-state had been politically weakened, that the ethnic conception of citizenship became an instrument of a revisionist policy—a policy that aimed at winning back settler territories of former German citizens and at "bringing home" ethnocultural Germans from Middle and Eastern Europe. As Annemarie Sammartino strikingly has put it in her contribution to this volume, in this phase the character of German citizenship as an "imagined community," which represents the ideal rather than the actual composition of society, becomes evident.[32] The imagination of the German community after World War I was different from the prewar period. Contrary to Eli Na-thans' interpretation,[33] it is not the case that the same fears and preju-dices inspired anti-Semitic and nationalist naturalization practices before and after the war. The lack of territorial stability and national self-consciousness, the changing structure of immigration, and the par-ticular state of international relations after World War I caused more rupture than continuity and provided a breakthrough for the gradual radicalization of citizenship politics under National Socialism.

IV. Concluding Remarks

The polarity and opposition of a "German" and a "French" conception of the nation rest upon constructions that became fully developed be-tween the proclamation of the French nation during the French Revo-lution and the founding of the German nation-state in 1870–71. The confrontation of an ethnic-objective and a political-subjective concept of the nation, however, was not synonymous with the confrontation of two principles of attaining citizenship, *ius sanguinis* and *ius soli*. Rather, ethnocultural and state-political elements in the citizenship law of both nations coexisted simultaneously. As my analysis has shown, at the end of the nineteenth century, the citizenship systems of both na-tions developed, above all, on the basis of two factors: (1) confronta-tional perceptions and the political reactions to these perceptions and (2) the differing political, economic, and demographic conditions in the two nations. Although the differing conceptions of the nation did make possible and easier the polarization of two different systems of citizen-ship, they only partially conditioned developments and exercised their effects with temporal delay. The "republican" citizenship law of the *ius soli* in France was established two decades after the defeat at the hands of Germany, at the beginning of a period of political and military up-swing; the dominance of the ethnocultural conception of the nation in the German *ius sanguinis* first emerged after the defeat—above all by France—in World War I. We have seen how much the leading concep-tions of citizenship in Germany and France in the twentieth century emerged from confrontations between the two nation-states at the end of the nineteenth century. There is much to be said for the thesis that, with the reduction of confrontation between the two nation-states, the path has been laid for a convergence of citizenship systems in Germany and France.

CHAPTER 3

The Citizen and the Republic
in Germany, 1918–1935

PETER C. CALDWELL

IN A PAMPHLET ISSUED IN 1919, Walther Rathenau proclaimed the need for a "new state": a "living construction from bottom to top, in constant renewal and motion," rather than a "static" and "formal" parliamentarianism.[1] Rathenau's writing fit within a broad cultural discourse (in the sense of an action-shaping rhetoric not necessarily founded on rational argumentation) that reached across the political spectrum from the Far Right to the Far Left. Opposed to the "dead" forms of parliamentary democracy, the new state would somehow be "living," an organism that connected real people to power. As opposed to the "static" and "formal" rules of parliamentary procedure, the new state would incorporate authentic voices of the people into government. The liberal Rathenau, like Oswald Spengler on the Far Right and Rosa Luxemburg on the Far Left, hoped for a different kind of citizen, one fully involved in the collective work of the *Volk* rather than an individual bearer of private and public rights: a citizen in substance rather than a private person, a bourgeois, making use of formal citizenship rights for his or her own gain.[2]

The criticism of so-called formal citizenship marked political debate in Germany between 1918 and 1935. The concepts of *citizen, public, law,* and *nation* were under dispute as political players took positions on which rights and procedures should replace monarchical rule with popular self-government. The term *citizenship* itself, however, conveyed a variety of different significations, as it does in the present book. Not all of these meanings are compatible: those focusing on the formation of identities and communities may point to a very different object of analysis than those focused on legal rules and institutions, for example.

In this chapter, I begin by asking what kinds of insights these different significations of citizenship provide. The second part of this contribution turns to the role that the notion of citizenship played at a critical juncture in German history. I argue that the search for a substantive citizenship as an alternative to parliamentary democracy could take many forms. Advocates of councils and corporate assemblies had an active notion of citizenship: they sought to extend the rights of active citizens to shape their surroundings. Carl Schmitt, by contrast, sought to restrict citizenship rights in the name of a leader-oriented republicanism that echoed Mussolini's emulations of Roman republicanism under fascism. Finally, the Nuremberg Laws implemented a citizenship that proclaimed status and identity, but notably set up no active rights. After examining different challenges to parliamentary democracy in the name of an active citizenship, I posit a correlation between the conception of citizenship as identity and the paucity of active citizenship rights.

I. Conceptions of Citizenship

Citizenship has at least four different meanings within contemporary scholarship. It may refer to a subject's belonging to a state, the objective set of rights that accrue to a citizen within a state, the citizen's subjective sense of which rights he or she is entitled to within the state, or a subjective feeling of identification with a certain state or community. Listing these four categories does not imply an impermeable division among them. In practice, observers tend to make use of the term *citizenship* in multiple ways. But the distinctions do remain, and lead to different descriptions in historical work.

In the context of international law, citizenship means simply being part of a specific state. (The German indicates this with the term *Staatsangehörigkeit.*) One might be a serf or a slave, a monarch or a magnate; one might be the subject of a despot or a republican citizen with active voting rights. All count as "citizens" of a certain state. As Georg Jellinek noted more than a century ago, citizenship from the point of view of international law is purely formal: it simply means "belonging" to a certain jurisprudence.[3] Whether a particular person feels like a citizen is irrelevant to the definition, and so this definition does not deal with a subjective sense of entitlement in politics. But for the international lawyer, the formal concept is necessary. It permits not only decisions on jurisdiction but also the ascription of legal responsibility to states in areas such as international private law and human rights. The formal notion furthermore does have a history that intersects with other conceptions of citizenship, one that overlaps with the growing regularization of international law during the past two centuries and with the accompanying problem of stateless refugees such as German Jews, stateless combatants such as those held by the United States at Guantanamo Bay, and territories without a state.[4]

Citizenship in the second sense refers to a wide body of rights and duties held only by those recognized as citizens by the state's own rules. The rights and duties of citizens may cover a number of different areas, including contractual rights, rights to have access to courts or other state authorities, social rights, and the right to shape the rights and procedures of the state itself.[5] Citizenship as a bundle of rights remains a relatively formal, legal concept—but by no means insignificant. From the point of view of legal actors, determining whether someone has legal rights and access to legal institutions such as a court is paramount. This definition of citizenship refers to a huge area—potentially to law in its entirety. But some rights, such as rights guaranteeing private property, serve to limit actions of citizens beyond the property owner, although others, such as voting rights, enable citizens to shape their own polity. A formal, legal definition of citizenship covers both the freedom to participate collectively in a polis and the freedom to act without reference to the other members of a polis.[6] A formal description of rights and duties highlights that relationship rather than covering it up. That is one reason why defenders of property rights were so disturbed by the formalist legal work of the period.[7] The Socialists in the revolution of 1918–19, furthermore, challenged precisely this relationship between private entitlements and public rights of citizens. Historical work that makes use of the formal definition of citizenship tends to focus on institutions and systems (frameworks within which actions take place). This is the approach of much constitutional history in Germany: it seeks to portray the development of state law as a set of rights and duties that develop within a specific historical context.[8]

There is no sharp boundary between an "objective" set of private and public rights possessed by citizens, the second sense of citizenship, and the subjective sense and active use of those rights in the third sense: law's "meaning" becomes clear through practice, through action.[9] People act as citizens when they justify their actions according to their subjective sense of having rights or entitlements within a certain community.[10] This sense of having rights, of being entitled to call upon the state to either act or not act in specific cases, may not line up with the rights of the citizen as determined by those empowered to enforce those rights in the name of state, city, or other community (from legislator to judge to police). Citizenship may take the form, then, of appealing to rights that are imaginary—just as it may take the form of appealing to rights that would challenge the status quo.[11] Law is mutable, and at moments when an entire system of law is under examination, as in the period 1918–36 in Germany, conceptions of citizenship influence how the legal community is imagined. Historical work that focuses on subjective notions of entitlement covers a broad area, from direct challenges to existing rules by those searching for a different kind of society (the councils theorists and corporatists whom I look at below) to conflicts in courts and other legal institutions over what is possible and what is not within a political system (e.g., fights over the limits to free speech in Weimar, or the issue of abortion rights, which is the subject of Cornelie Usborne's contribution to this volume). But these investigations of the subjective sense of entitlement of individuals require that the investigator consider law as it objectively exists as well. Claiming that women as citizens have the right to control their own bodies is not the same thing as having that right.[12]

Finally, one may separate citizenship from legal rights and duties completely. Citizenship in this fourth sense may serve as a category of identity, and in particular national identity: one feels oneself a citizen of a given community or state, regardless of whether rights or duties exist within that entity. I think that this is an important aspect of citizenship: one thinks of the image of the patriotic fighter, hand raised in allegiance to the republic, body set at its disposal as a soldier.[13] But it is only one aspect of citizenship, and has no necessary connection to the first three categories. Furthermore, historians already have articulated concepts of "national identity" and "collective identity" that are quite independent of the citizenship concept. Citizenship as identity needs to retain some distinction, perhaps a connection to the republican tradition, if it is going to add to the historical debate.[14]

One other use of the term *citizenship* should be mentioned, although I am not as convinced of its utility: as a category describing "social practices that define the relationship between people and state and among people within communities."[15] The notion of a "social practice" or "instituted process" is general enough to apply to a wide variety of societies: citizenship shifts from being a conception immanent in the object of historical analysis to being an abstract category describing societies in a transcultural and transhistorical way. Serfs and slaves are part of "instituted processes." That does not necessarily make them "citizens" as bearers of actual rights and duties in the second, third, and perhaps even fourth senses above. And even in the first sense, of belonging to a state recognized by an international legal order, the term *citizen* may not apply in certain contexts. If Afghanistan under the Taliban was not internationally recognized as a state, then women were not citizens even in the first sense of the term, although they played a role in the narrowly circumscribed "instituted practices" of home and community. Although the examination of the social foundations of citizenship is an important task, social history alone, without political, legal, and intellectual contexts, will not provide an adequate description of citizenship.

All the notions of citizenship laid out above have political ramifications within specific historical contexts; they are not merely descriptive terms employed by outside observers. Ethnicity was, of course, important for the discussion of citizenship in Germany, but by no means was it the only or even most important criterion for talking about "the people" as the Republic formed. Debates over the nature of the people and their representation revolved around the role of councils and revolutionary control, corporate assemblies and parliament, and whether republican unity permitted pluralism and parties.

II. State, Society, and Citizenship in Weimar Germany

Darauf kommt es an, zu wissen, was ein Volk, das durch den Zusammenbruch einer alten Herrschaft traditionslos geworden ist, eigentlich will.[16]

By July 31, 1919, when Friedrich Naumann uttered these words in the National Assembly, the main decisions had been taken to preserve a strong executive, private property, the traditional judiciary, and much of the old administrative structure within the context of parliamentary democracy. A good deal of Germany's tradition had, in fact, been retained. The question of what shape the German polity would take remained open, however, as the Kapp Putsch, Ruhr uprising, Beer Hall Putsch, and indeed the Republic's slide into dictatorship after 1929 show. In a sense, Naumann's words sum up the problem of citizenship from the point of view of democracy. First is the question of what and who a *Volk* is: who is the citizen empowered to take on responsibility for the *res publica*? Second, given that old traditions were challenged in the revolution, through what regular practices and institutions does a citizen take on that responsibility? How do citizen and state relate, and what are the means of representation? How do the multiple systems of civil society link up with the state? Indeed, does a clear distinction still exist between work and family, or associational life on the one hand and the state on the other—that distinction so fundamental to German political thought? And finally, what should the revolutionary polity look like?

A. Councils

The revolution produced a radical notion of citizenship: the immediate assembly of working men and women at their place of work, in the form of soldiers' and workers' councils. The councils broke the continuity of the German state's development; they overthrew not just the monarch but also the Reichstag, the government, and at the local level the power of administration. In some areas, such as Munich, they also restructured the judiciary to permit immediate justice by the people, not subject to appeal.[17] On November 10, the councils of greater Berlin appointed two bodies that would unify executive and legislative power in the hands of the Socialist parties. The Council of People's Deputies consisted of three moderate Social Democrats and three representatives of the Independent Social Democrats (USPD), also from the less radical part of the party. The Executive Council was staffed with more radical representatives; its initial function was supervisory, although the exact relationship between it and the Council of People's Deputies was unclear. At the General Congress of Workers' and Soldiers' Councils on December 19, 1918, deputies from across Germany mandated that a National Assembly be appointed to write the new constitution. In other words, the councils, not the "German people" as defined by principles of general and equal suffrage, would determine the political course of Germany. Friedrich Ebert sought to blunt the revolutionary challenge of the councils movement when he argued for a continuity with the wartime organization of the state: the Council of People's Deputies, under his leadership, in his estimation, would act like the monarchical government in wartime, and the leadership of the Central Council—elected by the General Congress of Councils on December 19 to replace the Executive Council—would act as a kind of interim wartime parliament, ceding most powers to the Council of People's Deputies.[18] Despite Ebert's interpretation, however, the fact remains that for a short time the councils were sovereign and this sovereignty rested on the factual assumption of power rather than on a carefully considered theory.

In the months after the revolution, a general theory of the councils gradually formed.[19] The radical journalist and councils delegate Ernst Däumig provided one of the most coherent defenses of councils as a system. He began his defense of a "councils republic" with a criticism of the "formal," "parliamentary-democratic-bourgeois" system.[20] The free press served only to reiterate the arguments of the big capitalists who controlled it; likewise, he asserted, the political parties would serve whatever system prevailed. They all served capitalism at present in order to maintain themselves.[21] Furthermore, they separated the people from power and artificially set the workers against each other.[22] Finally, Däumig rejected the constitutionalist doctrine of the separation of powers: executive and legislative power, he argued, should be permanently lodged in the hands of the councils, in direct contradiction to the foundations of "bourgeois democracy."[23] At its core, Däumig's argument, colored by the work of Revolutionary Shop Steward leader Richard Müller and others at the center of the movement, assumed that parliamentary democracy was a failure before it had even begun in Germany: the United States was ruled by trusts, Britain by imperialists, and France by finance capital.[24] For the defenders of the councils, the citizen played a *direct, unmediated, and active role* in self-government. Only those active in production, "workers of hand and head" (*Hand- und Kopfarbeiter*), could be full citizens.[25] The councils would extend the range of democracy from politics to production itself and would entail practical socialization: not the empowerment of state bureaucrats, but of workers at work.[26]

It is easy in retrospect to point out the naiveté of the theory of councils that sought to eliminate all bureaucratic control in a complex economy and to reconcile "planned organization of production" with "self-administration," in the words of the guidelines for the councils system adopted by the Councils of Greater Berlin on August 29, 1919.[27] But such unrealistic assumptions are part of a revolutionary experience. The workerist notion of citizenship posed bigger problems, both political and theoretical. The political Right, and not only the Right, pointed out that large factories do not encompass all those who work. The definition of the citizen as worker potentially excluded many in the population. Lower-level civil servants' and white-collar employees' positions in the councils were unclear; the notion of "workers of the

head" was vague and allowed for imprecision and caprice in drawing the line between "employee" and "manager," for example.[28] Well-
paid artisans and poorly paid servants were notably not part of any
firm. How did they fit into the councils system? And who defended
the rights of unpaid female domestic laborers and the unemployed?
The councils system, although overcoming "formal democracy," in
fact restricted citizenship. The call to unify the power of the people
in the form of a dictatorship of the proletariat, finally, represented one
of the fundamental errors of many on the Left in the twentieth century:
the belief that legality hinders progress.

Yet the pitfalls of the "councils system" should not obscure the challenge it posed to a notion of citizenship premised on the clear distinction between public freedom through representation and private domination (exactly the problem surrounding the political emancipation
of women). The danger of removing this distinction, of course, lay in
the compression of economics into politics. If a council had both the
political right to vote and the right to hire and fire within a firm, for
example, it could deny an opponent a vote by denying his or her job.[29]
Could there be a revolutionary notion of citizenship that attacked private power but nonetheless maintained the legal forms that distinguish
democracy from despotism? Alternatives were certainly available. The
Social Democrat Max Cohen, a member of the Central Council, for
example, developed a model of council codetermination of industrial
policy within the firm and at the level of legislation. His aim was to sal-
vage some aspect of the revolutionary councils movement for the new
democracy, and not to leave the claim to that movement to the propo-
nents of a dictatorship of the proletariat.[30] Workers and owners together
would form "chambers of labor" that would culminate in a second assembly alongside the Reichstag. A Chamber of Labor would represent
the "productive force and achievement of the people, of the people's
organism itself." Although it would not eliminate inequality between
workers and capitalists, it would, for the first time, bring workers into
decisions about production.[31] Cohen failed to find support in his own
party for this institution linking economics and politics through a legislative body.[32] The corporatist model, by contrast, did find its way into
the Weimar Constitution in the form of Article 165, which proclaimed
the existence of a National Economic Council. The National Assembly
discussion of Article 165 opened up another challenge to parliamentary
democracy and its conception of citizenship during the revolution—but
this time from the Right.

B. Occupational Estates

The first drafts of the new constitution contained no reference to councils and only minimal reference to basic rights. Only in the context of the radicalization of many workers in February 1919, culminating in the general strike of March, did the republican majority of the National Assembly seek a way to anchor the councils in the constitution. It aimed, however, to depoliticize the councils, to reduce them to a purely economic body in firms. These firm-based councils culminated in the National Economic Council, a sort of economics advisory committee on social and economic legislation. Article 165 left specific provisions to future legislators—who chose not to develop the institution further. Although it existed throughout the Republic, the National Economic Council in practice had little importance.[33]

Representatives to the National Assembly from both the Left and the Right sought to strengthen the councils. Representatives of the Far Left Independent Social Democrats and the Far Right German National People's Party (DNVP) became unlikely allies in their attempt to grant legislative power to councils. They meant different things by "council."[34] On March 4, 1919, Alfred Henke of the USPD called for councils based on the vote of "all those who want to work" that would exercise both legislative and executive power and would implement socialism. These councils, he asserted, were the product of the workers' own initiative and were not derived from the Russian Revolution; they represented a new form of polity, based on the 1871 Paris Commune, that would replace the parliament.[35] The Right rejected Henke's arguments and viewed the councils as a Bolshevik-inspired terrorist program. But, they argued, in the hands of German workers, an "inorganic," interest-based organization could be transformed into an "organic," "German," occupation-based organization. Hoping to bring about occupational estates, DNVP leaders argued for a robust Article 165 in the National Assembly and for similar assemblies in the *Länder*.[36] DNVP representative Adelbert Düringer called for a representative chamber based on corporate estates in his speech to the National Assembly.[37] DNVP leader Clemens von Delbrück proclaimed, although scornfully, that the councils represented the only innovation in the German Revolution of 1918–19. Though born of the Russian Revolution, he continued, they had taken on a different form of organizing the entire productive population of Germany and could serve as a corrective to an "exaggerated parliamentarianism." Their point, however, was not to dissolve

distinctions among workers, pulling everyone down into the faceless
masses, but to provide for parity among different groups to ensure that
all voices be heard.[38]

Unlike the advocates of workers' councils, supporters of occupational estates as an alternative to parliamentary democracy had been
considering such representational forms over the previous half century.[39] One of their clearest advocates, Edgar Tatarin-Tarnheyden, was
explicit in his rejection of "head-count democracy" (*Kopfzahldemokratie*).
In a parliamentary system, he argued, each individual citizen voted as
an atomized individual for parties representing special interests rather
than the interests of the whole; citing Lenin, he asserted that the democratic republic might be the best cover for the rule of capital.[40] Tatarin-
Tarnheyden, furthermore, called for active citizenship rights to be directly connected to productive activity, under which he included a wide
variety of occupations. Although the "drones" might thereby lose their
voice, he questioned whether that would be a loss to society.[41] The right
to participate in self-legislation would not be unstructured, formal, and
individualized but rather organic, where each person would be part
of a cell, in turn forming part of a great, productive organism.[42] That
organism, he argued, already existed in the thousands of corporate
organizations of German society. The organic future was embedded
in present-day communities of laborers in their trade unions, professionals in professional organizations, and employers in their societies.
Like a Gramsci of the right, Tatarin-Tarnheyden sought the sources for
a counterhegemonic challenge to political democracy and liberalism in
the subterranean development and self-organization of production. His
prime example for how these organic interests could rise to the level of
political entities was the Central Labor Community (*Zentrale Arbeitsgemeinschaft*) formed on November 18, 1918, between representatives of
labor unions and employers' organizations. This was, he proclaimed,
the Magna Carta of labor, citing union boss Carl Legien: it gave organized labor the right to participate in the social organism (but notably
not to take control of it).[43] It empowered labor to cooperate with capital
in a communal economy (*Gemeinwirtschaft*) while rejecting expropria-
tion as social policy.[44]

Unlike most theorists of the organic state—such as Rudolf Steiner
with his vague esoterica, Othmar Spann and his romantic conception
of community, and even Walther Rathenau—Tatarin-Tarnheyden was a
trained lawyer with specialized knowledge of interest groups in society.[45] His conception of the citizen embedded in an organic totality is

to be taken seriously—after all, it is precisely the corporatist conception that is at the heart of "citizenship" in a large complex institution like a university today. But just as colleagues, students, staff, and administration at my university stand in a complex and unequal relationship to one another (and in an essentially subservient relationship to the collective monarch of Rice University, the Board of Trustees), so the requirement of "parity" in the corporatist conception ensured unequal citizenship rights of professionals, workers, consumers, and managers under the state. The place of the marginalized, such as housewives, domestic servants, and part-time laborers, was ignored by Tatarin-Tarnheyden, as it had been in the work of Däumig.

Like the councils, occupational estates rejected the notion that an unstructured, formal, abstract, equal right to vote periodically was an adequate way of aggregating interests and reaching the general will. Both criticisms relied on the distinction between mere form and real substance, where substance represented some kind of coherent decision on political and social organization conceived of as a totality. That "totality" had a different relationship to existing society: whereas the councils' aim was to revolutionize capitalist society, the estates' aim was to conserve a social organization that had developed spontaneously within capitalism and to hinder "abstract" interference with that organization by a democratic legislature (whether in the hands of a capitalist or a socialist party). Form and substance were in fact slogans in a number of German academic fields after the turn of the century and took on a distinctly political meaning, especially in the political theory of the Republic. Carl Schmitt's search for the "substance" of the nation represented a direct attack on "formalism."

C. Plebiscitary Democracy

The organized Right remained relatively moderate in its demands during the National Assembly. The DNVP's call for a corporate assembly, for example, was far removed from the calls for a Führer and ideologies of extralegal violence being developed in the Freikorps and other Far Right groups. The party officially remained within the constitutional framework, although a few short years later some of its leaders would work behind the scenes to support the Kapp Putsch.[46] The period after 1920 saw some of the most fertile work of antidemocratic political thinkers on the Right.[47] Although some turned openly against the new democratic order per se, others constructed a theory of post-traditional authoritarianism on the basis of mass democracy.

Carl Schmitt's *Verfassungslehre* of 1928 stands as his most important contribution to constitutional theory. His work of the early 1920s openly admired the work of the radical Right; his work after 1928 was less theoretical than practical, laying the foundations for presidential rule. In 1928, however, Schmitt seemed for a moment to try to work within the parliamentary system to reconsider the foundations of constitutional thought in the light of the democratic revolution. Schmitt distinguished between the constitution as a set of mere rules and procedures, which he termed the "bourgeois" rule of law, and the constitution as a "concretely existing thing," as an "existentially existent will."[48] If the will, the power to decide, preexists constitutional rule, then the entire system of constitutional legality becomes subordinate to sovereign decision. The revolutionary subject is capable of superseding the constitution under certain conditions—conditions that by definition were not set down by mere constitutional statute.

Scholars do not disagree that Schmitt's *Verfassungslehre* contains valuable insights about the relationship between constitution and sovereignty. They disagree about the overall intent of the work: was it a neutral work of constitutional theory that laid out the problems facing the postrevolutionary order, or did it undermine parliamentary democracy by positing a deeper conception of the physical, willing "constitution" of the polity, one that might have led toward the authoritarian, presidential rule that Schmitt later defended under Brüning and Papen?[49] The conception of democratic citizenship that Schmitt developed, in my view, supports the latter conclusion: he did not describe constitutional reality so much as he sketched a different model of republican citizenship based on identity, immediacy, and homogeneity.

1. *Identity.* An authentic revolution, Schmitt argued, produces a constitution that cannot be a:

   contract between monarch and people or between some corporate (*ständisch*) organizations, but rather a political decision taken by the one and indivisible nation [*Nation*] determining its own fate. Every constitution presupposes this identity.[50]

   By *identity*, then, Schmitt meant a substantial unity, a *Volk* that is able to speak with one voice and act with one will. That, he argued, is the presumption of democracy. By implication, compromise and concession in the formation of a constitution necessarily reflect pluralism, the lack of identity.

2. *Immediacy.* Democracy, then, assumes a basic "identity" of the people, one that is better expressed collectively than by individuals:

"The natural form of the immediate expression of a *Volk*'s will is the affirming or rejecting outcry [*Zuruf*] of the assembled mass [*Menge*], acclamation [*Akklamation*]."[51] This immediacy furthermore presupposes a certain form of voting, on the model of the Roman forum or the Greek *ekklesias* or the assembled men (*Mannschaft*) of the Germanic tradition.[52] Truly sovereign voting is public, not private, open rather than secret, collective rather than individual.[53] Liberal democracy's protection of the individual's right to vote as an individual, in a closed voting booth, without communal influence, is by implication illegitimate and contradicts the political principle of democracy, Schmitt claimed.[54]

3. *Homogeneity.* "Democracy," Schmitt wrote, "is a state form that corresponds to the principle of identity (namely of the concretely present *Volk* with itself, as a political unit)."[55] Individual freedom is not a necessary part of democracy insofar as it may break the collective will.[56] "Equality" (*Gleichheit*), however, is. But "equality" here means "sameness"; it relies on the distinction between the same, the identical, and the not-same, the different, the unequal. *"Gleichheit"* is defined "substantively" as the fact of "belonging to a certain *Volk*," whose sense of belonging may be determined by very different moments: "conceptions of a common race, faith, common fate and tradition."[57] Whatever the common element, it is the political foundation of democracy. "Democratic homogeneity" is a "political principle of form" that contradicts the "liberal" idea of the equality and freedom of individuals.[58] Or, to provide one more quotation: "Democratic equality is essentially *sameness of type* [*Gleichartigkeit*] and, in particular, sameness of type of *Volk*."[59] Schmitt explicitly did not state here that the "same type" must be race; that is an argument he made after Hitler came to power.[60] The implication, at any rate, is that democracy is qualitatively different from the individualism and rights associated with liberalism and the "bourgeois" rule of law. The democratic citizen, by implication, is an *immediate part of a public, self-identical, homogeneous whole*: not a bourgeois, not a "private man."[61] Division of the people into interest-representing parties runs counter to Schmitt's notion of republicanism.[62]

The call for a strong, substantive notion of citizenship over against the mere formalism of parliamentarianism and the rule of law, as well as the distrust of parties and special interests in a representative system, mark the similarities between Schmitt's conception and those of the advocates of councils democracy and of corporatism. Over the next five years, Schmitt fleshed out an argument for a presidential democracy organized around the acclamation of the people and the exclusion of parties. But his notion of acclamation remained limited: the people as substantial unity can only say "yes" or "no" to relatively simple questions;[63] in practice, Schmitt's republican citizens cede authority to those who set the questions.[64] They are not active workers in the councils or active producers in the corporatist assemblies. It comes as no surprise that Schmitt admired Mussolini's executive control with plebiscitary affirmation.[65] An interesting contradiction appears: the most theoretically sophisticated critique of "merely" formal parliamentary democracy imagined a far more passive citizenry.

Beyond its political implications, Schmitt's theory was muddy at its core in the notion of the homogeneity of the people. The idea that a "people" has a unified relationship to some core attribute in each other and in its leader is, I think, empirically false. People identify with leaders and nation for many different reasons, and to assert otherwise is to affirm a myth of oneness, of collective identity. It takes brute force to give such a myth practical relevance.

III. The Nuremberg Laws: The Triumph of Passive Citizenship

The previous sections have outlined three challenges to "formal" democracy, political parties, and an "abstract," "individualistic," "headcount" notion of the citizenry. Radical advocates of a councils republic conceptualized the citizen as a *worker actively and directly involved in determining both polity and economy*. The corporatists saw the citizen as a *producer actively embedded within a structured, organic, social totality*, and shaping, once more, both polity and economy. Schmitt and other authoritarians saw the citizen as a *direct part of an already existing national totality* and, because the totality already existed, playing the passive role of affirming or rejecting executive decisions. Schmitt's notion of citizenship recreated the distinctions between public and private, and politics and property, that were characteristic of nineteenth-century liberalism—but rejected political liberalism, especially in its contemporary democratic form.

Liberal democrats, meanwhile, were deprived of utopian or mythic elements with which to defend the existing system. Parliamentary democracy existed, and the reality of democracy is generally not heroic but, rather, complex and messy. Its theorists doubted the existence of a national consensus on basic questions. The people (plural!) made their decisions through a procedure; will was formed rather than given. The question was how to organize the legislative process to reflect as many interests as possible. They argued that the best way to ensure that a polity remained open to change was to allow social groups to develop spontaneously, without state control. To facilitate social organization, rights applied to all citizens of the state—to all who "belonged" to the state, not just friends of the plebiscitary leader or those deemed worthy as workers and producers.[66] As Ian Shapiro has pointed out, the defense of democracy is a "relatively thin one," based on:

> its claim to our allegiance as the best available system for managing power relations among people who disagree about the nature of the common good, among many other things, but who nonetheless are bound to live together.[67]

Weimar democracy would fail, but what replaced it supports rather than refutes Shapiro's claim.

Hitler's coming to power ended democracy. The Nuremberg Laws shed light on the new notion of citizenship of the Nazi state. The Nuremberg Laws related to the first signification of "citizenship" developed at the start of this paper, the determination of who "belongs" to the state (*Staatsangehörigkeit*). The laws made a distinction between *Reichsbürger* and a mere *Staatsangehöriger*, which was a more general term for those who were within the state's jurisdiction. A *Reichsbürger* bore "German or like blood," and proved through his behavior the willingness and ability to serve "the German race and Reich" faithfully. The definition of German blood at the heart of the laws, as has been pointed out, often was ambiguous and anything but a clear guideline for legal decisions. However, other aspects of the laws are more important for the present paper. First, the laws broke with the principle of equality before the law associated with the German *Rechtsstaat*.[68] Second, the laws for the *Reichsbürger* created no rights or procedures for active participation. They flew in the face of political liberalism, the councils tradition, and corporatism. Citizenship meant the state of belonging, not the right to codetermine; it referred to the identity of Germans, not to the ability of citizens to organize socially.

In short, the importance of the Nuremberg Laws extends beyond their exclusion of Jews, other non-Aryans, and those not "willing and able" to serve the "race." As Carl Schmitt declared, the Nuremberg Party Congress and its laws represented "the first German constitution of freedom" in centuries; it defined the citizen in a substantive sense, not in the merely formal sense of the *Staatsangehöriger*, and it elucidated the foundation of the new order:

the German *Volk* with its Führer as head of state and highest judge over the nation; the order of the National Socialism movement as the defender of our constitution; the German army with the Führer as the commander in chief.[69]

Citizenship as identity rather than as a set of rights and duties was an essential part of Nazi despotism.

IV. Conclusion

All four notions of citizenship laid out in the first section of this paper played a role in the Weimar Republic. At stake was the relationship between citizen and state: who was inside and who was outside of the state (*Staatsangehörigkeit*); the objective rights and laws that enabled or limited action by citizens; the sense of rights and entitlement of those who considered themselves citizens; and, finally, citizenship as a component of national identity. Although the Nuremberg Laws fall outside of the official years of the Republic, they responded to debates within the Republic. They both broke with the liberal tradition of constitutionalism and asserted that a substantive and not merely formal notion of citizenship had finally been attained.

Rathenau, Däumig, Tatarin-Tarnheyden, and Schmitt all formulated their positions as critiques of formal notions of citizenship. *Formal* was a vague term in Weimar, of course (though not nearly so vague as the term *substantive!*). What it implies was first and foremost some kind of rule or procedure that allowed things to happen, no matter what "substantive" ethics might demand. Mere formal voting rights would allow those to vote who were perhaps communists or capitalists or Jews or "drones." Mere formal property rights would allow land to be purchased by a Jew or by a capitalist or by a workers' organization. Formal property rights, furthermore, allowed a variety of groups to make their views public through ownership of publishing houses: effective speech by marginalized groups (and by pornographers) in mass industrial society is probably inseparable from property rights. Mere formal citizenship rights allowed all of these groups, as well as women, access to the legal system, even if they challenged dominant values. The Nuremberg Laws as well as many other Nazi decrees ensured that the formal aspects of citizenship were subordinate to substantive values—which meant values defined by the clique in charge. Despotism justifies itself in terms of morality.

Which is not to say that all moral arguments about who is a citizen are necessarily despotic, or that all formal notions of the citizen are democratic (although in Weimar that correlation often held true). *Form* and *substance* are notably slippery terms; *formalism*, for example, may reflect a substantive respect for other people even when one disagrees with them—it may, in other words, be grounded in a moral conception. The point is that the conception of citizenship employed by German political actors in these years was implicated in a set of fundamental questions about democracy. And if, as this chapter has suggested, the usefulness of the term *citizen* for historical work draws on the conceptions developed within the object of historical analysis, then the notion of citizen and citizenship used by the historians of Weimar Germany is bound up with the challenges of citizenship at that time. Historians need to consider whether the concept of citizenship they employ, no matter how it might correspond to present-day concerns, unwittingly implies a position in the political debates of the times they are investigating. As my aside in this paper on issues of governance at Rice University shows, different institutional and historical contexts fundamentally alter the political function of certain concepts.[70] Focus on rules and procedures alone may result in a dry history that ignores or denies what was at stake in Weimar and the fundamental political challenge of what a (formal) democrat is to do when the majority of citizens use their rights against democracy. Focus on identity, however, runs the risk of moving into the realm of myth, which was, despite efforts by the Left, effectively controlled by the Nazis. Abstract concepts cannot save historians from the requirement of working out the methodological and ethical challenges posed by an object of historical analysis.

CHAPTER 4

Culture, Belonging, and the Law:
Naturalization in the Weimar Republic

ANNEMARIE SAMMARTINO

IN 1922, ARON GENKIN APPLIED for German citizenship. Genkin was a Jewish Ukrainian doctor who wanted to become a German citizen so he could be licensed to work as a doctor in Germany and thus better support his wife-to-be, a German war widow, and her three children. He initially submitted his naturalization application in Thuringia, which approved it and sent it to the other *Länder* for approval, as was required by the citizenship law of 1913. The Bavarians advised the Thuringians that they did not intend to support Genkin's naturalization because he belonged to a "foreign *and uncultured nation [fremdstämmigen und kulturfremden Nation]*."[1] As a result, his application was forwarded to the *Reichsrat*; a majority of delegates from each of the German states would have to vote to grant him citizenship if he were to be naturalized. Genkin's fiancée, Maria Berenz, hearing of the possible rejection of his application, appealed directly to Friedrich Ebert, the German chancellor:

I have struggled most terribly for eight years [since the death of her husband in 1914 on the front] and I am both spiritually and physically at the end of my strength. Herr Dr. Genkin, a noble man who is respected by all who know him and a selfless friend to my children, has come and wants to help us, four victims of the war. Herr Reichspräsident, shouldn't one greet this generous deed with generosity? Shouldn't the German state give this man citizenship so that he can fulfill the responsibilities that he has already taken upon himself with the engagement, and that he finds sacred? Here the state can also fulfill its sacred duty towards four war victims who would otherwise be doomed. . . .[2]

Despite Berenz's passionate appeal, there is no evidence that Ebert actually intervened in this case. Instead, at the first vote in the *Reichsrat*,

Genkin's naturalization application was denied by a vote of 5–4, with Prussia voting with Bavaria against granting citizenship. According to the Bavarian representative to the *Reichsrat*, the application was denied because Genkin's stated intent of helping his fiancée and her family, though noteworthy, was a private interest secondary to national concerns.[3] For the five states that voted against Genkin's naturalization, the link that Berenz had tried to invoke between the suffering of her family and the duties of the state was unconvincing.

Shortly after, the Thuringian representative, with Prussia's support, brought the case back to the *Reichsrat*. Berenz again wrote a letter in support of her fiancé's application, this time to the Thuringian representative. However, she changed her tactic: instead of emphasizing the suffering of her family, she wrote about how great a provider Genkin was, ending by noting that "it is not Herr Dr. Genkin's fault that he is of Jewish descent; he has a very noble-minded disposition and is a true friend of Germany."[4] In this later vote, the Prussian representative changed his mind and voted to grant Genkin citizenship. According to the Bavarian representative to the *Reichsrat*, Prussia's decision was based on the fact that Genkin had been admitted to the exam to get a German medical license, thus proving he was worthy of becoming a naturalized German citizen.[5] Ebert and the *Reichsrat* were unmoved by the suffering of Berenz and her children. What appeared to have changed the Prussian representative's mind was a decision on the part of other German authorities that Genkin was acceptable on his own terms.

Even those who opposed Genkin's citizenship application recognized that he was an upstanding man whose naturalization would substantially alleviate the suffering of a war widow and her three young children. Furthermore, as a trained doctor, Genkin was highly educated, and he appeared to hold no objectionable political views.[6] Genkin, moreover, had lived in Germany for years and spoke fluent German.[7] His personal character was not at issue during this debate; neither was there any reason to suspect that a denial of his citizenship application would have caused him either to end his relationship with Berenz or to leave German soil. Nevertheless, his citizenship application inspired heated controversy. Several German states tenaciously sought to deny Genkin the right to German citizenship, while others argued just as passionately that he deserved membership in the German national community. In the pages that follow, I explore the highly divisive debates about citizenship policy and practice that convulsed the

German republic in its first years. In other words, I investigate the reasons behind the initial rejection and ultimate acceptance of Genkin's naturalization application.

Although the citizenship law of 1913 and its *ius sanguinis* definition of German belonging remained in effect throughout the Weimar period, actual citizenship practice was much more heterogeneous. A complex set of concerns motivated local and national officials; a homogeneous ethnic community was one, but by no means the predominant, interest. In both theory and practice, officials held to seemingly contradictory beliefs in the determinative power of ethnic belonging, the responsibilities of ethnic solidarity, and a sense of the possibility for cultural assimilation. Germans from across the political spectrum—save the extreme Left—shared a belief that citizenship should only be available to those who had proven their German identity. Nonetheless, there was a striking lack of agreement as to what attributes—whether ethnic or cultural—constituted this slippery notion of "German identity." The issue of defining German identity was particularly fraught in the first years of the fledgling republic. Officials rewrote citizenship regulations to reflect the changing political imperatives of the post–World War I world, defining them more loosely due to the newfound political clout of the Socialists. At the same time, Germany faced the immigration of hundreds of thousands of foreigners who managed to cross its porous postwar frontiers in the first years of the new republic. Despite their best efforts, German border guards were unable to staunch this flow. Citizenship policy and practice thus were freighted with the symbolic burden of compensating for the unsuccessful boundary maintenance that so frustrated Germans during this period.

I. Citizenship as Imagined Community

World War I destabilized the relationship between German identity and German citizenship. An imagined community of Germans living within Germany's borders was replaced with a more complex and less settled image that had to encompass people of German descent living in Russia, Jews who had lived their entire lives in Germany, Germans who had renounced their citizenship for supposed economic reasons and now petitioned to have it reinstated, German Communists claiming membership in an international proletariat that transcended German borders, German women who married Russian POWs and lost their German citizenship although they continued to live in Germany, and many other groups. To be sure, at least some of this diversity had existed prior to 1918, but the combination of war and political upheaval made people confront it in new ways. The war and the revolution led people from across the political spectrum to think about both the community they were a part of and the community they wished to construct for the future. One of the most important ways that Germans dealt with these issues was through constructing and debating citizenship policy.

Working within a climate of economic scarcity and general hostility toward foreigners, the various German states attempted to negotiate thousands of applications for citizenship. According to Rogers Brubaker, this should have been an easy task. Brubaker and others argue that Germany's sense of citizenship and belonging was, and for the most part still is, located in an understanding of German identity dependent on German blood. This schema amounts to a teleology whereby the ethnic guidelines established by the 1913 law provided a framework for German citizenship policy but lead directly to the racism of the Nazi regime. Yet looking at both policy guidelines and the handling of actual citizenship cases reveals a substantially more complicated picture. Although some officials did subscribe to an, albeit not absolute, definition of German belonging based on ethnicity, others argued that, through long-term exposure to German culture, foreigners could express the cultural qualities that would make them worthy citizens. Ethnic solidarity and radical assimilation existed alongside one another as competing models for the adjudication of citizenship claims.

As a result of the process spelled out in the 1913 citizenship law, all citizenship applicants submitted their applications to a local office, where they were reviewed and then approved by the *Land*'s Interior Ministry. The *Land* then was required to submit a list of potential citizenship applicants for review by the other *Länder*, which were allowed to raise objections to those they felt undeserving of citizenship in the Reich. In cases of disagreement, the *Reichsrat*, a council made up of representatives from each of the *Länder*, decided by a majority vote whether the applicant would be granted citizenship.[8] Even in Prussia, which was ruled by a coalition led by the Social Democrats, only slightly more than half of citizenship applications were recommended for approval. The number of citizenship applications approved in Prussia rose 250% between 1921 and 1923—from 6,953 to 17,848. During those same years, the number of applications from "foreigners from the East of non-German descent" (*fremdstämmige Ostausländer*) that were approved decreased from 757 to 309,[9] while hundreds of thousands of foreigners arrived on

German soil. Based on these figures, no more than 30,000 foreigners were applying for citizenship in Prussia during any given year, most of whom were ethnic Germans from eastern Europe. Very few new immigrants—especially the Jews, who inspired the most fear—applied for citizenship.[10]

References to the refugee crisis nonetheless often served as the background for the development and application of naturalization policy. For example, citizenship regulations drawn up in 1920 and implemented in the following year stated that citizenship needed to be restricted because of the influx of foreigners and the demands that they placed upon Germany.[11] In a 1923 letter to the Bavarian representative to the *Reichsrat*, the Bavarian interior minister referred to difficulties created by the "flood of immigrants" to explain the necessity for a restrictive naturalization policy:

The economic difficulties created by the flood of immigrants of foreign descent, especially the damage to the apartment and job market, must be continually stressed. The danger is even greater since a large portion of these foreigners have built their existence on the destruction of the economic life of Germany and would not be able to advance under healthy circumstances. When others reply that only those foreigners from the East would be granted citizenship who have been in Germany for years and "adapted themselves to German culture," it is to be remarked that the renewed immigration of Eastern elements has meant that those who have been here longer have received so-called fresh blood and so need to be dealt with even more carefully.[12]

Neither this letter by the Bavarian interior minister nor the national guidelines for citizenship (which I will discuss shortly) make any references to the tangible benefits that citizenship would confer upon foreigners and why these would increase the danger posed by foreigners residing in Germany. For example, although citizens had the right to receive state unemployment benefits, the allocation of such benefits was not part of the discussion of naturalization. Nor did voting rights play a role in the discussion. Instead, those who opposed the citizenship of non-German foreigners argued that these foreigners would take precious jobs and housing away from Germans (although few steps were actually taken to deny jobs or housing to noncitizens). As I have discussed elsewhere, the German government was, in practice, both unable and unwilling to deport immigrants.[13] Considering the fact that most foreigners who were denied citizenship would remain in Germany and that most recent immigrants were not even submitting naturalization applications, what did citizenship mean for Weimar Germans?

Recent valuable work reveals that citizenship is an arena in which individuals actively engage in defining their own relationships to the state.[14] But citizenship is never merely a question of self-definition. It exists at the symbolic crossroads of the state and its citizens; thus, in analyzing this dialectic of citizenship, examining the importance of citizenship to the state is crucial.[15] According to Timothy Mitchell, the state uses its performance of a series of tangible tasks, such as naturalization, to project an aura of its transcendence above the very social forces that constitute it.[16] Naturalization procedures fulfill this symbolic role, even in cases where the granting of or refusal to grant citizenship would have little tangible effect on the state or its citizens. In other words, in the process of adjudicating citizenship cases, the state is simultaneously constituting and reinventing its image and, thus, itself. Mitchell's attention to the symbolic role of state projects usefully illuminates a peculiar but rarely mentioned quality of citizenship: although citizenship (and here I am referring to *Staatsangehörigkeit*) is ostensibly about defining who is or is not part of a state, it rarely, if ever, actually corresponds to the composition of the people living within a state's borders. States generally have neither the military strength nor the moral imperative to deport those foreigners who manage to get over the border. Because of this fundamental lack of correspondence between the population of a state and those accorded the rights of citizenship, citizenship is never only a question of legal membership within a community, nor is it solely an issue of civic behavior and self-understanding.[17] Citizenship is quite literally about an *imagined* community; rather than representing the actual composition of society, it represents its ideal.[18]

Because of the national convulsions of the war and the postwar period, Weimar Germans were particularly aware of the symbolic quality of citizenship policy—the disjuncture between the population of those who claimed a German cultural or ethnic identity and the population currently residing within Germany's borders. Those who held to a notion of citizenship solely defined by descent and those who promoted the possibility of an acquired connection to German culture were arguing about this ideal vision of who should constitute the German national community. Seeing citizenship in this light helps to explain one of the otherwise confusing aspects of citizenship rhetoric, namely, the fact that debates about citizenship often emphasized the competition for scarce resources within Germany, even though immigrants—who, for the most part, could or would not be deported—would continue to compete for these resources whether or not they were citizens.

Mitchell argues that the state's performance of its duties buttresses its "aura" of transcendence. But in Weimar, the state failed to perform many of its mundane duties, including but not limited to the protection of German territory against a massive refugee crisis from eastern Europe. In a reversal of Mitchell's argument, anxieties about Germany's failure to secure its physical frontiers were projected onto this symbolic form of boundary maintenance.

Citizenship policies and practices could not actually control the numbers or types of foreigners within Germany. Furthermore, Germans were willing to tolerate the presence of many more foreigners than the number to whom they were willing to grant citizenship.[19] Yet if citizenship policy could not control who resided on German soil, it did reflect who officials believed belonged within the German community. In a letter to the Interior Ministry in Mecklenburg, the Bavarian Ministry of the Interior referred to its twenty-year waiting period for all nonethnic German immigrants from eastern Europe (*fremdstämmige Ostausländer*) as a "test period," implying its at least theoretical willingness to grant citizenship if, after this twenty-year term, this "eastern immigrant" had proven his or her connection to Germany.[20] Similarly, when the Saxon representative to the *Reichsrat* complained of the hardships induced by the stringent citizenship policy of the Reich, the national interior minister replied that "there is an important difference between tolerance of immigration and the granting of citizenship," and that many residents had not yet proven themselves worthy of citizenship, even if they were to continue to be allowed to reside in Germany.[21] To return to the Genkin case, although Genkin's naturalization was highly controversial for the delegates to the *Reichsrat*, no official, not even the Bavarians, contemplated deporting him. At issue was whether he deserved membership in the German community, not whether he deserved to live in Germany.

II. Citizenship Policy and Practice

In 1919, Wolfgang Heine, the Social Democratic interior minister of the Prussian government, articulated some guiding principles for the adjudication of citizenship applications in the new republic. Heine negotiated a fine line between a statist and an ethnic definition of German citizenship. On the one hand, Heine stated that, with regard to the hundreds of thousands of Germans who were then immigrating, it was a national duty to "repatriate former Germans" without exception. At the same time, he added that foreigners were surely not requesting natural-ization in the postwar period for their own personal gain, because there was little a weakened Germany could give them; instead, they must be motivated by "a firm inner connection to the German state."[22] Heine therefore called for the naturalization of all applicants who had served in the war or had sons who had served, including Jews and Poles.[23] The nationalists in Bavaria, who took power after the crushing of the Com-munist *Räterepublik* in the spring of 1919, opposed Heine's articulation of naturalization policy.[24]

This conflict between the two largest states in the republic led to a conference and the drafting of national guidelines for determining the citizenship of the flood of applicants that accompanied the end of the war.[25] The guidelines released by the Reich's Interior Ministry ar-gued for a cautious approach to the granting of citizenship.[26] Keeping in mind the housing, food, and work shortages currently plaguing the German state, they instructed local governments "only to accept people that demonstrate a positive population growth in a political, cultural and economic respect." The most important demonstration of a foreign-er's suitability for citizenship was his or her

way of life, namely in Germany itself, that expresses a sufficient understanding for the German way of life and for his [or her] public-legal responsibilities in the *Land* and the community.[27]

The Interior Ministry said that the following were all positive indica-tions that a foreigner should be granted citizenship:

Birth in Germany and being brought up with German methods and in a German environment, having a German mother or marriage with a German in combination with a long-term, trouble-free life in Germany.[28]

German ancestry was an important test of one's suitability for Ger-man citizenship. But the ministry guidelines also listed other factors— such as residence in Germany, exposure to German methods of child-rearing and education, and so on—implying that ancestry alone was not a sufficient basis for a citizenship claim and that culture played an important role in transmitting this connection to Germany. The guide-lines noted the importance of the applicant having

proven that he possesses a German character [*Eigenart*] and the ability to fit into the German cultural community. Here too, it is certain that foreigners of German descent are more likely to fulfill this standard than are others.[29]

German descent was clearly important, but only because it was a sign of a commitment to Germany and of the internalization of German culture. These were the factors that ultimately were necessary for any successful application for German citizenship.

As interesting as what was said in the Interior Ministry's guidelines is what they did not say. A draft that circulated among the German states a year earlier contained two clauses that did not find their way into the final document—one that absolutely forbade the awarding of citizenship to foreigners from the east of non-German descent, and one that would only allow citizenship to be awarded to the second generation of such foreigners, a continuation of prewar policy. These two clauses foundered in the face of opposition from the Prussians. The Prussian representative at the meeting to finalize this document stated:

such clauses would signal a return to Prussia's earlier Poland policy and must be avoided. The applications of *fremdstämmige Ostausländer* must be reviewed along the same principles applied to other applications.[30]

Interesting as well is the fact that the Prussian willingness to grant citizenship to those who had fought in the German army was not directly reflected in the policy guidelines that were ultimately agreed upon. Ethnicity, service, and cultural assimilation all were to play roles in the adjudication of citizenship cases.[31] As it was, the citizenship guidelines so painstakingly argued over in late 1920 had little effect on naturalization policy in the individual states. There was no marked difference between the handling of citizenship cases before and after the release of the guidelines in 1921. Instead, as I will discuss, the same conflicts about the worthiness of *fremdstämmige Ostausländer* for citizenship, pitting the principles of cultural assimilation against those of ethnic determinism, continued after the guidelines went into effect.

Throughout the early Weimar period, Social Democrats controlled the Prussian Interior Ministry, and Prussia also had the largest number of foreigners in the Reich. As the debates about policy suggest, Prussian naturalization practice tended to recognize the potential for the assimilation of foreigners to a greater degree than the Bavarians. Prussia often ran into conflicts with Bavaria, which insisted upon longer residency periods than the Prussians were willing to agree to. Yet to say that Prussia was more accepting of nonethnic Germans does not mean that Prussia entirely ignored ethnicity in adjudicating naturalization applications. Indeed, Prussian officials turned to the *Fürsorgeverein für deutsche Rückwanderer* (Aid Association for German Return-Migrants), an organization founded in 1909 to encourage the migration of *Auslandsdeutsche* to Germany, to verify applicants' German descent. (It often denied applications of recent immigrants who were not of German descent.)[32] Officials routinely assumed that non-German applicants were trying to get German citizenship solely for reasons of expediency. For example, the police president of Berlin accused the "Russian-Polish factory worker, Abraham Halpern, Jewish religion" of only wishing to keep his job and avoid deportation and separation from his German wife.[33] He was doubtful that Halpern had demonstrated a sufficient "firm inner connection" to Germany, despite marrying a German woman, and did not sympathize with Halpern's desire to maintain his livelihood and family. Halpern's familial obligations were deemed to be entirely personal and were looked upon with suspicion.

It was possible for non-Germans (even Jews) to receive the approval of the Prussians for their citizenship applications. In 1920, Württemberg forwarded to the Prussians the application of a Jewish factory owner, Aisik Borodowisch, who had been resident in Germany since 1903 and had unsuccessfully applied for citizenship in 1908, 1909, 1911, and 1916. Citing his military service and the fact that his presence did not signify a danger to the public order, the Württemberg minister of the interior recommended that Borodowisch be granted citizenship, a recommendation to which the Prussian Interior Ministry agreed.[34] The police president of Berlin forwarded the application of the Jewish doctor Helene Eliasberg to the Prussian Interior Ministry after she submitted recommendations from the Charité Hospital and the Ministry for Science, Art and Public Education.[35] Yet even applicants who, on the basis of their names at least, appeared to be of German descent were sometimes denied citizenship because they were considered to be "foreign [*Wesensfremd*] to Germandom." In December 1921, a local official recommended that the Prussian Interior Ministry reject the application of the miner Johann Müller because he was barely competent in the German language despite his long-term residence in Germany. This official further stated that Müller was only applying for citizenship because he wanted to avoid regulations that applied to foreigners and was considering returning to Russia for work.[36] Much like Halpern, Müller's desire to secure his livelihood was a factor against recommending his application. Various *Länder* contested the citizenship applications of several suspected Communists although they were of undisputed German descent.[37]

At the same time, those who were of German descent could surmount obstacles that a non-German could not hope to overcome. In 1919, the Prussian interior minister approved the naturalization of a Russian citizen of German descent, Johann Bergerack, despite his robbery conviction and ten-day jail sentence in December 1914. The local official who sent the application to the Prussian Interior Ministry wrote: "As a German returnee, Bergerack is to be considered a desirable addition to the population. I am approving his application in consideration of his unobjectionable conduct because he was punished." With this recommendation, the Prussian Interior Ministry approved his application.[38] Unemployed factory worker Anna Donat, another person of German descent from Russia, similarly was judged a desirable addition to the population although she had only been in Germany since 1916 and was unemployed at the time of her application.[39] Finally, the Berlin police president recommended an applicant named Milsch, even though he was a "known homosexual," because he was of German descent and had served honorably in the war, receiving the Iron Cross and behaving, at least to the knowledge of the police president, "morally" during the time of his service.[40]

Although the Prussians were more willing to grant citizenship to applicants of German descent, descent was only one criterion among many, albeit an important one. It appears that Prussian officials generally followed Heine's dual citizenship policy, which saw citizenship as a privilege based on German descent and public utility. They favored those who had performed military service or, as in the case of Eliasberg, other publicly useful tasks. At the same time, Prussian Interior Ministry officials were wary of applicants whose grounds for applying for citizenship could be traced back to personal gain. Citizenship was to be awarded as a result of a lofty "firm inner connection" to Germany and not more limited personal goals. Thus, in the Genkin case discussed earlier, although his personal goal of helping the Berenz widow and her children was deemed admirable, the case was ultimately decided on the basis of Genkin's more abstract worthiness for German citizenship.

The case of Moritz Estersohn, a Russian citizen who applied for Prussian citizenship in 1919 after more than twenty years of residence in Germany, is interesting because it represents one instance where the Prussian Interior Ministry challenged the rejection of an applicant by local officials. It was not a clear-cut case, so it illustrates some of the tensions that underlay citizenship policy in the early Weimar Republic, and exploring its progress in some detail is worthwhile. Estersohn first submitted his application for naturalization in 1919. After the local government in Arnsberg rejected it in August of that year, the Prussian Interior Ministry inquired as to the reasons for the rejection, noting that, according to his name and religion, he appeared to be of *"German* nationality."[41] The mayor of Hagen, where Estersohn was living, responded that Estersohn had been punished while serving in the army because he was insubordinate and stole some potatoes. Furthermore, the mayor emphasized that Estersohn had been arrested by Freikorps units and warned that he "belonged to political circles that wanted to destroy the peace of the population." Finally, the mayor wrote, Estersohn was originally Jewish and had only converted in 1898.[42] Even when faced with this seemingly damning evidence, the Prussian government still considered forwarding Estersohn's application to the other *Länder* for approval. This leniency was challenged by the Prussian Commissioner for Public Order, who reiterated the objections initially raised by Hagen's mayor, stating that Estersohn was a Communist, a profiteer, and Jewish besides.[43] Estersohn was rich enough to have his own lawyer, who responded to these accusations by noting that Estersohn had served two and a half years in the army despite being a Russian citizen at the time. The lawyer furthermore denied that Estersohn was a Communist, writing that he was a member of the SPD, not the Communist party.[44] The records do not indicate if Estersohn ultimately was approved for citizenship by Prussia; even if he had been, it is highly doubtful that the Bavarians or other more conservative states would have approved such an application. Nonetheless, the bureaucratic exchanges over Estersohn's citizenship case continued for two years, through at least mid-1921. There are two ways of reading this indecision on the part of the Prussian Interior Ministry. On one hand, this case illustrates the obstacles placed in the way of a successful businessman, long-term resident, and war veteran.[45] At the same time, it is intriguing that the application was not immediately rejected. The Interior Ministry continued to solicit information and consider the application even after hearing the accusations that Estersohn was a Communist, a Jew, and a war profiteer. The Ministry was caught between these two seemingly irreconcilable images of Estersohn and seemed unable or unwilling to decide between them.

As the Genkin case illustrates, citizenship decisions were not made on the level of the state alone. Conservative states could veto applicants who had already received approval from their own more liberal states of residence. Indeed, the Bavarians, who were firmly committed to a *ius sanguinis* or ethnic approach to determining citizenship, proactively used their veto power to force votes in the *Reichsrat* on applicants they considered unacceptable.[46] Although the *Reich*'s guidelines set a ten-year residency minimum for the acceptance of citizenship applications from those of non-German descent, the Bavarians applied their own standard of a twenty-year waiting period to the applications of *fremd-stämmige Ostausländer* and rejected applications submitted in other *Länder* that did not fulfill this criterion.[47] In the *Reichsrat*, which had to approve all disputed citizenship applications, the German states tended to split between those that held to the Bavarians' more conservative line, such as Württemberg, and those that followed a more liberal policy, such as Prussia and Saxony.[48] The Saxons and Prussians repeatedly complained to the national Interior Ministry that Bavaria prevented them from exercising their own citizenship policies and used its veto power to enforce its more restrictive guidelines.[49]

Saxony, in particular, objected to the Bavarians' heavy-handed use of their veto power in the *Reichsrat*. The Saxons' lax approach to naturalization resulted from the SPD/USPD Socialist coalition that governed the *Land* throughout the first years of the republic. The Saxon Interior Ministry repeatedly sent to the other *Länder* for approval names of citizenship applicants who had been in the country fewer than twenty years or had other issues that meant that they were destined to receive a veto from the Bavarians. Opinion was divided in Saxony about this strategy. Although the Dresden District Office complained about the Bavarian veto policy, some within the ministry argued that Saxony should not recommend the naturalization of foreigners who were inevitably destined for a Bavarian veto.[50] In addition to protesting Bavaria's insistence on a twenty-year waiting period, the Saxon Ministry of the Interior continued to send cases for approval from the other *Länder* that had little hope of approval, even after Bavaria expressed its anger about this policy.

The case of Johann Goluchowski demonstrates the lengths to which the Saxon interior minister, Robert Lipinski, was willing to go to protest Bavarian intransigence.[51] Goluchowski had served in the German army for a little more than a year during the war but otherwise appeared ill-suited for German citizenship, especially according to Bavaria's strict standards. He was an illiterate and unemployed Russian-Pole who had only lived in Germany since 1910. When the Leipzig authorities forwarded his case to the Interior Ministry for approval in November 1919, they noted their reservations regarding his naturalization.[52] Nonetheless, in a May 1922 letter to the Leipzig District Office, Lipinski stated that he saw no reason to deny Goluchowski citizenship. Lipinski regarded Goluchowski's lack of employment as temporary; he countered accusations that Goluchowski did not speak German by stating that Goluchowski had spoken enough German to serve in the army; and he even explained Goluchowski's criminal conviction from early 1922 as a minor setback, one that was more than offset by the fact that he had not been punished for any other crimes.[53] Because by 1922 it was more than clear that Goluchowski had no hope of approval from Bavaria, Lipinski's insistence on Goluchowski's candidacy for naturalization can only be seen as an attempt to test the patience of the Bavarians. Furthermore, his promotion of Goluchowski's application reflects Lipinski's own conviction that citizenship should be decided along other criteria than those insisted upon by Bavaria.[54]

It is important to keep in mind that even the Bavarians were not denying the ability of Jews ever to become German citizens. An eastern European Jew could be considered for citizenship after twenty years, at least in theory. That time frame was, the Bavarians claimed, the minimum amount of time it would take for an *Ostjude* to acquire German cultural values.[55] This did not necessarily mean that the Bavarians were in practice willing to grant citizenship to Jews after that time, but it does show that the prevailing political climate in Weimar Germany was such that they felt that they needed to phrase their opposition to the granting of citizenship to eastern European Jews in terms of a residency requirement rather than a total ban. The Bavarian twenty-year waiting period was itself a departure from prewar practice, in which immigrant Jews were not usually able to gain citizenship until the third generation of residence in Germany.

When faced with a non-German citizen who had lived for a long period of time in Germany, the Bavarians occasionally relented and allowed him or her to be awarded citizenship. For example, David Linick, a prosperous Jewish businessman who had resided in Germany for eighteen years and "had an understanding for the German way of life and German values [*deutsches Wesen und deutsche Sitten*]," was awarded citizenship in 1921 despite Bavaria's initial objections.[56] Similarly, in 1921, Bavaria was willing to approve Hermann Rieder's citizenship application after Baden (his state of residence) offered his son's already approved German citizenship, his daughter's marriage to a German citizen, and his own active involvement in Jewish aid organizations as evidence of his commitment to Germany.[57] If involvement in Jewish aid organizations could be considered a positive criterion for citizenship, then the meaning of a commitment to the German cultural community was more complicated than it appears at first glance.

Tensions between a cultural and an ethnic definition of the German nation, and consequently of German citizenship, continued to play a role throughout the remainder of the Weimar Republic. This is most clearly the case in the relatively liberal state of Prussia. In 1925, the Prussians agreed to the Bavarian demand that foreigners from the east be subject to a twenty-year waiting period before being considered for citizenship.[58] Two years later, a new Prussian minister of the interior, Albert Grzesinksi, sought to replace the category of *Deutschstämmigkeit* (German descent) with *Kulturdeutscher* (cultural German). In doing so, he explicitly sought to remove the barriers to the naturalization of Jews. His definition of *Kulturdeutscher* included such features as a connection with a family resident in Germany, birth or upbringing in a German-speaking area or settlement, attendance of German schools, a German name, and maintenance of "German customs and language."[59] Against the opposition of most of other *Länder* and most national ministries, Grzesinski also sought to return Prussia's waiting period for citizenship applicants from the East to ten years, as it had been at the outset of the Weimar period—a decision that met with great resistance from the other German states.[60]

III. Conclusion

Aron Genkin—whose citizenship application was ultimately approved after two close votes in the *Reichsrat*—and other applicants for German naturalization found themselves caught in the symbolic politics of citizenship during the Weimar period. At a time when the Reich could not control its own borders, citizenship policy was an important arena in which Germans fought about the meaning of an ideal German community. The highly contentious debates surrounding naturalization reflected the lack of unanimity regarding what combination of ethnic and cultural factors constituted the German national community. Some officials were committed to an ethnically defined vision of the German nation, while others insisted on the possibility of assimilation, even for eastern European Jews. These competing visions corresponded to the fracture of the prewar ethnocultural consensus. Rather than assuming that ethnicity and culture were one and the same, officials fought over whether ethnic purity or cultural assimilation was the standard by which the German national community should be constituted. Nonetheless, few officials adhered to either of these extreme positions. Even Bavarian advocates of an ethnic standard allowed for the possibility of assimilation after twenty years of residence, and even Saxon Socialists accepted the ten-year standard residency requirement. Attitudes toward ethnicity and culture existed along a spectrum, rather than representing hard-and-fast extremes. Furthermore, regardless of the particular standard they applied, German officials were reluctant to grant citizenship to any but the most "deserving" applicants. Even if some officials believed in the possibility of assimilation, few foreigners could meet this high burden of proof. Foreigners might be able to remain in Germany, and a select few could become citizens, but true participation in German political life would not be granted to the great majority. Be it a result of tolerance or weakness or, as I argue, a mixture of the two, Germany would continue to have a large population of foreigners on its soil for most of the Weimar period. Due to its parsimonious granting of naturalization requests, few would become German citizens, instead existing in a legal limbo.

Finally, it should be clear that what I am referring to here as *citizenship* actually corresponds to the German concept of *Staatsangehörigkeit*, or belonging to the state. This chapter has not addressed the term *Staatsbürgerschaft*, which also is often translated as citizenship, but emphasizes the duties and rights accorded to members of a polity. Intriguingly, the German state in the Weimar period often bestowed limited rights to noncitizens; in particular, Russian Germans (even those without German citizenship) and POWs who married German citizens could become eligible for a certain amount of assistance from the welfare state. As a result, *Staatsbürgerschaft* was to a degree decoupled from *Staatsangehörigkeit* in this period. This divide further reinforces my thesis, namely, that *Staatsangehörigkeit* served as a symbolic form of boundary maintenance. As many of the other chapters in this volume demonstrate, cultural citizenship provided a means for articulating belonging within a community that often had different standards than those of the state. Yet from the perspective of the early Weimar state, "German" culture was the very ground upon which belonging to the state was articulated. In the citizenship practice of the early Weimar Republic, culture was a weapon, and cultural citizenship represented not the possibility of inclusion beyond the letter of the law but the very exclusivity of that law.

CHAPTER 5

Citizenship, Identity, and Community in the German Democratic Republic

JAN PALMOWSKI

BERLIN, 6:00 A.M. ON ELECTION DAY for the city council of Greater (East) Berlin, 1963. Grandpa Dolle, full of excitement, storms into the sleepy house. Holding on to his bunch of carnations, he rushes up the stairs and straight into the bedroom of his grandson and granddaughter-in-law. "Elfie, Paule, get up," he demands in heavy Berlin slang. "Come on, don't pretend to be tired. I have already voted." He darts into the rooms of the other family members to wake them up to this great day until he reaches his final destination: the bedroom of his son, Willi. Here, he slows down and assumes a more dignified position. Puffing out his chest, he presents the flowers. "Congratulations, my son," he beams. "I have already voted for you to become a councilor."

Despite the early hour, Willi Dolle is obviously more together than the other family members. He asks why Grandpa did not wait, because the family had planned to go after breakfast and vote together. "But then," Grandpa retorts, "the flowers [handed to the first voter] would have been gone, and I cannot congratulate you empty-handed!"

The scene described here constitutes the opening of the final episode of the four-part TV drama called *Dolle's Family Album*. Featuring some of the German Democratic Republic's most distinguished actors, *Dolle's Family Album* charted the evolution of the Dolle family under Socialism from 1945 to the mid-1960s. Produced at great cost, the drama was broadcast in the immediate run-up to the twentieth anniversary of the GDR's founding[1] and was billed as one of TV's great entertainment highlights.

This scene appears to celebrate one of the most fundamental acts of citizenship, the act of voting. In fact, it brings out very well the peculiarities of voting in the GDR. Grandpa Dolle managed to be the first at the voting booth—a particular sign of loyalty to the state. What is being celebrated also is the fact that Willi Dolle will be elected to the Berlin city council, even though voting has barely started. The way that this foregone conclusion is not just addressed but celebrated is striking.

It seems hardly surprising that the GDR has barely been considered in the context of citizenship. If *citizenship* is defined as a relationship between government agents and individuals based on mutual bargaining and leading to the negotiation of settlements,[2] the absence of bargaining processes in GDR elections appears as the very opposite of that definition. Indeed, the GDR fails to correspond to T. H. Marshall's blueprint of the evolution of citizenship from civil to political to social citizenship.[3] It may be possible to argue about the existence of social citizenship in the GDR. Political citizenship, by contrast, appears to be nominal, even if individuals like Willi Dolle, who agreed with the ideological precepts upon which the state was founded, could take up political office. Finally, civil rights such as freedom of speech, due process, and even rights to private property and freedom of contract were often constrained by ideology (as farmers found out in the collectivization drives of the 1950s).[4] Little wonder, then, that A. O. Hirschman attributed the apparent stability and the sudden collapse of the GDR precisely to the problems associated with "voice," of free participation and protestation between citizens and the state.[5]

Yet it is important to remember that the influential models of developing citizenship articulated by Marshall as well as Jürgen Habermas were developed against the background of the historical evolution of capitalist societies. Moreover, Marshall and Habermas have both been subject to criticism for the rigidity and the ahistorical nature of their respective models.[6] If we follow, by contrast, Charles Tilly's definition of citizenship as a "set of mutual, contested claims between agents of states and members of socially-constructed communities,"[7] then there is no reason why the GDR should be excluded from the study of citizenship. By directing the analytical focus to different forms of contention between state and citizen, citizenship may provide a unifying framework of investigation that is mindful of practices of domination assumed by state and party while focusing on how these interacted with everyday practices at the grassroots.[8] Such a perspective of citizenship can give full weight to the importance of ideology and the exercise of power, and it can establish a framework of comparison that is not restricted to the Third Reich, a comparison that currently dominates "totalitarian" approaches to the history of the GDR.[9]

Citizenship in the GDR is an important subject of investigation, not least because it was such an important construct in the GDR itself. Few terms can have had greater currency in official parlance than *citizen*. In the 1970s and 1980s, inhabitants of the GDR were constantly referred to as a *"Bürger der DDR"* (citizen of the GDR), or in short, *"Bürger."* This was in part due to the term's semantic advantage, because it allowed the state to refer to its subjects while avoiding the term *German*, and thus demarcate them solely with regard to the GDR. Still, the frequency with which the term was in circulation raises the question of what the state and its citizens had in mind when they used this term, and how compatible these connotations were.

In the GDR, citizenship became a central platform on which the ideology between the party, the state, and its citizens was constructed. The consequent involvement of the state in almost every walk of life meant that there were plenty of arenas for contention between state and citizens. However, because it was always the state that determined the boundaries in the contention of citizenship, the relations between the state and the individual never assumed the identity that the state desired. The more closely the state sought to construct its relations to the citizens, the more opportunities there were for the citizens to express differentiation from the state.

I. The Ideology of Citizenship

In the first two decades of the GDR's existence, citizenship had a very ambiguous formal status. The East German constitution of 1949 did decree, in Article 1.4, that "there is only one German citizenship [*Staatsangehörigkeit*]." However, it then proceeded to refer to its own citizens as the *Bürger*, whom the constitution implicitly defined as those who were subject to the GDR state and its laws. The term *Bürger* allowed the state to refer to its own subjects without referring to the vexed question of nationality. Indeed, throughout the 1950s and for much of the 1960s, the formal definition of *citizenship*, and its relation to nationality, was so politically sensitive as to be left open. For this reason, it was no contradiction if GDR officials expected the Spanish émigrés who had sought refuge from the Franco regime during the 1950s to remain loyal to their distinctive Spanish nationality even after they had been provided with GDR identity documents.[10]

As legal and constitutional thought developed in the new Socialist Germany, a distinctive conception of citizenship emerged that linked to earlier republican citizenship concerns, as discussed by Peter C. Caldwell in this volume. Hermann Klenner, one of the GDR's most influential legal theorists, argued that the essence of Socialist law was most evident in the relation of the citizen (*Bürger*) to the basic rights and freedoms. In capitalism, basic rights had a purely negative function: to protect the individual against external limitations to a nominal freedom, which was always constrained by inherent social and economic inequalities. In Socialism, by contrast, the individual was truly free because his social interests were no longer determined by material inequality. Basic rights were no longer necessary to guarantee freedoms because these existed already—instead, these freedoms helped transform the citizen's mentality and personality. For the more the individual participated in Socialism, the more he and the Socialist society became one, so that the development of the individual's personality and Socialism became identical.[11] Klenner's views on basic rights fitted well with an ideological orthodoxy advanced notably by Karl Polak, especially Polak's assertion that in Socialism there was an identity between the state, the *Volk*, and the individual.[12] The concept of the *Staatsbürger*, of the citizen, had clearly developed by the mid-1960s, even if the political-legal dimensions of citizenship had not yet been explicitly discussed.[13]

In 1966, the People's Chamber passed the Law to Protect the Citizenship and Human Rights of the GDR, in which these dimensions were demarcated clearly against West German political and legal assumptions.[14] The following year the Chamber passed the Citizenship Law of the GDR, and a distinctive GDR citizenship (*Staatsbürgerschaft*) was enshrined again in the 1968 constitution. The trigger for the legislation of a GDR citizenship was provided by the context of inter-German relations in the later years of the Hallstein Doctrine, notably the explicit West German denial that separate GDR citizenship existed. In one of the first East German books on the subject, published in 1967, Gerhard Riege justified and articulated the nature of GDR citizenship almost exclusively in negative terms in relation to the Federal Republic of Germany. Only in a short conclusion was Riege concerned to develop the positive content of citizenship in Socialism per se.[15] Both in origins and in its initial justification, the laws of citizenship in the GDR were originally constructed *ex negativo*, in relation to the FRG, and they were firmly rooted in the political context of the 1960s.[16]

The 1967 Citizenship Law defined all those as GDR citizens who had been on GDR territory when the state was created on October 7, 1949. Arguably, the Citizenship Law, both at the point of its creation and through its "backdating" of GDR citizenship (*Staatsbürgerschaft*), formally violated the assertion of a unified German citizenship (*Staatsangehörigkeit*) determined in Article 1.4 of the GDR constitution.[17] Even East German academics had to admit that the backdating of citizenship meant that in the early years of its existence, most inhabitants of East Germany would not have been aware of the existence and nature of their citizenship.[18]

East German legal and state theorists defended the retrospective application of citizenship by emphasizing the different notions of citizenship inherent in the ideas of *Staatsangehörigkeit* and *Staatsbürgerschaft*. The former, expressed both in the West German conception of citizenship and in Article 1.4 of the 1949 GDR constitution, was integrally linked to the concept of nationality. By contrast, in the East German conception, *citizenship* denotes the relationship between the individual and the state, so that when the separate East German state was created, a distinctive citizenship had come into being as well.[19] More importantly, scholars argued that the state itself had come into being as a result of the social transformation that had come about with the triumph of the working class. Thus a more comprehensive definition of citizenship, expressed through *Staatsbürgerschaft*, had been instituted that defined the individual's relation to the Socialist community in substantive ways. This term had made obsolete the formal and legalist conceptions that still determined the "imperialist" West German conceptions of citizenship as *Staatsangehörigkeit*.[20]

At the heart of the Socialist conception of citizenship stood the maxim that there was no distinction between the state and its citizens in Socialism. The state was a function of the leading role of the working class, which in turn expressed the rights and freedoms of its constituents. Citizenship therefore determined the relationship between the state and the individual citizen, but ultimately it also determined the relationship within society, among the citizens themselves. The function of citizenship was to help more and more individuals realize the perfect identity between state and society, between their individual interests, social progress, and the interests of the state.[21] Citizenship represented a special "identity" of the GDR in which citizens took pride not just in what they had achieved but also in being involved in co-determining social and historical progress.[22]

Intimately connected with the substance of citizenship was the realization of the citizen's basic rights and duties. Formulated in Article 19-40 of the 1968–74 constitution, these included political rights such as the right to vote and the "right" and obligation to protect the country, as well as personal freedoms such as the right to petition and the privacy of postal and telephonic communications. Basic rights also comprised social, economic, and cultural rights, such as the rights to work and to receive equal pay for equal work, as well as the rights to education and participation in cultural life. All these rights were also conceived of as duties. The right to cultural participation included a duty to enrich the cultural life of society. The right to work included a duty to contribute to economic progress to the best of one's ability. And the right to vote was also a duty to vote.[23] Clearly, citizenship in the GDR went beyond legally enforceable rights to include moral rights and duties.[24] For instance, although the state and the law could enforce the ending of discrimination at the workplace and in public life, it was the moral duty of each citizen to ensure that at a personal and social level there would be no discrimination.[25]

GDR citizenship, then, formally developed from the late 1960s, and its official definition remained relatively stable during the Honecker era. The GDR citizen was closely linked to the state and to the social and economic order that defined it. Put differently, GDR citizenship was inherently dynamic[26] because it was an expression, and an instrument, of constantly changing class consciousness toward Socialism. The individual's school efforts, his military service, his behavior at the workplace, the way he socialized with his friends, and, as Toby Thacker notes in this volume, his visits to a concert were all manifestations of citizenship.

Through the integral connection between the individual and the Socialist community, the concept of citizenship was doubly vulnerable once the GDR citizen ventured abroad, especially to non-Socialist countries. First, citizens could renounce their citizenship by changing their GDR passport immediately for a West German one. In theory, the GDR refused to recognize this act of renunciation, but in practice, in 1971 and 1981, the ministerial council twice withdrew GDR citizenship from those who illegally stayed in the West. In each case, this action was justified through the assertion that those who had stayed in the West had contravened the moral and legal rights and duties of GDR citizenship.[27] Second, the moral essence of GDR citizenship was particularly difficult to maintain if GDR citizens lived or worked in a capitalist country. Abroad, scholars argued, citizens had to be particularly mindful of their obligations and duties toward their Socialist community back home. Through their work abroad they had to contribute to the GDR's economic benefit, while at all times and in all spheres acting morally as representatives of the Socialist community, the GDR.[28]

GDR citizenship was primarily acquired through birth,[29] but its function as an expression and instrument of Socialist consciousness had two important legal consequences. First, it meant that citizenship technically could be acquired by those of any national origin who declared their wish to subscribe to the rights and duties expressed and conferred through citizenship. There was no legally enforceable claim to citizenship, but if those requesting citizenship were considered worthy, conferment was granted by the ministerial council on a case-by-case basis.[30] The absence of legal accountability meant that, in practice, the decision to confer citizenship was rather arbitrary and rested with high-ranking party officials, rather than state officials.[31] A second consequence, which proved to be much more significant in practice, was that citizenship could be withdrawn. This could occur by mutual consent between state and citizen if the citizen lived abroad and asked to be released from GDR citizenship. This was, however, not applicable to citizens living in the GDR or to citizens who had left the country illegally. Furthermore, the conferment of citizenship could be withdrawn within five years if the individual concerned failed to fulfill the basic obligations of a Socialist society. Finally, citizenship could be revoked unilaterally by the state if an individual who lived or traveled abroad flagrantly and consciously offended against the duties and rights conferred by GDR citizenship.[32]

II. Citizenship Between Ideal and Practice

The Socialist ideal of citizenship that developed first through its social and cultural constructions and then in its explicit political-legal definitions allows us to consider the scene portrayed above from *Dolle's Family Album* in its proper context. The fundamental act of citizenship that we witness here is not simply Grandpa Dolle's act of voting, important though this was. What is crucial instead is his joy at having voted and his excitement about his son's election. The Dolle family's story began in the first episode in 1945, with Grandpa Dolle ready to fight the Red Army because he sees Socialism as the worst thing that could happen. Grandpa Dolle's joy at the beginning of the final episode marks the completion of his remarkable transformation. Through Socialism and the rule of the working class, his own class, he has been liberated and his consciousness transformed. It is Grandpa Dolle's joy at voting that represents the most significant manifestation of citizenship in this scene.

The rest of the episode charts Willi Dolle's work as a city councilor and deals with the tensions this generates in his private life. The episode thus introduces a second important motif: in Socialist theory, the key to the realization of citizenship in practice is participation. From this perspective, what distinguished citizenship in the GDR was the active, "democratic" assumption of duties that impacted upon the community in the everyday and that helped realize Socialism in practice.[33] Article 21 of the 1968 constitution (in its 1974 version) stated that every citizen had the basic right to political, economic, social, and cultural participation in the Socialist community and the Socialist state. As the *Legal Handbook for the Citizen* asserted, "[T]his basic right of codetermination [*Mitbestimmung*] takes the central place among the political, and beyond this among all basic rights and duties."[34]

An important sphere in which codetermination was to help translate the theory of citizenship into practice was the law. Even if many areas such as civil, family, and labor law did not usually have direct political implications,[35] the perspective of citizenship illustrates the political and ideological importance even of minor breaches of the law. Law had an educative function, as it guided individuals in their self-education as Socialist citizens and created a stronger bond with the state.[36] To this end, Socialist law aimed at involving lay citizens, for instance, through tribunals or as assistants to the justices. Here, lay citizens could add a critical social and local dimension to the proceedings, and this would allow the law to exercise its educative function on transgressors more effectively than purely professional courts.[37] For lay participants and for the contesting parties, the law was conceived as an important tool for social and moral improvement, as an instrument of citizenship.[38]

If the law was to act as a fundamental instrument in achieving identity between the state and its citizens in practice, there was one crucial problem: no law existed to protect the citizen against arbitrary administrative acts. Although during the 1950s a number of academic lawyers at the University of Jena and elsewhere worked on the development of administrative law, Walter Ulbricht's speech at the 1958 Babelsberg Conference at the Academy of State and Legal Science put an end to these attempts.[39] Consequently, the GDR had no administrative law because in theory bureaucratic actions were always expressive of the identity between state and citizens. And yet poor, slow, and often arbitrary administrative practices were difficult to deny. A new generation of legal academics began to demand the formulation of administrative law in the early 1980s,[40] but a new law that introduced judicial review for some administrative acts did not come into effect until July 1, 1989.[41]

It was never going to be easy for law in the GDR to act as an agent of citizenship. All too evident was its function as a tool of state power, from the shaping of the judicial system in the beginning to the evident manipulation of justice in the trials against political opposition.[42] Yet, the majority of the population would have direct encounters with the law not in such cases of all-out opposition but in the "nonpolitical" spheres that dealt with cases of divorce, parental rights, minor civil law transgressions and so forth. By linking *all* aspects of the law to Socialism and the creation of a Socialist citizenship, the state could hope to impact upon the individual directly.

From the point of view of the state, the law did help to reduce the distance between state and citizens. From the point of view of the citizens, this had a very different effect, however. It is impossible to be sure about this point, because we still know very little about the impact of Socialist law on communal relations, for instance. Yet it is clear that the closeness between the law and the party led the population to distance itself from the law. Despite the growing size of the state security services and a sizeable and visible police force, there was a marked disrespect for the law in many spheres of life, from nudism in the 1950s to the illegal construction of garages and vacation cottages to the disposal of trash in the countryside and to free-riding on public transport.[43] Because of its connection to Socialism, transgressing the law could signal distance from the official definition of citizenship and hence from state and party.[44] For this reason, it is precisely the closeness between the law and the state that emasculated the law in its ability to help realize the Socialist conception of citizenship.[45]

Because of the assumed identity between citizen and state in Socialism, there was no reason why, in principle, citizens should not address the state directly with their concerns. Indeed, in the absence of distinctive administrative courts, the state created an extensive right to petition, a basic right articulated in Article 103 of the 1968 constitution.[46] In principle, petitions (*Eingaben*) represented the citizen's active participation in the state.[47] Petitions spoke of the trust the citizens had in the state by turning to it, and helped fulfill the identity between the concerns of the individual, the Socialist community, and the state.[48]

Petitions were indeed a popular way to try to address individual concerns. In 1956, almost 100,000 petitions were sent to the GDR's highest authority, the state council and the party leader. During the 1960s, this figure declined markedly, reaching a low of around 40,000 in 1973. In the following decade, the number of petitions rose again to an average of around 65,000, until it rose dramatically from around 1985, reaching a figure of almost 140,000 in 1988.[49] These numbers are impressive, but only represent the tip of the iceberg. Additional petitions were sent to the popular television show *Prisma*, which aimed at uncovering shortcomings in the realization of Socialism in everyday life. Scholars have looked particularly at these national arenas for petitions, but it should not be forgotten that writing to members of the state council most often represented a last resort. The first address for petitions frequently was state and party administrations at the local and regional levels. Many petitions were only sent to the state council if the local administration had failed, in the eyes of the petitioner, to address the subject of concern in an appropriate manner.

Petitions gave the state access to important information, which enabled it to respond to many of the small and large crises which evolved in the everyday life of the citizens.[50] Yet we know very little about the impact of petitions on the everyday lives of citizens, and their attitudes toward the state. Contrary to the ideals expressed at the Academy for State and Legal Sciences,[51] it is not clear that petitions actually encouraged the citizen in feelings of trust, responsibility, and a sense of protectedness (*Geborgenheit*) vis-à-vis the state. The state was constantly concerned to improve the petitioning process, but this concerned the form, not the content, of the state's responses. Ultimately, the state's word was final, for it alone represented the Socialist community. This meant in practice that the success of petitions was uneven, and often depended on the individual decisions of local officials.[52]

Indeed, some petitions were more likely to succeed than others. Other things being equal, a petition made in the arena of social welfare could often have a successful outcome. By contrast, the petitions protesting against officials' decisions to deny individual access to the five- and 0.5-kilometer exclusion zones along the border had virtually no chance of success, because the officials concerned usually represented the border troops or the state security service. In such instances, petitions speak volumes about the frustrations caused by the state's treatment of its citizens.[53] Moreover, petitions also impacted upon the mutual relationships between citizens. This is shown with particular clarity by the petitions sent in at the local level. Such petitions were often written by neighbors complaining about each other, or disgruntled individuals blowing the whistle on malpractice in their local agricultural cooperatives. Laying open such daily conflicts to the state could either contribute to their resolution or could exacerbate existing conflict. In other words, petitions could ameliorate individual frustration, but they also could heighten frustration against the state (in the case of unpopular decisions) and against other members of the Socialist community of citizens.[54] Petitions did bring the state closer to the citizens, but whether the citizens were brought closer to the state and to each other remains, in light of current research, at best ambiguous.

Petitions were an important, but by no means the only, form of citizenship participation. In 1979, a textbook written on behalf of the Academy of State Science and Jurisprudence numbered those active in politics and society at over three million. This included 194,200 members of local, district, and statewide parliaments; 500,000 participants in local commissions; 680,000 parents active in school councils; and almost 100,000 workers contributing to production councils at the workplace.[55] The actual numbers are worth noting for the impression that the party sought to create—that Socialist democracy was alive and well, and that its well-being was evident through participation at the local level.

Local politics as an agent of citizenship invites immediate cynicism, because in democratic centralism, decisions were handed down from the center and local organs were relegated to executing national and district decisions. And, as much as the state tried to encourage participation at the grassroots, holding out the possibility of individual political careers leading to the state council was simply never an issue. The local arena thus was always removed from political decision making at the center.

And yet, even here, in a system of democratic centralism, Adelheid von Saldern's point in this volume about the significance of the locality for determining the meanings of individual citizenship holds true. From the point of view of citizenship, the local level was crucial—it was here that central decisions had to be communicated to the citizens.[56] Although most policy decisions may have been centralized, state policy was experienced at the local level: local officials were the most frequent addressees of petitions; they allocated precious housing space; they could influence the use of limited resources in building and other materials; and, not least important, the ability of a mayor to rally and organize could have a crucial impact on the success of local community projects and festivals.[57] Moreover, Socialism was about the application of "objective" and "scientific" criteria in economy, society, and culture. Prejudices and traditions persisted most tenaciously at the local level; hence, citizenship needed to overcome the parochialism of the locality.[58]

In the absence of any research on the administration of a small or medium-sized community in the GDR, evaluating the practice of citizenship is difficult and speculative. Even if official figures for local participation were clearly overstated, there is no question that citizens could be enticed to engage themselves in their community, even if this did not necessarily represent a full-blown commitment to Socialism. Many grey zones existed at the local level. The localization of the newspaper press (every county had its own edition of the district newspaper!), for instance, allowed a degree of debate about strictly local issues that would have been inconceivable in a broader context. In the form of readers' letters, or even of series of "investigative" articles, the quality of local services or the behavior of individual citizens could be articulated and discussed.[59] Hence, it is possible to speak of elements of a public arena at the local level that could contribute to the citizens' sense of belonging and engagement.

There were two conceptual problems with the connection between citizenship and the local arena. First, by encouraging local political participation, the state had to accept some degree of variation in the way in which its decrees and laws were applied. However, these variations in administrative practice were effectively overshadowed by the vastly different resources allocated to different localities, depending on their economic structure (and output) and their political significance. The hierarchy that existed in the cultural and material provisions for citizens in Berlin and the rest of the GDR was a palpable and incalculable source of irritation to "provincial" citizens, as were differences in allocation among different provincial towns.[60] Local inequalities made the ideal of a single cohesive community much more difficult to achieve and belied the idea of an equal Socialist citizenship.

Second, the ideal of citizenship within the local community has nothing to say about a problem that proved crucial in practice—the relationship between state and party. Careful appeals to the party against local administrative practices often became an acceptable way to voice criticism, as local functionaries of the Socialist Unity Party (SED) usually trumped local state officials in the decision-making process. Hence, even though local politics provided another avenue through which the state could approach its citizens, in practice local politics could encourage strategies to pursue individual aims in contradistinction to the state.

The ideal of Socialist citizenship through grassroots participation at the workplace, in the local school, or in the village council was extremely wide-ranging as such. Yet, much more was at stake. According to Hermann Klenner, social and cultural attitudes had "withered away" (*verkümmert*) at the local levels, and here the challenge of effecting personal transformation was at its greatest.[61] As a result, citizenship could only be achieved through a further important sphere, that of the "Socialist *Heimat*." This ideal covered all aspects of the individual's free time and aimed to ensure that this was spent "sensibly," in other words, to the benefit of individual and social improvement. Individuals could participate in the Socialist *Heimat* through their enthusiasm for the environment, their passion for local history, or their desire to collect stamps. Through these pastimes citizens could enrich their knowledge of the *Heimat* and use it for the greater good through restoration projects, exhibitions, and publications.[62]

Through *Heimat*, the ideal of citizenship was expanded to the private sphere. By aiming at educational and cultural improvement, *Heimat* contributed further to the growing identity between the individual and the community. And, not least importantly, participation in and for the *Heimat* was supposed to lead to a love of the immediate surroundings. *Heimat*, in other words, opened up a new dimension of citizenship, its emotional side.[63] It led to an identification with the GDR that was based not merely on an understanding of social and historical processes but on a love for the immediate locality and the entire Socialist fatherland.

In practice, the distinction between citizenship through emotional or rational identification with the community was often difficult to make. One important example concerns the annual "Take Part!" competitions, in which citizens were encouraged, with varying degrees of intensity, to participate in the beautification and improvement of their *Heimat* communities. Because it promoted the "voluntary" participation of citizens in their communities, the competition's organizer, the National Front, considered participation to be the most important manifestation of citizenship, second only to participation at the workplace.[64] In practice, the construction of the community in this manner allowed the community to act as a system of inclusion as well as exclusion of those whose participation was not considered desirable.[65] As a result of communal work conducted by the "in-group"—the citizens—swimming pools were built, gardens weeded, and apartments repaired. In the "Take-Part!" movement, citizens improved their relations with one another, and they demarcated themselves against Germans to the west of the border, who could not relate to this participatory movement. Ideally, what emerged as a result was a Socialist community that was not just closer-knit but also identified more closely with the Socialist GDR.

Through the Socialist *Heimat*, the state attempted to appropriate the citizens' private sphere and claim it for its construction of citizenship. In a number of respects, this proved to be quite successful. The "Take Part!" competition did allow many communities to undertake projects for themselves, which not only responded to the social objectives of citizenship but often contributed to its economic aims as well. Once again, however, there was a downside. Projects often could not be realized because of a lack of available tools or construction materials. Moreover, not all citizens were skilled laborers, and popular initiatives for the preservation of historical monuments in particular, but also work for the upkeep of public buildings, was often of poor quality and of little practical value. The initiative also divided citizens between those who participated and those who did not want to join in the effort, so that the "Take Part!" movement strengthened some communities, but weakened others.

One example must suffice to illustrate the themes considered above and how these could interact in practice. Peter Apel grew up in the western district of Eisenach, whose inhabitants formed a close-knit community. Following his marriage, Apel stayed in the family house and during the 1970s and 1980s became one of the western districts' leading spirits. When I asked him in an interview about what caused individuals to be active for their community in the GDR, Apel responded with the example of the *Waldschlösschen*, a dilapidated communal pub that was torn down in the early 1970s. The pub's destruction triggered local consternation and resentment, which the residents expressed by collecting signatures for a petition that was sent to the district authorities. The residents argued that this pub had been crucial as a meeting place for their football club and for meetings of the official residential districts (*Wohnbezirke*) that composed the western district. The petitioners felt they had powerful backup, not least through Willi Ostermann, a local resident who was the bearer of the patriotic medal in bronze.[66]

The petitioners were successful. In response to the petition and in connection to upcoming elections, district officials visited the community and agreed to sponsor a new pub. In return, the residents committed themselves to participate in its construction, as part of the "Take Part!" movement. Apel organized the residents' labor on Saturdays and recorded the amount of labor contributed, for which the state paid five marks per hour. The laborers in turn donated the money they earned for their football club's kitty.

One Saturday, the newly appointed head of Apel's residential district appeared at the building site. He was seen as a young party hack appointed from outside to replace Ostermann.

Imagine this guy standing there on Saturday morning in a suit, we all wore working clothes and were busy in the construction. And he stood there and wanted to take over the bookkeeping. This guy had no chance. I told him, "Boy, if you don't take a hike, there will be a big bang here."[67]

I asked Apel why he didn't let the new official do the books so the state would be satisfied everything was in order and his companions would be left alone. "But what use," Apel replied, "does a community like ours have for an idiot like that?"[68]

Eisenach's western district was not a community like any other. Apel and his friends were pivotal in the organization of the *Sommergewinn*, the annual local festival and pageant that was the GDR's largest spring festival. The western district's long history of dealing with state and party authorities in the organization of this event and their participation in, and contribution to, cultural citizenship clearly emboldened them to demand rights in relation to their community. The way in which they approached the authorities demonstrates an acceptance of the nature of political citizenship in the GDR. To challenge a decision made at the local level, Apel and his friends petitioned the local authorities in the language of GDR citizenship.[69] They were successful, and through direct negotiation with the local authorities, they achieved their aims. The state, in turn, demonstrated what it perceived as the "democratic" nature of citizenship, and it effected the citizens' further participation in the construction of the new pub through the "Take Part!" effort. Finally, the "Take Part!" effort demonstrates how it could lead to a tightening of community ties—the money earned went straight into the kitty of the football club.

So perfect does this example of practical citizenship appear that it is easy to overlook the fact that its ultimate object was the construction of a communal pub, whose contribution to the ideal of Socialism is arguable. More importantly, Apel and his friends accepted the rules of Socialist citizenship, but there is no evidence that their citizenship brought them closer to the state. The Communist Willi Ostermann was accepted because he integrated himself in the way his successor did not. Ostermann had been a worker,[70] whereas the new head of the residential district appeared on the building site in a suit, signaling distance and authority. Citizenship could indeed strengthen a feeling of community and identity in the GDR, as this example illustrates very well. Yet, the strength of such a community in turn could embolden it to demarcate itself clearly against encroachments by the state.

III. Conclusion

We, as citizens, want to be asked if we agree . . . every individual is important who articulates herself openly and who is supported by others, because only together, in groups, associations, parties, will we gain a legal sphere of resistance and contestation.[71]

When Bärbel Bohley expressed her protest on the GDR's fortieth anniversary, she did so in terms of citizenship. Clearly, this was not simply about the right to vote. It was about overcoming resignation through articulating discontent. It was about regaining "voice." Bohley insisted on her GDR citizenship, but she wanted this citizenship on different terms.

By expanding citizenship to arenas that came to include social welfare, the quality of consumer goods, and the provision of culture, the state opened up channels of communication and—limited—contention to those who did not necessarily subscribe to the ideals of Socialism. For as long as state provision of culture, social services, and consumer goods improved during the 1960s and 1970s, the citizenship ideal may well have enhanced the GDR's stability. Indeed, it even allowed the state to offset a shortcoming in one area (such as supply shortages of consumer goods) with advances in others (social welfare). Once the state's economic base deteriorated sharply in the 1980s, the state was unable to realize the expectations of citizenship in all the cultural, social, and material arenas that it had created.[72] Then, citizenship could reinforce feelings of frustration against a state that failed to fulfill its own citizenship ideal.

Evidently, the state had failed to realize its own citizenship ideal. In this ideal, citizenship was constructed as the expression of a GDR identity. Accordingly, citizenship was the crucial tool through which the objective reality of the identity between state and society was translated into individual consciousness. At an objective level, the identity between state and citizen was manifest through basic rights and duties in the economy, at the workplace, in social relations, in cultural life, and in the private lives of the citizens. In 1989, the state's failure to realize its citizenship ideal became manifest. Neither the few in whose name Bohley spoke, nor the many whose lethargy she criticized, conformed to the party's ideal of individual participation in and for Socialism.

In fact, the more the state tried to overcome the gap between ideal and reality, the more it multiplied the opportunities for individuals to signal distance to the state or its ideology. Not going to the theater, ending work on Fridays at 2:00 p.m., or throwing litter in the public park could be simple life choices, expressions of *Eigen-Sinn*.[73] Whatever the original intentions, such acts moved into the political and ideological sphere through the ideal of citizenship. The ideal of citizenship multiplied opportunities for, and expressions of, dissonance.

The close relationship between citizenship and identity suggests a measure of continuity between the GDR and the Third Reich. In both dictatorships, there existed an ideal of the "identity" of citizens. In the Third Reich, this was conceived as the *Volk*, whereas in the GDR the identity was rooted in the Socialist community. This had implications for the law, which in both systems served to help realize the ideals of the respective dictatorships.[74] There was an even more direct parallel: the Third Reich had been the first German state to withdraw citizenship rights from those who did not correspond to the identity ideal between state and citizens.[75] The State Council of the GDR, too, assumed for itself the right to withdraw citizenship from those who had shown themselves to be not worthy. In practice, of course, the GDR used its powers far more sparingly than did the Third Reich. When the State Council decided to exclude Wolfgang Biermann from GDR citizenship in 1976, this action was controversial even among the most loyal of SED members, precisely because it invoked the precedents set by the Third Reich.[76]

The parallels to the Third Reich, therefore, did mean that the state could only withdraw citizenship unilaterally in extreme cases. Moreover, on closer inspection, the differences in the identity concept assumed by each dictatorship become more apparent. National identity during the Third Reich was based exclusively on race, and this identity was, as academic debates in the Third Reich progressed, increasingly represented and expressed by the will of the Führer.[77] This gave way to an arbitrariness and a brutality of the state and the law that, notwithstanding the brutalities of the *Stasi*, was quite impossible under the East German conception of identity.[78] In the GDR, the party recognized the imperfect state of the identity between state and subjects, and the point of citizenship was precisely to help overcome the dialectic between "objective" reality and individual consciousness. Where dialectic reigned, there was room for argument, while the state could never afford to ignore, at least publicly, the rules by which the party proclaimed it should act.[79]

At first glance, Bärbel Bohley's concerns of mid-1989 relate directly to Albert Hirschman's model of exit, voice, and loyalty. By insisting that citizens only could be induced to stay in the GDR if they received a say in the country over their own future, Bohley clearly relates the alternatives of loyalty and exit to the possibility of "voice."[80] Yet this chapter has shown that opportunities of "voice" existed on many levels. True, citizens had no choice at the polls, but they were encouraged to participate by sending petitions and engaging at the local level. At least in the absence of further research in this area (e.g., into the potential for, and impact of, agency in local politics), this possibility to engage should not be dismissed out of hand. Those who were at the head of the local agricultural production community (*LPG*), the local cultural league organization, or the local branch of the party could have a significant impact on the quality of life of the local community.

The problem in the GDR was not the lack of "voice" as such. After all, it is important to remember that in "all sorts of regimes, most of the time political participation goes on without contention" as individuals go about their business of paying taxes, receiving benefits, and so on.[81] The problem in the GDR related to the *ways* in which contestation could take place. In the GDR, citizenship was contested chiefly in a local context, with a narrow focus on particular circumstances, through direct appeals to state and party as powerful patrons. This corresponds very well with Charles Tilly's model for "undemocratic" repertoires of contention.[82] In such regimes, the strong public prescriptions for contention left a huge area of technically possible claim-making interactions that were forbidden. As a result, "contentious politics rarely overlapped with state-prescribed forms of political participation," while those areas of overlap that existed were most common in the local arena.[83]

Tilly's model has to be considered with caution in this context, not least because it is based on an analysis of the Iberian peninsula and the

Low Countries between 1650 and 1850. What it does show, nevertheless, is that the perspective of citizenship can be usefully applied to the undemocratic GDR in order to better understand processes of differentiation, contention, and contestation between state and citizens in a noncapitalist system. Citizenship opens up a perspective that allows direct comparisons with the state-citizen relationship not only in the Third Reich but, just as importantly, in the Federal Republic of Germany, in other German states in the nineteenth and twentieth centuries, and in other countries. Indeed, Tilly's observations about the elevated significance of the local as a principal arena for contention in undemocratic regimes reinforces Adelheid von Saldern's more general point about the importance of the locality in analyzing individual meanings of citizenship. It suggests that in the GDR, precisely because of the centralist and authoritarian nature of the regime, the locality acquired a particularly significant role in the development of citizenship at the level of the everyday, even in relation to other historical contexts.

As a result, the citizenship ideal could contribute to feelings of community in practice. At a local level, the different opportunities to realize specific goals, often through community action, undoubtedly encouraged many communities to stick together. In this sense, citizenship was a crucial factor in the creation of the community spirit that looms so large in the memory of the GDR and is apparent, for instance, in oral history interviews. There is little evidence, however, that this feeling of community led to a greater identification with the state or with the Socialist community at large. By encouraging contention at a local level, the state reinforced localized communities that were distinguished not through Socialism but by preexisting ties of tradition, local milieu, and individual leadership. In practice the all-embracing ideal of citizenship as the identity among state, society, and the individual produced unintended consequences because it provided a large sphere in different local contexts in which individuals could develop their own meanings of citizenship.

PART TWO

The Politics and Culture of Citizenship

CHAPTER 6

The Citizen at Home:
Wohnkultur Before World War I

JENNIFER JENKINS

IN HIS ANALYSIS of the emergence of capitalist modernity in the nineteenth century, Walter Benjamin drew attention to the shifting relationship between public and private life that attended large-scale processes of political and economic transformation. "Under Louis-Philippe," he wrote in his characteristically elliptical fashion, "the private citizen entered upon the historical scene." This sentence, and what followed in his text *Paris: Capital of the Nineteenth Century*, traced a twinned development. The broadening of the franchise, "the extension of the apparatus of democracy by means of a new electoral law," corresponded to the emergence of the middle-class interior as a site for the expression of new forms of subjectivity.[1] These could be emotive, furtive, and deeply individualized—Benjamin characterized them as obsessed with secrets, covers, and traces—but they were not purely private; they were not separate from public life or from political culture. Rather, the transformation of political life under a broadened franchise and the emergence of the interior were mutually constitutive developments. At the same time as the interior became the preferred "casing" of the citizen, Benjamin wrote, cities took on the character of living rooms.

Benjamin's remarks refer to the environs of Paris, but they productively raise issues for analyses of culture and politics on the other side of the Rhine, particularly for exploring the intersection between ideas of the modern, the everyday, and the political in Wilhelmine Germany. Following Benjamin, this chapter poses questions about the emergence of new visions of the modern interior and concurrent articulations of citizenship and public life in Germany before 1914. How did discussions at the turn of the century on the proper shape and design of living spaces—the debate on what was called *Wohnkultur* or the "culture of dwelling"—produce new ways of imagining a national public? How did interiors become preferred "casings" for German citizens? Recent studies of Imperial Germany have made such questions possible. On the one hand, explorations of political life—on elections, suffrage laws, and reform movements at both a local and national level—have yielded a dynamic picture of political culture in 1900 as a work in progress. Political life in the Empire is now seen as more open, diverse, and multiple in its meanings, as essentially unfinished rather than fatally set on a path leading toward 1933.[2] New studies of citizenship, on the other hand, while not focusing specifically on Germany, have expanded the concept beyond its juridical frameworks; their emphasis on cultural practices offers particular possibilities for studies of Wilhelmine Germany.[3] Because a modern conception of national citizenship (in contrast to municipal and regional variants) had not been made but was in the process of being defined before 1914, the ways that German culture was being imagined by associations, institutions, and individuals as both modern and national was central to its development.[4] These imaginings updated an older discourse on "national character," which had been fundamental to definitions of the polity in Germany since the late eighteenth century. Images of modern interiors, as will be discussed in this chapter, reveal visions of national identity in formation, in which the individual subjectivity formed through this space articulated and reflected the cultural mores that bound the nation together. In this arena, citizenship and national belonging were posited as cultural codes, sets of norms and behaviors held privately and performed publicly.

Between 1890 and 1914, a broad discussion on how people should furnish their homes and conduct themselves domestically filled the pages of journals on "art and public life" and instigated the activity of associations both nationally and locally. A central concept in the midcentury discussions of craft reform that had stemmed from the poor showing of German goods at Europe's "great exhibitions," by 1900 *Wohnkultur* held a significant place in the lexicon of architects, designers, politicians, and social reformers. Connected to programs for the moral uplift of the urban working classes on the one hand, it also became a locus of discussions about how to manage the effects of Germany's new consumer culture on the other. In short, many topics were viewed through this lens. For example, the Third German National Arts and Crafts Exhibition, held in Dresden in 1906, defined national culture through design. Introducing the functionalist aesthetic that the Bauhaus would make famous, the exhibition showcased sets of private and public rooms as visions of national strength and industrial power. Yet the show in Dresden was about more than shapes and objects. Under the rubric of architecture and design, architects, social reformers, industrialists, and politicians discussed national consolidation, the development of an expansive, export-oriented economy, political transformation, and the evolution of Germany from an agrarian into an industrial state. Exhibiting the close connection between culture and politics characteristic of modern German political culture, in 1906 debates on *Wohnkultur* went beyond the style or function of particular objects to address topics of self, state, society, and nation. If citizenship is understood as a cultural code, as a way of imagining self, community, and nation and the relationships between them, Dresden's pedagogical displays clearly instructed viewers on modern lived forms of "Germanness." They presented, to use the words of Lauren Berlant, "normative technologies of citizenship," which sought through instruction "to create proper national subjects and subjectivities."[5] Such "normative technologies" were not limited to exhibitions of modern design but were a predominant feature of Germany's new consumer culture. Anxieties about mass consumption spurred the production of taste manuals, specialized magazines and exhibitions that were deliberately pedagogical in tone and effect, guiding viewers and readers through the issue of what they should desire and why. Even department store windows incited consumer desires within instructional frameworks. In 1902 displays of furniture at the Wertheim Department Store in Berlin presented their wares not as simple objects but as pedagogical visions. Tables and chairs became larger than themselves through their positioning in an "exhibition of modern living spaces."[6]

"All modern nation states, because of their dependence upon mass popular armies for their defence, taxation for their economic survival and mass suffrage for their legitimacy," writes Leora Auslander, "need to instill a sense of belonging, of shared responsibility and of loyalty in their citizens." Because modern nation states "rely on voluntary compliance and participation," they are compelled to take on this "pedagogic task."[7] This occurred through various avenues. The codification of official national rituals, the instituting of compulsory and universal primary school education, and the introduction of conscription into a national army were three ways for the state to mass-produce modern national citizens.[8] The creation of the modern citizen-consumer was another. As will be shown here, *Wohnkultur* followed an "activity of national pedagogy" meant to lead to the "production of a national culture," and it was the associations of civil society, rather than the state, that directed the process before 1914.[9] The "nationalization of the everyday," which Auslander has studied for France, was the stated aim of the *Werkbund* in Germany. This association of architects, industrialists, and politicians had the "conspicuous intention to create a national idiom for modernity."[10] Auslander's work ties citizenship and national culture in France to specific practices of consumption.[11] This chapter sketches out what this terrain looked like in Germany while acknowledging the strong element of fantasy ("national fantasy") tied to *Wohnkultur*'s instructive images for modern living. In pictures and in prose, *Wohnkultur* envisioned citizens at home, the nation as lived in an everyday sense of the term.[12]

* * *

Taste manuals and journals of interior decoration were widespread in Wilhelmine Germany's expanding consumer society. Together with the construction of luxury department stores such as Alfred Messel's flagship Wertheim building on the Leipziger Platz in Berlin (1904–6) and the presentation of modern design at international exhibitions in Paris (1900), Turin (1902), and St. Louis (1904), arts and crafts journals and taste manuals framed the products and spaces of consumption as sumptuous instructional displays.[13] Often loaded with images— photographs and lithographs—the manuals opened onto the international world of modern design, or so it is thought. In 1910 one such manual, remarkable only for its length, gave in addition to pictures an extensive amount of advice on matters of interior decoration. Here viewing was secondary to reading, the images following the manual's prosaic and prescriptive text. The work of the cultural critic Joseph August Lux, this nondescript book, entitled *Taste in Everyday Life*, bombarded its audience with information. Copious suggestions for reform were mixed with an equal number of warnings. National culture, by which Lux meant the living spaces of the middle-class home, was in crisis. Filled with inauthentic (read "foreign") and unaesthetic (read "industrially produced") things, it posed a danger to the sensitive (read "imperfectly formed") national sensibilities of German citizens.

A member of both the arts and crafts reform movement and the German *Werkbund* of 1907, Lux used hundreds of pages to instruct his audience on how to reform aesthetically their homes and their persons: from the design and construction of living spaces to their furnishings, decorations, and everyday objects. Lux wrote on the home as a complete aesthetic environment; he also wrote a text that is astonishing in its combination of the trivial with the national, the aesthetic with the disciplinary. *Taste in Everyday Life* ranged over topics from the correct construction of a wall to the ins and outs of wallpaper. He covered the importance of suitable lighting, the design of visiting cards, and the proper operation of a camera so that it produced art rather than kitsch. Foregrounding the fruits of the modern movement in architecture and design, the book did not take its cues from an international discussion on art. Arts and crafts journals placed German works into international contexts, but this was generally done in the service of national concerns. Obsessive and anxious, Lux's manual located interior decoration and private space at the center of a complex of national problems. These had to do with markets, publics, production, and consumption. Taste was no longer a purely individual quality, wrote Lux. It was not the expression of a single personality, not even the exalted individual personality of the artist. Taste was a collective entity, a national good, and an economic force, hence the seriousness of the book's tone.

Lux started from the premise that German national culture was both incompletely formed and inwardly weak. National culture referred to interior spaces, namely the domestic spaces of the middle-class home.[14] Using the language of "national character," in which the script for belonging was written privately through the expression of manners and mores, Lux foregrounded everyday interiors as his chosen site of intervention. Nothing escaped his notice, and everything—from the design of a teaspoon to the arc of an iron lamp—had a direct connection to the national economy and to the modernization of national life. Exhibiting a deep suspicion of unguided acts of consumption and creativity, Lux wrote that taste was a "cultural power" too important to national life to leave unschooled. "We have to recognize in good taste a spiritual force," he wrote, "that creates a harmonious picture of life."[15] It was a property of material objects and a spirit that surpassed them. An entity both individual and collective, it was a code of behavior and a program for action. Lux often started with the small in order to progress rapidly to the big. For him, questions of taste, encapsulated in the term *Wohnkultur*, were an entry point into the largest national and social issues of his time. "[E]verything is dependent on dwelling," he wrote, "health, the strength of the nation and the beauty of the land."[16] If a home's inhabitants were properly educated, Lux believed, the domestic interior would be safely and powerfully modernized. If successfully reformed, the contradictions of modern life—which he saw as a battle between *Kultur* and *Zivilisation*—would be harmoniously overcome.

The *Werkbund*, of which Lux was a minor but tireless member, is most often analyzed for its contribution to the development of a progressive design culture that reached its zenith in the Bauhaus.[17] The organization brought together artists, architects, industrialists, journalists, and politicians for the purpose of improving the quality of manufactured goods.[18] Its leading figures—Hermann Muthesius, Fritz Schumacher, Henry van de Velde, Peter Behrens, and others—sought to translate the fruits of the international movement in arts and crafts to Germany and to adapt them to national and local contexts of production. While the nationalism and imperialist politics of the organization have not escaped scrutiny—particularly in studies focusing on one of its most famous members, the left liberal politician Friedrich Naumann and his concept of *Mitteleuropa*—these are often seen as secondary to its role in the creation of a modern industrial aesthetic.[19] Its meaning, in other words, has been seen as primarily artistic and cultural rather than social or political. Moreover, its importance for modern German history is often seen as straightforwardly progressive, a perspective that stems from a one-sided view of the organization.[20]

Recent literature on the *Werkbund* has highlighted the framework of national questions within which the association cast its discussions on the meaning and importance of modern art.[21] For members like Lux, the creation of a modern design culture was a necessary step in a larger program aimed at the nationalization and modernization of German society. The transformation of the domestic interior was an integral part of the larger desire to design new spaces for mass society. These spaces were to obey acknowledged laws of form and function; visions of them were prescriptive rather than descriptive. The publications of the *Werkbund* do not provide a look at modern life as it was lived but at modern life as it should be lived. This said, the designs and images produced by its members often have more of the character of the wish image than that of documentation or evidence. These wishes were also eminently middle-class (*bürgerlich*). Rather than being an example of what Benedict Anderson has called the "official nationalism" that motivated late nineteenth-century European states, the *Werkbund* provides a glimpse of a bourgeois nationalism that was quasi-public and quasi-private in organization.[22] It operated primarily through the channels of associations, pressure groups, and businesses rather than through the state (although the state was an addressee of its programs), and it aimed to transform public and private lives according to the principles of science, technology, and industry.

Publicity was an indispensable tool in this project. Members focused on educating numerous publics of producers and consumers. In this way they conceptualized an emergent national public organized around issues of economy, technology, and culture. Lux's book was, in a clumsy way, an attempt to systematize the realm of taste: to take it from its chaotic individual state to one based on rules, principles, and collective forms of behavior. It was an effort to define taste "scientifically" and to anchor this conception of taste in a broad middle-class public. Bringing art into the home—one of the organization's stated goals—was a starting point for binding the artist to the organizations of modern industry and binding the living spaces of German citizens to one another by creating a standardized, if high-level, culture for all. As such, the *Werkbund*'s aim to transform the spaces and things of everyday life can be seen as a central episode in how the national question was defined and "seized," to use Geoff Eley's term, in the years before 1914. Lux's recommendations on how to transform what one wore, saw, or used are concrete examples of what Eley has called a "politics of continuous nationalist pedagogy."[23]

This pedagogy focused on the transformation of private spaces and everyday objects: how people lived, dressed, and conducted themselves. A national culture was not conceived of as abstract or distant but as personal and concrete. Questions of national strength, health, and belonging were posed as issues to be addressed in the interior of one's home and on the body of one's person. Hermann Muthesius's famous study of English architecture, *The English House* of 1904–5, which provided a model for the reform of the German domestic interior, collapsed private and national space together; this move was characteristic of the *Werkbund*'s efforts to infuse the objects, space, and time of everyday life with the monumentality of national feeling. Citizens were exhorted to engage in a process that would make them more sufficiently national; a new form of national community, it was thought, would be built from their efforts. By posing national belonging as a question of consumption and character, Lux and others saw Germany's modern national culture emerging out of a reform of everyday life.[24] They focused on educating the middle-class consumer, who would fulfill his or her patriotic duties through an active awareness of the connections between consumption, community, national economy, and national culture.

*   *   *

With its drawings and photographs of objects of all sorts—door handles, vases, fireplace screens, book covers, lamps, dishes, and furniture—*Taste in Everyday Life* takes us into the world of art and architectural reform before 1914: the work of Karl Schmidt and Richard Riemerschmid, Henry van de Velde and Peter Behrens, the Darmstadt artists' colony at the Mathildenhöhe, the Dresden Workshops, and the garden city at Hellerau. All of these projects grappled with "the problem of modern dwelling" and focused on the creation of interior spaces as complete aesthetic environments.[25] The domestic interior was an organizing framework for discussions of social reform at the Universal Exhibition in Paris in 1889. Through the 1890s, bourgeois reformers in Germany focused on transforming working-class homes into sites of "ethical culture" through affordable and hygienic household décor, pictures, books, and furniture.[26] The *Werkbund*'s focus on reforming craft production emerged out of these discussions, but soon diverged from them. One of its main points of focus became the project to reverse the perceived national decline of the middle-class interior caused by the mismanaged industrialization of home furnishings. As commentators liked to state, mechanization and mass production had made the German interior into a place of national alienation. In his assessment of the sources of cultural decline, Hermann Muthesius wrote that:

scientific and technical thinking had weakened the feeling for form so substantially that it could no longer react. It was the result of current developments that over decades we have arrived at a complete failure of humanity's aesthetic judgement, such that has never before been observed in history.[27]

A founding member of the *Werkbund*, he was invested in reversing this process.

Critics such as Muthesius and Lux analyzed the crisis in the same way. Historicism had led to an inauthentic copying of the styles of the past, and industrialization had furthered the spread of shoddy goods made in Germany but also in foreign lands. "A crisis of taste is simultaneously a moral crisis," wrote Lux, who blamed the mass distribution of industrially produced art nouveau objects for social ills ranging from individual irritability to hatred between the classes.[28] The industrialization of everyday objects had swamped middle-class consumers with products of poor quality, questionable function, and inauthentic design. Lux saw historicist decoration as physically as well as aesthetically harmful, for dust and bacteria collected in its cutout corners and embellished surfaces. He drew moral lessons from the poor quality of the objects, claiming that "fake material" and "shoddy manufacture" were synonymous with a "cheating sensibility."[29] Through such things, he wrote in his sweeping manner, corruption, rather than authenticity, and slavish dependence, rather than self-conscious virtue, had taken over the German interior.

Journals of art and design that began publication in the 1890s took this crisis as their starting point. Writing in the inaugural issue of *Deutsche Kunst und Dekoration* in 1898, its editor, Alexander Koch, claimed national culture to be insufficiently developed and internally weak. The German consumer was at the mercy of inauthentic styles and under the pressure of foreign markets. His journal would address this problem. In his editorial manifesto he declared:

> For this reason the editor of this paper, after careful consideration, set himself the task to create *a journal for artistic German work in the area of technical art* that will strive in general for the *promotion of a truly authentic and modern German language of art and forms* for those appliances and decorations that fill our lives.[30]

Koch consciously addressed a broad public of readers, consumers, and interested participants. He exhorted artists reading the magazine to send in "sketches, drafts and photographs of completed works . . . of the most modern conception." Among these he especially desired "those things and artistic objects that stand in service to the 'home.'"[31]

Koch was a major supporter of the Mathildenhöhe exhibition in Darmstadt in 1901. For examples of an "authentic German language of art" he pointed toward the work of Peter Behrens and the other architects and designers who displayed their work there.[32] The artists' colony built on the Mathildenhöhe took its inspiration from the English Arts and Crafts Movement and promoted the heightened presence of art in everyday life. Designers went beyond the single object in their attempt to create entirely new aesthetic environments "from the whole plan down to the last detail . . . streets, gardens . . . chairs . . . plates and spoons."[33] Yet this exhibition's focus on the individual artistic expressions of the architects made the display insufficiently national for some. The modern movement as shown in Darmstadt revealed "the new movement [as] a movement made up of individual men," wrote the architect Fritz Schumacher. It showcased their particular artistic sensibilities (their *Sondergeschmack*) rather than providing a set of guidelines that would be suitable for national cultural reform.[34] Koch wrote that he also wanted his journal to focus on practical cultural reform rather than on "fine art" as removed from everyday concerns. In order to become modern, wrote Schumacher, art had to become both more collective in its experience and more practical in its function. Rather than taking one away from everyday life, art had to grapple with it, heighten its meanings in a public and collective direction. It had to move from a concern with decoration and "come to more objective foundations."[35] In the language of the first decade of the twentieth century, art (*Kunst*) had to become "designed space" (*Raumkunst*).

The idea and project of *Raumkunst*, or the designed environment, brought the topics of art, industry, space, and nation together into one programmatic concept. It was the operative term for the Third National German Arts and Crafts Exhibition, organized by Fritz Schumacher and held in Dresden in 1906.[36] With *Raumkunst*, designers moved from creating the single object to focusing on the transformation of public and private spaces. Through *Raumkunst* national culture was grasped in both its spatiality and its totality. Conceived of as an organic and aesthetic whole, it also was reconciled with the power of industry. Through this concept reformers clearly articulated the connections between aesthetic reform and its national purpose. The Dresden exhibition showcased 142 spaces of different kinds: "halls and rooms, ground floors, corridors, and courtyards." In this "series of designed spaces," wrote Erich Haenel, "hardly any of the practical questions remained unanswered."[37] *Raumkunst* collapsed the differences between the arts, bringing them together in the service of an organic whole. According to Haenel, the rooms in which one "works and eats, plays music and sleeps, are not a random assortment of ceilings and walls, windows and doors." Rather, the arrangement had a cultural and spiritual function. Designed environments defined the spaces of everyday life as artistic and industrial "organisms" through which a national style was sought and defined.[38] For architects and designers such as Haenel, Schumacher, and Muthesius, style (*Stil*) was shorthand for an ideal form of national culture; its unified expression would place it in opposition to the inauthenticity of foreign "fashion."[39] The aesthetic "unity" encapsulated in *Raumkunst* sprang, in Haenel's words, from "a strong national life force."[40]

Muthesius saw 1906 as a turning point in the forging of Germany's new culture, writing a few years later:

After a few years we had already achieved clarity of expression in arts and crafts. Those things that were shown at the Dresden exhibition in 1906 took on an almost unitary national stamp. The initially purely artistic arts and crafts movement became a much larger general movement that had as its goal the reform of our entire everyday culture [*Ausdruckskultur*].[41]

National culture, in this conception, was totalizing in scope. *Ausdruckskultur* referred to the things of everyday life, breaking down distinctions between "high" and "low" culture. It referred to theater, literature, music, and the fine arts as well as to the design of a chair and the layout of a garden. In this terminology, all of these things were national cultural "expressions." In his inaugural lecture in 1907 as head of Berlin's Handelshochschule, Muthesius continued the promotion of interior decoration as a national project. From his writings and those of Friedrich Naumann, it was clear that the exhibition of 1906 had made, and publicized, two important facts. First, it showed that art and machines could enjoy a harmonious, even beneficial, relationship. Machine production would be guided by artists (in their new role as designers), its power contained by the shaping influence of aesthetic categories. Second, it revealed that an authentic national style could, and should, emerge from industry, from industrial thinking and industrial values.[42] As Muthesius implied, the new style did not have to be created as such. Rather it emerged as one stripped away the ornament and decay of centuries. It stepped forth from the interior of objects, from their bones and blood, so to speak: from their materials (glass, wood, paper, iron, clay, textile), their function, and their adherence to timeless laws of proportion and form. Through the machine, this style could be brought into every home, strengthening the German economy and disseminating German culture. As he wrote, "taste" was a more suitable concept for this program than was art. "If the issue was only one of art, we would have founded an artists' group then and left the industrialists outside," he said referring to the founding of the *Werkbund*:

But it has to do with the practical application of art, the bringing together of artistic, industrial and business goals in order to produce a working together of the forces of art, industry and distribution. And in this sense the word "art" is simply too pretentious a choice for many areas of our work. Often only taste [*Geschmack*], good and suitable form, and propriety [*Anstand*] are at issue.[43]

Competitions, in addition to exhibitions, were useful ways of publicizing "good taste" in order to raise consumer awareness and elevate public education on these matters. The numerous competitions run by associations and specialized journals were a popular way of teaching consumers to recognize new styles and value new standards. In 1908, for example, the periodical *Die Woche* staged a competition for garden design. Approximately three hundred entries arrived from all over Germany. Muthesius, Bruno Paul, Richard Riemerschmid, and Paul Schulze-Naumberg sat on the panel of judges. With titles as literal as "Garden on the Rhine" and as sentimental as "Forget Me Not" and "O

Tannenbaum," the entries were remarkable in their acquiescence to a set of architectonic standards thought to be modern, national, and disciplined. Gardens were pictured and described as rooms and represented architecturally through blueprints. Although the entries came from all parts of Germany, regional differences in botany and landscape were not prominent. Rather, a more standardized vision of the modern garden emerged from the entries, showing their adherence to an evolving vision of "good taste."[44]

The education of consumers was carried forward in the taste manuals. In *Taste in Everyday Life*, Lux went for the direct approach. He juxtaposed unreformed, art nouveau objects with their undecorated and properly industrially produced counterparts. Throughout he set forth principles of consumption, the so-called *Käuferregel*, exhorting consumers to pay attention to quality and form before price.[45] Alexander Koch went Lux one better and published an entire series of books dealing with all aspects of interior design. Each book in his series *Handbooks to Modern Living* (*Handbücher neuzeitlicher Wohnkultur*) dealt with a different room in the middle-class home. One publisher praised the publication of the books as "a national act," claiming that they "belong in every German home." As a contributor to a collection of Koch's wrote, putting the issue in a more pointed fashion:

> We are citizens [*Bürger*] *of our own time* and have with respect to it not only the rights of citizens but the duties of citizens. We would be traitors, if we did not help our time to reach its proper expression.[46]

*   *   *

"Modernity is easy to inhabit but difficult to define." This pithy summing-up by the historian Dipesh Chakrabarty speaks of the complexities of defining the relationship between modernity and nation.[47] Members of the *Werkbund* would have turned the sentence around. For them, modernity—the space of the nation—was easy to define but, as yet, hard to inhabit, at least in its wished-for form. As Eley writes:

> Eventually nations attained a presence independent of the political practices that originally proposed them—they acquired an instituted and renewable everydayness, which built them into the underlying framework of collective identification in a society, part of the assumed architecture of political order and its common-sense intelligibility.[48]

What Eley describes as an end result, early twentieth-century nationalists like Lux and Muthesius saw as a future outcome. Their desired nation was not yet made in a uniform and powerful sense. It existed as dream and as program. This dream was shared by nationalists in other countries. An organization of everyday life in terms of rationality, productivity, and hygiene, complete with its corresponding aesthetics of industrial form, recently has been described as the core of "the modern," as project and as experience.[49] In many countries, as in Germany before 1914, such an organization of the everyday was identified with national definition and renewal.

This everyday, however, had a small sociological compass. Between 1907 and 1910, the *Werkbund* moved from its original project of reforming manufactured goods to focus primarily on issues relating to consumption. In this shift they parted ways with the goal to "raise" the working classes by improving conditions of production and training for artisans. At the organization's yearly meeting in 1910, a lecture appeared on citizenship and the German worker. Given by Adolf Vetter, and with the title "The Meaning of Quality Work for State Citizenship" (*Die staatsbürgerliche Bedeutung der Qualitätsarbeit*), this lecture connected citizenship to the conditions under which "quality" work would be produced. "The worth of productive work for state citizenship," Vetter stated, inhered in improved working standards and protections for labor. Yet, by 1910 his talk was out of step with the others on the program.[50] Citizenship, and the concept of the national everyday to which it was connected, devolved more closely on a specific conception of German culture and its promotion by the German consumer. As the early history of the *Werkbund* reveals, members took seriously the writings of Georg Simmel and Werner Sombart, which analyzed consumption as the strongest area of Germany's modern economy. It was also the most undetermined realm of capitalist culture. As Frederic Schwartz has written, members of the *Werkbund* saw Germany's capitalist culture as "an open field whose nature could still be altered, shaped and negotiated."[51]

The *Werkbund* is often described as "overcoming" the "opposites" that divided modern German culture: the material and the spiritual, art and industry. While this language is both too heroic and too indebted to the organization's own view of itself, it does highlight the members' conviction that different spheres of modern life obeyed the same principles of organization. Uniting these areas consolidated and strengthened national life.[52] The uniting of culture and power was seen as an ideal form of organization for both German industry and German culture, and the *Werkbund* imagined an enlightened and educated middle-class consumer as both the creator and the occupant of its vision of national reality.

From the Chopped-off Hand to the Twisted Foot: Citizenship and Police Violence in Twentieth-Century Germany

THOMAS LINDENBERGER

"LA POLICE EST INSTITUÉE pour maintenir l'ordre public, la liberté, la proprieté, la sûreté individuelle" (The institution of the police is charged with maintaining public order, and with ensuring individual liberty, property, and security), according to the concise definition in the 1795 "Code des délits" of the young French Republic.[1] Even if individual rights of security and property are situated above public (read: state) order in today's democracies, one issue was determined unambiguously in the formative period of modern central-state power in late eighteenth-century France: public policing affected the rights and prerogatives of citizens, be it in concrete physical and material terms (with regard to security or property), or in the all-encompassing sense of granting every individual the ability and right to autonomous thought and action (freedom). And from that period onward, this function of the police led to the assertion that they enabled the promotion of general welfare and even the individual life chances of citizens, a standard justification used to legitimize the police in any political order, ranging from democratic liberal to totalitarian systems.

Although the institution of the police, which is omnipresent in daily social life, represents an immediate expression of the legal relationship between the citizen and the state, it is rarely considered in theories and historical surveys on citizenship. Scholarship on the history of the police instead has been traditionally fixed upon the police as part of the state order, as one of the larger bodies vying for power in the state, or as signifying and constituting the external relationship between state and society. As a result, historians of the police have only recently begun to consider the concept of citizenship, in decidedly "revisionist" police histories.[2] In this chapter, I will consider a fundamental structural component of any police practice, namely, recurring violent interactions of the police with citizens, in order to outline some possibilities of considering the historical significance of citizenship in its relationship with the police. I will focus on the regular and publicly applied means of violence available to the police, which—as a working hypothesis—signify normative understandings of citizenship, that is, of the relationship between state and citizen.

I. Police and Citizens in Urban Environments

The implementation of legitimate state power in modern societies originally was characterized by a fundamental ambivalence. On the one hand, citizens' rights, including property rights, had to be protected and safeguarded. Individual private property became the norm, privileging a minority of propertied classes against the aspirations and claims of the vast majority of expropriated classes. All police activity inevitably thus became, and still is, associated with contributing to the maintenance of social inequality. On the other hand, institutions such as the public police are needed in the market economy for technical reasons: they regulate and guarantee general access to public spaces and their various uses to the benefit of productive relations. But this requires a minimum of practical egalitarianism with regard to the man on the street. At least in theory, rules of behavior must be applicable to more or less everyone who uses public streets and places in order to minimize friction and to further business life.[3]

Seen from below, from the street users' perspective, this particular function of state executive power could gain legitimacy depending on whether it could meet a slightly different set of expectations. First, regardless of their differing social status, everyone should be entitled to use public streets for diverse purposes, including those transcending economy-related activities, such as recreating, socializing, and demonstrating, without facing risks to their life and sanity. Furthermore, in order to enforce rules and standards of behavior against rule breakers, the police should intervene impartially, their measures should be commensurate and pertinent to the matter involved, and they should be accountable for their actions to legal procedures, as is every other citizen.

These expectations became quite popular among German city dwellers beginning in the second half of the nineteenth century, often inspired by the legendary model of the British bobby and the establishment of a nonmilitary police in England. Because they were continually disappointed, in particular in the case of Prussian state authority, everyday police–citizen interactions developed into a particular field of negotiations about what it meant to be recognized as a fully entitled, "regular" citizen subject to no discrimination. In these interactions, lower- and lower-middle-class individuals would challenge such discrimination and articulate their visions of a just and fair (*recht und billig*) police.

The idea of legitimizing state power by standards of impartiality and egalitarian citizenship, however, was alien to the German and Prussian elites' idea of state sovereignty. In their worldview, the state had to serve the *bürgerliche Gesellschaft* only to the extent that the latter's development would entail the perpetuation of their own, essentially preconstitutional, position of domination. The police thus had to serve the state, not the actual public in the streets. Both social discrimination by the police (against workers, women, and minorities) as well as the insistence on the state's prerogative being the prime and ultimate goal of the executive were often repudiated by a broad coalition of city dwellers. *Polizei und Publikum* (police and public) therefore was a common topic in the urban press, to the extent that it constituted a journalistic genre of its own, including reports on police misbehavior and arrogance, inadequacy of bureaucratic practices, and partiality and provincialism of the personnel (the majority of police officers in large cities originated from the countryside). The most recurrent point of complaint in these debates were instances of the abuse of police powers, abusive by virtue of their lack of justification and their excessive scale.

Because police violence was part of both everyday life and spectacular political events, I will use it here as an indicator of the changes in the citizen–state relationship over time and in notions of citizenship as it was practiced and negotiated in this field of interaction. To reduce the empirical basis of this long-term perspective to a practicable size, I will focus on the technical side of how police inflicted violence on citizens in standard situations, that is, on police weaponry: sabers, hand guns and carbines, truncheons, fists and tonfa sticks, complemented by passive protection (leather, steel, and plastic helmets, shields, and protection gear).

Looking at Germany in the twentieth century, from the *Kaiserreich* of the 1910s to the Federal Republic of the 1990s, the picture of a road to successful civilization seems to be inevitable. This goes hand in hand with the common assessment of contemporary interactions between the police and citizens as less violent and less risky. In order to understand such historic achievements of formal democratization and legitimacy without resorting to a self-serving success story of civilization, I will look at changes in the bodily conduct of the interacting parties and how, or if, they are related to one another. It is not sheer philanthropy or spontaneous conversion that enabled police officers and citizens to settle their conflicts with less dangerous weapons and less lethal results over the decades. Looking at German politics of the twentieth century, I will argue that the growing proximity of the interacting parties made possible less violent interactions between police and the public, a growing proximity in terms of their physical conduct, their standards of behavior, and their way of life in a more general sense.

II. Contrasting the Extremes: Two Case Studies on the Late *Kaiserreich* and the Recent Federal Republic

In order to substantiate my argument, I will present a double narrative. First, I will describe two cases of excessively violent encounters between civilians and police officers that establish my thesis about fundamental differences by their contrasting contexts—the late *Kaiserreich* versus the Federal Republic in 1994—within a *longue durée* perspective on German police history.[4] In picking these two examples, I focus on periods that were marked by *relative* peace and stability, both externally and internally, compared to the decades between and in the perception of the actors themselves. The two cases therefore represent two variants of "normality" of peacetime that can be compared in terms of the norms of bodily conduct that underlay "relations in public"[5] between police and citizens.

In a second, rather summary, narrative, I will then outline the development during the decades stretching from the November Revolution to the coexistence of the two German states.[6]

A. The Saber as the Symbol of a Preconstitutional Order

Berlin, during a hot weekend in July 1906, in one of the typical working-class districts of the capital—today's Kreuzberg—with its overcrowded tenement housing:

A major crowd gathered in the streets Saturday night at Reichenberger Straße. As constabulary Reichenbach ordered the crowd to disperse, he was insulted by the worker Karl Schade from Reichenberger Straße 149, so that the latter was to be summoned to identification. On the way to the police station, worker Wilhelm Rau from Köpenick and worker Paul Haase from Niederschönweide attempted to free their comrade [*Genossen*] by force. As they did not succeed, Haase set on the crowd against the constabulary with the words, "After all, we are not in Breslau with the chopped-off hand," adding "that 'the blue' ought to give free Schade." (This gave the signal for the crowd to throw stones at the officers.)[7]

That same night, but on the other side of the Spree River, in the Strahlauer Viertel, a fire brigade fighting a fire in a factory courtyard was attacked by a crowd, resulting in an extended street fight between hundreds of rioters and the police. The mounted commander of the police squad, a police captain named Kubon, became the specific target of furious attacks. The *Vossische Zeitung* reported that during the eviction of the Strausberger Platz, Kubon

was thrown at with stones, one hit his shoulder and thereby tore off the epaulette. Simultaneously, he was attacked by a gang of young lads heading directly at him, so that he had to put out of action the first of them, later to be identified as the butcher Schumann, by a sabre stroke, at the very moment when the latter was about to throw a paving stone at him.[8] . . . Without delay, it was rumoured that the police had cut off someone's arm, and several rioters immediately shouted: "Revenge for Biewald!"[9]

Regarding Schumann's injuries, the Social Democratic daily *Vorwärts* reported:

The saber stroke hit Schumann while he was actually picking up his hat. It had completely cut through the wrist, the sinews and the artery; an amputation, however, had not been necessary.[10]

Set against the background of street politics in Berlin in those years,[11] both events can be characterized as rather "nonpolitical" by the standards of that time. They were based on traditional hostility between the urban lower classes and the royal Prussian constabulary, the *Schutzmannschaft*. Such events merely represented two of the numerous violent episodes in a long decade of guerrilla-like warfare between the police and a mainly proletarian street public, which was fought over standards of public order and "proper" behavior in public. Contemporaries were familiar with such incidents. They formed an integral part of urban everyday sensation, reported quite regularly in the local section of the newspapers along with crimes and other miscellaneous affairs.

Nevertheless, some details reported in a rather casual way point to political meanings and deserve closer attention. What do "After all, we are not in Breslau with the chopped-off hand" and "Revenge for Biewald" stand for?

* * *

Franz Biewald was a worker who lived in Breslau. During a protracted labor dispute in the local metal industry in April 1906, the police were called in several times against strikers. Not unusually for this period, uninvolved persons were adversely affected as well, including Biewald. Fleeing from police officers storming by with drawn sabers, he retreated onto an open staircase. A policeman followed him, and with one stroke of his saber chopped off Biewald's hand—an outrageous occurrence even by the public standards of 1906 Prussia, where mistreatment by constabularies was well-known.

Within a short time, this incident gained symbolic significance, particularly among the Social Democratic public and therefore among workers in big cities and industrial communities such as Berlin. It represented the essence of the brutality of the Prussian police system and inspired numerous caricatures, sarcastic jokes in cabarets, and satirical comments. In 1908, police informers reported that a small police horror exhibition had been set up at a Social Democratic summer feast, displaying among other things a replica of the "chopped-off hand of Breslau." The trade union and party organizations distributed a postcard that showed Biewald with his maimed arm.

Back to Berlin and the hot weekend in July 1906 discussed above: Two weeks earlier, the trial for the Prussian state to gain indemnity for Biewald had started and of course was covered meticulously by the Social Democratic press. By contemporary standards, the fact that the trial had even materialized meant that the police had already admitted that the attack on Biewald had lacked any legal justification. Adversaries of the police referring to "Breslau's chopped-off hand" to justify their resistance against police measures could count on the approval of a working-class public: everyone would immediately see the connection between a policeman's drawn saber and the arbitrary treatment of harmless workers, with the potential for mutilation and mortal injuries.

On the other side of the class divide, the saber represented the fears and anxieties that pervaded the state's authority and those on whose behalf it acted, the ruling elites of Prussia. The fact that the Prussian elites did not want to give up the usage of military weapons as police weapons was rooted in the unstable and precarious legitimacy of the Prussian state and its executive forces, and this lack of legitimacy was furthered by the everyday usage of military weaponry in policing. In conflict situations, the constabularies were not regarded as the citizens' police, and they were deliberately not meant to be such in the eyes of the authorities. The royal constabulary was meant to protect the power of the existing order, including the monarchy, property, and the census suffrage. Any aspirations to put this order into question, be it as such or in some minor respect, were to be fought immediately and energetically in an old-fashioned, soldierly manner.

In the perception of both the ruling elites and the police in the streets, such aspirations lurked everywhere. The cops on the beat knew it from their work: in many cases, particularly in conflicts on the streets and on weekends, when alcohol also might play a role, mere persuasion based on the prestige of the police function definitely would not work. When witnessing a conflict with the police, the crowd of onlookers always seemed prepared to engage in counterattacks and, if necessary, to throw stones, punch, or stab. If a situation deteriorated in this manner, the police usually were in the minority. Left completely on their own, they had to resort to the saber, swinging it around to keep the shoving crowd at a distance.

This readiness to resort instantly to potentially life-threatening violence was part of the defensive mentality of a besieged collectivity that permeated all executive levels of the Prussian state. According to Alf Lüdtke's pioneering work on the practice of state violence, this mentality of *Festungspraxis* was forged during the nineteenth century and became the unquestionable mindset of the police as they sought to enforce public order using a military model. Following the underlying worldview of *Festungspraxis*—maintaining the semi-absolutist state order—existing property rights and discrimination against workers were identical.[12] Consequently, every smaller industrial conflict involving disputes between strikers and strikebreakers could escalate within a short period of time into a larger riot in which footed and mounted police alike would draw their sabers, or *blankziehen*, as they were called in contemporary vocabulary, and hit indiscriminately into the crowd (*einhauen*).

Of course, there were less dangerous ways of using the saber in everyday police practice. The blade remaining in the sheath could be used to push back the crowd. Moreover, drawing the weapon below the dangerous level known as *scharfes Einhauen* would allow hitting with only the flat side of the blade, and in "normal" times, the blade was not honed sharp.

Although such subtle ways of using sabers existed, in the eyes of enlightened police "clients" the fact of using sabers as a police weapon per se had become a grotesque atavism belying the modernity of highly industrialized and urbanized Germany. It sharply contrasted with the widespread ideas of and desires for a decidedly nonmilitary police practice, which was mainly inspired by the English model.

At the same time, precisely these experiences of state violence contributed to the creation of a civil, asoldierly countersymbolism by the Social Democratic party. The party and its organizations were determined to avoid images of violence and disorderliness at any price in terms of their interacting and socializing, their self-representation. Leaders and functionaries were constantly at pains to teach their followers the virtues of strict self-discipline to achieve this goal. This was particularly true when they took to the streets. A separate body of guards (*Ordner*) and a meticulous organization when marching to and leaving the mass meetings were established in order to display appropriation and usage of public places that was exemplary not only for its peacefulness but also for its respect for traffic regulations and police orders.

The civilized appearance of hundreds of thousands of workers in their Sunday suits with white shirts and ties was also a means of protection during demonstrations, as it was well known that the police instinctively would treat people in bourgeois outfits less badly. All in all, this way of staging mass events was meant to be a symbolic attack on the narrow-minded militaristic understanding of executive state functions held by the ruling elites. It created a specific image and symbolism of citizenship in the people's state (*Volksstaat*): sober, rational, self-disciplined, egalitarian, one that included both men and women.

B. The Twisted Foot of the Radical Reporter, or Police Violence in Postindustrial Society

Today, gruesome episodes such as the "chopped-off hand from Breslau" seem like horror stories from a remote country, or from the Stone Age of a nation-state still ignorant of citizen and human rights. Despite contemporary cases of abusive violence by the police, which are regularly and justifiably investigated and made public by police critics, we presuppose *grosso modo* that the exertion of police violence is contained in particular by the logic of *Verhältnismäßigkeit der Mittel* ("appropriateness of the means"), which implies that the degree of police violence inflicted on an individual has to be in reasonable proportion to the goal to be achieved. Such logic is in direct contrast to military logic, which uses violence to annihilate the opponent. Following this rule of *Verhält-*

nismäßigkeit, police violence may be employed only insofar as it is absolutely required to avert imminent endangerment of public security. The restrictive elements of this definition are *appropriate, imminent, required*, and also the more restrictive, purely "technical" notion of *security* instead of the traditional and deliberately diffuse "order and security" (*Ordnung und Sicherheit*).[13]

But what do *appropriate, imminent*, and *required* mean today? And what does "civilized" or demilitarized violence look like?

* * *

Downtown Hamburg, May 30, 1994. Oliver Neß, a journalist who has repeatedly published reports about abuses of foreigners by the Hamburg police, is observing a right-wing rally at which the Austrian politician Jörg Haider is expected to deliver a speech. Because left-wing demonstrators have announced their participation, numerous police officers are present in order to prevent confrontations between right- and left-wing demonstrators.

Among the police are groups of plainclothes officers who are dressed rather casually and are taking action against so-called left-wing "disturbers" in a massive show of force, which repeatedly leads to smaller brawls. While only observing one of these incidents, Neß is attacked by a uniformed officer and pushed to the ground. As he gets to his feet, an officer in civilian clothes pushes him down again, holding his neck and kicking him in the hollow of his knees. Then the first cop holds him on the ground by kneeling on his chest. Meanwhile, another uniformed officer intervenes: He kneels down near Neß's feet and applies a foot-twisting lever (*Fußdrehhebel*), a method—as the *Hamburger Landgericht* will state later—that he had learned in a training program and by which, according to the *Landgericht* decision:

persons lying on the floor and offering resistance can be put either in a supine position or on their belly by inflicting pain in a controlled manner through holding the foot of the stretched leg at the heel and the forefoot, and then, while fastening the heel with one hand, turning the forefoot with the other in the direction desired.[14]

At the first attempt, this lever failed because the shoe slipped off Neß's foot. The policeman took hold of his foot again:

[F]astening the heel of the witness Neß with one hand, he bent the forefoot with a force of 25 kilopounds so quickly inwards, that the witness Neß still lying halfway on the right side couldn't follow the sudden turning of his foot and therefore could not bring himself into a supine position, especially because he was hindered by another policeman. Consequently the ligamental structures, consisting of only 1mm thick ligaments, of the witness Neß's right talar joint were severely disrupted, including rupture of two of the lateral ankle ligaments.[15]

Neß had to undergo a complicated operation and protracted physical therapy for several years until his broken foot had more or less healed. During the following years, the Neß case appeared on Amnesty International's list of human and civil rights violations in Germany. The infamous spirit of comradeship in the Hamburg Department of the Interior prevented any commensurate criminal investigation of the case—the two uniformed police were acquitted in 1998.

The question of whether Neß actually had been the victim of an illegal attack was resolved in favor of the accused policemen by two court decisions. We can leave it open for the moment whether he was the victim of a revenge act of a particular police unit against a nasty police critic, carried out with the aim to inflict exactly this kind of injury—as Neß and his lawyer stated in several publications—or of an act of negligent injury within an illegal arrest procedure. (Some evidence, indeed, seems to speak in favor of the first interpretation.) In the context of our problem, some details of the incident that are less questionable merit closer attention.

First: The police entered the stage in double appearance: uniformed and equipped with additional passive protection (helmets, shields, leather jackets), plus the so-called "pushing-off stick" (*Abdrängstab*), a long police baton. In addition to the uniformed police, there were officers who wore plainclothes of a particularly cool and sporty kind. They worked *with their bodies only*, using no passive or active weaponry at all.

Second: Besides the long stick, which is also used for hitting, of course, the main device of police violence consisted of applying certain holds at the neck and other parts of the body, pushing with the hands, imposing the weight of the body, and the disastrous foot-twisting lever (*Fußdrehhebel*). Direct body contact played a key role. Modifying another expression, we can speak of an intensive body-to-body interaction that characterized the whole course of events from the outset. Thus, in its decision, the court did not find any term better than *"Schlägereien"* (brawls) to describe the interactions between the police and left-wing participants of the rally. This term refers to a rather informal form of police action, but it merely described what happened: a confrontation carried out with bare hands and, at least on the side of the police, not unprofessionally. Pulling the legs, twisting the foot, and holding the neck while kicking in the back of the knees were techniques referred to as a separate register of physical violence belonging to the realm of combative sports and, more specifically, to martial arts.

Of course, elements of martial arts did not enter German police practice with its relative civilization under the Federal (or also Democratic) Republic. On the contrary. Jiujitsu and judo had long been popular among the German police, both via a canon of specific police holds (*Polizeigriffe*) and as a recommended but not obligatory way of physical training. But during the previous decades, the main emphasis had been placed on knowing elementary holding techniques, not on acquiring comprehensive and elaborate fighting techniques, which would require time-consuming practice to maintain and apply appropriately.

Beginning in the 1970s and intensifying in the 1980s, techniques of Eastern martial arts were implemented more systematically in police training. Not only were many police officers practitioners of sports such as judo, karate, taekwondo, and ninjutsu during their free time, but martial arts had also become part of their obligatory professional training. A new style of martial arts was created approximately thirty years ago that integrated elements of different fighting techniques and included common practices such as belt examinations, championships, and so on. The sport was named jujutsu, and it was popularized by police athletic trainers for the explicit purpose of their practice. New U.S. variants and schools of martial arts were specifically tailored for the needs of police work and were disseminated throughout the international police community.

We have to bear in mind a crucial fact when discussing this phenomenon: The growing popularity of Eastern martial arts beyond the extent to which it was traditionally limited within police training programs is by no means a peculiarity of the police community. Enthusiasm for judo, karate, taekwondo, kung fu, and all the other martial arts with their esoteric ritualism has pervaded society, especially (but no longer exclusively) the adolescent male section from which most police officers are (still) recruited.

Moreover, one of the most recent innovations in German police weaponry—the tonfa, a 61-centimeter-long hard plastic stick with a 14-centimeter-long hold, which allows more flexible and effective applications than the traditional rubber or wooden truncheon—originated in jujutsu as practiced in the United States. When used with skill, the tonfa is considered to be much more harmful than conventional truncheons (although no severe or lethal incidents of tonfa use have been reported in the Federal Republic so far).[16]

With regard to their respective contexts, the decisive difference between our two examples of police violence can be determined as follows. The saber as a police weapon symbolized and executed an enormous cultural distance between the dominating state authority and the predominantly lower-class urban public. It represented the essence of the aristocratic soldiership and professional military as a privileged state of society (*Stand*). By contrast, the body-to-body techniques borrowed from the arsenal of martial arts belong to cultural practices and experiences shared by both sides of the conflict: the body as a fighting instrument, cultivated by sports in general—more particularly by combative sports and martial arts—and by young men in general, be they police officers or left-wing street fighters.

III. Civil War Impending? Policing the State of Emergency and Citizenship Between 1918 and 1969–89

Before discussing the long-term sociocultural changes underlying this secular development, let us first turn to the intervening period between the two events. This brings us to the second, much more abstract and comprehensive narrative of this essay: policing within the horizon of the emergency state.

A. Revolution and the Weimar Republic

Even before 1918, insightful practitioners among the Prussian elites acknowledged the anachronistic nature of the saber as police weapon. It seemed evident that violent industrial conflicts and demonstrations could no longer be suppressed by mounted saber attacks. Anticipating class struggle as civil war, reactionary modernizers such as Berlin's infamous police commissioner Traugott von Jagow ordered handguns for every policeman. A quantum leap came about during World War I and the uncompleted revolution of 1918–19: the police officer who chivalrously fought man-to-man or man-to-crowd was replaced by small, flexible detachments armored with machine guns, hand grenades, light armored cars, and light artillery. Until the demilitarization of West German police training during the 1970s and the dissolution of the East German *Volkspolizei* in 1990, these became the standard equipment of ordinary police forces (*Bereitschaften*) for extreme cases of public unrest. Underlying this armament was policy makers' concern that threats to the state order could be imminent at any given time, that civil war remained a real threat.

Of course, such a means of prevention could not inform everyday policing during calmer periods. As amply described in the literature, Weimar police history was marked by a profound dichotomy between the (social-) democratic reformism among the civil leadership and the stubborn militarism of the officers' corps.[17] During their professional training in *Bereitschaften*, policemen were trained by former professional soldiers to become modern civil war soldiers and were subjected to antirepublican indoctrination. On the beat, however, they had to adapt to the new republican zeitgeist. *"Die Polizei—Dein Freund und Helfer"* ("The Police—Your Friend and Helper") went the new slogan, promising a citizen-oriented and service-minded way of policing. It was within this context that the new standard weapon for everyday use was finally introduced on a general scale in Germany: the (rubber) truncheon.[18] Truncheons had been in use previously, but only in 1924 did rubber truncheons become standard weaponry for daily service. Sabers remained part of the equipment, although with a diminishing practical significance: As long as the military were allowed to parade with sabers as a symbol of their soldierly self-esteem, police officers would stick to these symbols during ceremonial events. In the legal, state-oriented minds of some Prussian police leaders, the rubber truncheon's introduction was aimed primarily at reducing the harmful effects of violent intervention. But, as Christian Sturm has shown in his recent study on the history of the police truncheon in Germany, in practice use of this innovation remained half-hearted. Some reports about successful uses in crowd control contrast with the widespread view among the police that firearms would remain the final argument in dealing with public unrest. Despite some gains in the direction of demilitarization in everyday practice, the militaristic core would survive during the short Weimar epoch.

However, one should not blame the state exclusively. Incomplete demilitarization was not just the problem of the state but of all citizens. Firearm possession remained widespread, even after wholesale actions of disarmament that terminated anti-insurgency measures. The new constitutional political culture of the Weimar coalition parties never gained hegemonic status; at the same time, the other political camps were breeding new cults of political soldiers who wore uniforms and were armed with clubs and, if necessary, handguns. As a consequence, one precondition for implementing a less risky and less violent way of policing in everyday life remained precarious: the effective and socially accepted monopoly of violence in the hands of a state under the rule of law.

B. Policing Racialized Citizenship

Nevertheless, the populist appeal of a *Freund-und-Helfer* police gained wider acceptance as a promise of nondiscriminatory policing in everyday life. The Nazis continued to exploit and cultivate this, but within a completely different notion of whose *Freund-und-Helfer* the police should be: that of the *Volk*, of course, but along the lines of inclusion and exclusion of the racially and politically purged *Volksgemeinschaft*. After the institution of a permanent state of emergency in February 1933, this deprivation of rights of particular groups was combined with a gradual fusion of state and party apparatuses of violence, dissolving the very notion of exclusive powers of the legal state. This became evident both in the secluded sites of terror and annihilation in the concentration camp system as well as at the grassroots level during "normal" times and under "normal" circumstances. Recent research on public rituals of humiliation and violent abuse of Jews, political opponents, and offenders of the Nuremberg Laws have stressed not only their widespread popularity but also their unmistakable tolerance and/or support by the regular police.[19]

Volksverbundenheit in this sense, however, went hand in hand with a rhetoric of general remilitarization of the police. The truncheons were stored away and reserved for crowd control in particular situations. Police officers carried sabers and small swords (*Seitengewehr*) again. Using the truncheon was dismissed as non-German: "[I]t is unworthy for a German to be beaten with a truncheon" stated a circulated order of the Reich Ministry of the Interior in 1935.[20] The very notion of *Verhältnismäßigkeit* had to step back in favor of "higher" ends when the journal *Deutsche Polizeibeamte* declared:

It had thus a deep symbolic meaning when the policeman was allowed to take off the truncheon: The character of a German man is not beating; however, he fights if necessary. The one who turns against the Führer, nation and fatherland will be struck with the gun [*mit der Waffe*], but then until annihilation.[21]

The divisive nature of the Nazis' notion of citizenship at once freed the *Volksgenosse* from the humiliating experience of being beaten like an ordinary dog and stabilized the self-image of the soldier-policeman, who was empowered to annihilate the Führer's enemies immediately in a "manly" and "German way"; that is, with a true weapon, the gun. Inside detention institutions, however, this argument lost its pertinence. Out of the public view, policemen as well as experts from other institutions used a broad range of violent techniques to terrorize detainees, including blows with bare fists as a means of deliberate humiliation.[22] The apogee of the institutional fusion of police and military violence on behalf of the racial state was reached during World War II, with large police units participating at different stages in the murder of European Jews.[23]

C. Policing Under Allied Control

The total defeat of Nazi Germany and the Allied control of all public affairs after 1945 marked a short interregnum of poorly armed German state institutions. Policing by Germans was supposed to pick up some of the civil habits that had been partially introduced during the Weimar Republic. In all occupied zones, truncheons again became the standard; handguns for self-protection were cautiously added, following Allied discretion. As the Cold War dynamic unfolded, a rearmament of police forces took place in both parts of Germany, the East preceding the West by three years (1948–51). In both cases, an anticipation of civil war situations determined the concepts of training and actual police practice, particularly of crowd control, although, of course, under completely different legal and political conditions.

D. East Germany: Reaffirming Authoritarian State Ideology

In the East, the type of emergency anticipated by Communist military experts turned out not to be what actually occurred on June 17, 1953: a spontaneous revolt of the working people against their "own" workers-and-peasants state. Police armament and training (such as it was) instead had been focused on settling a state of guerrilla warfare induced by infiltration from the outside.[24] Despite the bitter lesson of the June uprising, this continued to be the focus, for two reasons. First, the uprising had made it clear that Soviet military force was needed to guarantee the regime's survival. However, underneath this factual rule of force, a routine of negotiation in order to avoid any violence between the regime and the working class could establish itself in the following years and decades. The exclusive site of negotiation was the state's Socialist enterprise, not the public space of streets and squares. Second, the canonical interpretation of June 17 as a fascist coup attempt and consequently the absolute taboo on popular agency as its actual motor became an integral part of the reclaimed legitimacy of Communist power, prefiguring future riot prevention policies. This perception was reaffirmed by the Hungarian Revolution in 1956, which actually was an armed insurgence against Communist rule that received considerable moral, although not military, support from the Western world. Throughout the rest of the GDR's history, policing concepts remained fixated on the possibility of a violent uprising and guerrilla warfare within the GDR, triggered by West German infiltration. The stubborn intactness of this fantasy is proven not only by secret police minister Erich Mielke, who in 1989, the night before the now-legendary October 9 "Monday Demonstrations," asked his general staff, "Comrades, shall it be the 17th of June tomorrow?!" It is also evident from the fact that military leaders and security experts had no idea how to deal with a citizens' movement that, by 1989, consciously subscribed to the tenets and tactics of strictly nonviolent actions.

Therefore, everyday police–citizen interactions in the GDR took on a rather peaceful appearance: With no effective right to contest state action through formal procedures and deterred by a harsh prison regime, GDR citizens did not want to jeopardize their modest "normal" lives when running into conflicts with the police. This imposed pacification of police–citizen relations reached its peak after the seclusion of the GDR from the West in August 1961. The Berlin Wall closed an exit option for those who lived in open conflict with Communist state authority, while relieving state leaders of some of their tasks: no one could remain on the run for long within this small, sealed-off country. That further reduced risk-taking behavior on the civil side and also reduced the need for police to apprehend persons violently, as the ordinary citizen could not get far. From a comparative perspective, no wonder the GDR was a paradise of extremely high police clearance rates.

That image of superficial peacefulness (which contrasted sharply with the widely publicized violent police–citizen confrontations in the West) was a result of the way in which the exertion of state violence was structured, namely, concentrating its life-threatening potential at the territorial borders of the polity and, to some less dangerous but nevertheless deterring degree, in its prisons.[25] But it was also a result of the SED's policies of social homogenization: *Werktätige* and ordinary police officers resembled each other in terms of class origin and lifestyle to an extent unprecedented in German police history. This undoubtedly *could* have contributed to easier communication in everyday policing in many instances. But *Volkspolizisten* and GDR citizens shared more than the common language of "ordinary" people; they also shared factual impotence within Communist state machinery. The public police branch, the *Volkspolizei,* was the least prestigious of the *bewaffnete Staatsorgane,* ranking below the army and of course the secret police (*Stasi*), let alone the overall authority of the party and the Soviet Union. Although *Volkspolizei* officers were effectively protected against citizen violence by the threatening power of an arbitrary legal system, for that same reason they were not respected as actual bearers of authority. Everyone knew that the real threat to citizen rights originated from other institutions. So it came as a shock to the demonstrators of October 1989 that this seemingly harmless *Volkspolizei* actually confronted peaceful but unauthorized demonstrations with "conventional" crowd control devices that had been in place since the end of the 1970s (truncheons plus passive armament, tear gas) and massively abused the arrested demonstrators.[26]

E. West Germany: Leaving Behind the Emergency State Paradigm

The Western zones and the Federal Republic underwent a much more complex process of reinventing policing, in the end leading to a revised notion of citizenship within the police–citizen relationship. Briefly, it can be treated in three phases:

1. Reeducating the police. During their direct control over the German police, the British and American occupation powers tried to implement fundamental police reforms at the institutional, legal, and practical levels. Sticking to German state culture, their German partners—including anti-fascist politicians and legal experts—remained skeptical about a reorientation that would put forward civil rights as the primary object of policing. But, although tradition won the upper hand when the Allies gave sovereignty back to the newly founded Federal Republic, reeducation actually left some marks on the police force in the long run. They were shown other ways of policing through invitations to visit American metropolises; they learned to value systematic "public relations" strategies in order to win citizens' acceptance; they were confronted with the expectation to subscribe to a strictly legal state orientation as the basis of policing. Therefore, it is commonly ac-

knowledged that, although a particular fixation upon the sovereignty of the state and the status of police officers as *Beamte* were reintroduced immediately after regaining partial sovereignty, some long-term effects of reeducation did remain among the police.[27]

2. Policing the "Cold Civil War."[28] In the Cold War logic of reciprocal escalation, remilitarization took hold of West German police training from 1951 onward. *Bereitschaften* were to be trained to respond to internal insurgencies or to supplement the regular army in the event of an attack from outside, because army deployment was restricted to regular states of war. Tactics for crowd control that evolved during the Weimar period (truncheons) were complemented by some novelties (water cannons, tear gas). Sometimes local police leaders would resort to tried-and-true ways of impressing riotous crowds, such as during consumer protests in Munich in 1953–54, when the *Bereitschaftspolizei* occupied the streets in "traditional" gear with *Wehrmacht* steel helmets and carbines.[29]

At the same time, the reconstruction- and "normalization-" minded society of the young Federal Republic was disarmed to an extent that German society had never been before. Until the revolts of the late 1960s, the opposition of rioting rock-and-rollers and beat fans to such anachronistic shows of force therefore remained relatively tame and "unpolitical" compared to the Weimar years. The early success of economic recovery and the prospects of *Wohlstand für alle* furthered the decline in aggression levels between police and citizens. A major shift in the nature of this interaction took place through motorization, as traffic control became the standard situation in which an adult German would be addressed by a police officer. The issue of citizenship, with regard to fair treatment by the police, found new symbolic representation: the citizen's egalitarian participation in public space as a driver was intertwined with egalitarian participation in the nation's wealth as a car owner and was efficiently organized in semi-official lobbying organizations such as the ADAC (*Allgemeiner Deutscher Automobil Club*), which promoted "partnership" between the driver and the police and, therefore, between the citizen and the state.[30]

The full potential of a police force informed by emergency state concepts became evident only with the challenge of the Federal Republic by the student and youth revolt in the 1960s. As if falling into old habits, parts of the elites still informed by the Weimar disaster reacted as if that revolt constituted an actual threat to the state itself (only to be outdone by a minority among their opponents who opted for real guerrilla warfare in the years to come).[31]

3. From *Notstandsgesetze* to *Innere Sicherheit*. It is one of the subtle iro-
nies of the turbulent 1960s that, according to more recent scholarship,
one of the most contested projects of the Grand Coalition of the decade,
the emergency laws (*Notstandsgesetze*) from 1968, turned out to be a cornerstone for the development of a new understanding of policing in the
years to come.[32] Against all alarmist expectations by left-wing contemporaries, these laws did not result in a general curtailing of civil rights.
On the contrary, the deployment of the army in specific situations of inner insecurity, which these laws codified, unburdened the police from
being prepared for this kind of emergency. Vocational training in the
Bereitschaften was consistently demilitarized (no more light artillery,
machine guns, and hand grenades). Instead, instruments of modern
crowd policing (in particular, passive weaponry such as plastic helmets
and shields) were introduced on a systematic basis.

With the upsurge of a broad variety of new social movements in the
aftermath of 1968, police and citizens had ample opportunity to experience various occasions of more or less confrontational interaction. To
make a long story of debates within the citizen movements and among
police experts short: In the end, both parties learned to "read" and
use the other side's intentions and priorities as a lever to further their
own goals. Tacticians of civil disobedience and nonviolent rule breaking counted on the police's moderate intervention in order to publicize
their own agenda more effectively. Protest policing, which was not fixated on "the state" as the immediate normative object of protection, allowed new ways of negotiating partnerships with demonstrators based
on the principle of "deescalation."

The background of this development can be seen in debates of the
1970s about *Innere Sicherheit* in the community of security and police
experts.[33] *Innere Sicherheit* initially was conceived of as an integral part
of state social policies, defining citizens' entitlements to secure and reliable conditions of existence. However, the changing norms and values
in society rendered this notion highly dynamic, reflected, for instance,
in a number of constitutional court decisions. By the end of the 1970s
and especially after the constitutional court's decision on the supreme
priority of the right to demonstrate in 1985, a new "policing philosophy"
established itself: Rather than banning demonstrations because single
criminal acts had to be expected, the police were obliged to isolate the
minority of "disturbers" in order to safeguard the majority's right to
demonstrate, and they had to do so—again—according to the principle
of *Verhältnismäßigkeit der Mittel*, at least in theory.

IV. From the Saber to the Tonfa: A Successful Story
in Civilizing Police Violence? Yes, But . . .

Guaranteeing the peaceful citizen's right to demonstrate by extracting individual *Störer* was exactly the philosophy brought forward by the Hamburg police in order to legitimize the attack on Neß, the journalist, in 1994. Subtle police techniques adapted to broader ends would not preclude gross abuses if specific individuals were targeted for specific motives such as revenge, racism, or just fun. Although citizens had some opportunities to bring such abuse to court, the Hamburg case has amply shown how limited such attempts can be, even in a fully fledged legal state such as the Federal Republic. Even under pressure of public criticism, the police always have been able to sidestep criminal prosecution by mobilizing the traditional values of manly comradeship and solidarity typical for "cop cultures"[34] everywhere in the world.

In conclusion, then, how should we interpret the observable changes in violent police–citizen interactions between the 1910s and 1990s? It would be too easy to register this as net progress in the direction of renouncing the use of violence in our intersocial conflicts. We should not limit our attention to purely quantitative aspects. In order to understand the overall nature of the process, we also must look at changes in the cultural codes that inform and set the standards for the use of violence, standards that in turn inform the notion of citizenship. At the beginning of the century, both cultivating and, within the same process, disciplining male aggression followed unquestioned military and soldierly patterns, be it in the realm of gymnastics or military training. These realms of male socialization also furthered the stereotypes of obsolete chivalry—*Ritterlichkeit*—embodied in the saber as a symbol of state authority. Whether the noble ranks handled their disputes of honor using guns or sabers[35] or the rabble was to be held down, keeping distance and inflicting bloody wounds were the rule.

By contrast, in today's postindustrial hedonistic society, dealing carefully with the body has acquired paramount importance as a moral obligation as well as an individual entitlement. Protection against accidents has increased drastically, as have ways of minimizing their consequences. (With some luck, surgeons today could have sewed on poor Biewald's hand, although at immense cost—which, however would be regarded as appropriate.)

This comprehensive valuation of the body—valuation in the financial sense as well—is extended to norms regarding our lifestyle and behavior. We constantly are reminded to keep our body healthy as long as possible, investing significant money and time in this, not just by renouncing drugs and excessive food but also by maintaining a high-quality diet, systematically protecting ourselves against injury, and exercising. In contrast to the time of the Emperor, sports are no longer attuned to the requirements of the military but to the well-trained individual who must be prepared to deal physically and emotionally with the modern struggles of existence.

This code forms an essential part of our culture of the self: it bears upon violence in conflicts between citizens and the police and thereby on the identities of citizens when they interact together in public. Looking at the interplay of both levels—the first one regarding institutions of violence, the second one regarding the sociocultural standing of the self and the body—allows us to reconstruct the significance of violence in the public sphere as the interface between the state and the individual insofar as this interface is represented and executed by the police. We thus can reconstruct historical changes and their influence, for instance by looking at the actual changes in the political structures and sociocultural patterns of a long-term civilization (in the normative sense). That does not mean assuming a teleologically derived, irreversible process of modernization. Rather, this perspective takes into consideration decades of violent encounters in German society. Although these experiences with violence, however long ago, happened to former generations, they still underlie present-day interpretations of reality, representing a permanent state of impending or actual emergency that no one wants to return to.[36]

Nevertheless, these experiences do not constitute a homogeneous and definite positive norm in the present. They do not by themselves preclude the discriminatory application of the rule of law in conflicts determined by ethnic, social, sexual, and political cleavages. This is why police actions remaining within the conventional range of socially accepted violence are more likely to target "non-German"-looking or marginalized civilians than "German-looking" or "normal" civilians under similar circumstances. While the degree of abusive violence is contained by historical experience in a given society of citizens, discrimination against those with a precarious status is not. The norms that manifest in the violent relationships between police and citizens, and the institutions and practices of citizenship in which these norms are embedded, require ongoing negotiation and renewal. Citizenship remains a historical risk in the relationship between state and society, both for the individual and for the state as a whole.

Body Biological to Body Politic: Women's Demands for Reproductive Self-Determination in World War I and Early Weimar Germany

CORNELIE USBORNE

MUCH HAS BEEN WRITTEN about the vehement campaigns to liberalize the abortion laws during the Weimar Republic. Although historians used to concentrate on the medicolegal, demographic, or political aspects, female scholars more recently have paid attention to the implications for women's rights.[1] This chapter, however, seeks to situate struggles for reproductive freedom within the larger topic of women's citizenship. It will tease out the manner in which an issue formerly regarded as private became part of public policy and gained political centrality and how women utilized this for their own ends. Contesting official population policies, they started to participate passionately in the debates about fertility control and thus found a voice in the democratic process and the construction of female citizenship at a time when the language of citizenship was barely developed.

On May 18, 1926, the German abortion law, §§218–20 of the penal code of 1871, was liberalized. The three existing clauses were replaced with a single new clause, §218, and the penalty for the aborting woman and her accomplice was mitigated from penal servitude to plain jail. But commercial abortions, those performed without consent, or abortion that ended in the death of the woman were all to be punished much more severely.[2] Campaigners for a more radical reform at the time gave the 1926 amendment only faint praise, and most historians have tended to agree.[3] I, however, have always regarded the 1926 revision as a remarkable achievement. Germany, together with the Soviet Union, had the most lenient abortion regulation in the developed world; the new law protected many thousands of women from long prison terms and, remarkably, it came about as a piecemeal reform ahead of the revision of the entire penal code, which had been planned since 1909 and which the government was most anxious to process as a whole.[4] Apart from a Supreme Court decree in 1927 permitting abortion on strict medical grounds, the 1926 law remained unchanged until 1933; legalized abortion was introduced only after World War II, first in the German Democratic Republic in 1972 and then in the Federal Republic of Germany in 1976.[5] The 1926 law also had an important practical and symbolic significance. If there were extenuating circumstances for women having abortions, their penalties could be as little as a single day in jail or a very small fine. Furthermore, they were no longer tried by a jury but by lay assessors, who were usually more sympathetic to female defendants. Much to the outrage of the two Christian churches, after May 1926 simple abortion was no longer regarded as murder but as a misdemeanor. The amendment finally signaled a remarkable shift in official attitudes toward women's reproductive rights and, by implication, women's social role, the family, and maternity. This important change was the result of years of strenuous campaigning initiated and to a large part supported mainly by women themselves; they fought to be permitted to terminate an unwanted pregnancy as a basic human right, especially crucial during World War I's years of hardship and the immediate postwar period. If the campaign was fuelled by women's sense of physical and psychological survival, it also provided them with an unprecedented opportunity to carve out a new political space. It served as a powerful means by which women renegotiated their relationship with Germany's first democracy and redefined a gender identity that often transcended occupational, generational, regional, denominational, and class differences. Newly enfranchised in the revolution of 1918 and buoyed by their contribution to the war effort, women placed the body female at the center of the body politic and ensured that reproductive rights, especially the right to intervene in unplanned pregnancies, remained at the top of the political agenda.

Much of the historiography of the abortion rights struggle concentrates on the period of the depression at the end of the Weimar years, when public protest was spectacular but no longer effective.[6] I will instead focus on the period of World War I and the early Weimar years, when the transformation process of gender and civic identities was most marked. The exercise of female action was often mediated by third-party public figures such as female politicians, as well as by left-wing party officials who appropriated fertility control as a tactical tool. Female action was also mediated by left-leaning doctors and sex reformers, who eagerly supported campaigns because they promoted their own ideological and professional struggles. Historians have usually concentrated on all of these groups.[7] But women's campaigns are more remarkable for having expressed their attitudes directly and independently of tactical or political considerations, and this will be explored below.

The question arises as to why such passionate campaigns for reproductive rights took place in Germany when women in other western European countries largely shied away from confronting the issue as openly. The answer is a conflux of extraordinary circumstances in Germany. Some preconditions did occur in other countries, such as the professionalization of medicine and the medicalization of society, increasing secularization, and a rising number of people leaving both Christian churches;[8] but what singles out Germanys is the degree of change and the way in which this change coincided with other events. For example, in Germany, the revolution led to the disestablishment of the Protestant church. Added to a temporary lifting of censorship followed by more liberal attitudes toward sexuality, this benefited an already vibrant sex reform movement that included a number of fearless feminists with an excellent record in the public debate about body politics. Helene Stöcker, founding member and long-term leader of the radical sex reform organization the League for the Protection of Motherhood, had campaigned since 1905 for the rights of unwed mothers and their children, for sexual equality, a new moral order, and women's control of their own bodies. She believed that a radical new interpretation of human sexuality was the best means to solve not only the women's question but also the social question as a whole.[9] Such ideals of bodily autonomy, which were articulated frequently and persuasively in Imperial Germany, anticipated and facilitated the successful campaigns in the more congenial climate of the Weimar Republic. Also important was the numeric strength of the German women's movement and its two branches of bourgeois and proletarian organizations; they were concerned not just with extending the franchise but, among other things, with achieving reproductive rights.

But questions of procreation and fertility control were propelled up the political agenda first and foremost by radical demographic change. Since the 1880s, the crude national birthrate had been in steep decline, yet the impact of this was not fully appreciated until the 1910s. Other western European countries experienced a similar demographic trend, but the change appeared to be most dramatic in Germany, which re-acted more uncompromisingly than its neighbors. Imperial and state statistical offices excelled at fine-tuning information that fuelled alarm about "a race suicide." Unusually, some German physicians conducted surveys about sexual behavior among their working-class patients and recorded astonishingly frank answers of intimate thoughts and prac-tices, revealing that the use of contraception and abortion among the urban and rural poor was very widespread.[10]

Imperial Germany was determined to reverse the population deficit by any means possible: by collecting "scientific" data, deploying suf-ficient resources, and educating, cajoling, and intimidating the popula-tion to breed more and better children. After 1912, when the first results of the Prussian inquiry into the causes of the declining birthrate were published, the project to reverse this trend became one of the most im-portant tasks of government. Eugenic and pronatalist ideas were em-ployed to launch an aggressive policy to boost procreation and rule out "unfit" breeding, with few qualms about violating individual rights. Although this originally was conceived as a carrot-and-stick policy in which material incentives were to sweeten a tough regime of punitive measures, economic and military concerns soon ensured that the latter far outnumbered the former. It was during the last two years of peace and throughout World War I that corporeality began to dominate do-mestic politics, and because the government was authoritarian, body politics subjugated the individual to the perceived interests of the com-mon good. In the words of one cultural historian, the body is "where power has historically assumed its most monstrous and its most libera-tory incarnations."[11] In Imperial Germany, the effect on women was de-cidedly double-edged. On the one hand, pronatalist and eugenic poli-cies commodified women as providers of the future generation. On the other hand, they promised women new political significance, as their reproductive capacities conjured up the notion of women as saviors of the race, an image frequently employed by women themselves. Let me flesh this out.

The language of Wilhelmine pronatalism and eugenics certainly de-based and disempowered women by attempting to restrict their identi-ties to that of mothers. So did repressive programs that pathologized nonreproductive female sexuality and "dysgenic breeding," calling both harmful to the social body. Attacks on the alleged deterioration of female sexual morality became more frequent, as were attempts to fight it by judicial means. For example, in 1916, the president of the Prussian

Commission to Combat Fertility Decline, Dr. Otto Krohne, blamed the "alarming change of attitude toward the institution of marriage and task of procreation in wide sections of our population" firmly on the "increasing agitation in public for unlimited sexual activity" and on "contraception and the so-called free love." This was a veiled reference to the League for the Protection of Motherhood, by then much feared in government circles, and also to the new reproductive behavior of German women in general. Abortion was singled out for special condemnation. Krohne was not alone in complaining that such "unnatural and criminal" behavior threatened "state and church authority."[12] With this in mind, the Reich Minister of the Interior issued a circular to all public prosecutors the following year that stressed the importance of judicial proceedings against abortion in order to "eradicate this evil at its root" and urged them to prosecute with severity all those "persons who perform abortions habitually or commercially or give advice...."[13] The apogee of the repressive Wilhelmine population policy was three government bills introduced in early 1918 to outlaw contraception and voluntary sterilization and tighten abortion regulation. Their adoption was a foregone conclusion when the revolutions in 1918 intervened, and they were abandoned, never to be revived.

These unprecedented attempts to regulate individual sexual behavior and family life provoked a strong protest by the women's movement in July 1918 in a rare display of unity between the bourgeois and proletarian women's organizations, which were usually at loggerheads. Using the language of civil rights, they appealed to the Reichstag Select Committee on Population, demanding that the bill to outlaw contraception be scrapped, as it was an "unsupportable interference in the free right of women's self-determination."[14] This feisty stance was by no means the only time women's voices were heard. Thus I disagree with Elisabeth Domansky's judgment that the "newly gained national importance of women's reproductive work" during the war, far from empowering women, served to marginalize them from official influence.[15] True, women's real empowerment came under the more propitious circumstances of the Weimar Republic, but even during the war, women benefited from the high profile of female sexuality. Fertility suddenly had become a legitimate issue to be aired widely, and it fostered the blurring of boundaries between private and public sphere in civil society. The possibilities this opened up for politics were recognized as early as 1912, when two Social Democratic physicians from Berlin called for a national "birth strike." They called on working-class women to stop bearing children as cannon fodder and a reserve army of labor and hoped that thereby the ruling classes and capitalism itself could be defeated. But their plan was foiled by the Social Democratic Party of Germany (SPD) leadership, who condemned a birth strike as anti-Socialist, even though there was considerable enthusiasm for it within the women's grassroots movement.[16] Although during the war there was a notable all-party political consensus to stimulate the birthrate, this united stance did not preclude the possibility of also pressing for more support for women, often cloaked in terms of a just reward for their war effort. For example, a 1916 article in *Vorwärts* supported the official pronatalism but suggested it be tempered by welfare measures and the introduction of an eight-hour day for all female workers in munitions factories.[17]

At first sight, though, early twentieth-century German population politics did look like the eighteenth-century civil body politic described by Carole Pateman, which was formed solely in the image of male citizens, with women's bodies entirely absent.[18] Typically, in October 1915, *Vorwärts* joked about the pompous inauguration ceremony of the Society for Population Policy, founded at the instigation of and with support from the highest quarters in Prussia, as an assembly of "a large number of gentlemen [and] only a few women"; the speeches were informed, it wrote, "by the desire to remain exclusive in this undertaking and to be disturbed as little as possible by women."[19] Other populationist organizations proceeded likewise.

But this is not the whole picture; women did play a part, if only a small one, and they appeared all too eager to please. At the inaugural meeting of the Society for Population Policy, described above, there was at least one official female speaker; true, Paula Müller of the German Protestant Women's Federation was the token woman and one hardly known for radical feminist ideas, but she was there and she did speak for women. Gertrud Bäumer, the president of the vast bourgeois umbrella organization the Federation of German Women's Associations (BdF), and other leading women frequently contributed to the official debate, sometimes in very prominent locations. There is no doubt that they used very cautious language and expressed their support for the government's call to protect the *Volkskraft* (population strength) and *Wehrkraft* (military strength), but they were nevertheless able to introduce a different tone and represent a female point of view. For example, at a meeting in October 1915 in the Prussian House of Representatives, Bäumer pointed out that reproduction was more than a national question; it was "a problem which reaches deep into the emotional life of women and which equally can only be solved with the help of women's innermost being."[20] Unlike some prominent male commentators, such as the Social Democratic professor of social hygiene, Alfred Grotjahn, who admonished women to serve their country in wartime by procreating and called "pregnancy . . . a woman's active service" on a par with men's sacrifice in battle,[21] Bäumer stressed women's nature, their innate and God-given mission of maternity. The problem of a declining birthrate could only be reversed, she argued, if one promoted "the holy will to motherhood in women."[22] Bäumer here used an essentialist rhetoric relegating women to their prescribed biological task. But at the special war conference of the BdF in 1916, she shrewdly adopted racial hygiene terminology seeking to capitalize on the importance of women's procreative abilities, demanding an improved legal and social status for women befitting "the mothers of the race." During this time of censorship and expected display of patriotism, it is not always clear whether such statements stemmed from genuine pronatalist/eugenic convictions or from tactical considerations of securing an audience and then imperceptibly subverting official ideology. Certainly, some feminists managed to use male arguments to their own advantage. Rosa Kempf, for example, another prominent BdF leader, adopted the notion of pregnancy as women's "sacrifice to the fatherland"; she did so less to encourage procreation but rather to draw attention to the shamefully high and rising rates of death in childbed and perinatal mortality and morbidity that had received little official attention.[23]

The wartime pronatalist climate even emboldened perfectly ordinary women to put pen to paper, convinced that they too could help solve Germany's demographic dilemma. Although this should not surprise us given the high public profile of the population question, and although we should not be astonished that women seemed sympathetic to pronatalism, it is indeed surprising that they felt able to address themselves to the Imperial Chancellor himself and that the Chancellor's office read and annotated such letters and subsequently filed and archived them. For example, in May 1917 von Bethmann-Hollweg received a long communication from one Margaret Schrott-Matern of Magdeburg urging "the German government to care for and educate illegitimate children by German soldiers and women of the occupied territories, especially if these are boys." They would be useful for the fatherland and for future German reconstruction. Furthermore, to boost the birthrate, she recommended "wives' trains" to transport German women to their husbands at the front and permit soldiers to fulfill their marital duties. These trains should be equipped, Frau Schrott-Matern wrote, with individual compartments for use by married couples in hourly rotation; wives should bring the necessary blankets and pillows. To prevent the embarrassment of "satisfied couples" coming face to face with couples who were still waiting for their turn, there should be a one-way traffic through the train carriage, with the waiting couples entering from the left and leaving on the right once their time was over.[24]

A few years later during the Weimar Republic, a period noted for widespread agitation for women's reproductive freedom and for better access to termination of unwanted pregnancies, it would have seemed inconceivable that such sentiments could have been so confidently advocated. So what had changed since Imperial Germany that brought about such a radical shift? Or was the shift indeed radical? Is it not more plausible to regard the wartime experience and the patriarchal discourse as having laid the foundations for women's determination to remain in control of their own bodies, and to suggest that the changed political and social circumstances in 1918–19 made this possible, even promoted such ideas of personal autonomy? I would argue for this latter view, which entails recognition of the influence of the war as well as the dramatic changes brought about by the new democracy. For a start, the German birthrate continued to decline very sharply during and after the war despite the combined efforts to the contrary by the Imperial government and the military authorities. The marriage boom in the first postwar years did not result in enough children to make up for the wartime losses, and the peak in postwar national fertility in 1920 was below that of 1913, the last year of peace. At the same time, official estimates suggested a sharp increase in the annual abortion rate. Medical statistics informing government policy put the number of illegal terminations in the range of between 200,000 and 500,000 per annum in the immediate postwar years and up to one million by 1930.[25]

The refusal to submit to government exhortation was of course linked to economic and social hardship. But it should also be read as a rebellion by women, often supported by men, against stereotypical notions of women's social role. Certainly Adele Schreiber-Krieger, the radical feminist, sex reformer, and SPD Reichstag member, thought the phenomenon of rapidly declining national fertility was "the greatest, non-violent revolution" by women and one that "put the key to the control of life firmly into the hands of mothers. Thus a woman in bondage becomes master and determines the fate of the family, the *Volk* and humanity."[26] There is no doubt that thousands of women agreed and adopted the political issue of better access to birth control, and especially abortion, to carve out a new role for themselves in the new state. Remarkably, the impressive campaigns to reform §218 started as spontaneous actions by ordinary women and only later became part of more organized political campaigns mediated by male and female politicians, doctors, and reformers. After the revolution, it was women from the grassroots who appropriated the issue of fertility control long before a new population policy was formulated or the different parties had their own programs in place. In this way women, in their new role as voters and citizens, ensured they were heard by policy makers and legislators and influenced their projects.

What gave women the confidence to speak out in public about an issue that was still regarded by many men as embarrassing and personal rather than political? First, body politics had already assumed political significance in Imperial Germany by the government's decision to make reproduction central to domestic policy. This significance had been heightened during the war. Second, women's perception of their own role had changed as a result of their wartime experience, which had profoundly transformed the Wilhelmine notions of gender roles. Women had replaced absent men in the labor market and moved into traditional "male" jobs, and they had often become the head of the household as sole wage earner and lone figure of authority vis-à-vis their children, which promoted women's sense of independence and power.[27] The material and emotional hardship they had suffered during the war also fuelled their disillusionment with the authorities for their inability to protect families from deprivation. All women, but especially those who worked for twelve hours or more in factories, suffered physically, a condition aggravated for the many mothers who volunteered for night shifts "to be free during the day" for child care. Women's deteriorating health was reflected in the steep rise of female morbidity and mortality, a result of the strain from the triple burden of waged labor, housework, and maternity.[28] There is no doubt that these experiences had radicalized women politically. As Ute Daniel has shown, women were at the forefront of social protest against war, hunger, and insufficient wages. Such protest took less the form of organized strikes and demonstrations, rather erupting spontaneously in streets or the workplace,[29] a pattern that was to repeat itself in postwar protests against §218. Women's insistence on protecting themselves against unwanted pregnancies was just another form of self-help to maintain a measure of control over their lives and to ensure survival of the family in difficult times.

Third, the promises of the 1918 revolution and the Weimar constitution of a new gender and social order suggested a world turned upside down, where the formerly disenfranchised now had influence, and where the new civil rights emboldened women to speak out for themselves. Many thousands of women demonstrated for the decriminalization of abortion and thereby ensured a continued high profile for reproduction in domestic politics. To be sure, the draconian penalties meted out to those who were detected and tried for illegal abortions, especially in the early years of the Republic, and the mass violations against what seemed an unjust law turned many left-leaning politicians against §218. Still, it was ordinary women's own public form of protest against §218 that did much to define their new sense of citizenship. "Down with §218!" was the battle cry with which the newly enfranchised female voters made themselves heard. In the new democracy, the language had changed from one of duty and forgiveness to one of entitlement: bodily autonomy, reproductive self-determination, the right to choose.

How did ordinary women organize their protests? The strategy employed during the war, the development of informal networks among family and neighbors to help with food acquisition and child care, was also adopted in the postwar protest movements.[30] This ability to pool resources helped women survive the difficult postwar years: it would help them locate a tried and tested abortionist who was prepared to help when the need arose.[31] The same strategy of cooperation also helped channel women's anger with the law enforcement agencies' response to their plight toward political protest. The campaign against §218 arose apparently spontaneously from such local networks.

Popular movements are difficult for historians to trace unless they happen to have been recorded in the press or unless petitions have survived in official files. There is, however, important evidence of ordinary women voicing their demands to rate the body female above that of the body politic very early after the war. What is striking is the boldness of the language employed and, just as during the war, the lack of inhibition in contacting the highest authority of the land. For example, as early as February 1919, a month after the election to the National Assembly, a group of women in Berlin met to discuss how best to "curb coercive procreation to save Germany." They followed this with a resolution to the National Assembly expressing concern that the "increased difficulty of employment and rising consumer prices would lower the marriage rate and boost extramarital sex . . . [and] the surplus of women." They demanded a decree for abortion law reform: married women with three children should be allowed to terminate any further pregnancy, as should single women "who can prove that they had been a victim of seduction or of their own irresistible passion."[32] Although worded unconventionally, this petition anticipated the future standard demand adopted by most abortion reformers for legalized abortion on health, social, and moral grounds. Intriguingly, the petition also wanted women's sex drive to be recognized as valid grounds for a legal termination, thereby disputing the dictum of many doctors that only men were ruled by sexual compulsion. The Select Committee for Petitions of the National Assembly duly considered this resolution in "a lively debate" in October of the same year. Although the committee of six men and three women could not reach agreement on whether to pass it on to the floor of the house,[33] it was reported in the local and national press and undoubtedly encouraged others to follow suit.

Only four months later, in June 1919, a petition from Erfurt in Thuringia was sent to the Prussian Minister of Justice. It was entitled: "Many women are urgently requesting the revision of §§218 and 219 of the BGB [Civil Code]" [sic] and signed: "many women." The abortion law, it said,

should have been repealed a long time ago. For wealthy childless women have the means and ways to do this and a poor woman is branded a criminal and punished with penal servitude. This, too, should be remedied. Every woman should do with her body as she wishes.[34]

The notion voiced here, that §218 was class discriminatory, would later become a routine argument by left-wing reformers. The surprising reference to bodily autonomy in the final sentence had previously only been used by feminist sex reformers like Stöcker but later became the staple of feminist arguments; during the Depression, it was modified into the famous Communist Party of Germany (KPD) slogan "Your body belongs to you!"

In addition to those pioneering efforts, discourses about reproductive rights were mediated by third parties. Records reveal numerous women's protest meetings and demonstrations in the early 1920s, but they were almost certainly instigated by trade unions, the sex reform movement, or female politicians. Demanding a substantial liberalization of the abortion law, such demonstrations crossed denominational, regional, and very often class boundaries; they took place in Protestant Thuringia and Prussia, in Catholic Bavaria and Württemberg, and were supported by the working and the middle classes. In 1922, for example, "mass rallies" were reported in Stuttgart, Munich, and elsewhere in southern Germany, apparently sparked off by "monster abortion trials" that had taken place there that year. Such trials frequently led to public agitation because of the police raids that often subjected all known female patients of a doctor or lay abortionist to humiliating investigations, regardless of whether they were implicated in terminations.[35] In one such case in 1922 in Württemberg, it was claimed that more than 2,000 female patients of a physician suspected of crimes against §219 were interrogated by the police; 400 subsequently underwent a pretrial investigation, but only six were finally tried. Another famous case that caused a number of protests was that of the Berlin chemist Paul Heiser, who was tried in January 1925. Heiser had admitted, somewhat fancifully, to having procured abortions for 11,000 women, many of whom were investigated by the police. Eventually, only 400 women stood trial.[36]

Some of the rallies were likely to have been organized or at least helped by the KPD or SPD, which had by then adopted proreform tactics. In March 1924, hundreds of proletarian women assembled in front of the Reichstag to await the outcome of an urgent motion by the Communist parliamentary party to abolish §§218 and 219 and to declare an amnesty for the victims of these clauses. At the same time, the press reported "large protest demonstrations by women" in eleven working-class districts of Berlin in favor of the abolition of the abortion clause.[37] Women also attended rallies by pressure groups such as the League for the Protection of Motherhood. At a public meeting in the Berlin town hall in February 1924, the League managed to have the hall "filled to overflowing." This demonstration, too, called for an emergency decree repealing §§218 and 219 and for an immediate amnesty for all "those pregnant women convicted under §§218/9."[38] All these activities received wide press coverage and probably encouraged other activists to organize similar events.

Abortion law reform soon took hold of party politics. The issue was ideal to attract female party members and voters; given the importance of attracting their electoral support, especially as female voters were numerically outstripping male voters after the war, all parties took women's issues very seriously. Naturally, it was the political Left and the group of newly elected female members of the Reichstag and the state diets who listened most attentively and took up the cause of reproductive choice. They had reason to woo women because the first democratic election held with universal suffrage showed that women had favored the parties of the Center and the Right. In 1922, the KPD urged its party workers to adopt "the concrete problem [of abortion] to mobilize women and to win them for the class struggle," which proved successful. At the party conference in 1924, it was noted with satisfaction that rallies against §218 had indeed attracted "thousands of women" and even "many new party members."[39] The party also made use of the International Women's Day in March for annual demonstrations against the existing abortion law, with specially designed posters, including the famous 1924 poster adorned by a Käthe Kollwitz drawing, as an effective device for its recruitment drive.[40] The SPD, too, made use of the topic to win new women members. An SPD women's leader frankly admitted that whenever a party meeting was announced promising to discuss §218, it always attracted a large female audience and secured new members, but that retaining them later was more difficult.[41] In 1922, for example, local SPD branches arranged over 5,000 women's meetings to debate §218 in Eastern Saxony, which had apparently all been extremely popular.[42]

Trade unions, not to be outdone, employed similar tactics. For instance, in May 1925 the Berlin section of the Association of Clothing Workers held a well-attended rally, attendees of which voted unanimously to petition the Prussian Minister of Justice and demand the repeal of §218 as well as an amnesty for all those convicted under it.[43] Sex reform organizations and local sections of the women's movement did the same. In November 1925, for example, the Hanover branch of the Neo-Malthusian League against Compulsory Maternity used a promotion meeting to petition the Reich Ministry of Justice. The handwritten letter read as follows: "The assembled c. two thousand men, women and girls . . . demand the total repeal of §§218 and 219, because women of the working classes do not want to bear children if they cannot feed them."[44]

At the same time, significant sections of the bourgeois women's movement remained opposed to a total decriminalization of abortion and voiced their views accordingly: various local branches of the German-Protestant Women's Federation petitioned the State and Reich Ministers of Justice in late 1920 and early 1921 conveying "full understanding for tragic individual cases and wishing for lenient sentences" but expressing their strong disapproval of any attempt to abolish the abortion clauses completely. This, they argued, would be tantamount to approving moral decline. Naturally, the German Catholic Women's Organization also objected to a radical liberalization of the law.[45]

Although women's organizations clearly were divided over the desirability of abortion law reform, I would nevertheless argue that any kind of high-profile participation in the public debate, whether for or against reform, did much to sustain a debate about bodily autonomy in particular and women's role in general that was started not by prominent but by ordinary women in the very first years of the republic.

Left-wing politicians of both genders reacted very quickly and took the issue to parliament. In March 1920, just five months after discussion of the first resolution to the National Assembly by the group of Berlin women to repeal §218, a motion was introduced in the National Assembly by Luise Schroeder of the SPD to permit termination of pregnancy on social and eugenic grounds. It was signed by six female and five male comrades with the additional support of Marie-Elisabeth Lüders of the German Democratic Party (DDP). Shortly after the first Reichstag convened in July 1920, a motion was introduced by the Independent Social Democratic Party of Germany (USPD) and another by SPD delegates for radical abortion law reform, but the motions were not debated. They were followed by a further nine Socialist reforming motions in different versions, introduced at regular intervals until 1926 when a debate was secured in the Reichstag select committees that resulted in the amended law of May 1926 with which this chapter began. This law is a testimony to the success of grassroots pressure but also to the responsiveness of the Left, which understood that this issue was central to working-class politics. Female parliamentarians and party activists, in particular, were committed to reproductive choice and led the fight in the Reichstag, in diets, and within their parties. The cause also helped them to establish their own careers. Politicians like Martha Arendsee and later Helene Overlach of the KPD and Klara Bohm-Schuch of the SPD became well-known by speaking up for law reform on the floor of the Reichstag or diets, in town councils, at mass rallies, and at annual party meetings. The Dresden Social Democratic physician Anna-Margarete Stegmann even dedicated her Reichstag maiden speech to the topic of maternity and fertility control. Many of the new female politicians had made social policy their specialty and influenced, sometimes chaired, the appropriate parliamentary select committees to ensure that reproduction and fertility control were debated. The Select Committee of Population Policy of the Prussian Diet, for one, had a majority of women. Significantly, the committee backed abortion law reform early on, concluding that the law was "bankrupt" and that prosecutions appeared to the public to be entirely "arbitrary" because of the imbalance between "one million offences a year and only c. 10,000 convictions."[46]

Female parliamentarians also helped to lay to rest the crude pronatalism of Imperial Germany. Whereas for some male Socialists a declining birthrate was an "ideological expression of materialistic necessities," their female colleagues went so far as to praise smaller working-class families as a sign of social responsibility. Particularly Adele Schreiber-Krieger, a member since 1920 of the Reichstag population select committee for the SPD, welcomed the end of the "erratic and haphazard productions of proletarians." In a keynote speech to the 1919 SPD women's conference, she called birth control, including abortion, an essential human right:

> I demand a woman's right of self-determination about her maternity, I demand full enlightenment for women on all these questions; I have demanded for years . . . social-hygienic women's advice centres.[47]

As I have shown elsewhere, the medical profession was at the center of the official discourse and government policy;[48] writers, artists, and filmmakers also responded to the heated debate by addressing abortion issues in cultural productions.[49] This latter development reflected the fact that the previously unquestioned link between women's procreative capabilities and the *Volkskörper*, the national body, had in Weimar Germany increasingly been replaced by women's sexual freedom and the reproductive choice embodied in the alluring concept of the New Woman that so enthralled Weimar popular culture. For the younger generation in particular, birth control shed its negative image and could now be celebrated as a means of enhancing women's well-being and sexual pleasure.

The new concept of reproductive autonomy and the concomitant process of reshaping gender identity invariably had a considerable impact on the political process and the sense of citizenship in the new republic. As I have shown, reproductive rights contested the old boundaries between private and public spheres and made the personal political: questions of sexual activity and procreative choices ceased to be relegated to the private (female) realm of nature. Such questions were no longer assumed to be outside the legitimate concerns of the state; they became a profoundly public issue. The process of politicizing reproduction, and with it the redefinition of the role of the family unit,[50] started in World War I and continued during the Weimar Republic, culminating in the Nazi population and racial programs. The recasting of the relationship between state and society both entailed an unprecedented intervention into individual women's bodies and also provided a new discursive space for women to voice their concerns about their bodies. Female civic participation challenging the abortion law changed the language of politics from one of nationalism, law, and science to the more culturally informed language of the everyday: from population policy to politics of the body, even of women's wombs. Blunt references to fertility brought to the fore the visceral aspects of women's gynecology and sexuality and frequently proved unsettling for men. Such references also proved to be a profound challenge to the patriarchal state. The separation of sexuality and reproduction that birth control promised instilled in many men the fear that women would misappropriate the kind of sexual license traditionally afforded to men and conjured nightmare visions of unleashed female sexuality. It fuelled tension between men and women at home, in the workplace, and in politics. The new woman-initiated discourse about abortion was indeed, as one historian put it, "the fulcrum of a much broader ideological struggle"[51] offering women a new subjectivity and challenging views of women's place within the body politic.

This chapter, it is hoped, has demonstrated the usefulness of citizenship as an analytical tool. If we take *citizenship* to mean both status and practice or if we, as Kathleen Canning and Sonja Rose put it, embrace it in its discursive and experiential dimensions,[52] we can appreciate German women practicing citizenship, even though they may not have been fully aware of it, in the way they embodied their convictions and as a result mobilized to attain bodily autonomy. Four categories of citizenship are commonly cited: a political status within a state; a set of rights that accrue to citizens; the citizen's subjective sense of entitlements; and a subjective feeling of identification with a certain state or community.[53] In this schema, the ordinary women's protest movement against §218 during our period belong to the third and fourth categories: during World War I and before attaining the right to vote, but also in the Weimar Republic when formal political and social citizenship was bestowed on them, women "sensed their subjective rights" and began to subvert accepted gender roles and adopt illegal strategies by their mass violations of §218 and their protests against this law. They strove to sweep aside the old distinctions between private and public, family and government, individual procreative decisions and state regulation of fertility control, thereby redefining the boundaries of citizenship and influencing newly emerging public spheres.[54] Reproduction and abortion was and is of course a deeply gendered issue, and women who participated in the campaign against §218 recognized this by identifying with a "gendered community" of like-minded sisters, sometimes linked purely by geography, as in the protest meetings that sprang up in certain localities of working women, sometimes by political affiliation, as with women's sections of SPD or KPD. Thus, they shed their traditional role as reproducers who were relegated to the realm of nature and became agents in their own right.

Creating the Nazi Marketplace: Public Relations and Consumer Citizenship in the Third Reich

S. JONATHAN WIESEN

THE GROWING LITERATURE on consumer society is raising new questions about the meaning of modern citizenship. Citizenship, some scholars suggest, reveals itself not only in an individual's legal status or civil rights but also in a seemingly mundane act: shopping. In their power to buy a product or respond to a marketing campaign, individuals exercise certain fundamental privileges accorded to them as citizens. At the same time, these privileges are accompanied by a set of obligations that consumers have to the nation. Through their purchasing power, they support the government in its economic and political missions. This support can be ongoing, but it becomes particularly crucial during periods of crisis, upheaval, or transition. As Konrad Jarausch and Michael Geyer have suggestively argued with respect to a divided Germany, it is "'getting and spending' in the large and small dramas of everyday choice and their public display" that make up what they have called the "secret of citizenship." [1]

This rendering of citizenship is contentious and could be subjected to several critiques. One could argue that the notion of a "consumer citizenship," with its emphasis on private acts of choice, forces the concept of citizenship well beyond its accepted meanings. [2] One could also argue that the notion becomes meaningless if it is not analyzed within the framework of a wider set of political and civil rights and obligations that traditionally has defined modern citizenship. What is citizenship, after all, if not the opportunity to have one's voice heard and to fulfill one's civic duties in a visible and transparent public arena? Yet recent conceptualizations of "consumer citizenship" raise several significant questions about the connections between ostensibly private choices in the marketplace and transformations within the formal political arena. These conceptualizations suggest that, at certain historical junctures, the "citizen-consumer" can become a key figure in broader debates about the political, social, and economic order. For example, Lizabeth Cohen has argued that during the New Deal era of the 1930s, the American citizen-consumer emerged as a powerful embodiment of both the economic necessity and symbolic force of personal consumption during a time of scarcity.[3]

This concept of the citizen-consumer is also relevant to the history of modern Germany. In recent years, scholars have constructed the consumer marketplace as a space where shifting definitions of German citizenship have been articulated, revised, and contested.[4] In West Germany, the years of the "Economic Miracle" in the 1950s and 1960s saw a successful reconstruction of a post-Fascist democracy as linked to an emerging consumerist mentality among war-weary citizens.[5] And despite limits on competition and consumer choice, the GDR also cast the Socialist citizen as a consumer of quality goods that could be produced without the attending evils of capitalist exploitation.[6] In both East and West, the consumer played a vital role in articulations of postwar German citizenship.

But what about the years of National Socialism? Can one speak of any viable "citizenship" in the context of a dictatorship defined by racial exclusion and the collapse of political pluralism? Answering this question requires moving beyond political and legal conceptions of citizenship and turning to the cultural ideals that surround the notion of citizenship itself; that is, the ways in which individuals maintain a perception of themselves as citizens even as freedoms and rights are being taken away. Even as it obliterated the citizenship rights associated with modern democratic states, the Third Reich continued to appeal to the cultural idealizations surrounding the meaning of citizenship. This chapter looks at one dimension of this process: how private institutions appealed to Germans as citizen-consumers through drawing on a racialized message of privilege and responsibility in the marketplace. The question of who was allowed to take part in the economy—to buy and sell goods, to purchase and maintain property, and to see themselves as part of a modern, industrial society—was fundamental to cultural conceptions of citizenship, not only before and after the Nazi period but also during its twelve years.

Recent literature on consumer society in the Third Reich has revealed how the *Volksgemeinschaft* (racial community) was premised not only on economic revitalization but also on visions of mass consumption.[7] The regime's construction of a racially exclusive modern society did not displace fantasies of mass consumption and leisure, but rather relied upon and mobilized these fantasies.[8] In the planned vacations of the Strength Through Joy (*Kraft durch Freude*, hereafter KdF) movement, in the advertising of luxury items during a period of scarcity, in the manufacturing of "people's products" that would merge consumerism and *völkisch* ideology, National Socialism stimulated consumer desire and imbued it with nationalist significance.[9]

This recent scholarly attention to state and party initiatives that were designed to incite consumption and leisure in the Third Reich begs certain questions about how consumerist messages are circulated, promoted, and voiced under a political dictatorship. Perhaps most significantly, they shift our attention to an actor that is often overlooked in both cultural histories of consumption and broader histories of National Socialism: the company itself. How, specifically, did private companies—the very institutions responsible for producing and marketing consumer goods—mediate among state demands, business interests, and consumer desires?[10] How were firms both purveyors of official state ideology and protectors of their own corporate reputations? To what extent did companies contribute to the construction of the marketplace as a site of what we might provisionally call an "ersatz citizenship," one that existed in the absence of true democratic participation and civil rights?

This chapter addresses these questions by focusing on corporate public relations as an expression of what Charles Tilly has called the "vocabulary of citizenship."[11] Focusing on the so-called "peaceful years" from 1933 to 1939,[12] it offers a glimpse into typical corporate publicity efforts as exemplified by Henkel, a German company celebrated for its chemical and household products and its cutting-edge advertising. At a time of tight censorship and governmental intervention in the private economy, Henkel confronted a series of contradictions. On the one hand, it aligned with the state, using its own public relations as a medium for National Socialist propaganda. On the other hand, like all corporations in modern, industrialized nations, it invoked ideals of consumer empowerment and self-fulfillment that were hallmarks of capitalist democracies. In company newspapers and industrial films, in manuals for traveling salesmen and at trade fairs, Henkel appealed to consumers as simultaneously members of an exclusive race-based community and citizens who continued to exercise certain cultural and economic privileges associated with modern capitalism and liberal democracy. Thus corporate public relations revealed the multifaceted and often contradictory nature of the Nazi marketplace. Companies issued calls for racial unity and public sacrifice even as they referenced a private sphere of consumption, one ostensibly detached from state terror and ideological conformity.

I. The Meanings of Public Relations Before 1933

In order to analyze corporate public relations under Nazism, it is important to provide a cursory history of the concept of PR and to distinguish between public relations as a normative concept and the practice of the professional public relations advisor.[13] While the 1910s and 1920s saw an explosion of public relations agencies in the United States, the self-conscious use of the English phrase *public relations* did not become commonplace in Germany until the founding of the Federal Republic in 1949.[14] Yet historians of modern Germany have located the *practice* of modern PR in the latter half of the nineteenth century. More than simply product advertising, the project of public relations revolved around the dissemination of a positive image of the corporation and the national economy *writ large*. In 1851, the Krupp concern unveiled its modern form of *Öffentlichkeitsarbeit* when it displayed its massive cannons and won a number of prizes for quality production at London's Great Exhibition of the Works of Industry of All Nations (the Crystal Palace Exhibition).[15] Krupp's "publicity work" soon entailed the advocacy of business-friendly government policies, close links to the news media, product advertising, and careful exercises in damage control when members of the much-followed Krupp family misbehaved. In the late nineteenth century, Krupp and other large companies founded their own news and press offices, as well as in-house advertising and cultural branches.[16] Company literary bureaus and historical archives were created to build links to industry's new discovery—"the public."[17]

But what, exactly, was the nature of this relationship between the company and the public? Today, many PR experts see their work as a mutual dialogue with rational consumers, who maintain considerable power to accept or reject the offerings of a given company.[18] But this idea of public relations as a "two-way street,"[19] one grounded in the open exchange of ideas, did not represent the views of early corporate publicity experts. In the 1920s, American writers like PR counsel Edward Bernays (who was Sigmund Freud's nephew) portrayed public relations not as an exercise in democratic discourse but rather as company-driven "propaganda."[20] As the number of public relations counsels and advertising agencies mushroomed in the United States and abroad, their chief spokesmen, eager to craft a scientific rationale for publicity, drew upon concepts culled from modern psychology, including "herd instinct," "suggestion," and "mass persuasion."[21] These works anticipated the contradictory understandings of "the public" that would inform modern PR. Publicity experts also turned to earlier studies of "the masses," notably the fin-de-siècle works of French sociologists Gustave Le Bon and Gabriel Tarde. Whereas Le Bon saw Europe as entering an "era of crowds," defined by a collective and dangerous irrationality,[22] Tarde charted the transformation of these "masses" into a more rational "public." While "the crowd" could be gathered in a discrete physical space, the "public" was a metaphysical entity, composed of widely dispersed individuals venturing into the market with shared values and demands for personal fulfillment.[23]

Le Bon and Tarde provided two different models for understanding group psychology, and in the early twentieth century companies reflected both in their publicity strategies. Responding to the latent needs of the "masses" while satisfying the more rational demands of the "public" became a fundamental challenge of public relations, and companies met this challenge through advertising, marketing, and the projection of their own integrity.[24] With the onset of mass consumption in the 1920s, company publicists studied and debated Fordist ideas of production and consumption and pursued the practices of "psychotechnics" and "human relations," in order to chart both factory workers' and the broader public's shifting desires.[25] While the United States was the undisputed front-runner in public relations practices, Weimar Germany saw similar, if also more ambivalent, attempts to understand citizens as consumers whose sense of entitlement hinged on their ability to make choices in the marketplace.[26]

If PR entailed new understandings of the modern citizen, it also called for the recognition that the fates of big business and the nation were entwined. This link between the company and the nation endowed publicists with a sense of mission: companies would have to instill trust in the institutions of government and industry at a time of political and economic upheaval. Thus corporate publicists and professional advertisers were concerned not only with the promotion of specific products but also with the potential power of a company name to induce feelings of national superiority or tap into consumers' unspoken desires for comfort and safety. What made people choose one product or company over another? Were consumers more receptive to subliminal enticements or to more transparent accounts of a product's advantages? How could the health of a company be tied to national vitality? By the early 1930s, these were the defining questions for public relations advisors in the United States and practitioners of *Öffentlichkeitsarbeit* in Germany.

II. Public Relations, Henkel, and the Consumer

The National Socialist ascension to power came at a critical moment in the evolution of public relations. Just as Germans were exploring their identities as private consumers and public citizens, the new regime recoded "the public" along racial lines.[27] Moreover, the Great Depression greatly challenged the population's trust in the institutions of capitalism. Extreme economic devastation meant that Germans now sought to obtain basic essentials rather than luxury items or name brands. At the same time, the intense political propaganda of the period elevated "mass persuasion" to a daily ritual. Managing public opinion through sloganeering, pamphleteering, and violence challenged the already blurry boundaries between art, commercial advertising, and politics.

In 1933, company executives wondered how these changes would affect their own marketing and publicity activities. On a superficial level, there was no immediate cause for alarm. Indeed, there were affinities between Nazi propaganda and corporate attempts to woo the public. Nazi leaders studied the works of Le Bon and other crowd psychologists, and in 1933 Propaganda Minister Goebbels met with Ivy Lee, the most sought-after PR advisor in the United States, who worked for an American affiliate of IG Farben at the time.[28] In both theory and practice, there were similarities between fascist propaganda and company publicity—from the use of advertising, billboards, and slogans, to marketers' creation of "mental weapons" to instill brand loyalty in consumers.[29] Historians have even described the creation and dissemination of the "Hitler myth" as its own form of modern PR.[30]

Despite the parallels between state propaganda and company public relations, the Nazis made it clear that they would monitor carefully industry's publicity practices, particularly advertising.[31] Shortly after Hitler came to power in 1933, the government established the *Werberat der deutschen Wirtschaft* (Advertising Council of the German Economy). Placed under the auspices of the Propaganda Ministry, the *Werberat* regulated advertising, aryanized ad agencies, and attempted to set uniform ethical standards in order to expunge seemingly dangerous practices from the industry.[32] For example, using patriotism in the service of commercial interests was disallowed, such as the formulation "Anyone loyal to Germany uses X-brand 'German' gasoline."[33]

State intervention in the economy posed other challenges to company publicists. While the market economy was left intact, the removal of Jews from business life, the enactment of price controls, and the setting of limits on competition revealed the foundations of the economic recovery in the 1930s to be "autarky and armaments."[34] This was a far cry from the economic model that undergirded PR in the United States, where Fordism promoted mass production, high wages, and mass consumption. With the proclamation of the Four-Year Plan for war readiness in 1936, German companies focused on raw-materials procurement and economic self-sufficiency. Finished goods and luxury items did not disappear, but consumerism became associated with the regime's sponsorship of "people's products" like radios, refrigerators, and not-yet-available Volkswagens. Per capita spending on consumer goods never reached Weimar levels, and the Nazis increasingly undermined the consumer sector in the run-up to war.[35]

In their reordering of the economy, the Nazis appear to have made it more difficult for companies to communicate with their customer bases. Yet this would be an oversimplification. Even if the Nazi economy was based on, in the words of Avraham Barkai, "dictatorial state interventionism,"[36] profit motives remained, and advertisers and economists freely explored the latest methods and rationales for selling their products under National Socialism. Experts in branding and corporate publicity, like Carl Hundhausen, Hans Domizlaff, and Wilhelm Vershofen, continued to discuss the applicability of business practices from the United States, where flourished the mass democracy that the Nazis formally critiqued. Hundhausen, in particular, articulated the view that modern "American" PR could be imported to a National Socialist setting.[37] Hundhausen argued that while Germans had always engaged in public relations, companies would be wise to follow the lead of American firms in promoting "Good Will." More than simply advertising, public relations sought to circulate a "truthful" interpretation of a company, so that its reputation would match its inner character. Hundhausen did not ignore the differences between Nazi Germany and the United States, "the land of so-called civil liberty," where economic individualism and a "Judaization" of society undermined communal thinking.[38] But he detected in his country the same "desires for security," and he called upon companies to attend to "the sociological aspect of human relations" in their attempts to earn public confidence.[39] The notion of "winning public trust," as articulated by both Hundhausen and Hans Domizlaff, would become central to public relations theory in postwar West Germany.[40] But by the late 1930s, it already resonated with Nazi ideology, which celebrated the concept of trust (*Vertrauen*) in the name of racial and national unity.[41]

Even with the constraints imposed by the regime, corporate public relations in the 1930s proceeded from the idea that international practices of publicity could ultimately be reconciled with National Socialist goals of inspiring confidence in the *Volksgemeinschaft*. Indeed, the more companies were forced to follow the dictates of "noncompetitive" or "non-egotistical" advertising, the more they relied on PR conventions that transcended national boundaries.[42] For example, in conjunction with the Society for Consumer Research (*Gesellschaft für Konsumforschung*, hereafter GfK) in Nuremberg, large companies like Bayer, Opel, and Siemens, as well as numerous smaller, finished goods firms, conducted market research to gauge the reception of their products and to chart the resonance of their company name. Their correspondents went undercover into drugstores, perfume shops, and beauty salons, interviewing customers or mentioning the name of a product to see what reaction they would get.[43] They would then report on their findings to the headquarters in Nuremberg. Dozens of reports were prepared between 1936 and 1945, containing thousands of observations about consumers' daily lives. Next to this so-called *Verbraucherforschung* (consumer research), companies relied on a combination of psychological mechanisms and standard marketing strategies: Siemens called upon Hans Domizlaff to design logos that would penetrate the "mass brain."[44] Hot air balloons bore the image of the "Bayer Cross"; companies christened ships bearing their names; and business leaders led Nazi leaders, visiting foreign dignitaries, and Olympic athletes on factory tours.[45] At its peak in 1938, Henkel led 80,000 visitors on such tours, where they could watch workers at their stations and view high-budget promotional films that they might have missed in their local theaters.[46] All of these gestures at once reinforced confidence in a company name and contributed to the visual spectacle that accompanied economic renewal in the 1930s.

Henkel was particularly skilled at adapting its public image to the new political setting, and it offers a glimpse into the common workings of public relations under Nazism. Already famous for its advertisements, particularly its 1922 *Weiße-Dame* (White Lady)—the stylish "new woman" clad in a flowing white dress and hat and holding a box of Persil detergent—Henkel saw numerous opportunities for publicity under National Socialism.[47] Like most firms, the company aligned itself with Nazi aims and reported on Hitler's public events and proclamations with great fanfare. But Henkel also promoted the virtues of its own products and its ethos of customer service in an increasingly global marketplace. Throughout the 1930s, the company set up "Persil instructional institutes" and "Mother Schools" in Germany and abroad.[48] There, housewives learned how to "soften the water" with the help of Henkel's lime removers and produce the cleanest laundry possible with Persil detergent. Along with these hands-on promotional efforts, Henkel also hoped to reach "in-house" consumers and company salesmen through employee magazines, which made creative use of its Persil trademark. In a regular feature column, readers followed the travels of their wide-eyed protagonist "Persil," who regularly wrote a letter to his *Lieber Reiseonkel* (globetrotter) to report the company's many exciting public events, like the unveiling of the Henkel Pavilion at the 1937 World's Fair in Paris. "Persil Knights" saved the housewife from back-breaking labor, "Persil Pioneers" forged new paths in research and production, and "Persil fighters" later entered battle on the Western Front for "Führer, firm, and fatherland."[49] At trade fairs and in the accompanying literature, poets and songwriters paid homage to Henkel products, while company employees complied with managers' requests to use the slogan *"Persil-gepflegt"* ("cared for by Persil") whenever possible in conversation.[50] The overwhelming presence of Persil can be compared to product saturation today, carrying in the 1930s a comforting message of familiarity and reliability: in the face of rapid change, to invoke the famous slogan, *"Persil bleibt Persil"* ("Persil is still Persil").[51]

These examples of Henkel's marketing and advertising were standard methods of product placement and self-promotion; publicity practices, notably advertising, from the Weimar years could not simply be abandoned overnight with the Nazi takeover of power. But German companies faced the challenge of reconciling their image as international firms (which depended on marketing strategies that transcended domestic concerns) with the reality that they now operated in a radically new, hypernationalist political setting within Germany. Even as companies celebrated international solidarity in their advertisements or in their participation in world fairs, corporate public relations served the racist and paternalistic aims of the Nazi state. As a self-avowed

Leistungsgesellschaft (performance society), the regime joined with companies to project images of strength and quality production. This ideological goal rested on the "education" of the public through organizations like the Reich Committee for Economic Enlightenment and in KdF events. A Persil teaching institute could at once serve the needs of the company by cultivating brand loyalty and the broader goals of the state, which saw itself as instructing the people in the virtues of sacrifice and hard work.

Despite companies' employment of common publicity methods of the 1930s, one cannot overlook the racist setting in which they were produced. For every routine article in a company magazine about brand familiarity, there was another that honored the Nazi leadership and the company's contribution to the building of a "racial community." Companies like Henkel and Bayer manufactured health-care and cleaning products that indirectly supported the Nazi vision of a healthy *Volk*. In addition to calling upon widespread images of unsavory, money-hungry Jews, Henkel mobilized colonialist stereotypes of African savages cleansing themselves of their blackness by bathing in or drinking Henkel detergents.[52] In Henkel's advice to traveling salesmen, the company indicated that if a customer complained that the quality of soap had declined (something that would become increasingly true under the Four-Year Plan), the representative should respond with a flat-out denial.[53] First, however, the salesperson should remind the customer of how "dangerous" it was to "spread unsubstantiated rumors about the products of German industry."[54] When a biography was too critical of a company, as was the case with Bernhard Menne's 1937 history of the Krupp firm, the book was referred to the Gestapo and censored.[55] When assessing public relations in the Third Reich, then, one cannot forget the larger picture of racism, repression, and intimidation.

III. The State and Industry: Consensus and Conflict

Thus far, I have demonstrated how multiple forms of corporate publicity, emerging from transatlantic practices before 1933, dovetailed with the aims of the Nazi state. By linking shopping, company reputation, and national renewal, firms applied prevailing methods of public relations to a Fascist setting and turned average Germans into patriotic consumers who served the public good by supporting the economy. But the operation of public relations under National Socialism also embodied certain tensions. As Nancy Reagin has shown in her study of the

Four-Year Plan, propaganda aimed at the consumer was more complicated than it first appears. Even though the consumer sector was curtailed during the late 1930s, the state continued to appeal to shoppers,
particularly women, by mobilizing the grammar of personal and social
empowerment. By sustaining the private sphere of the home through
their thrifty purchasing decisions, women were contributing to the autarkic aims of the state in their capacities as "housewife-consumers."
While women's choices were ultimately limited by the poor selection
of consumer goods, the identification of domestic self-sufficiency with
the public good accorded women a measure of social power, however
limited.[56]

The symbolic connection between the public good and private consumption was not unique to National Socialism. Indeed, the United
States in the 1930s saw similar rhetorical links between consumer empowerment and the recovering health of the economy. But this connection took on a unique cast in a totalitarian setting where the boundaries between the private and the public were continually—and often
violently—breached. Corporate public relations appealed to the domestic, private sphere as a locus of personal gratification at a moment
when this sphere was highly permeable and vulnerable to the state.
This reliance on the private sphere was particularly evident at trade
fairs and national exhibitions. In 1937, Henkel played a premier role at
the *Schaffendes Volk* (A People at Work) exhibition in Düsseldorf. Billed
as the first *Reichsausstellung* to celebrate the rebirth of the economy,
the exhibition was a showpiece of the Nazis' Four-Year Plan for economic autarky, and it highlighted the role of the country's companies
in providing jobs and promoting technical ingenuity. On the exhibit
fairgrounds, visitors flocked to the Henkel pavilion, which contained
a model home filled with Henkel's products and sanitized with Henkel cleansers. Sparkling kitchens gave way to dining rooms and living
rooms decorated with furniture made from synthetic materials. Walls
were adorned with placards explaining Henkel's products in detail. A
child's bedroom was spruced up with Henkel paint, its furniture was
sealed with Henkel glue, and a bathtub was made of Henkel plastic.
Visitors could browse through a photo exhibit highlighting the life and
achievements of company founder Fritz Henkel, watch a demonstration of Henkel's scientific laundering methods, or view a film about
the firm's contributions to national productivity.[57] In an internal memo
about the exhibition, the Henkel management asked its employees to
promote these displays in the spirit of both a "propagandist and skilled

worker."[58] They should take care to emphasize that Henkel products were the result of individual craftsmanship, not impersonal assembly-line manufacturing, and they should employ whenever possible the company slogan "*Wer Henkel wählt—wählt Qualität*" (loosely, "Choose Henkel—Choose Quality").[59]

The exhibition's appeal to the domestic realm suggests a tension at the heart of Henkel's public relations undertakings in the 1930s. In its model house filled with time-saving devices and sleek furniture, Henkel put the private sphere and the possibilities of personal satisfaction within it on dramatic display. Even though it was billed as evidence of a collective altruism, *Schaffendes Volk* relied upon notions of individual gratification within the private realm. By consciously selecting Henkel products, men and women could enhance their leisure activities and fill their homes with objects of their desire. In the process, they would support the nation's economic, hygienic, and racial revitalization, and public sacrifice was to be rewarded with personal satisfaction.

In addition to foregrounding privacy, PR appealed to notions of difference and heterogeneity. Here, too, there was a tension between public relations and Nazi ideology. This could be seen in the training tips that Henkel gave to its traveling salespeople. Despite the regime's official promotion of social conformity, Henkel advised representatives to personalize the sales experience by addressing their customers' sense of individuality and their human need for respect.[60] "We must not forget," wrote Henkel's advertising director Paul Mundhenke, "that people are all different—different in character, in disposition, in temperament. They are different in manners of thinking and logic, and different in age, sex, and origin."[61] This respect for diversity, according to Mundhenke, ought to inform not only the company's promotional efforts but also its intimate contacts with clients. Let the customer "mother" the salesperson in her own home; give her a sense of control over the conversation; let her show off her knowledge of a product; and be sure to impress her with small details about her personal life on subsequent visits.[62] This advice about personalizing the sales experience was echoed in the work of other companies. Bayer advised its traveling salesmen to heed "twelve tips," including taking time to learn about the customer's desires.[63] In its in-house publications, the company encouraged its representatives to heed the "voice of the public" in ways that honored individual differences.[64]

The use of standard marketing and sales strategies suggests that company publicists were trying to navigate a number of tensions within Nazi Germany: tensions between the national and the global; between the private and the public; and between manipulation and consent. While Hitler wanted to see Germans as "the masses," a single entity that would respond in unison to certain visual and rhetorical cues, private companies had a stake in appealing to people as individuals with their own idiosyncrasies. By proclaiming the consumer's right to choose from a variety of products or to be treated as special, companies played to people's sense of personal entitlement and uniqueness. At the same time, publicity experts understood that modern marketing required homogeneity: by buying a particular car or detergent, the customer satisfied personal desires while making the same choices as millions of others. This interplay between individuality and conformity is a key component of modern marketing, but, again, it was uniquely pronounced in the Third Reich.[65] If "the masses" were vulnerable to manipulation through a few rote slogans and more subtle persuasion, "the public" was much savvier, holding greater power to disrupt the ideological status quo through expressions of consumer dissatisfaction. The challenge for company publicity experts in the 1930s, therefore, was to determine exactly when people acted as rational consumers and when they relinquished their individuality and became part of the crowd.[66]

A final tension that shaped the operation of PR under National Socialism concerned the boundaries between Nazi ideology and company self-promotion. While the regime welcomed expressions of National Socialist ideals in commercial publicity, any attempt to *exploit* Nazi ideology for publicity purposes would be confronted head-on by the state. Henkel discovered this after embarking on one of its most elaborate PR undertakings, namely, the production and screening of the 1938 Ufa film *Henkel—ein deutsches Werk in seiner Arbeit*. Directed by Walter Ruttmann, famous for his studies of film and rhythm and his 1927 classic *Berlin: Die Sinfonie der Grosstadt*, the film used typical KdF images of clean factories and joyful workers to highlight the company's products and its contribution to the greater social good in order to create a "monument to the name and concept 'Henkel.'"[67] Scenes showed *Henkelaner* checking out books from the company library, engaging in group calisthenics, relaxing on park benches, and taking walks on the company grounds.[68] In early 1939, the Henkel management was particularly excited about its plans for screenings in one hundred cinemas around Germany, including the Ufa-Palast in Berlin.[69]

At first glance, the film did not appear controversial. The Nazi years saw a steep rise in the number of industrial and advertising films, often produced by major movie companies and involving major actors.[70] Henkel's advertising director Paul Mundhenke praised the medium for offering "new methods of mass influence."[71] The censors in the propaganda ministry approved the film at the end of 1938, but it ran into trouble with the *Werberat*. The Advertising Council accused the film of exploiting National Socialist ideals to promote Henkel's own reputation. In particular, Henkel was showcasing for marketing purposes the social benefits and leisure opportunities that every company should be providing for its workers. Henkel was directed to remove all images relating to company social welfare; otherwise, it would have to cancel its nationwide screenings and show the film only to its employees.

Henkel management was dumbfounded. After spending many years conforming to the regime's ideological standards for workplace camaraderie, cleanliness, and leisure, the company argued, it was now being asked to remove any visual depictions of its successes.[72] Nor was it easy to excise this major portion of the film without destroying the work's integrity and coherence. In its written protests to the *Werberat*, the company was careful to celebrate the Nazi factory community and its ideological import. But management could not avoid airing its frustration about the regime's prohibitions against economic "opportunism." Wrote director Mundhenke: "What's the point of even making a company film if it can't be used for advertising purposes?"[73] If the company had just shown people in their work clothes at their stations, the management insisted, Henkel would have been accused of *failing* to portray National Socialist principles. Henkel also posed to the *Werberat* a series of questions that exposed the shakiness of Nazi policies regarding public relations. Should the company sports team carry flags with the swastika, the company logo, both, or carry no flags at all? If it was acceptable to tout the company's ideological contributions in anniversary volumes, firm histories, and brochures, why could it not do so in ads or in films?

The *Werberat* did not have immediate answers, but it did demand further alterations to the film. In keeping with its laws against competitive advertising, the *Werberat* found other problems with the film. Henkel had to remove the statement "Persil is in every case superior," unless it could document that this was true. Henkel could not present its antibacterial soap as essential to fighting infant mortality, given that there were other methods just as effective for lowering the death rate among children. Finally, in showing crosses to depict death, Henkel was coming too close to promoting Christianity.[74]

In response to these complaints, the company scoured back issues of the *Werberat*'s advertising journal *Wirtschaftswerbung*, looking in vain for indications that these scenes from the film violated Nazi policy. It compiled worldwide statistics and presented bacteriological studies on mortality to defend its claims about soap and infant deaths, and it besought the Advertising Council to consider the Henkel movie more as a "filmed rendition of a factory tour" than a publicity work.[75] In the end, faced with Henkel's exhaustive defense of the film, the *Werberat* appears to have backed down;[76] in the course of 1939, the film was shown to 37,000 viewers in fifty-one cities. While the war interrupted the screening, the film event resumed in the winter of 1940 to much critical praise.[77]

The eventual resolution in favor of the company reveals a flexibility within the regime's censorship apparatus. But the controversy also exposes the challenges of public relations in Nazi Germany. Henkel, which had built a name for itself as a producer of quality goods and images, hoped after 1933 to continue its marketing and advertising traditions in order to promote itself and maintain its sales. Yet, with increasing demands for ideological conformity, the company found itself frustrated in its attempts to speak to the public without violating the state's anticompetitive dictates. In effect, the firm was expected to promote itself in an entirely selfless manner, which, to the company management, was oxymoronic. The conflict between Henkel as a capitalist firm and Henkel as a standard-bearer of Nazi ideology came into full relief. Despite calls for a modernization of commercial publicity in the Third Reich, companies confronted several challenges by the late 1930s: How did one market goods and induce brand loyalty in a regulated economy? More importantly, was there a *need* to maintain aggressive publicity efforts in a society marked by limited economic choices, price controls, and censorship? While Henkel reconciled itself to—and even benefited from—National Socialist mandates, the company management made it clear in 1939 that it wanted not only to sell the ideals of the *Volksgemeinschaft* but to actually sell itself.

*   *   *

The practice of corporate public relations in Nazi Germany entailed a number of contradictions. At one level, PR was very much aligned with the state in its visual celebration of the *Volksgemeinschaft* and economic rejuvenation. At the same time, the basic tenets of a democratic, capitalist marketplace—freedom of choice, personal fulfillment, corporate self-interest—were filtered back into Germany in ways that were inconsistent with the Nazis' communitarian aims. But what do these tensions and affinities ultimately tell us about the status of "consumer citizenship" under National Socialism? There are two possible answers to this question, both of which ultimately hinge on how narrowly or broadly one defines modern citizenship, and whether one believes it is even possible to provisionally disentangle certain notions of political, economic, civil, and social rights. One might argue that, in the end, corporate public relations only worked to undermine proper notions of modern citizenship under the Third Reich. By depicting profit-driven business interests as serving the common good, PR was built on distortion and manipulation. It deluded consumers into believing that their purchasing decisions were socially responsible exercises in rational choice. This "engineering of consent"[78] reveals the authoritarian tendency of public relations and its challenge to older notions of "publicity" that worked to expose true political domination through public discourse. Writes Jürgen Habermas: "Because private enterprises evoke in their customers the idea that in their consumption decisions they act in their capacity as citizens, the state has to 'address' its citizens like consumers."[79]

There is certainly much that is compelling in this view that German companies during the Nazi years mobilized public relations to create only the illusion of choice—whether to ensure state patronage or to increase sales. As a site of personal and material gratification, the Nazi marketplace offered Germans a compensatory citizenship, but one stripped of its democratic and discursive possibilities. An open consumer marketplace was more fiction than reality, calling on the language of civic participation in the absence of true political expression. To be sure, there existed in the Third Reich what Lizabeth Cohen has described as a "triangular relationship between consumers, government, and business."[80] But while this triangular relationship was linked to the power of the "citizen-consumer" in the United States, in Nazi Germany it was premised on ideological conformity rather than the freedom to criticize—and thus have a real effect on—the behavior of a company or the state. Consumers did voice discontent with products, ad campaigns, and economic deprivation more generally, and they often resisted the guidelines of the state regarding resource- and cost-saving measures.[81] But absent the possibilities for a broad consumer activism that could take shape in the political realm, public relations emerges as little more than company propaganda. Ultimately, as Colin Crouch and others have argued with respect to contemporary Europe, the market is an impoverished substitute for a more genuine citizenship based on civil rights and social welfare.[82]

But there is another line of argument, one that moves us away from the formal political rights associated with modern citizenship and asks about the more psychological, anticipatory, and subjective elements in the model of consumer citizenship that took shape under National Socialism. Embedded in PR, even in certain practices aligned with Nazi aims, was the foreshadowing of a post-Nazi consumerist ideal—a promise of the world that would come later during the "Economic Miracle" of the 1950s and 1960s. Public relations could collude with the Nazi state through mechanisms of manipulation and distortion. But it simultaneously reintroduced visions of a society outside the parameters of the Nazis' anti-individualist ideology, linking people's pre-Hitler experiences of private consumption to the economic revival of the 1930s and to expectations of future material gratification. Through corporate PR, the glimmers of the society from which PR primarily emanated—the United States—also slipped back into view. I am not claiming that public relations enabled a liberatory or open form of civic participation. Nor can one celebrate the United States or Weimar Germany as bastions of democratic freedom. Rather, by appealing to notions of private life, a protected domesticity, and personal idiosyncrasy, corporate public relations reminded Germans of a different social order, even as their political and civil rights slipped away.[83] As we have seen, this could have undoubtedly benefited the Nazi regime, which used these contradictions to support its own goals of racial conformity and social integration. But even under Fascism, Germans were able to indulge in their own consumerist fantasies, whether in touring a Henkel pavilion, buying a luxury item, or shopping for their family. Industrialists promoted their company's creations while workers and housewives prided themselves on their contributions to the economic recovery of the 1930s.[84] In the ideological jumble that was National Socialism, people carved out spaces for the expression of a consumer citizenship, attenuated in regard to political rights but endowed with psychological dimensions nonetheless. This expression referenced the past—namely the pre-Depression experiences of consumption—but also present expectations of a sustained material abundance as a reward for hard work and national service.

Ultimately, this "psychological citizenship," merging responsibilities to the country with expectations of gratification in the marketplace, was not unique to the Third Reich. It prefigured the language of sacrifice and "prosperity for all" that accompanied West Germany's economic reconstruction after World War II.[85] While many Germans already believed in the 1930s that a vibrant consumer society would arise under National Socialism, any such development was halted by the realities of a war economy.[86] It would only be in the late 1950s and 1960s, in the context of a political democracy, that West German citizens would experience the reality of "better living," a reality that had been promised—but only partially realized—in the Third Reich.[87]

"Gesungen oder musiziert wird aber fast in jedem Haus": Representing and Constructing Citizenship Through Music in Twentieth-Century Germany

TOBY THACKER

THE CONNECTIONS BETWEEN MUSIC, citizenship, and identity are complex and indeterminate. They are not codified in legal statutes, and are not easily subjected to statistical or quantitative analysis. We can be sure, though, that the connections do exist, and that music and music making of different kinds have functioned in Germany as potent symbols of identity, often linked to specific concepts of citizenship. This has been recognized by a growing body of academic work, including the 2002 collection of essays on music and German national identity edited by Celia Applegate and Pamela Potter.[1] The differing perspectives and methodologies in this volume reflect a larger concern within both academic history and musicology to explore the social and political contexts in which music of different kinds has been produced and received. The last twenty years have seen the emergence of a sophisticated body of analytical work on music in Weimar Germany and the Third Reich, and this is now being extended to the postwar occupation period and to the GDR. Most recently a conference on *"Musik und Macht"* in Potsdam sought to challenge these long-standing chronological and geographical boundaries and to consider new thematic approaches to the role of music in twentieth-century Germany.[2] In this chapter, I will explore two ideas that lie at the heart of a specifically German relationship with music and that allow us to examine different ways in which music has been used to represent and construct citizenship during the twentieth century. The first is the notion of German musical superiority, and the second is the attempt in the GDR after 1949 to construct a Socialist ideal of active musical citizenship.

The idea of German musical superiority has been examined in a stimulating essay by Albrecht Riethmüller. Laying bare some of the central assumptions of this discourse as it has developed since the eighteenth century, he concludes that "the illusions live on," supporting this with alarming contemporary examples of insularity, arrogance, and ignorance.[3] I want here to qualify this sense of continuity, not by denying the validity of Riethmüller's examples or the central thrust of his argument but by enlarging it to consider further dimensions of the problem. I agree that in the first half of the twentieth century, the idea that the "Germans" were the most musical people in the world was widely accepted, outside Germany as well, and that it went largely unquestioned. I will argue, though, that from 1945 this idea was challenged from several different directions, and that it has since then survived only among declining circles of reactionaries and nationalists, increasingly to be found among older and more middle-class sections of the German population. To an extent, this can be seen as one aspect of larger paradigm shifts: in the arts from modernism to postmodernism; in music specifically from nineteenth-century concepts of "national" music to a wider concern with ethnomusicology and with what is now called "world music." It also reflects the changed position of high culture, increasingly confined as a matter of importance and concern to a declining minority. In terms of identity, we can see the decline in the propagation and acceptance of German musical superiority as one reflection of the shift that Eric Santner (following Habermas) has charted from a "conventional" sense of identity, "rooted in a specular relation to particular norms," to a "postconventional identity" based on a "more distanced and critical dialogue with the intensely ambivalent cultural legacy of recent German history."[4] Thus, this shift in Germany is part of the double post; post-Holocaust and post-modernist. It can finally be placed in the wider context of the globalization of cultural production and reception.

I will focus here on specifically German factors that have contributed to this shift, and ask how far the decline in the belief in German musical superiority was also prompted by political changes and by military occupation of Germany itself. It was, after all, a stated goal of Allied "Music Control" in Germany after 1945 to challenge this idea and to replace it with a broader internationalism. How was the idea of musical superiority affected by the division of Germany in 1949 and the positioning of the two new states founded as cornerstones of antagonistic superpower blocs? How has it fared since reunification in 1990?

Let us briefly chart the evolution of this discourse. It emerged during the eighteenth century and was consolidated during the nineteenth. By the early twentieth century, the understanding that the "Germans" were particularly musical people, that the music of great "German" composers expressed not only something particularly "German" but also something universal and therefore of much wider significance, was commonly held among German-speaking peoples, and far beyond. It was rarely challenged or subjected to critical analysis. After 1919, the idea was articulated with a more frenzied urgency, which can be understood as a defensive reaction to an embattled sense of identity after the perceived disaster of the Treaty of Versailles. A representative example can be found in a small volume, *Der Deutsche Genius*, published in 1921–22, and addressed to *"Deutsche Vaterlandsfreunde"* (and notably to ethnic Germans living outside German borders, *"Auslandsdeutsche"*). This contained a series of essays about various aspects of "German" culture. In the introduction, Georg Steinhausen presented some of the central pillars, or clichés, of the discourse of musical superiority: the music of the great German composers (Bach, Handel, Gluck, Haydn, Mozart, Beethoven, Weber, Wagner) has qualities, identified here as *Tiefe* (roughly translated as *depth*) and *Innerlichkeit* (inwardness) that are not fully comprehensible to "non-Germans." Nonetheless, these non-Germans recognize music as the art that is particularly German and in which the greatest creative spirits have been German.[5] In a later section devoted to music, one of Germany's leading musicologists, Alfred Heuss, developed these ideas, adding that music was widely acknowledged as the art form in which a people expressed "the ways of its soul most purely, most clearly, and most incomprehensibly," before sketching a now-familiar canon of great "German" composers from Schütz to Wagner who exemplified this. Repeating the claim that this canon had been a gift to the whole world, Heuss urged his readers to take pride in this peculiarly German achievement. His account, though clichéd and superficial, was not obviously racist. Heuss included Mendelssohn in his canon, and made no comment on his racial origin.[6]

In other publications during the Weimar years, the discourse of German supremacy took on a marked sense of inclusion and exclusion, fitting easily with *völkisch* philosophy and an emergent pseudoscientific racism. Before 1933, the most aggressive and offensive articulations of German musical superiority displayed a crude anti-Semitism. An example with the most terrible implications for Jewish musicians in Germany was the chapter "Das Judentum in der Musik" written by

Erich Müller, which appeared in editions of Theodor Fritsch's *Handbuch der Judenfrage* published between 1932 and 1934. Müller followed Heuss and others by describing a "German" musical canon, but modified this to exclude those of Jewish origin like Mendelssohn and Schoenberg, who, he argued, threatened to destroy the canon from within. In an ominous development—which culminated in 1940 in the publication by the NSDAP's *Hauptstelle Musik* of the infamous *Lexikon der Juden in der Musik*—Müller in 1932 presented lists of supposedly "Jewish" musicians who were allegedly contaminating different areas of "German" musical culture.[7]

The doctrine of musical superiority was taken as axiomatic by the Nazis, but was modified along the lines developed by anti-Semites like Müller to include only those of "Aryan" origin. Racist ideas, many of which appear patently absurd today, were used to underpin the idea that "Aryan" Germans were particularly musical and creative. The "racial scientist" Hans Günther had already pronounced that the "Nordic race" was particularly musical, and archaeological findings of pairs of bronze lures were used to substantiate this, "proving" that Germanic tribes had developed harmony at a very early stage.[8] By the late 1930s, these pseudoscholarly ideas were commonplace not only in academic German musicology but in condensed form in popular reference books as well. An example is the multivolume *Meyers Lexikon* published in 1937–38. Here we find, in an article on "Deutsche Kultur," all the clichés of the doctrine of musical superiority, embellished with a line drawing of two interlinked bronze lures.[9] A striking poster by Lothar Heinemann in 1935 combined visual imagery with the doctrine of musical superiority. The Nazi eagle's head, shoulders, and outspread wings merged imperceptibly with the pipework of a large organ above the slogan *Das Land der Musik*.[10] By 1943, when that prolific writer, Hans-Joachim Moser, complacently asserted on behalf of the Propaganda Ministry that music was a unique part of German cultural life because of the "supreme musical talent of our people" (*Höchstbegabung unseres Volkes für Musik*), the sense of hubris was overwhelming.[11]

Music was also used as a basis for exclusion from the *Volksgemeinschaft*. Many scholars since 1933 have commented on the way in which music was at the forefront of the public Nazi persecution of the Jews.[12] If Jews could not be German citizens, they certainly could not be part of the German musical community—indeed, they threatened to undermine that community's superiority and had to be excluded from it. The earliest published demands in Nazi Germany for the exclusion of

Jews from musical life were couched in metaphorical terms that might be interpreted as demanding nothing more (!) than professional exclusion, but that certainly hinted at something much worse. As early as April 1933, Germany's leading musical journal, the *Zeitschrift für Musik*, reprinted a brief article by the same Erich Müller that celebrated the exclusion of Jews from musical composition, performance, publishing, criticism, recording, and broadcasting in Germany. In 1934, Müller revised his contribution to the *Handbuch der Judenfrage*, praising the way that Hitler was driving Jews out of German musical life with an "iron broom."[13]

If the ideal member of Hitler's *Volksgemeinschaft* was a lover of Bach and Beethoven and perhaps an enthusiastic and capable musician as well, he or she could not at the same time be a lover of jazz. The Nazi hatred of jazz and swing has been analyzed in considerable detail. Of interest here is the way in which jazz, the attitudes that appeared to accompany it, and the bodily movements it provoked were characterized, for example, as a "manifestation of a general degeneration of healthy German bodily feeling."[14] The conviction that listening to, dancing to, or performing jazz music was un-German led directly to a range of prohibitive measures that, although ultimately unsuccessful, had appalling consequences for many individuals and indicate how far purely musical affiliations were taken as symbols of identity. The many Jewish musicians who suffered at the hands of the Nazis might have suffered equally as nonmusicians, but some of the young men and women dispatched to Moringen, Uckermark, Ravensbrück, and Neuengamme might well have escaped persecution were it not for their involvement with jazz and swing.[15]

At the same time, the Nazis worked hard to make sure that the slogan *Das Land der Musik* had some foundation in reality. Their support for a wide range of musical activities—from the overseas tours of the Berlin Philharmonic and the Reich Music Chamber's financial grants to individual composers, to the promotion of *Hausmusik*—has been well documented. It is indeed impossible to imagine Hitler's Germany without music. The 1937 *Handbuch der Reichskulturkammer* expressly linked state support for music with the doctrine of supremacy, stating: "The German reputation as the first musical country of the world and the German view of music as the 'most German of the arts' is founded on the great blossoming of concert and choral activity."[16] After 1939 in parts of occupied Europe, "German music" was consciously promoted as representing a universal ideal. Commenting on a performance by the Berlin Philharmonic in Chaillot at the end of a European tour in June 1944, Heinrich Strobel (later so influential as director of music at the *Südwestfunk*) wrote that this was a testimony to "the inviolable heights of German artistic practice and the ethical power of German music which encompassed the continent."[17] Until the final collapse of the Third Reich in May 1945, active music making continued in Germany as an assertion of a particular national identity. This not only can be seen in the significance attached to such well-known events as the final wartime concerts of the Berlin Philharmonic,[18] but it also appears in the memoirs of ordinary citizens who saw continued music making in the face of adversity as an activity of great importance. In Göttingen, as the townspeople anxiously awaited the arrival of the Americans on Good Friday 1945, the town's premier choir, the *Stadtkantorei*, performed Schütz's *Matthäus-Passion* in the overcrowded *Johanniskirche*.[19] True to their reputation, the Germans went to total defeat in 1945 still singing and playing.

As part of the reeducation project, all four occupying powers in Germany after 1945 were dedicated to the internationalization of the arts and therefore to challenging the idea of German musical superiority. They sought to do this not by denigrating "German music"—most Allied music control officers themselves had an enormous regard for it—but by introducing their own national music and that of other countries alongside the traditional German concert repertoire. The French linked the idea of German musical superiority most directly to racism and therefore worked most actively to dismantle it. In a report on the French cultural program in Germany, Jean Arnaud, head of the Direction de l'Information in the French military government, argued that the German sense of racial superiority had been founded partly on a conviction that they were "the only truly musical people." If this could be challenged, he wrote, "immediately one of the fundamental premises of racist and pan-Germanist philosophy collapsed."[20] Acting on this belief, the French banned the performance, live or broadcast, of symphonic music by Wagner, Richard Strauss, Bruckner, and their epigones in the French zone of occupation. The British, Americans, and Soviets censored music that they interpreted as "Nazi" or "militarist," but the French went further. Explaining why the music of contemporary composers like Müller, Trunk, and Kilpinen was banned, Arnaud wrote: "We are trying to eliminate from our programmes musicians spiritually compromised by German pride."[21]

What of the Germans themselves? It is tempting to argue that the doctrine of musical supremacy survived the chaos of 1945 remarkably well and was rapidly reasserted. Many writers have commented upon the resumption of concert life and of amateur music making all over Germany after the *Stunde Null*. The regional and municipal pride manifested in the reconstruction of concert halls and the reopening of musical academies after May 1945 has been used to support the idea that music—above all, German classical music—served as a locus of refuge and as an acceptable way of reasserting national pride, a connection with another, better Germany. The development in Western zones of institutions devoted to international musical modernism has been evinced as further evidence of this remarkable recovery.[22] By 1951, when the Bayreuth Festival resumed, in studiously apolitical guise, it might seem that German music, now repackaged in the West as *abendländisch*, had resumed its former undisputed supremacy.

This should be qualified. Many Germans undoubtedly saw their musical tradition as something hallowed that was untainted by Nazism and were glad to turn to it in their hour of need. For instance, in Munich in July 1946, the blacklisted Hans Pfitzner was given a long standing ovation by an enthusiastic audience after a performance of his music, even though the conductor, Hans Rosbaud, refused to allow him onto the stage to accept the applause.[23] Nonetheless, there is overwhelming evidence to suggest that among many German music lovers and administrators, Allied internationalism in music was very welcome, and that the doctrine of German supremacy was badly battered, if not a thing of the past. When in 1950, municipal and *Land* authorities in West Germany met to consider public support for music, they prefaced their report with the infinitely nostalgic statement, "Germany was the most musical country in the world."[24] Behind this there may well have lurked desires for a reassertion of musical hegemony, or longing for a vanished past, but there was a frank recognition that times had changed. Open expression of the pre-1945 assumption of German supremacy, with its xenophobic and exclusive overtones, was increasingly confined to the private sphere and was left as the preserve of reactionaries.[25] In the context of early Cold War rivalry between East and West Germany, when composers, like other "great" figures from Germany's past, were avidly fought over, it is notable that as the Mozart anniversary in 1956 approached, the government of the Federal Republic decided that public celebrations in Germany should have only a regional, and not a national character. It was left to the newly sovereign Austrian state to claim Mozart as its national composer.[26]

Although the early Federal Republic has been celebrated, and indeed mythologized, as the home of the international postwar avant-garde, many of those most active in its musical life were overcome by a sense of crisis. This was manifested not only in private correspondence and in wider public debate about generational and cultural conflicts but also in documents about music education and professional and amateur musical life. By 1953, a body called the Working Group for Music and Musical Education felt sufficiently concerned by the emergent culture of materialism to report to the federal government and to public authorities at every level in West Germany on the "emergency situation" of musical life there. The report spoke of "alarming symptoms of the decay of our musical life" and argued that it was no good giving people housing if they were "empty inside." [27]

Behind this rhetoric of crisis and of stated concern with "mass pleasures" was the changing position of high culture in society, very different today than at the beginning of the twentieth century. If not all Germans in 1900 were intimately familiar with the German classical music tradition, most were proud of it and saw it as worthy of great esteem. With a growing international dimension to communications and culture, this respect significantly diminished. In Germany, the clear distinction between "serious music" and "entertainment music"—between high and low culture—has steadily eroded since the 1950s; intimate knowledge of "serious music," and the conviction that it is something of great importance, has become the preserve of a tiny minority in Germany, as elsewhere. The changes in broader social attitudes identified by the Working Group in the early 1950s have continued, altering beyond recognition the social context in which the discourse of musical supremacy operates.

If 1945 marks a distinct break in the propagation and reception of the idea of German musical supremacy, it also led directly to the assertion in the eastern part of Germany of a new Socialist ideal of active musical citizenship. The most striking articulation of this idea appeared in the GDR's musical journal *Musik und Gesellschaft* in 1951. The GDR's leading musical theoretician Ernst Hermann Meyer, the journal's original editor, prefaced the first issue with a concise manifesto. Posing the question "What does this journal want?" Meyer wrote: "It wishes . . . to encourage the working masses to active music-making in the spirit of the reconstruction of our intellectual life." [28] The ideal GDR citizen was not to be merely a consumer of "the classical inheritance" and its contemporary descendants in the GDR and the other "peoples' democracies" but an active Socialist musician. Great efforts were made to realize this ambition, particularly in the GDR's early years. Cultural functionaries and music experts had high hopes that the GDR could create an entirely distinctive musical culture untainted by the commercialism of the entertainment industry that was apparent in West Germany, or what the SED, the Communist Party of East Germany, saw as the "formalism" of the Western avant-garde. Of course, the idea of the active musical citizen was not new. It derives from a long German tradition of amateur music making, which had taken a number of distinct forms since the eighteenth century. The tradition of *Hausmusik* had a long pedigree, and as recently as the 1920s, composers and administrators had sought to minimize the gap between the professional musician and the ordinary citizen. With the emergence in the late nineteenth century of a Socialist choral movement in Germany, amateur music making had taken a more overtly politicized form, and it was indeed in this tradition, during the last years of the Weimar Republic, that Meyer himself had found the synthesis of music making and active politics to which he dedicated his life.[29]

In a sense, the idea of the active musical citizen was linked to that of German supremacy, not least through the notion that all Germans, more than other peoples, were innately musical and likely to play or sing together. Despite the fact that the musical culture of the GDR also developed intensely nationalistic overtones, it is noteworthy that originally Meyer further developed the idea of active musical citizenship not in Germany but in England, the land often paraphrased in musical circles as the *Land ohne Musik*. As a refugee from Nazism, Meyer lived and worked in England between 1933 and 1948 and was active with the Workers' Musical Association. His long involvement with amateur choirs made a lasting impression on him, and in later writings, he portrayed the English amateur choral tradition as a model that the GDR might follow.[30]

This ideal of active musical citizenship held considerable appeal to Socialist musicians in Germany after 1945, and we can see an emphasis on it in documents from the occupation period. With the creation of the GDR in 1949, there were new possibilities for its realization, and, particularly in the early years of the Socialist republic, a concerted series of measures were taken to achieve this. Above all the GDR sought, while preserving and developing the highest standards of elite music making, to erase the gap between professional and amateur musicians. It therefore supported a hierarchy of ensembles, ranging from orchestras and choirs important throughout the GDR to the *Kreiskulturorchester,* an orchestra at the county level that had semiprofessional status, and the *Gemeinschaftsorchester,* community orchestras that acted to train musicians for higher levels of performance. The SED's preferred compositional form in the early 1950s was the oratorio, in which a didactic narrative was set to music, ideally performed by a professional orchestra and a large amateur chorus. Music was given high priority in the school curriculum, and extensive efforts were made to provide *Kulturhäuser* (cultural centers) in small towns and villages where professional and amateur music could be performed. Unsuccessful efforts were made in the 1950s to develop a new electronic organ that could be used in *Kulturhäuser* and other buildings that lacked a pipe organ. Music was an integral part of all party ceremonies, and other compositional forms for large bodies of amateur musicians, like the "mass song," were given extensive state support.

Between August 1951 and December 1953, this campaign was supervised by the *Staatliche Kommission für Kunstangelegenheiten* (or *Stakuko,* as it became known internally). A feature of this body's work was its practice of regular local inspections. The reports from *Stakuko* inspectors chronicled the development of musical life in different parts of the GDR and also provided revealing insights into the mindset of the GDR's musical functionaries. Typically, the reports oscillated in tone between a frenzied optimism and despair; their principal concern, revealingly, was with musical standards. The inspectors often catalogued failings and shortcomings at the local level, mixing musical and political concerns. Local "culture orchestras" were criticized for failing to produce a homogeneous string tone, which then was blamed on the "reactionary attitude" of the conductor, not yet freed from the "trammels of formalism." Inspectors frequently reported problems with the development of active musical citizenship. In this context, one report, from Mecklenburg in 1952, stands out. Among the normal host of complaints and problems, the inspector noted: "there is singing or music-making in virtually every house" (*Gesungen oder musiziert wird aber fast in jedem Haus*).[31] Here, for a brief historical moment, it appears that the GDR's ideal was realized.

Although after 1953 the GDR's musical establishment increasingly was forced to compromise with non-Socialist influences from the West, it continued to celebrate the ideal of active musical citizenship. In 1965, Ernst Hermann Meyer spoke in Bombay about musical life in the GDR.

A central theme of his talk was how widespread amateur musicianship was; to support this, Meyer proudly described how many GDR work-places had their own choirs and instrumental groups.[32] Well before this, though, as Meyer knew, a serious problem had developed that had set the GDR authorities on a collision course with a significant group of its active amateur musicians.

The renewed interest in and performance of jazz in Germany af-ter 1945 was as notable in cities like Leipzig as in Western zones. Even before the foundation of the GDR in 1949, trade unionists and SED of-ficials were concerned by the competition posed to professional dance orchestras by young amateur jazz and dance bands. By 1951, when the *Stakuko* put this problem on its musical agenda, the problem was even more acute. Young amateur musicians, above all in the SED's youth movement, *Freie Deutsche Jugend*, and the universities, favored west-ernized forms that were considered "degenerate" and "formalist" or dismissed as "noise" by SED officials. The main thrust of the *Stakuko*'s campaign to repress this music was, as I have analyzed elsewhere, not to control what was played but to regulate who was allowed to play.[33] By insisting that musicians who wished to perform in public should be licensed, the SED hoped to exclude from the public sphere those who were insufficiently qualified and thus protect the interests of profes-sional musicians. Despite the evident failure of this policy as early as 1953, it was persisted with until the GDR's collapse in 1989.

The problem was straightforward. The successive waves of Anglo-American popular music that reached the GDR were all forms that in their original contexts derived from spontaneous amateur activity. In the late 1940s, this meant jazz; in the early 1950s skiffle, and after 1956, rock and roll. In the 1960s, music by the Beatles and the Rolling Stones was enormously popular in the GDR; in the 1980s, punk rock and its associated attitudes had considerable appeal to some young people. Each of these musical forms appeared more horrible and dangerous to the GDR authorities than the last, and no matter how they tried to react, they were constantly outflanked. From the start, the hostility of the SED and its musical establishment to these westernized musical forms and their determination to repress them in the GDR meant that the state was at odds with a significant number of its most musically active younger citizens. This was no mere disagreement about musical taste, involving as it did larger issues of lifestyle and value formation. There is no doubt that the SED's hostility to Western popular music contributed significantly to the alienation of successive generations of young people from the regime and its larger goals.

After the abject failure of *Stakuko*'s campaign of outright repression of jazz and sentimental dance music, the GDR embarked upon a policy of co-option, seeking to bring young amateur musicians under the tutelage of the party and to make their music supportive of rather than hostile to Socialism. Thus, in 1957, official efforts were made to accommodate jazz music and musicians; in 1965 to co-opt "beat" groups; and in the 1970s to support what became known as "GDR rock." The Academy of the Arts even formed a "Rock Music Section." By the 1980s, GDR musical theorists celebrated this home-grown rock music as a positive symptom of their activist musical culture.[34] The utter bankruptcy of the policy of co-option was in fact repeatedly demonstrated and at times put GDR functionaries in the most convoluted of positions. This is well demonstrated by an incident at the very start of this policy.

In 1957, a number of amateur GDR musical groups were allowed to take part in the VI World Games in Moscow. The list of these groups testifies to a lively culture of active music making, one that was determinedly Western in its orientation. Bands from Rostock, Saalfeld, Dresden, Jena, and Juterbög, including Klaus Steckels New Orleans Jazz Band, the New Orleans Jazzband Halle, and the Hochschulgruppe Ilmenau Sextett, were due to participate. Several GDR magazines publicized this, one of them, *Zeit im Bild*, running an article accompanied by a picture of one of the young musicians with his washboard, describing this as a "classical jazz instrument."[35] This provoked a reaction from one GDR citizen, who angrily wrote to ask the Ministry of Culture, "Do we need this nonsense?" His complaint focused on the role of the washboard in these bands, and its portrayal in the press as a musical instrument.[36] It generated a correspondence that tells us much about the tensions surrounding the concept of active musical citizenship in the GDR. The complaint reached the desk of Hans-Georg Uszkoreit, a young SED musician who had attained high office in the Music Department of the Ministry of Culture. He penned a tortuous defense, sending copies to the magazines that had publicized the use of the washboard by GDR musicians:

The use of the washboard or other household articles as musical instruments is indeed from the standpoint of our musical practice to be seen as mischief, or a primitive seeking for effect. That does not give us authority to take action against it with state measures.

Pointing out that black slaves in the United States had, out of necessity, used washboards as musical instruments, Uszkoreit continued:

That indeed a regression to primitive forms of musical practice is taking place in Germany, even more in the socialist part of Germany, in which an honorable and proud tradition of nearly a thousand years' musical culture exists, is shameful for those who play in washboard orchestras, and also for the "concert-goers" who listen seriously to such music.[37]

Here, in a few lines, we see the GDR's distaste for Western popular music; its confusion over the origins of this music among black slaves; its exaltation of a peculiarly German musical tradition, one continued above all in the GDR; its characteristic use of a racist discourse; and its unconcealed contempt for many of its own musically active citizens.

Even explicitly Socialist amateur music making could attract the ire of the GDR authorities, concerned with channeling active musicianship into acceptable forms. The poet and songwriter Wolf Biermann has described how in 1960 his "agitprop" setting of the Brecht text *Die Partei hat tausend Augen* (*The Party has a thousand eyes*) was characterized as "political shit" by the members of the Ernst-Hermann-Meyer Ensemble at Humboldt University and criticized by the GDR's musical establishment. Only by forming his own ensemble, and by enlisting the support of Hanns Eisler, was Biermann able to get his "agitprop" songs performed. This kind of grassroots activism was unwelcome to the authorities, and Biermann was banned from performing in 1965.[38] He later left the GDR.

Similar tensions can be found in the GDR's attempt to co-opt pop groups like the Guitar Boys and the Klaus-Renft Kombo in the 1960s,[39] and in the persecution of the punk band Nameless (*Namenlos*) in 1984. The protestations of GDR writers notwithstanding, the SED and the old guard of the GDR's musical establishment were always at odds with this stream of active musical citizenship, characterized, for all the differences between skiffle, pop, rock, and punk, by spontaneity and amateurism. The GDR could never wholeheartedly adopt the Western European and American strategy of commercializing these emergent forms and packaging them in sanitized forms acceptable to a mass consumer market. The SED had a vision in which music would be performed in every house, but the party never found a coherent and successful response to the agency that this gave to the music-making citizen.

As the introduction to this book explores, citizenship has commonly been discussed in its "thin" and in its "thick" conceptions. This chapter has focused on some of the "thick" dimensions of citizenship, notably, the citizens' multifaceted relationships with music. Proscriptions about these relationships have not been written into constitutions and only rarely into legal codes.[40] In that sense they might be seen as having much more to do with identity than with citizenship. It is clear, though, that for much of the twentieth century, many Germans in elite and subaltern strata have believed that music, and their relationship with it, says something imprecise but essential about being German and about being a German citizen. Attitudes toward music and music making have been seen as markers of an ideal or exemplary citizenship to which all should aspire, and conversely as evidence of a deviation from an ideal citizenship that is not to be tolerated.

Surveying the century, it is clear also that ideas about music and citizenship in Germany have changed considerably. As Riethmüller states, the illusion of musical superiority does persist, but only, I would argue, in limited circles. Increasingly, the ideas that underpinned this discourse have been cut away. Central to this belief was the sense of a rigid canon, structured around a chronological progression of German composers. As we saw earlier, this was defined by nationalists as running from Schütz to Wagner. In the GDR, Meyer, in a keynote speech to composers and officials in 1951, neatly defined it as "from Bach to Brahms."[41] Although Celia Applegate and Pamela Potter have argued recently that this canon still dominates contemporary perceptions,[42] here I part company with them. The canon has been subverted, and recognized as an intellectual construct. In Germany and elsewhere, it has been revised in different ways, both chronologically and geographically. Of these two, the former is more significant. Introducing a symposium on German music in the 1970s, Hans-Hubert Schönzeler recognized the importance the "early music" revival had for the idea of German superiority. He wrote:

Whilst it is true that for a period of more than a century Germany enjoyed a certain measure of predominance in western music, it must not be overlooked that this rise to pre-eminence was largely based on the achievements of the Flemish, Italian and English polyphonists which preceded it.[43]

Geographically, there is now a much wider understanding of what constitutes, and constituted, European music, although extra-European influences upon this are recognized as important only from the late nineteenth century onwards. We must nonetheless now place the idea of "German" musical superiority, or indeed "European" musical supe-

riority, in a wider postcolonial context, one in which the "provincializa-
tion of Europe" is being discussed.[44]

As for active music making, understandings have to move with
broader societal changes. The cherished German ideal of the skilful
amateur musician playing string quartets with friends and family in
domestic settings or singing in the village choir has already, as we have
seen, been challenged by young people playing washboards, electric
guitars, and drums in garages and cellars. It may be more constructive,
rather than hankering after an imagined past, to recognize that mixing,
sampling, and sequencing now constitute equally valid forms of music
making, and that the thriving and extraordinarily diverse postmodern musical culture of Germany today does not necessarily represent a
falling-off from past greatness. It should rather be seen as one expression of a new ideal of citizenship in a world where the boundaries of
the nation-state, real or imagined, no longer hold the importance they
once did.

PART THREE

Citizenship in German History

Conceptualizing Citizenship as a Biopolitical Category from the Eighteenth to the Twentieth Centuries

PASCAL GROSSE

ONE OF THE MAJOR PITFALLS in conceptualizing citizenship(s) in the West has been the tendency to equate the category of the nation with that of the nation-state. Although these three categories unquestionably relate to each other, they, nevertheless, do not collapse into one single coherent concept but refer to different registers in the political-legal sphere. In principle, the nation has no territorial boundaries, in contrast to the nation-state. However, the nation-state can confer citizenship on individuals living outside its territory, or exclude individuals who live within the confinements of that state from citizenship. The boundaries between the two fundamental principles upon which citizenship in modern Western nations is based, nationality (in the sense of a nationalized citizenship, as opposed to, for example, universal human rights) and territoriality, consequently become blurred. As such, the nation as well as the nation-state is inherently—and paradoxically—transnational, if one considers the nation to be an ideal unity between state population and territory.

It is evident that seemingly culturally defined categories that cut across national boundaries, such as religion or ethnicity (in the sense of *Volkstum*), have posed a challenge to the idealized unity between state population and territory. Indeed, this challenge has been even more profound as a result of paradigms based on biological traits such as "race" and "sex." From this perspective, citizenship has to be regarded as much as a biopolitical category as a political-legal construct. Yet the biology at stake here is quite complex. For example, citizenship conferred through genealogy implies the idea of biological (in today's phrasing: genetic) lineage through (usually patrilineal) descent. And it is certainly true that a biology-based divide was at the core of these constructions, because the status of men and women had been conceptualized as essentially different in all Western countries. However, in the German case after 1870, there was no ethnic or racial bias in this construction as long as no practices of expatriation were established along the lines of ethnicity, and no legal restrictions on marriage or offspring between German fathers and ethnically or racially different mothers were implemented. Interestingly, the German colonial context between 1885 and 1914 served as a decisive platform for probing new trajectories of biologically inspired citizenship policies in order to replace "sex" by "race" as the leading genealogical principle upon which to base inclusion.[1] As such, German colonialism bore the nucleus for superseding notions of the classical nation-state by a new variant of a transnational organizational principle, that is, a "racial state," which then became a reality under National Socialism.

In the course of modern German history, National Socialism unquestionably represents the most salient example of how biologistic principles of state formation subverted the classical nation-state as it was set up in the nineteenth century. Instead of merely buttressing notions of national citizenship, racial concepts contested those political-legal notions of citizenship bound to the territorial nation-state, because *race* inherently has no correlate in entities defined by territoriality handed down through history. Crucially, prior notions of (nationalized) citizenship came to be replaced entirely after 1933 by criteria of racial inclusion in or exclusion from the community of Germans (e.g., through enforcing measures such as expatriation, expulsion, marriage restrictions, sterilization, murder, and naturalization, all along assumedly racial lines). In terms of classical participatory rights and duties, the notion of *German citizenship* thus became entirely hollow, and ultimately the category *German* itself became bare of any relevant meaning, as the latter does not refer to a biological but to a linguistic entity. National Socialism, however, should not be regarded as the only or even the final reference point for understanding how biopolitics and issues of citizenship have become intertwined. Newly emerging biological concepts and technologies have always challenged traditional notions of citizenship.

If we accept the fact that citizenship can be regarded as a biopolitical category, we then need to examine more closely its intellectual foundations and how biological categories such as "race" or "sex" have become connected to notions of citizenship at all. In this chapter, I shall attempt to expand notions of citizenship in the latter sense by taking the biological side of biopolitics quite literally. However, I shall do so through exploring some of the more basic philosophical and political foundations of biologized citizenship, rather than scrutinizing the biological implications in the political-legal process. Such an attempt almost unavoidably relates to the history of the neurosciences, which began in earnest as a scientific project about three hundred years ago, and which today in the Western world has led to the dominant biopolitical framework of cerebralizing human existence. Thus, the core of my argument will explore how notions of power have become "cerebralized," in particular, how a notion of *cerebral citizenship* emerged as a new and decisive platform within the project of civil society. As I plan to show, *citizenship* has evolved from biopolitical ideas since the seventeenth and eighteenth centuries and has always transcended the idea of a nation-state bound to a single territory at the level of familial and local as well as globalized communities.

My inquiry in some ways resonates with arguments made by Foucault and others working in a similar vein, most notably Agamben. These thinkers have pleaded for conceptualizing an alternative analysis of power beyond the judicial and institutional sphere, in particular at the level of the modern human body as an interface of subjective techniques and objective procedures.[2] Their central point of departure has been that Western modernity has integrated and heightened subjective techniques for individualization at the same time as it has developed objective procedures for totalization as a paradoxical political "double bind" in the foundation of modern structures of power.[3] This presumed double bind is the obvious intellectual site for conceiving of citizenship(s) as embedded in social and cultural practices as well as their subsequent judicial codifications through which status is conferred. I want to suggest that the brain has become in fact the particular (bodily) site where subjectivity and objectivity, individuality and totality, inwardness and outwardness, the sense of Self and Other, have been represented.

In principle, this approach is in line with recent scholarship seeking to contest reductive understandings of *citizenship* as connoting primarily membership in a community bound together through the nation-state. For instance, Kathleen Canning and Sonya Rose as well as Gisela Bock and Susan James have called for expanding the definitions of citizenship as an analytical category for conveying subjectivity along with a sense of individual identity or for relating citizenship to bodily experiences.[4] Because they place the site of inquiry outside the framework of the nation-state, their and similar approaches essentially reflect postmodernist attempts to reconcile competing notions of equality and difference within the concept of citizenship, which is inflected by intrinsically normative categories such as religion, class, race, and gender.

Definitions of bodily and mental/cerebral functions, as represented by categories such as race and gender, have served as major avenues for social engineering as a constituent of Western civil society. More recently, novel biotechnological interventions, for example, in human biological reproduction, might eventually change practices of inclusion and exclusion in radical ways that go beyond the methods that have been used up to now, such as social exclusion or physical annihilation. In what follows, I want to address three primary questions. First, what connects biology to the philosophical and political-legal constructions of citizenship(s)? Second, do biological concepts correspond with the nation-state as the primary location for citizenship in the nineteenth and twentieth centuries? And, finally, how do biotechnological developments interact with notions of citizenship? Rather than giving detailed answers to these questions, I shall respond by sketching out a more general conceptual framework that, nevertheless, refers back to this set of questions.

I. Citizenship and Biopolitics: Mapping a Problem

There can be little doubt that some of the seventeenth and eighteenth centuries' emerging categories in ontological and political philosophy, such as volition, intentionality, and autonomy, were intimately linked to the idea of citizenship rights and access to the public sphere. In this logic, exerting (self-) control could pave the way to power—over oneself as well as in society. At the same time, researchers in the field we would call today the neurosciences— neurology, psychiatry, and cognitive psychology—began to probe the biological basis for these political-philosophical concepts. Variations of biophilosophical materialism, which came about in seventeenth-century Britain as empiricism and in eighteenth-century France as sensualism, offered a new epistemology for shaping citizenship(s). In opposing ideas about the divide between mind and body, it sought biological foundations to essentialize the human condition and human behavior in models that revolved around nerves and the brain. Subsequently, in different but specific historical and political constellations in Western societies, citizenship has been gendered, racialized, psychologized, related to age, or otherwise defined on biological grounds by assigning, implicitly or explicitly, specific qualities to the mind, or more precisely to its material basis, the brain. In other words, if "the body" were in fact involved in the historical realizations of citizenships, the most central facet would be the brain.

An example from our times can perhaps best illustrate this line of thought. For about thirty-five years in the West, an individual has been considered dead when his or her brain is "dead," even if all other organs are still functioning properly.[5] The idea of "brain death" may seem commonsense to us today, but it is in fact a radical departure from a tradition going back several thousand years that equates death with the cessation of the heartbeat and respiration, irrespective of an individual's mental state. As such, Western societies have come to acknowledge the new paradigm, that brain functions alone provide the material basis for a life worth living because the brain confers subjectivity as the threshold to individuality. Though the medical construction of brain death and its subsequent legal codification came about in the 1960s and 1970s to serve the purposes of the emerging field of transplantation medicine, it also reflects contemporary attitudes toward constructions of individuality and subjectivity. At another level of reflection, this move has inserted the classical controversy about the legal and ethical nature of a "conventionally" dead body (is it still a human, or a thing, or something in between?) into the brain-dead body with living organs. In Western societies, an entire corpse with its brain is usually more than a thing, the physical integrity of which is to be preserved, although its status is not that of a person in the legal sense. Conversely, the living body of a brain-dead individual is equated with a thing without proper (citizenship) rights, and thus the removal of organs from such a biological entity is not criminalized. By implication, then, the brain alone accrues all (citizenship) rights. The current concept of brain death marks something like the provisional final point in a 250-year development to equate citizenship rights with cerebral function.

It is possible, in the case of brain death, to accept that an individual whose unconscious mind no longer properly functions cannot exert his or her rights, because these rights are based on volition, which requires wakeful consciousness. But the question of brain death is just one extreme case in which biology has substantially shaped questions relating to citizenship. Suicide is another classic example, because suicide has been associated with mental/cerebral dysfunction and with a state of limited volition for some two hundred years.[6] In the same way, obsessive-compulsive disorder, posttraumatic stress disorder, eating disorders, depression, and many other behavioral phenomena have been psychologized in the course of the last decades as expressions of compromised volition. In this line of thought, biological psychiatry and the neurosciences are realigning individuality along the lines of a postmodern expression of citizenship with a "normalization" of volition and subjectivity. The other major avenue that has already begun to dramatically reshape notions of citizenship is genetics and reproductive medicine. Disentangling biological reproduction from sexual intercourse, choosing the qualities of the offspring, or modifying the process of biological aging are just some of the examples that illustrate how biotechnological developments may eventually reshape our current understanding of inclusion and rightful participation in different communities.[7]

Taking all this together, it is tempting to view the neurosciences as well as genetics as relatively new developments shaping citizenship(s). However, from a historical perspective, the neurosciences and genetics have been intertwined fields of bioscientific research for the past two hundred and fifty years, because both are bound together through evolutionary thinking that relies on the idea of a universal genealogy of humankind. The shared central premise is that faculties of the mind as represented in the brain are inborn and cannot be changed through environmental factors. This variation of biological materialism only came about at the end of the eighteenth century and strongly opposed previously dominant models of (nervous) materialism propagated, for example, by those British empiricists and French sensualists who held that individual experiences shape and mold the nervous system to some extent. The very idea that mental qualities are inscribed in the brain constitutes the core of the biological construction of the citizen, who was, of course, male, white, (economically) autonomous, and heterosexual (in the sense that heterosexuality establishes participation in a biological genealogy). It is a biogenealogical construction of power that encompasses the inward perspective, that is, power over one's self, together with the outward perspective based in power over others. Thus, it is important to turn to the basic categories of volition, race, gender, and sexuality, as, since the eighteenth century, they have become the crucial components in the cerebralization of human existence.

II. Cerebralizing the Human Condition

For the project of civil society, volition was the one and only avenue for achieving individual success in life—at least for white, economically autonomous males. For the rest of humankind, success was defined through other avenues. In this broader context, scientific secularism reformulated the human brain from the "organ of the soul" to the material basis of mental power, that is, the "modern" brain that thinks, sees, hears, feels, and speaks.[8] In other words, philosophical notions previously ascribed more generally to the "mind" were translated into distinct cerebral functions. The brain subsequently became the site for representing virtually every expression of human behavior and cognition.

As an empirical research project, this line of thought was first reflected in the work of the German-born anatomist and psychiatrist Franz Joseph Gall in the last decade of the eighteenth century. Gall put forward the deterministic idea that "moral and intellectual qualities are innate" in each individual. He also proposed that the brain was "the organ of all faculties, of all tendencies, of all feelings,"[9] of which he counted around thirty.[10] Since then, the cerebralization of human existence developed into such a powerful discourse because locating the essence of human existence in the brain became a dominant epistemology and a normative agency in itself. Because this process postulated the existence of natural laws operating in every individual, it offered a radically egalitarian understanding of the human condition. In theory, it fundamentally challenged the social inequalities born out of a feudal system based on birth prerogatives. It also countered unreasonable superstitions, which in the West were mostly attributed to the churches. In Germany, this tendency was most pronounced in the early works of archliberals such as Rudolf Virchow (1821–1902), specifically around the time of the 1848 revolution.[11]

However, cerebral biologism contained an inherent paradox. Its internal logic postulated that any existing social or cultural difference must have a neurobiological correlate. This happened because brains were now thought of as representations of the whole of the individual as well as the individual's controlling agency. Nineteenth-century developments of race biology, gender biology, and social biology essentially constituted a neurobiology of difference that continually questioned biological egalitarianism based on the very same intellectual foundations. Moreover, the introduction of evolutionary thought into assumptions about how brains operate created a seemingly permanent hierarchy among different behavioral patterns. Each individual, then, carried quite diverse biological ancestry in which specific human cerebral features were only accrued over the course of evolution. The animal thus still resided inside every human and could be unleashed. This theorem could also be reversed so that humankind appeared as merely humanized animals, which corresponded to the idea of the domesticated animal. The term *race* became synonymous with this biological genealogy in its double meaning. On the one hand, the *human race* represented a biological species different from animals, a meaning that stressed the universality of humankind. And on the other hand, *race* also served as a taxonomic category, a meaning that stressed difference. Despite all universalist and environmentalist claims, the project to cerebralize human existence was differentialist right from its outset, because it inserted "volition" and intentional acts as a normative paradigm and a prerequisite to becoming a citizen. This move stratified humankind into humans who exercised more will over themselves and those who exercised less—and who consequently had more or less inherent right to exercise power over others.

A. Volition

In the course of the eighteenth century, volition became the centerpiece of an argument to distinguish humans from the rest of the living world, most notably animals. This idea was certainly not new, but the intellectual and cultural contexts in which it developed were novel. In particular, it became a self-reflexive code for the bourgeois project because it was intimately linked to notions such as freedom, emancipation, and civil rights. To assign volition a cerebral basis, as, for example, Diderot had detailed in his "Éléments de Physiologie," [12] in which he drew on contemporary medical opinions, was just a logical extension to frame a counternarrative to religious creationism. But the idea to ground volition in the brain only took off with the work of anatomists, such as Franz Joseph Gall and Samuel Thomas Soemmering, [13] who dissected human and animal brains in a comparative fashion, and the French physicians who set out after the Revolution to reform institutionalized psychiatry by postulating that mental alienation was based on cerebral alterations, [14] a view that was adopted internationally in the early nineteenth century.

In Germany, the psychiatrist Wilhelm Griesinger took the ultimately decisive step in the 1840s by locating any mental alienation in the brain itself, without attributing causality to any external agents.[15] He instead claimed that any expression of human behavior, not just reason, must have a cerebral correlate of its own. However, biological psychiatry established a double-edged program because, lacking any positivistic proof of the cerebral basis of volition, it only defined volition *ex negativo* as the absence of instincts (*Triebe*). As such, it remained a sociocultural construct, though one with substantial normative implications, because any behavioral variation and deviation from the norm could be psychologized as a "disease of the will." The only expression of willful human behavior that Griesinger positively identified was intentional movement, which led to action (*Handlung*; movements resulting from reflexes were considered instinctive).[16] But action did not exist independently; rather, it was in a constant struggle with instincts, which were related to perceptions (*Vorstellungen*) and could only be overcome by an obsessive effort (*innerer Zwang*). The more humans realized that they "must want" (*müssen wollen*), the more likely they were to achieve human freedom (*menschliche Freiheit*), which remained equivalent with intentional physical action in the absence of instinctive movements, based on the possibility of exerting self-control (*Selbstbeherrschung*).[17] All this supposedly happened in the brain, so that independent action and human freedom resulted from an interplay among different cerebral strategies. From this point of departure, any human behavior could be classified as either the successful achievement of volition over instincts or, as in the behavior of social delinquents, the mentally ill, and children, a form of compromised volition. Even more importantly, however, this model produced a new, narrow understanding of *natural*, for freedom was only "natural" in the sense that it had a biological basis, not because it came about automatically on its own. As a result, this reasoning represented a major departure from earlier ideas of natural reason and, by implication, natural human rights. Because freedom could only be achieved through (cerebral) self-control and not by any other agency, this reductive model also singularized each individual and made introspection a worthwhile enterprise.

Within this concept of volition were constant intrinsic disruptions by states of altered consciousness, such as sleep, dreams, intoxication, fever, dizziness, fits of all kinds, and orgasm. These altered states of mind did not obey the dichotomy between volition and instincts because they were seen as transitory states of mind in which volition was compromised. In particular, a physiological state such as dreaming was not easy to reconcile with essentialist and static notions of volition and reason, because it occurred in everyone. Although these issues contested the overall theory, the dividing line between those whose identity was grounded in volition and those who were compromised in this regard was not conceptualized within the individual but was organized through the categories of race and gender.

B. Race

The study of *race* was certainly the most comprehensive scientific project in the humanities since the eighteenth century, at least until the Human Genome Project came into being. It was totalitarian because it attempted to classify comprehensively every single variation of humankind and every expression of human behavior as a synthesis between the human body and human culture. However, one of the main differences between traditional studies of race and the Human Genome Project is that the former assigns individuals to typological groups defined through averages, whereas the latter deals with the individual and his or her genetic makeup without necessarily resorting to classificatory systems such as *race*. Moreover, scientific studies of race have always been self-referential because they can only replicate their own assumptions (i.e., that an individual belongs to a certain race because he or she shares some qualities that are prevalent in this type) and cannot deal with variation at the individual level, as DNA testing does by identifying the individual.

But what was really at stake when physical anthropologists measured arm lengths and skull indices or cultural anthropologists pondered totems? Through the explosion of race studies in the first half of the twentieth century, most researchers lost sight of the intellectual core of their studies. Interestingly, the geneticist Fritz Lenz, one of the founding fathers of German eugenics, reminded his scientific community in the 1920s that all race studies essentially dealt with the study of different mental faculties and that the variations in bodily makeup are just a surrogate measure for cerebral difference.[18] As such, right from the beginning, the study of the human brain implied a taxonomic approach involving the categories of race and gender.[19] It took the question of the genealogy of humankind seriously, because asking about the innate cerebral qualities of human races and how they were linked with each other was paramount to this line of research. However, the immediate study of human brains encountered many methodological barriers, especially because only the dead could be studied. Thus, other avenues proliferated. The first major path was to study the skulls of the living and the dead, which implicitly followed Gall's phrenological assumptions that the content of the skull was in some way reflected by the skull's morphology. Throughout the nineteenth century, skulls became almost synonymous with studies of race, but also with studies of the brain. From the mid-nineteenth century onward, the other major avenue pursued was a more sophisticated set of psychological laboratory experiments on elementary functions such as perception, reaction times, and the like. All these methodologies formed a synthetic research agenda, in which the search for "cerebral difference" became the common denominator.

Importantly, the study of such cerebral characteristics according to race could serve dual and contradictory purposes: either to stress similarities among the races or to refute them. The latter was much more common, but one of the best-known examples of the former was Friedrich Tiedemann's 1836 study "On the Brain of the Negro, Compared with That of the European and the Orang-Outang."[20] Based on his anatomical research, he took a strong abolitionist stance because, as he wrote, "neither anatomy nor physiology [of the brain] can justify our placing [Negroes] beneath the Europeans in a moral or intellectual point of view." And taking the larger political view, Tiedemann concluded that "Hayti [*sic*] and the colony of Sierra Leone can attest that free Negroes are capable of being governed by mild laws, and require neither whips nor chains to enforce submission to civil authority."[21] Quite similar arguments for the cerebral likenesses of humankind can be found elsewhere, most notably in the wake of the U.S. Civil War, when the federal government tested the aptitude of African Americans for military purposes and advocated their future recruitment.[22] Nevertheless, all these egalitarian claims did not imply equality, neither in the physical nor in the legal sense. All they concluded was that nonwhites were humans.

C. Gender

Significantly, the concept of the gendered brain established not only a science of difference but also a biological science of polar and complementary genders. The construction of cerebral gender polarity since the eighteenth century can be viewed as one of the overarching principles in the construction of civil society since the eighteenth century, which followed the scientific study of biological gender differences, specifically in the genitalia and the human skeleton, in the early modern period.[23] Crucial to the idea of cerebral gender difference was a distinct model of human evolution, within which women were considered to have imperfect brains. From the mid-eighteenth century onward, this line of thought was followed in research on nerves and the brain, with the idea at its core being that men and women represent different steps in cerebral evolution, an argument that remained in the air throughout the early twentieth century. Few new insights came out of this discourse in terms of concepts attributed to the category of gender, because at its core it only reiterated the opposition between emotions and reason. However, the cerebralization of gender difference nevertheless constituted an important intellectual step, incorporating human behavior into a binary evolutionary model based on nervous functions. As such, neurobiology did not merely add a new line of inquiry; more importantly, it aimed to explain the essence of gendered humans, because the workings of all bodily elements were linked through the nerves and controlled by the brain.

The internal logic of gender polarity in the nervous system asserted that males' nerves and brains were harder than females' nerves and brains. Based on the learning process in humans, it was contended that men were less impressionable, both mechanistically and electrically, and hence less prone to overwhelming sensory stimulation; women's imaginations were more vivid, which led to less stable emotional states. This, in short, was the reasoning of the materialistic Montpellier school of medicine, complemented by some fashionable mid-eighteenth-century theories on nerve irritability as well as some sensualist ideas. However, despite these seemingly new insights into biological polarities, this theory was not based on systematic observation, let alone experimentation. Rather than developing new content based on the emergent principles of organ physiology, it essentially adopted the principles of humoral physiology, which itself was based on the inner balance of polar opposites such as warm–cold, hard–soft, strong–weak, dry–moist, and the like. This basic approach was extended in the topographical work of later anatomists such as Emil Huschke, who in his influential 1854 study on cerebral gender and racial differences concluded that the frontal brain, equated with intelligence, was dominant in men, while the overrepresented prominence of the parietal lobe in women (and black Africans) accounted for their excessive sensibilities and passions.[24] Huschke essentially appropriated the dichotomous character of human personality traits, such as reason–emotion, active–passive, action–passion, and so on, and found them to be unequally distributed in the brains of men and women. But it was not only brain weights and brain anatomy that counted. The inquiries became broadly extended, particularly through the use of the new psychological laboratory methodologies, so that the field of gendered neuroscience was established by the beginning of the twentieth century.

Nevertheless, what at first glance seems to be a straightforward history of cerebral difference was regularly disrupted on both the theoretical and empirical levels. The belief that brains could shift, for example, from male to female or from black to white subverted any deterministic model. The German anatomist Jacob Fidelis Ackermann asserted as early as 1788 that "one can find skulls, brains and breastbones of the feminine type in men."[25] And even Emil Huschke, the godfather of cerebral gender and race anatomy, proposed thinking of humans in androgynous terms, stating:

often a woman is organized in a male way, a man in a female way, both physically and psychologically. At least in civilized people, the constitution of each gender is rarely encountered in a pure fashion in body and mind. In part, the big variety . . . exists because of the many transitions to the other gender, and most men and women are in this sense true hermaphrodites.[26]

Thus, the question at stake was how to deal with hybridities in rigid, bipolar classificatory systems. The realm in which this quest became paradigmatically modeled in cerebral terms was sexuality.

D. Sexuality

The scientific forum where sexual behaviors were linked to the nervous system was the extensive debates on masturbation and nymphomania from the mid-eighteenth century onwards. Both behaviors embedded sexuality in a psychiatric setting, while other forms of sexual expression were less explicitly commented on. However, medical philosophers considered sexual behavior to be the cornerstone of the gendered brain, and they considered the brain a sexual organ whose only use in women was biological reproduction. For example, Gall drew only on sexual behavior to develop his own views on gender difference, which he linked to the "instinct" to raise children (*l'amour de la progéniture*) as a distinct cerebral function. Similarly, he considered friendship, attachment, and romantic love, which would ultimately lead to marriage, as cerebrally based.[27] What Gall finally developed was in fact a translation of very common views of polar and complementary genders into a theory of a cerebral basis for biological reproduction.

After the mid-1850s, however, these simple views were fundamentally challenged when doctors started addressing variations in sexual behavior, most importantly same-sex practices both in men and women. Why this quite sudden interest came about remains unclear, but the contexts in which this happened were almost exclusively medicolegal. Next to hysteria, epilepsy, and neurasthenia, variations in sexual behavior became the most important avenue for redefining masculinity and femininity within a cerebral framework. The inner logic with which neurologists and psychiatrists explored sexual behavior was simple, because it had already been agreed upon that any sexual drive must have a cerebral grounding.

Following the template of constitutional hermaphroditism, researchers attempted to determine whether individuals engaging in same-sex practices had a female brain, a male brain, an intersex brain based on both male and female components, or a completely different brain altogether that was neither male nor female but specific to same-sex desire. There can be little doubt that these questions put epistemological pressure on the binary understanding of the gendered brain, which only allowed for a distinction along the male–female axis. Most answers to the question were inconclusive, erratic in their argumentation, or inconsistent regarding the observations they were based on. But one line of thought can clearly be distilled: the dichotomy between the male and the female brain was to be preserved—hence, the construction of sexual inversion (*conträre Sexualempfindung*), a term invented by Berlin neurologist Carl Westphal in 1870[28] and then propagated throughout the Western world. This notion came to represent a mismatch between sexual assignment as determined by the body, namely, the genitalia, and sexual assignment as represented by the brain. In short, sexual inversion came to represent a male body with a female brain and vice versa, as some kind of body-brain hermaphroditism. The hypothesis of cerebral male-female hybrids was dismissed in order to reassert a binary gender model as the only organizing principle for assigning sexual status. Thus, to identify the brain unequivocally in terms of sex was more important than the assignment of the whole of a body to one sex. It was an intellectual move that compartmentalized the body by disentangling the brain from the rest of the body. And it was the brain that supposedly conferred status, social representation, and identity.

III. Individuality and Totality

The sketches above show not only that since the eighteenth century citizenship required a brain but also that the qualities inscribed into the brains of citizens were quite specific. From a biological standpoint, the centerpiece of citizenship was constituted by the conscious and volatile act, which expressed individual will and freedom but was constantly disrupted by instincts. Yet the individual brain also represented the whole of humankind in at least two ways.

First, evolutionism asserted that each individual brain carried the genetic history of humankind. Each individual thus was trapped in a journey through time, inasmuch as he or she harbored the very representation of evolutionary time in his or her brain. The eighteenth-century notion of internal travel back through time strongly resonated with the scientific representation of non-European people as the material embodiment of earlier evolutionary stages of humankind. Thus, the "primitive" or the "savage" original state of humankind could still be unleashed in the form of instinctual behavior, in particular in women, while only men had the potential to develop beyond that. This logic created a specific tension between the animal and the human, in men of course more so than in women. Freud took up this line of thought in very much the same way when he paralleled neurotic development with cultural practices outside the Western world.[29] In essence, these evolutionary ideas presupposed that each individual harbored earlier expressions of animal and human life, but also that certain brains were capable of superseding and controlling these atavistic forms.

Second, the brain constituted a sexual organ in its own right because it harbored all the elements intrinsic to biological reproduction (lust, sense of fatherhood and motherhood, etc.). Biological reproduction established and transcended a genealogy at the level of the family, the nation, the race (in the taxonomic sense), or humankind. With this interpretation, biological reproduction became detached from the genitalia as the traditional site related to sexuality, and sexuality was assigned to the integrative and gendered brain. But these principles of biological reproduction only worked when the cerebral organization corresponded with the gender of the rest of the body. As in the case of same-sex practices, body-brain hermaphroditism implied a position outside this genealogical chain. As should be clear by now, I am suggesting that biological reproduction was one principal way to confer citizenship—though in a different way from acts of volition—because it placed the individual in a genetic community.

Does it matter at all that Western minds have tried to ground their identity on a material basis that is the brain? It might be that citizenship, with its connotations as we know them today, does not refer to law only in the sense of a judicially institutionalized status of existence that relates individual to groups, be it under the heading of the nation or of other communities. Notions of citizenship have also been modeled on the biological existence of humans, supposedly based on natural laws in analogy to the sciences. The project of civil society since the eighteenth century has incorporated both kinds of law as its intellectual guidelines.

The utopia of mid-nineteenth-century medical reformers in Germany such as Virchow was an imagined state organized according to the natural laws reigning in the human body; hence the constant likening of the state to a body in which cells represent individuals.[30] Thus, the body as the perfect representation of natural laws served as a template for organizing civil society, not just because it was thought to reflect the natural order of things but, more importantly, because natural laws opposed human despotism, arbitrariness, and superstition. However, this state was by no means conceived of as egalitarian or democratic. It was to be oligarchic in nature because the brain was supposed to control the different parts of the body, which all had different values for the whole of the organism. These were the basic concepts that were subsequently influenced by Darwinism, eugenics, and other strategies of social engineering. From this perspective, biopolitics is not just the addition of biology to classical politics. Biology does not merely legitimize specific social politics. Instead, biopolitics must be considered a synthetic, and yet paradoxical, constituent of Western modernity.

The key paradox is reflected in the cerebralization of human existence. The brain is construed as the site of ultimate subjectivity and individuality, in the twentieth century more so than in the nineteenth. At the same time, the individual brain should also represent the totality of humankind because it is a product of evolution. In the past two centuries or so, this specific tension has been assimilated into the construction of citizenships, which are themselves negotiations between equality and difference as well as between individuality and totality. In this sense, constructions of cerebral citizenships are expressions of

Foucault's double bind between techniques of individualization and objective procedures of totalization. And it is possibly not mere coincidence that the exploration of the Self as it started in the seventeenth and eighteenth centuries paralleled the development of Western-dominated globalized networks equating the unconscious Self with the "dark continent" and the "true inner Africa."[31] After all, both projects have grounded themselves on different modes of coercion, against the self as well as against others, thus defining the broader intellectual framework of modern biopolitics.

Citizenship in Twentieth-Century German History: Chances and Challenges of a Concept

ADELHEID VON SALDERN

I. The Concept

The concept of citizenship is highly complex indeed.[1] At first glance, its complexity resembles five "spinning tops." The first spinning top symbolizes citizenship in the core areas of the nation-state.[2] While historians have mainly analyzed the development of the connections between citizenship and the nation-state, other scholars have been interested in integrating into this concept not only the local and regional levels but also the transnational and global dimensions of belonging.[3] The second spinning top is related to nongovernmental places and spheres where interactions of citizens actually take place, such as the private and the public spheres, the areas of culture, media, and consumption, the workplace, people's informal networks, and so on. The third spinning top, the biggest one, placed in the middle, consists of agents such as individuals and groups. Companies, organizations, institutions, and authorities at all levels of society can also be seen as acting agents. The multivalent meaning in German of *Bürger* as a representative of his class and *Bürger* as citizen directly reveals the class orientation of the citizenship concept in the nineteenth century. When political citizenship was uncoupled from bourgeois class position by the revolution of 1918–19 and universal suffrage was introduced, all German adults, male and female, were defined as *Bürger* in the sense of "citizen" or *citoyen*. The fourth spinning top comprises all sorts of activities, such as various kinds of participation,[4] protest demonstrations, petitions, and discourses. It also includes social practices of exclusion or inclusion, as well as of civil courage and solidarity, of giving someone voice and of making private matters public. As recent studies have shown, people's feeling of belonging forms a part of this context.[5] The fifth spinning top, related to the first one, represents the overall framework of laws and rules and also the contexts given by the existing order of society, state, economy, and culture, as well as by special circumstances like periods of war.

These spinning tops are always in motion, some quicker, some slower, while they are dynamically spiraling, some of them simultaneously in the same direction. They rotate and touch each other; at other times, they are distanced from each other. They penetrate the circle of other spinning tops; they move against each other or they move in harmony; in short, they exist in a relational setting. The relations between the individual on the one hand and the communities and the state on the other are at the center of this setting. These relations also stood at the *core* of the introduction, maintenance, and expansion of civil rights, and they determined social citizenship, including rights of public education, social entitlements, and welfare provisioning.[6] The metaphor of the spinning tops suggests that there is no clear hierarchy among them. Moreover, citizenship is not only a stable status of individuals but a *permanent* process in which networks of memberships, relational social practices in public spaces, and active contestations for an expansion of citizenship play central roles.[7] Citizenship affects rights and obligations whose actual differences between individuals often correspond with their differing status. Furthermore, the image of the spinning tops suggests that there is no topic, no area, no sphere, and no agent that does not touch the concept. Thus, the concept is a kind of super-umbrella. And that is not only an opportunity but also a dilemma that characterizes the concept. If this is true, the consequence would be that a topic's relevance to citizenship depends only on the specific perspective of investigation.

Constitutional rights, political rights, procedural rights, and basic rights have been at the center of the concept of citizenship for a long time. The first wave of extension of the concept in the 1970s is connected with Thomas H. Marshall, who included individual claims in economic and social areas within the concept of citizenship.[8] The present second wave of extension, focusing on citizenship in the cultural area, has been due not only to the *cultural turn* but to theoretical insights deriving from gender studies, migration studies, and race studies.

In this regard, an important area within the cultural sphere is the media, and this includes advertising. Media do not only convey the image of citizenship to other audiences, but they also "produce" cultural citizenship.[9] These "productions" do not always coincide with the dominant political doctrine, not even in dictatorships. In his chapter in this volume on the advertisements of the Henkel company, Jonathan Wiesen has shown that the advertisements appealed to personal fulfillment and individuality. This not only demonstrates the relevance of media but also highlights that the imageries offered by the media during the Third Reich were complex and differentiated and addressed more than just communal life (*Gemeinschaftsleben*) in groups and camps. Clearly, the Nazi period must be seen as more complex and inconsistent than the image portrayed in many historical studies of this period.[10]

There were, of course, other aspects to citizenship in other periods of German history. The following paragraphs deal with the extension of the concept of citizenship toward the regional and local levels. Furthermore, they focus on the interrelationships between citizenship and gender, migration, and race. Finally, they explore the links between citizenship and other concepts, such as social engineering, governmentality, and civil society.

II. The Extension of Citizenship: The Regional and Local Levels

With the exception of the Nazi and most of the GDR periods, Germany has been organized as a federal political system with relatively strong regional states (*Land, Länder*). The states also affected citizens' rights, as Annemarie Sammartino's chapter shows. She demonstrates that it was states such as Bavaria and Prussia that adjudicated the eastern European migrants' applications for citizenship in Weimar Germany. Moreover, if the concept of citizenship were to be extended to include people's right to education, for instance, which was in the domain of the individual states, the states also would come into the focus of research on citizenship.

There is a similar tension between the regional and the national levels in the sphere of political culture. To be sure, there were strong movements dedicated to the nationalization of culture, as Jennifer Jenkins shows in her contribution on the early twentieth-century reform movement the *Werkbund*. The nationalization of culture is also suggested by the imageries of *Heimatfront* in World War I, by the interwar promotion of "national high culture," by the Nazis' centralization of cultural policy, and by the "nationalization" of everyday objects in the Federal Republic after 1949.[11] Indeed, even music could serve as an important instrument of national identity policies, as Toby Thacker's chapter shows. The areas of the economy, the labor market, and the welfare state developed in transregional contexts. These developments and the striving to nationalize people's mental maps certainly were successful in creating a common national feeling of belonging.

There remained, however, religious and other cultural differences among the various regional cultures, such as dialects, traditions, and mentalities. There have always been tensions, competitions, and mutual animosities among the different regions. Because Prussia had dominated the Reich policy for a long period, Prussians were the special focus of such tensions and animosities. For instance, during the German Empire, Bavarians often distanced themselves from a culture and politics perceived to represent the hegemony of Prussia-Germany and Berlin. "*Saupreuße*" ("Lousy Prussian"), for example, was a common swearword in Bavarian *Stammtisch* milieus for many decades of the nineteenth and twentieth centuries, even after Prussia as a state had ceased to exist in 1932. Research on political culture and citizenship thus must focus not only on the national but also on the regional level and must outline the congruities and incongruities between the two.

This research task gets even more complicated because the view on the local, subregional level is also important. The national becomes local and vice versa, as Geoff Eley and others have put it, because individuals experienced the state in everyday life mostly through the local arena, for instance, in their dealings with state bureaucracies or, as Thomas Lindenberger's chapter shows, with the police. Moreover, local authorities have to execute state laws and prepare state decisions, writing reports on many issues, for example. Annemarie Sammartino's chapter clarifies how important local assessments of an application for citizenship could be. Furthermore, Germany has had a distinctive tradition of local self-governmental rights since the civic ordinance designed by Freiherr vom Stein in 1808. To be sure, the rights of self-government were always more or less restricted by the states and by the Reich or federal state, and during the nineteenth and twentieth centuries, both the states and the Reich or the federal state acquired many tasks that originally had been reserved for the locality. Nevertheless, during the twentieth century there remained various areas for local self-government.[12] For instance, the last stage of the welfare system (*Fürsorge*) in the Weimar Republic was implemented by local authorities who, for this reason, checked their potential clients intensively before paying them.[13]

Despite the increasingly restricted rights of self-government, a city was always about more than the experience of citizenship at the everyday level. In the cities during the nineteenth century, the aspiring bourgeoisie became powerful *citoyens*, acquiring political, economic, and cultural dominance. The cities also were important arenas for the progress of women's empowerment in the nineteenth and twentieth centuries. Although women generally could not become formal citizens of a city and could not vote until 1919, they were anxious to expand their concept of "motherhood as profession" from the private sphere to the local public sphere, especially through voluntary work in local welfare agencies.[14]

More recent significant examples of local citizenship, are the social movements of the late 1960s and the 1970s. Active local citizens strove to participate in various local decision-making processes in all areas of politics.[15] Despite the tensions between the decision-making rights of the local parliaments and administrations on the one hand and the decision-making demands of active citizens on the other, the cities and their public affairs offered, more than ever before, important and lively occasions for social practices. In sum, cities have been an excellent place for men and women, whether residents or immigrants, to gain manifold experiences as active citizens.[16]

Moreover, city residents have taken great pride in their city's specific achievements and peculiarities. Although professional public relations work and modern city marketing management only arose in the 1960s, city identity policies were a phenomenon of the entire twentieth century and contributed to the development of people's multiple identities. Many citizens have not only felt German and Saxon but also have identified as citizens of Leipzig or Munich. The hybrid identities often were asymmetrically patterned, especially during periods of dictatorship. As Jan Palmowski underlines in his account of the centralized GDR, the local level was crucial. Grey zones existed here that stimulated people's common activities. According to Palmowski, cultural citizenship strengthened people's ties to the local communities rather more than to the state. Thus, the sense of belonging of a GDR citizen could be stronger toward his or her *Heimat*, or city, than to the GDR, or nation. In sum, the more closely research focuses on the citizens' own experiences, the more relevant the local level, the cities or villages, become.

III. Citizenship: Impacts of Migration, Race, and Gender Studies

There is no doubt that migration and gender studies have influenced the concept of citizenship, and this is also true for studies on race. This work has demonstrated explicitly that, as a rule, individual rights have been embedded in group rights and that both gender and ethnicity must be taken into consideration when full citizenship is on the agenda.[17]

Although in different contexts, both migration and gender studies provide insights into the preconditions of active citizenship, between empowerment and contractions of potential civic rights. Moreover, migration studies have clearly shown the multiple and hybrid identities of ethnic minorities, which encompass a broad range, from diasporic communal belonging to transnational identities.

Migration studies also have demonstrated the historical relevance of the policies of assimilation and adoption, although in different contexts. To become accepted, migrants often were expected to assimilate to the new country's culture. However, people of other races were seen as not being capable of assimilation—remaining the "others"—even if they had equal political rights. As Pascal Grosse outlines in his article on Imperial Germany, even the allegedly substantial biological differences between male and female brains were relativized as scholars offered explanations of the "differences" between black and white brains.

The enrichment of the concept of citizenship that developed through migration studies can be seen if one looks at the minorities of Imperial Germany. German politicians did not regard the Polish and Russian migrants, among them many Jews, as capable of assimilating to German culture. Instead of liberalizing the idea of assimilation and the concept of citizenship, the *Reichs- und Staatsangehörigkeitsgesetz*, carried through in 1913, was based on the principle of *ius sanguinis*. But, as Dieter Gosewinkel points out in this book and elsewhere, the citizenship law of 1913 was flexible enough to be applied either in a more liberal or in a more restrictive way.[18] Partly for this reason, this citizenship law existed in the Federal Republic until the end of the twentieth century.

The relative flexibility of the 1913 law does not mean, however, that ethnic contentions of citizenship were overcome, as policies toward and public disputes over the migration to West Germany in the 1970s demonstrate. After the law of 1973 eliminating the right of migration by application (*Anwerbe-* and *Zuwanderungsstop*) and as a consequence of the European Social Charta, families of former guest workers were permitted to move to Germany. Although the migrants were expected to become assimilated through some integrationist projects, many Germans continued to refuse to define Germany as a migration country.[19] The ideal of a preeminent ethnic identity has determined the political culture and public debates in the old and new Federal Republic with respect to migration policy. The GDR also experienced the legacy of the idea of pure German ethnicity in its own ways, as foreigners remained strangers there as well.[20] But there were some differences: while East Germans "seem never to have lost their sense of ethnic nationhood, young West Germans developed a more cosmopolitan and inclusive idea of Germanness."[21]

Migration studies have emphasized the multiple or hybrid features of the migrants' sense of belonging. *Hybridity* not only refers to migrants as noncitizens; it can refer to naturalized citizens as well. In general, *belonging* must be seen as a dynamic process of altering and oscillating among various units. People feel that they simultaneously belong to their families, their neighborhoods, their associations, their towns, their countries, their religions, and more. All these feelings can fit together or contradict one another. In the era of imperialism around 1900, for example, individuals became newly conscious of the peculiarities and common features of Europe, which stood in contrast to the United States, Asia, and Africa. As a consequence, people acquired a strong awareness of their belonging to Europe, believing in Europe's cultural superiority (Eurocentrism). This, however, did not mean that individuals lost their positive feeling of belonging to their nation-state. Instead, it made them more conscious than ever of their particular countries' alleged real superiority within Europe—the United Kingdom for the British, France for the French, Germany for Germans. Evidently, this was not a natural feeling but a result of cultural policies of identification, as Toby Thacker argues in his chapter.

Gender studies also have influenced the expansion of the concept of citizenship. The mainstream scholarly view considers full emancipation of women accessible within the project of civil society without a basic transformation of the society. Against this view, feminists hold that even if this were so, the transformation could only be realized under the restrictive condition that men remain the normal model of the human being (*Allgemeine des Menschengeschlechts*), and that women would have to adapt to, and accept, this man-centered model of citizenship.[22] This would not reflect a genuine openness of society toward different groups—an openness necessary for a society that seeks to be character-ized by the ideal of civility.

Looking at gender studies, we all agree that the ideal of citizenship is embodied in men and women who are committed to the common weal, the *Gemeinwohl*, and who are therefore willing to engage in vol-untary work. There are two dangers inherent in this ideal. The first is the gendering of labor, with the development of the regular, paid labor market for men and the voluntary, unpaid labor "market" for women. The second is a segregation within volunteer work itself: Certain posts, especially those that are representative and popular, such as chairmen or presidents, have been occupied by men, while the subordinate and "silent" tasks traditionally have been done by women. Thus, the issue of segregation, which has been the topic of so many gender studies, remains crucial and relevant to the history and future of citizenship.

Gender studies have also shown that the differentiation between pri-vate and public issues was connected to the rise of bourgeois society in the late eighteenth century. As the private and public spheres were highly gendered, it was easy for men to suppress women's concerns with the argument that they were private issues. Thus, it is highly sig-nificant that women used the overall changes after 1918–19 to acquire public voice for their concerns, as Cornelie Usborne illustrates in her chapter in this volume on abortion. Another radical step forward oc-curred in the late 1960s and 1970s. The reason for this huge time gap is to be found in the National Socialist policies toward women during the Third Reich and the aftereffects of these policies in the early years of the Federal Republic. The slow pace of progress was also due to a highly antiquated family law that was created in 1900 and outlasted all changes of political systems—except the GDR—until it was eventually eliminated in the 1960s and 1970s.

IV. Citizenship, Social Engineering, and Governmentality

At the center of the mutual links between the concept of citizenship and the concepts of social engineering and governmentality is the ques-tion of whether the latter are necessary and appropriate to make people "good citizens."

It was Michel Foucault who developed the concept of governmental-ity[23] and argued that liberal societies have functioned not only by direct state power but also by nonstate power and by the power of science and knowledge. As a kind of "conduct of conduct," various forms of self-technologies and self-organizations in society have arisen to "govern others and ourselves in a wide range of contexts."[24] Contemporary neoliberal theorists of governmentality use Foucault's critical insights for their neorealistic argument that people must transmute themselves into a complete *homo economicus* if they want to succeed.[25] This raises the question of whether governmentality could have similar impacts if used to create a "good citizen" and diminish violence in society.

Historians of Germany are more comfortable with the concept of social engineering or social rationalization than with the concept of governmentality. Although educational strivings "from above" are old phenomena, the concept of social engineering, developed in the context of Fordism, crucially belongs to the 1920s. New organizational processes of work and production forced employees into the dictatorial rule of the machine and the principles of rationalization. As with Darwinism, Fordism was transferred into other areas of society and labeled variously as social rationalization (*Sozialrationalisierung*), social Fordism (*Sozialfordismus*), social planning, and social engineering. Not only were the factories and companies adapted to the new principles step-by-step but modern architects were fascinated by the possibilities of social engineering in terms of the residents who had moved into their new housing estates. New Living (*Neues Wohnen*) encompassed rationalized and disciplined behavior achieved by regulations, "good advice," and exhibitions, as well as by "silent" educators in the form of highly rationalized and functional floor plans and by people's education of themselves and of each other. The idea of a rationalized conduct of living (*Lebensführung*) was derived from the idea of forming the society in the spirit of social reform. It was also based on the ideal of the emancipation of human beings and on the principles of the Enlightenment. To be sure, all these concerns had forerunners before 1914, so that Fordism, for instance, was foreshadowed by Taylorism. In the period before the war, the *Werkbund* was, for instance, eager to make private space a national space and to nationalize taste in everyday life through education, as Jennifer Jenkins writes in her chapter. It was education in the spirit of an opposition against historicism and in favor of nationalism, modernity, and socially rationalized citizenship in the private sphere.[26] Similar ideals can be found in city planning, especially after World War I, and were eventually incorporated in the Athens Charta of 1933.

Examples of social engineering can be found in other areas, such as population policy (*Bevölkerungspolitik*), eugenics, and health care. In these important areas of modernity, social engineering depended on the crucial role of the sciences quite in the way that Foucault and others have suggested. Scientific progress in the humanities—such as hygiene, health care, and medicine—led to the idea of planning in all aspects of society. The core question in this context is whether "race purification" and eventually the Holocaust also should be considered in the context of modern social planning, as Zygmunt Baumann and others have argued.[27] Baumann emphasized the Janus face, or the ambiguity, of modernity and interpreted radical racism and the Holocaust not as typical features of premodernity but as components of modernity: its darkest side.

It would be problematic, however, if we were only to take the darkest side of social planning and social engineering into consideration. Social engineering as a concept of modernity fits into various political-cultural systems and can serve different goals. This makes it attractive to historians of the German twentieth century, because the country faced five different political systems. Thus, as Geoff Eley highlights, research on the history of social engineering provides an opportunity for a long-term view of twentieth-century German societies as well as of the peculiarities of each political system and society.

The assumption of the total success of social engineering has often been expressed as a critical objection to Foucault's thinking in total dimensions. We must take into consideration that people select the components they want by appropriating them and giving them a meaning of their own.[28] Certainly, in Foucault's view, such patterns of behavior fit exactly into the concept of governmentality and are only superficially seen as acts of individual freedom of self-decision.

These divergences cannot be brought together. However, there are some arguments that in any case are important for empirical research. Social engineering has never been unidirectional in its effects but has been carried through by a multiplicity of agencies.[29] Even social engineering itself has had various goals and means. Thus, there have always been strongly contested areas of divergent influences in state and society, even when considered in the context of cultural hegemony.[30] For example, population scientists in Weimar Germany demanded three- to four-children families in order to regenerate the German population, while architects and housing reformers wanted only one- to two-children families because of the small apartments. Another example of an area contested because of the actors' different goals is the conflict between the ideal of effectiveness, which was an integral part of *social engineering* and was ideally directed by authorities, and the ideal of a lively democracy, which was held by nonstate institutions and associations.[31] The latter ideal is not effective or time- and energy-saving in the sense of social engineering[32] but is considered crucial to the exercise of democratic procedure through learning, discussing, and finding compromises.

Another kind of "proof" of the limits of social engineering is that sometimes it took a long time before people adopted certain values.[33] A good example of such a long-term process is the value of cleanliness. Although popularized before and during the interwar period by references to new knowledge in medicine, health, and hygiene, real progress in cleanliness occurred slowly, with the greatest advances only coming during the 1960s, in tandem with the rise of consumer society and technological progress. The *Werkbund*, as another example, had educated people throughout the twentieth century but could not convince all strata of the population.[34] To be sure, the complexity and selectivity of people's appropriation (*Aneignung*) always can be integrated into the concept of governmentality, but it does not completely mirror people's hybrid patterns of behavior, including their capabilities for cultural resistance. An "appropriate" *habitus* might be seen as a precondition of "good citizenship,"[35] but the question arises again of whether a *habitus* of "good citizenship" can be developed and, if it can be developed, how that could be done.

In trying to answer this question, we must recall the ambiguity of the concept of social engineering, which cannot be eliminated even if its agents have "good goals" in mind. That is not only a theoretical answer, but also an interpretation of practical work: Hodgson speaks of a "manufactured civil society" when looking at the multiagency working of a British project called Sure Start, which was designed to help young children in deprived areas. Although the program was couched in liberal language, the agents' educational practices were committed to norms set by the state.[36] The author concludes: "The evidence from this study suggest that manufactured civil society undermines social capital rather than encourages it."[37]

This critical view on a concrete project confirms the strong role of the state and the norms set "from above." Further, it indirectly leads to the necessity of differentiating education from social engineering. To be sure, the two are closely related in modern liberal societies. In Foucault's view, education, including "civic education," is always an integral part of governmentality and cannot be disassociated from it. However, differences remain. Education is a much more open concept than social engineering. It respects the value of the individual, does not want to manipulate him or her, and is (or at least should be) based on intensive interactions between the educator and the educated.

V. The Concept of Citizenship and the Concept of Civil Society

The concept of civil society, which received a new topicality following the emergence of the civil movements in the GDR and Eastern Europe before, during, and after 1989, has many features in common with the concept of citizenship.[38] Citizens as agents are the crucial components in the concept of civil society and vice versa: civil society is regarded as the desired result in the concept of citizenship. Furthermore, both concepts have similar difficulty in coping with their inherent normative dimensions. Power and interests, destructive or not, are to be regarded as the opposite of civil society and of citizenship, as well as being integral components of citizens' activities and civil societies. Despite this importance of power, both concepts are also predicated on ideals such as the civility of deeds oriented toward the values of tolerance and peace, the acceptance of difference, and the refusal of violence, as well as participation in rational public communication processes.

At the same time, of course, there are differences between the two concepts. Although the concept of civil society derives more from a view of society as a whole, the concept of citizenship focuses more on individuals as agents and their links to state and society and vice versa.[39]

To be sure, there are many definitions of what civil society is or should be. One definition concentrates on spheres and their interconnectedness. The assumption is that there is an intermediary area between the state, the private sphere, and the economy. Although these areas are strongly interrelated and although the intermediary area is infiltrated by power and interests, the intermediary area is considered to be (or should be) a sector of non-profit-oriented voluntary activities and self organizations, as well as rational communication processes (in the sense of Habermas). This is the area where active citizens can act.[40] Although researchers on civil society are also committed to the study of agents, their intensive focus on these spheres and the relations among them is central to the concept of civil society.

Studies of civil society also take into consideration the market economy as the third public sphere. According to Anthony Giddens, only a balance between these three areas could create a well-organized society. In his idea of balance, "good citizens" and citizens' commitment to *Gemeinwohl* tasks are regarded as essential counterparts to the *homo economicus* in the economic sphere. Moreover, companies should be convinced of the necessity of *corporate citizenship*, which could bridge the differences between the economic sphere and the sphere of citizenship.[41]

Some other differences between the two concepts of citizenship and civil society concern views of the role of the state. The nation-state is placed on the negative side or even neglected in many studies of civil society. In comparison, it receives more attention in an analysis of citizenship. The state is seen as responsible for the right of citizens to act and therefore plays a crucial role as the center of policy, legislation, and administration. According to the ideal of citizenship, governments are supposed to strive to extend the empowerment and participation of nongovernmental organizations in order to give the merely representative parliamentary democracy an underpinning. These associations and institutions, regarded as an ideal-typical category, "tend to be nonviolent, self-organizing, self-reflexive, and permanently in tension with each other and with the state institutions that 'frame,' constrict and enable their activities."[42]

A brief look at the German state in modern history shows that it has been characterized by its excessive and authoritarian bureaucracy and its strong power, buttressed by theories in which the state was seen as acting beyond the partial interests of social groups. The powerful German state sustained a political culture an integral part of which was people's devotion to the state. This peculiarity of German modern history permeated people's mental maps and diminished their chances of developing a mentality of self-confidence. Looking at the modest national resistance against the Nazi regime, one recognizes the great mental difficulties resistance fighters faced in attempting to disassociate themselves from their traditional loyalty and obligations toward the state. To be sure, some phenomena in German societies did work to counter the fixation on the state, such as the cohesive social milieus of workers, Catholics, liberals, and national conservatives of the early and middle twentieth century. These milieus were communities in which citizenship could be cultivated, although they were often hierarchically ordered, gendered, or contested by other groups. Even if they were, in general, primarily related to different worldviews (*Welt-*

anschauungen) and embedded in daily life experiences, milieu-oriented citizenship could be combined with state orientation. Furthermore, the social milieus showed their inner divisions and limits as early as the 1920s, evoked above all by mass culture and the new self-discovery of young people's and women's interests (the so-called New Woman). The rapid erosion of social milieus continued during the Third Reich under the impact of the racist policy of *Volksgemeinschaft*. They experienced a partial and temporary reconsolidation in the 1950s despite the settlement of new citizens (*Neubürger*), that is, the German refugees and the *Vertriebene* (expellees) from former parts of East Germany. The great break only came in the 1960s and the 1970s, when the transformation of individual mental maps accelerated. This was due in part to the social movements of that time, but also to more fundamental processes of individualization and community building in postmodern society. These processes were triggered simultaneously by a loss of state power due to new fiscal spending limits, the transnational Europeanization of decision making, and the expanding power of globalized companies. Nowadays, this new constellation not only offers the chance of an extension of civility but also contains hidden dangers of depolitization and economization of all societal areas as well as the development of egocentric lifestyles.

The genesis of the concepts of citizenship and civil society has been strongly related to communitarian concepts, whose protagonists pursue the idea that the state, the society, the "social," and the welfare state must be transformed in favor of smaller communities.[43] Only such a transformation could expand people's participation and encourage their best use of their chances in life. Restrictions in the areas of welfare rights and social citizenship are partly tolerated or even welcomed when weighing pros and cons. Individuals' isolation could be diminished by self-aware communities situated between the state and the individual.[44] Dangers arise, however, if communities are conceptualized as socially and culturally homogeneous. This is particularly true with respect to German history and the continuous strands of thinking about culturally homogeneous unities expressed in different ideas of *Gemeinschaften* (German *Wesensart*, regional *Landschaft/Stamm* or unity, idea of "German" *Volksgemeinschaft*). The longing for homogeneity and harmony in a "true" *Volksgemeinschaft* was widespread in the Weimar democracy of the 1920s. At that time, people were critical of democracy with its party feuds (the so-called *Parteienhader*), often contrasting it with an idealized unity experienced at home (*Heimatfront*) and in battle

(*Fronterlebnis*) during World War I.[45] *Parteienhader* was used as a negative catchword in different political settings, but at the end of the Weimar Republic it became more and more a catchword for the desired German *Volk* community. This concept tended to exclude Jews, although many of them were state citizens.[46] These trends toward a policy of inclusion and exclusion of citizens would be exploited by the Nazis for their radically racialist purposes.

VI. Norms of the Concept and Historical Research: Final Remarks

As already mentioned, normative aspects cannot be disassociated from the idea of citizenship and of a society based on active citizens. Although every concept is loaded with overt or hidden norms, the concept of citizenship faces the problem that, at first glance, the term *citizen* is not neutral but has a positive meaning.[47] The normative features of the concept of citizenship, related to the basic principles of the Enlightenment, should not, however, make historians uninterested in discovering the many citizens who did not fit into these normative values. Power, force, interests, and even destructive motives have belonged to the real world of citizenship, and it would be illusionary to imagine that these kinds of attributes could ever be eliminated. It would, however, also be naive to differentiate only between "good" and "bad" citizens. Instead, the presupposition for historical accounts of citizenship should be a view in which citizens have a *habitus* that leads to often inconsistent activities characterized by a broad variety of qualities that can be investigated.

Even active membership in a nonstate association does not mean that one contributes to the value of civility. Belonging to an association or a nonstate community does not signify a life lived according to the normative values of "good citizenship." On the contrary, as the history of 1920s Germany shows, many associations accepted or even glorified violence against the "other." The civic activities of right-wing individuals and Nazis endeavoring to destroy the Weimar Republic and the many attempts to motivate people in the spirit of the *Volksgemeinschaft* and racism during the Nazi period[48] demonstrate the analytic insight that the concept of citizenship has a double face: it is both a concept for normative positive values and a concept for investigating the "other" realities. Grassroots activities and "decentered citizenship" on diverse levels and in a variety of contexts[49] are to be regarded not as a guarantee but only as the potential of creating a citizen who corresponds to the positively normative values of civil society and renewed democracy.

When these and other problems are given enough attention, the concept of citizenship can genuinely emphasize new aspects, and it can draw new connections between separate phenomena. The concept of citizenship connects history and politics and can even structure the narratives of German modern history in a new way. All these chances, however, are bounded by the limitlessness of what may be called *citizen* and *citizenship*, as is expressed by the metaphor of the five spinning tops.

CHAPTER 13

Reflections on the Vocabulary of Citizenship in Twentieth-Century Germany

KATHLEEN CANNING

I. Citizenship vs. National Identity in Modern German History

The relationship between citizenship and national identity is character-ized by a fundamental ambivalence, one reflected in the papers for this volume and in the historiography of twentieth-century Germany more broadly. The *and* between citizenship and national identity suggests a certain reliance of the two concepts upon one another. In some of the contributions to this volume, for example, citizenship and national identity are used almost interchangeably to designate the kind of na-tional belonging encompassed in the German term *Staatsangehörigkeit*. Although *Staatsangehörigkeit* and *Staatsbürgerschaft* often stand in for one another, it is worthwhile to distinguish them: *Staatsangehörigkeit* usually encompasses the legal assignment of national belonging and the accompanying identities, entitlements, and obligations (passport, right to state protection, military service) that distinguish members of one nation from those of another; *Staatsbürgerschaft*, by contrast, signi-fies a political status *within* nations based on differential bundles of rights and duties ascribed to distinct categories of citizens. Although it is true that both of these terms are routinely translated into English as *citizenship*, the catalogs of participatory rights and claims that the En-glish term *citizenship* usually denotes are not central to either.

The presumption that national identity and/or belonging constitutes the real or most meaningful German citizenship has its correlate in a fundamental skepticism about the relevance of participatory citizenship for much of Germany's twentieth century. For one, Germans did not become citizens in the full sense of possessing civil, political, and social rights until the twentieth century was well underway—1919. Not long thereafter, the Nazis dismantled the democracy that gave rise to these rights and launched a violent assault on the civil and political rights, first and foremost of German Jews, but also on those of significant segments of the German populace. As I have argued elsewhere, in modern German history citizenship has served as an uncontroversial analytic only for the history of post-1945 West Germany;[1] Jan Palmowski's chapter elaborates its complex place in the very recent history of the German Democratic Republic.

The fact that *nation* and *national identity* serve as a kind of default mode for understandings of German citizenship is in part a legacy of the German *Sonderweg*, which indisputably privileged nation and state over citizenry and civil society. Against this standpoint, Geoff Eley has elaborated the "complex interpenetration of the two ideas—nation and citizenry—in the political languages of the nineteenth century." In his view, the German nation was conceived from its outset "simultaneously as a political community of citizens."[2] Although a certain interpenetration of nation and citizenry may aptly describe the new German nation-state in its founding phase, it is less clear that this ideal was ever realized on the ground of everyday politics or that it could be sustained through the ruptures and fractures of both nation and state during Germany's turbulent twentieth century.

During the last decade, new interdisciplinary studies of citizenship have significantly widened the terrain of citizenship studies, critiquing and transcending both modernizationist paradigms advanced, for instance, by T. H. Marshall, and binary models pioneered by Rogers Brubaker. New scholarship on social groups that do not fit easily into either of these models—women, minorities, immigrants, and colonized peoples—has prompted rethinking of both facets of citizenship and has helped to sharpen the distinction between them.[3] Although most of this work has taken place in the fields of cultural studies, American studies, and feminist and gender studies—that is, at a considerable distance from German history—these new interventions have informed recent critical engagements with histories of German citizenships, including some of the contributions to this volume.[4] The introduction of these perspectives, however, expands the study of citizenship considerably beyond the nation-state to local publics and social protests, to the spheres of consumption and self-representation, and the formation of individual and collective subjectivities.

One significant impetus of this volume is to unshackle citizenship from its fixed location in law and the practices of the German state, emphasizing instead its contingent construction and contested practices at various points in Germany's twentieth century. For one, this approach enables a critical engagement with the terms of national belonging (*Staatsangehörigkeit*) as defined by Brubaker. At the same time, it unlocks new arenas of participatory citizenship—some directly relating to the nation-state, and others well beyond its reach, where those lacking full or formal citizenship rights articulated claims, engaged in contest, or made their own meanings of citizenship. Hence one imperative outcome of this collection of articles is sharpening the analytical distinction between the different kinds of belonging that tend to blur and blend together in the term *citizenship*. Instead of allowing citizenship to stand in for either or both national belonging/identity and participatory citizenship, the relationship between these two facets of German citizenship should be explored as variable across historical time and space, as distinct political identities and articulations in some instances, and as overlapping or cohering with one another at other moments. Discarding the presumption that German citizenship was always primarily expressed in terms of national belonging/identity opens the way for more serious consideration of non-national identifications, of participatory claims or oppositional politics as articulations of citizenship.

Detaching citizenship from a deterministic relationship to state or nation remains controversial among German historians. The standpoint that citizenship is a meaningless category without the state or that there is no space for citizenship beyond "the nation" or "national identity" still finds considerable resonance among historians of modern Germany, including some of the participants at the conference in which the contributions to this book were first presented.[5] Adelheid von Saldern's examination of citizenship in twentieth-century Germany offers an important corrective here, underscoring the powerful citizenship identities that were located in regional cultures, both provincial and urban. Not only did these regional cultures create distinct sites of everyday citizenship experiences but they also took shape at a considerable distance from the national state.[6] Other articles in this volume take the notion of citizenship into even more explicitly cultural arenas further removed from the state, national or local. The chapters by Toby

Thacker and Jennifer Jenkins, for example, analyze the cultural objects, traditions, or practices that forged affinities and identifications of individuals or collectivities with the nation. The introduction of culture into the study of modern German citizenships represents a significant expansion and redefinition of this term, widening its scope from legal prescriptions and practices to the cultural milieus in which meanings and affinities were negotiated. Yet at the same time, the explorations of "cultural citizenship" featured in this volume tend to posit the nation, rather than the civic polity, as forming the primary site of belonging and identification in modern Germany. The pronounced association of culture with nation in these essays (and in modern German history more broadly) means that the cultural dimensions of participatory politics remain largely unexplored here.

The emphasis on citizenship as contingent or "under construction," as situated not only in politics but also in culture, widens the scope of citizenship considerably, rendering it both a more pliable analytic and more dynamic object of historical study.[7] Attention to the disparate dimensions and articulations of citizenship should not produce a notion of citizenship that is wholly indeterminate, but rather identify its historically specific meanings and manifestations. My own research on the debates and contests that produced the legal categories of citizenship in the Weimar constitution, its resonances in local politics, press, and public sphere, its politicization of spheres well beyond parliament or political parties, such as consumption, mass culture, or reproductive politics, seeks to illuminate this process of construction for the early years of the Weimar Republic.[8] Hence a second crucial imperative that emerges for me from this book is to delineate recognizable parameters for citizenship, both conceptual and historical, and to situate citizenship analytically in relation to terms such as *civil society* or *public sphere* upon which it impinges or depends. These parameters might be defined in a number of different ways, as the chapters here suggest. So, for example, the languages or rhetorics of *Staatsbürgerschaft* among historical actors might be examined and their referents distinguished (territorial nation or state, civic polity or public sphere). Peter C. Caldwell suggests, too, that the notions of citizen or citizenship that historians postulate are "bound up with the challenges of citizenship at that time."[9] Citizenship could be further specified as a discursive (legal) postulate or as a realm of experience, a habitus, or subject position; as an assigned (inhabited) status or as a (lived) practice. It could be explored as a tool of governmentality or as a space of resistance; as shaped by traditions and past practices or as arising from a new state–society constellation/ revolution/rupture; as situated in either civil society or the state or as defining the space they mutually constitute. Adelheid von Saldern proposes a reciprocal view of citizenship and civil society in which citizens "as agents are the crucial components in the concept of civil society" while "civil society is regarded as the desired result in the concept of citizenship."[10] Rather than a comprehensive paradigm or model of citizenship, the ensemble of case studies featured here offers historically specific insights into the distinct temporal, spatial, and discursive locations and manifestations of citizenship and national belonging. They also trace the lines of connection between the institutional and legal prescriptions of citizenship that "defined the terms for political action"[11] and those individual and collective subjectivities that congealed around claims of citizenship and national belonging in late nineteenth- and twentieth-century Germany.

II. National Belonging/Identification as Citizenship

Although not all sites or forms of modern German citizenship are encompassed within the nation-state, it remains a crucially important framework for historical exploration of citizenship, as the chapters by Dieter Gosewinkel, Geoff Eley, and Annemarie Sammartino show. Approaching nations as "epoch-specific constructions," as Gosewinkel suggests, illuminates the fluidity and volatility of the relationship between nations and states. What Eley describes as the "radical indeterminacy" of Germany as a territorial and political unit meant that citizenship itself was defined and recast in the interplay between nation and state. Both Sammartino and Gosewinkel suggest that a decoupling of nation and state, of national belonging and citizenship, took place in the aftermath of the German defeat, the revolutions of 1918–19, and the drafting of the Allied peace terms. Challenging Brubaker's premise that nations are comprised of "particular bounded citizenries," these case studies point instead to the mutability of the boundaries of national inclusion and exclusion both in the realms of law and in everyday practices.

The essays by Eley, Gosewinkel, and Sammartino offer pointed criticism of the stark polarity that Rogers Brubaker posits between a state-centered, assimilationist citizenship in France and a restrictive, differentialist citizenship informed by ethnocultural understandings of nation in Germany. Contending that "ethnocultural *as well as* nation-state elements existed side by side" in the citizenship laws of both countries from the early nineteenth century on, Dieter Gosewinkel analyzes the particular demographic and socioeconomic conditions that led to the embrace of disparate cultural idioms—*ius soli* in France and *ius sanguinis* in Germany. The contingencies of French borderland politics, industrial development, and fears of depopulation in the last third of the nineteenth century, rather than a republican principle of citizenship, fostered the assimilationist citizenship law of 1889. Despite its adherence to the principle of *ius soli*, Gosewinkel notes, this law remained ethnically coded in its exclusion of indigenous Muslims in the French colony of Algeria.[12] Rejecting the notion that citizenship in the modern German nation-state was informed by the "prestate concept of the people (*Volk*)" formed during the wars against Napoleon, Gosewinkel explores the process by which German citizenship became "nationalized" in response to an array of political, social, and economic transformations—from the mobilizations of Polish nationalist movements on its borders in the 1860s to the population shifts and waves of immigration that fueled Germany's rapid industrial growth in the Wilhelmine period.

Gosewinkel considers not only the "differing sets of demographic, economic, and nationality policy conditions" in the two nations, but also contends that their respective ideals and practices of citizenship were formulated in direct relation to one another, indeed, in competition with one another, particularly after 1870.[13] Jan Palmowski's study of the semantics of socialist citizenship in the former German Democratic Republic offers an intriguing parallel, for the distinctive conception of the *Bürger der DDR* was deeply inflected by the terms of West German citizenship, including its refusal of all references to nationality.[14] These case studies further undermine the notion of a nationally bounded citizenship and suggest rather that citizenship took shape not only amidst the shifting relations between nation and state but also in the interstices of transnational relations among and between nation-states (or between imperial states and their colonies).

A crucial turning point in the nationalization of citizenship in Germany was indisputably the passage of its 1913 citizenship law, which definitively rejected the territorial principle of *Staatsangehörigkeit*, a decision that, in Gosewinkel's view, represented the culmination of the preceding decades of nationalization rather than the reversion to a preexisting "ethnocultural" model of citizenship.[15] Eley also situates the origins of the 1913 law in the "immediate Wilhelmine context rather than deeper in the nineteenth century." Recent historiography on the pre-1914 era, he notes, has cast "severe doubt on the dominance, pervasiveness, and cohesiveness of the 'ethnocultural' idiom."[16] Despite the narrow *juridical* terms of citizenship, Eley argues, the late Wilhelmine period was one in which "ever more Germans made themselves into citizens by actively claiming a place in the nation."[17]

At stake in the debates about the 1913 citizenship law is not only its fulfillment of the ethnocultural idiom of citizenship but also Brubaker's focus on the place of this law on a continuum of restrictive citizenship that culminated in the Nazi racial state. If the 1913 law was the outcome of the *nationalization* of citizenship, a process of *"ethnicization"* was initiated, in Gosewinkel's view, by "the separation [from the nation] of large territories with former German citizens" after World War I.[18] Eley argues in a similar vein that the Nazis enforced "immeasurably more radical" ethnocultural boundaries than those encompassed in the 1913 law. For Gosewinkel, the Nuremberg Laws of 1935, which racialized citizenship by fundamentally redefining notions of descent, mark the decisive rupture in the history of German citizenship.[19]

Annemarie Sammartino also provides intriguing evidence of the discontinuities and disruptions in both the laws and practices of German citizenship from 1913 through the late Weimar Republic. In the aftermath of World War I, she suggests, the "ethnic guidelines established by the 1913 law" proved scarcely enforceable as Germany's borders contracted and it confronted an unprecedented influx of refugees from its former borderlands and the Russian Empire. Whereas Gosewinkel perceives this crisis as formative of an ethnic conception of citizenship that became "an instrument of a revisionist policy," Sammartino points to the marked disparities and contradictions in the practices of citizenship between and among different levels and agencies of state.[20] Although citizenship policy, she argues, ideally sought to limit citizenship "to those who had proven their German identity," her study makes clear that the task of determining the boundaries of German identity was a daunting one in the aftermath of World War I.[21] Instead, citizenship policy itself came to represent one ideological and bureaucratic site at which Germans confronted the task of remaking state and society amidst the shifts of borders, populations, and politics. The porosity of citizenship resulted, in Sammartino's analysis, from the state's very inability to enforce its boundaries: it could neither deport all of those who "did not belong," nor could it refuse provision of certain social citizenship rights and benefits to noncitizens, particularly as the

Weimar welfare state expanded its reach in the early 1920s. Rather than upholding a singular, coherent "ethnocultural principle," the practices of citizenship in early Weimar Germany were divergent and contradictory, pitting the "principles of cultural assimilation against those of ethnic determinism" in the ascription or denial of citizenship rights to Jewish or Eastern European émigrés and refugees. Rather than unleashing a process of progressive ethnicization, citizenship policy during the postwar crisis of both federal and state governments during the 1920s was sufficiently heterogeneous as to allow consideration of a foreign applicant's "public utility" in the absence of "German descent." Sammartino thus offers an insightful corrective of the trajectory of German citizenships from 1913 to the Nazi period, making clear that contests continued throughout the Weimar Republic between "a cultural and an ethnic definition of the German nation."

Certainly these articles offer important correctives, not only of Brubaker's specific citizenship paradigm, but also of the residues of *Sonderweg* that left many presumptions in place regarding the power of nation-states and their laws to bound citizenries. These articles reveal the specific contexts and contests in which one aspect of citizenship— *Staatsangehörigkeit*—took shape, both rendering it "under construction" throughout the period under study and making clear that it was shaped as much by ruptures and disjunctures as by traditions and continuities. The concern of most of the articles discussed thus far has been politics, law, and the practices of states and bureaucracies. The articles by Jennifer Jenkins and Toby Thacker analyze the cultural terms of national belonging, the realms of culture in which Germans designated and recognized themselves as citizens.

In the case of Jenkins's study of private space as formative of national publics and citizenship before World War I, the state recedes as the mediator of citizenship. Instead, Jenkins focuses on attempts to foster national belonging through the production of a new national aesthetics, oriented not toward the public culture of monuments, museums, and national symbolics but to the interior spaces of private homes. The modern design culture promoted by the *Werkbund*, for example, aimed to disseminate new standards of taste, style, and techniques for fashioning interior spaces that could serve as "casings" of national culture, thereby innovatively linking production, consumption, and aesthetic display in the "nationalization and modernization of German society." The goal of the *Werkbund*'s nationalist aesthetic pedagogy was to "infuse the objects, space, and time of everyday life with the monumentality of national feeling."[22] In Jenkins's analysis, the term *citizenship* appears to denote the positioning of family and self in a visualized and spatialized landscape of nation, in webs of emotional, subjective attachments to the nation.

The *Bürger unserer Zeit* to whom taste manuals and other projects of nationalist pedagogy were directed formed a community and social identity of citizens that were most likely class-specific and localized, despite the recurrent referent of nation. Jenkins expands the concept of citizenship to encompass not only the interior domestic spaces, where the display of cultural goods gained the capacity to symbolize and unify the nation, but also a new subject position of *Bürgerlichkeit*, circumscribed by national aesthetic standards but lived and practiced in local and class-specific terms. This subject position was formed at the crossroads of national pedagogical projects that took up an available rhetoric of *Bürger* and *Bürgerlichkeit* without intersecting with the juridical or political arenas of citizenship in Imperial Germany. Yet this variation of "cultural citizenship" also involved a refiguring of the politics of production, consumption, and aesthetics.

Toby Thacker's analysis of music as a foundation for national belonging and identification in Germany offers an interesting parallel to Jenkins's exploration of *Wohnkultur*: both cases involve pedagogical projects that instill national belonging and aesthetic projects that project or perform national belonging for specific publics. Although the *Werkbund* activists may have sought to establish German superiority in the realm of tasteful consumption and display of everyday goods, the presumption of German musical superiority is precisely why music could serve to foster or deepen ties of national identification or belonging. Read against the postwar ruptures in both the policies and practices of citizenship analyzed by Sammartino, it is easier to comprehend why German musical superiority "was articulated with a more frenzied urgency . . . after the perceived disaster of the Treaty of Versailles."[23] The recurrence of musical superiority, Thacker suggests, appeared to stabilize a sense of Germanness at the moments of its greatest indeterminacy (1918–19, 1945–49). Although, as Jan Palmowski demonstrates, the German Democratic Republic eschewed or effaced all references to nationality in its postulation of citizenship, we might conclude that its embrace of new arenas of sociability centered around music relied upon and reinvigorated a sense not only of nationality but of national superiority.

III. Citizenship between Governmentality and Agency

In this section, I will take up the task of locating and distinguishing participatory citizenships along a continuum stretching from state to civil society, while at the same time heeding Geoff Eley's call to assess the "complex intermeshing" of the two logics—governmentality and individual/collective agency—that shaped citizenship in twentieth-century Germany. The term *participatory citizenship* is meant to distinguish objective and subjective belonging to a nation or state from (1) those realms of citizenship that define or enforce the terms of participation in politics, society, or culture—the state in the guise of law, administration, welfare, military, police, and/or the ideologies, norms, or practices outside of the realm of state, such as those of natural or social science that coalesced to produce biopolitics; and (2) the citizen's subjective sense of possessing rights, entitlements, and duties within a state as well as the capacity of citizens and those with merely partial or incomplete citizenship to stake claims that widen or alter the terms or meanings of *citizenship*. These categories emerge from my own historical research, but they also address the differentiations Peter C. Caldwell posits in his chapter between "the objective set of rights that accrue to a citizen within a state" and "the citizen's subjective sense of which rights he or she is entitled to within the state." His distinction suggests that participatory citizenship takes shape in this subjective realm.[24]

These arenas broadly align around the concepts of governmentality and agency. Between them are many possible sites of citizenship on the long trajectory from (national or local) agencies of state to citizens as individual or collective subjects—public sphere and political parties, parliaments and courts, social reform and social welfare, consumption and popular culture, to name a few. This approach takes the juridical and ideological framings of citizenship seriously, while explicitly opening the study of citizenship to sites and spaces along this trajectory. I also intentionally leave the causal relationship between governmentality and the agency/subjectivities/self-fashioning of citizens open and subject to the kind of historically specific investigation offered by the chapters in this volume.

If we take governmentality as the starting point of this discussion of participatory citizenship, the articles by Peter C. Caldwell, Pascal Grosse, Thomas Lindenberger, Jan Palmowski, Cornelie Usborne, and S. Jonathan Wiesen each analyze a different form or aspect of governmentality in twentieth-century Germany. While Lindenberger and Palmowski in-

vestigate citizens' confrontations and communications with authoritarian states under conditions of relative stability—workers' protests and
police violence in Lindenberger's study, citizens' petitions (*Eingaben*) on
everyday affairs in the Socialist GDR in Palmowski's case—Caldwell
explicates the competing definitions of citizenship that emerged from
a dissolution of governmentality in 1918 that required the reassembly
of both nation and state in its aftermath. Usborne explores the mobilization of newly named female citizens against the intensifying incur-
sions of the state into matters of birth control, abortion, and sexuality, a
realm of governmentality that increasingly defined the terms of female
citizenship in Weimar Germany in the course of the 1920s. The realm of
governmentality Pascal Grosse examines is one removed from particular states but constituted by the intricate links between biological and
political-legal theory that made citizenship the core of a larger biopolitical framework in the post-Enlightenment West.[25]

Grosse's analysis of the biological underpinnings of modern citizenship makes clear that the definition of its boundaries was never the
task of the nation-state alone. Rather, Grosse argues, "racial concepts
contested those political-legal notions of citizenship bound to the territorial nation-state, because *race* inherently has no correlate in entities
defined by territoriality handed down through history."[26] Instead, its
criteria involved the capacity for self-control over volition and emotions, for autonomy and competency, which were fundamental prereq-
uisites of citizenship. Grosse demonstrates that the "cerebralization" of
citizenship was "differentialist right from its outset," stratifying society
along racial, sexual, and class lines into groups that "had more or less
inherent right to exercise power over others."[27] Thus, the governmentality that Grosse is interested in is much more comprehensive than
any particular nation-state, yet it still has important German particu-
larities, including those of German colonialism and National Socialism.
Here Grosse refers to the history of German colonialism as "a decisive platform for probing new trajectories of biologically inspired citizenship policies" that the Nazis later realized through racialization.[28]
While Grosse probes the intriguing test cases of citizenship that arose
from colonial liaisons and mixed marriages, I might add that the coin-
cidences between German colonial expansion and the scientification of
the social arena at home framed the responses of state and elites to the
mass mobilization of new publics and their growing claims for participatory citizenship during the 1890s. Moreover, many of these publics
were constituted by those social groups whose biological capacity for

citizenship was now more scientifically questioned—politicized workers, radical and liberal women, immigrants, and colonial subjects.

If governmentality in Grosse's case is both more comprehensive and more diffuse than that projected by a singular nation-state, Jan Palmowski's study shows that even in the highly centralized state of the GDR the rules governing citizenship were often learned, tested out, and subverted in the "grassroots" arenas of local politics involving schools, workplaces, or town and village councils.[29] The lessons of citizenship in the GDR were instilled in the sphere of *Heimat* and "covered all aspects of the individual's free time," including the private, familial sphere. Thomas Lindenberger's comparison of citizenship and police violence in the *Kaiserreich* and the Federal Republic points to the ways that the rules of citizenship, spelled out textually in law, become inscribed in the bodies of citizens through their everyday—and often violent—encounters with the police as agents of the state.

In a somewhat different vein, S. Jonathan Wiesen approaches the marketplace of the Third Reich as a site of "ersatz citizenship," which became crucial to Nazi deployment of citizens in the project of consumption as national renewal. Here, too, citizenship was learned and practiced not according to the letter of formal citizenship laws, but through intermediary institutions that criss-crossed the spheres of family, marketplace, and state. In projecting the myth of consumers' free participation in "the Nazi marketplace," public relations experts both advanced their companies' profits and allowed customers to satisfy their own individual desires.[30] One conclusion we might draw from Wiesen's analysis is that the sphere of consumer fantasy constituted a site not only of "ersatz citizenship" but also of alternative governmentality. One key difference between Wiesen's case study and that of Lizabeth Cohen for the postwar United States is the wider context of citizenship.[31] In Cohen's case, consumption became the most decisive articulation of citizenship (in the sense of both identification and participation), but it was never its sole manifestation; nor did it substitute for the rights of political participation of which citizens were violently dispossessed.

These disparate logics of governmentality called up distinct "fronts of citizenship," each entailing different capacities for and articulations of agency.[32] A significant contribution of this volume is the insights it offers into the salience of participatory citizenship—until now a merely secondary guise of citizenship in the history of twentieth-century Germany. At the heart of Thomas Lindenberger's investigation are contests over public space and public order that informed everyday interactions between would-be citizens and the police in the *Kaiserreich*. The stakes of the contests he examines were not only citizens' rights to public assembly but the insistence of Prussian workers, still deprived of equal rights by the Prussian three-class suffrage, that they receive just and fair treatment—as citizens—at the hands of the police. Lindenberger probes the larger field of relations between the public and the police, examining specific instances of police violence. During both the *Kaiserreich* and the Federal Republic, this arena of contested citizenship was defined as much by the "bodily conduct" between state and citizens as by the prescriptions of law.[33] Yet the excesses of the Prussian police that led to "Biewald's chopped-off hand," Lindenberger argues, evoked in its Social Democratic opponents an intriguing "soldierly countersymbolism," a self-representation that "was determined to avoid images of violence and disorderliness at any price."[34]

If bodily contact was one means by which the state inflicted its power upon its citizens and subjects during the *Kaiserreich*, Lindenberger presents the case of journalist Oliver Ness's twisted foot to emphasize the shifting relations between citizens and the police in the Federal Republic of Germany. The intactness of the body, as a core part of the contemporary "culture of the self," he suggests, has become a premier right of citizenship in postindustrial societies. Despite the state's unquestioned monopoly on violence, citizens and would-be citizens sought to define their own rules of bodily engagement with the police as the most tangible face of the state for most citizens of the lower classes. Lindenberger's case studies thus suggest that the terms of citizenship are established mutually: by states that wield violence but are simultaneously compelled to consider the appearances of fairness and justice; and by citizens whose actions internalize, resist, or force revision of these standards. Crucial to the interplay between governmentality and agency here is the very publicness of the contests over the bounds of citizenship—from city squares to the bodies of individual citizens—and the necessity for both state and citizens to legitimate their relation in the sphere of the public.

Jan Palmowski explores similarly public fields of contention between state and citizens in the former German Democratic Republic, weighing the "practices of domination assumed by state and party" against the "everyday practices at the grassroots." The starting point of Palmowski's skillful probe of the meanings of citizenship for the history of the GDR is the linguistic designation of citizenship—the *Bürger der DDR* that invoked a new Socialist participatory citizenship while wholly circumventing "the vexed question of nationality" that defined the terms of West German citizenship from 1949 on.[35] The GDR in his rendering was a society in motion, a model of participatory citizenship, with over three million citizens actively assuming citizens' duties in the 1980s.[36] The culture of participation at the heart of GDR citizenship law was fostered by the identity it posited between state and citizens, which was exemplified in basic rights like codetermination (*Mitbestimmung*) and the right to petition the state on everyday matters through the submission of *Eingaben*.

An indisputably rare example of participatory citizenship, citizens' petitions represented a both formal and vital channel of communication between citizens and state in which the claims and expectations of both sides were continually exchanged and renegotiated. Although the willingness of citizens to submit *Eingaben* to the state attests to their basic trust in the state, Palmowski points out that the petitions also enhanced the capacity of party and state governmentality, feeding it with a steady stream of critical information about citizens' everyday lives. The citizens' petitions constitute one example of how participatory citizenship was lived in the former GDR, of how it came to saturate factories, schools, neighborhoods, and village councils, spilling into leisure time and private lives—where the culture of participation was to be anchored by emotional affinities with party and state.[37] Palmowski's case study of the western town of Eisenach, however, reveals the fissures and fractures in the purported identity of citizen and state in the GDR, which would lead eventually to the collapse of party and state in 1989. Although citizens of the GDR apparently accepted "the rules of Socialist citizenship," Palmowski argues, this acceptance failed to bring them "closer to the state." Instead, as the case of Eisenach illustrates, it strengthened the local community, emboldening its members "to demarcate themselves clearly against encroachments by the state."[38] Thus the Socialist ideal of citizenship "multiplied opportunities for, and expressions of, dissonance,"[39] a dissonance that arose, in Peter C. Caldwell's terms, from the citizens' own "sense of having rights, of being entitled to call upon the state to either act or not act in specific cases."[40] Palmowski's analysis of citizenship, along with that by Cornelie Usborne, views citizenship not as effecting social closure (as per Brubaker), but as encompassing the meanings citizens made of their status and the subject positions they adopted in this process.

The citizenship that Peter C. Caldwell examines was not merely "participatory," but actually came to define the larger project of reinventing state and nation in the aftermath of defeat, revolution, and the collapse of the *Kaiserreich* in 1918. If the state was to be remade "as a 'living construction from bottom to top,'" a new and different citizen was required, one who was much more than "the individual bearer of private and public rights" and was instead "fully involved in the collective work of the *Volk*."[41] Caldwell, like Sammartino, analyzes citizenship in a moment of prolonged rupture, when it was not only "under construction," but when competing notions of citizenship jockeyed to fill the unprecedented vacuum of political power created through defeat and revolution. The agency of citizenship at this juncture in German history encompassed the widespread embrace of citizens' rights "to shape their own polity"—in this case to overthrow "not just the monarch, but also the *Reichstag*," local governments, and in some areas the judiciary in the course of the revolutions of 1918–19.[42] Members of the revolutionary councils also sought to derive theory from the lessons of the revolution, postulating a radical redefinition of citizenship that harnessed civil and political rights to a thoroughly reconceived politics of production. Although the citizen was to play "a *direct, unmediated and active role* in self-government," the rights of citizenship were dependent upon and restricted by a citizen's location or relation to production. The restriction of full citizenship rights to "'workers of hand and head'" amounted to an attempt to ascribe citizenship rights along class lines.[43] This council vision of citizenship was radical in another sense as well—in its rejection of the constitutional doctrine of the separation of powers, and its concomitant refusal of a "clear distinction between public freedom through representation and private domination."[44]

That the founding of the republic did turn, for a time at least, around competing notions of citizenship is revealed in the efforts of the National Assembly—and key figures like Hugo Preuss—to distance itself from this radical conception of citizenship and then ultimately to depoliticize the role of the councils in the blueprint it drew up for the new republic.[45] Not only radical Socialists and liberal democrats but also corporatists and conservatives took up the "search for a substantive citizenship" during the republic's formative phase. Yet their conception of citizenship was one based on "identity, immediacy and homogeneity" that could constitute a vital "alternative to parliamentary democracy."[46] The democratic citizen, according to Schmitt, is "an *immediate part of a public, self-identical, homogeneous whole*: not a bourgeois, not a 'private man.'"[47] Despite the distinct political outcomes evoked by each of these visions of citizenship, Caldwell identifies the intriguing parallels between conservative and council conceptions of citizenship—

"the call for a strong, substantive notion of citizenship . . . against the mere formalism of parliamentarism and the rule of law, as well as the distrust of parties and special interests in a representative system."[48]

The radicalism and the affinity of these new visions of citizenship with one another narrowed the conceptual and political space in which citizenship could be reimagined in the early years of Weimar Germany. Although historians of modern Germany, with the exception of Caldwell himself, have scarcely analyzed the founding of Weimar in these terms, the fact that citizenship was not only theorized but also tested out in unprecedented and revolutionary practices lends it a crucial place in the founding of Weimar democracy (and, by implication, also in its subsequent struggle for survival).[49]

Cornelie Usborne's chapter examines the particular kinds of agency that the naming of new citizens in the Weimar Republic engendered. If Pascal Grosse's paper made clear that imperial German citizenship was shaped by the competition between the biological principles of sex and race and their ascription to the bodies and minds of potential citizens, Usborne highlights a different kind of embodiment of citizenship, fostered by the active participation of women themselves, who "placed the body female at the center of the body politic" during the late 1920s.[50] As female activists from competing political parties struggled to define a space of female autonomy on matters of reproduction, they both embraced and immediately sought to expand their rights as newly enfranchised citizens. Although Usborne claims that many women learned the lessons of citizenship in the hunger protests and on the strike lines during the war, she also suggests that they were radicalized by the transformations of their bodies—by their deteriorating health and the bodily costs of "the triple burden of waged labor, housework, and maternity."[51] Also crucial in Usborne's analysis were the prewar constellations of medical and social reformers, eugenicists and feminist activists, who brought "the politics of the body" into public view in their search for the causes of Germany's declining birth rate. The female body came into public view as a site of state intervention and potentially subversive citizenship when debates about a potential birth strike erupted among Social Democrats on the eve of the war. Feminist scholarship in the home front in World War I—the older works by Ute Daniel and Elisabeth Domansky, as well as the forthcoming dissertation by Lisa Todd—suggest that this process only intensified during the war, when the sexual behavior of war wives was actively scrutinized by military authorities.[52] Although the transformations of subjectivity at the heart of Usborne's argument are exceedingly difficult to document, Usborne musters compelling evidence that women gained not only rights in 1918–19 but also a new capacity to speak boldly for themselves about sex and sexual pleasure, birth control and abortion.

Usborne's analysis leaves little doubt that citizenship rights, deliberated across parties, organs of state, and civil society during the early Weimar republic, were explicitly gendered, embodied, and sexualized. The ideal of universality that had inflected republican citizenships in Europe since the French Revolution was effaced by the urgency of the postwar crisis and the widespread perception that women had earned the rights of citizenship through their active service, endurance of hardship, and sacrifice of male family members to the war. Here it is useful to distinguish the citizenship that was hastily decreed in November 1918 amidst the crisis of defeat and revolution from that which was deliberated and finally inscribed in the Weimar constitution of 1919. Significantly, none of the visions of citizenship bandied about in the National Assembly—whether radical, liberal, corporatist, or nationalist—made a pretense of universality. Rather, each approached the negotiations over citizenship as one site for the (re)articulation of norms and ideologies of gender that would realign the relations between the sexes and thereby resolve the postwar "gender crisis." The inscription of explicitly differentiated, embodied citizenship rights now assigned women a particular place in the founding of republican democracy and the rejuvenation of the nation. The deliberations of reproductive rights—albeit under the guise of "population politics"—in the National Assembly and first sessions of the newly elected Reichstag placed them at the crux of both citizenship and republican governmentality. Usborne's analysis of female activists' petitions and the appeals of "average women" to the Chancellor on matters of reproduction offers an intriguing parallel to Palmowski's study of *Eingaben* in the GDR. Both cases illustrate how citizens could both take the terms of citizenship seriously and yet form subjectivities that profoundly questioned and expanded its terms.

IV. Conclusions

One of the formidable achievements of this book is to have pried apart the distinct German citizenships, probing their disparate locations and manifestations, and detaching both national belonging and participatory citizenship from necessarily deterministic relationships with the nation-state. The case studies assembled here point to wider contexts of law, ideology, and power that conceived of rights in terms of capacities and affinities of citizenship that often transcended the bounds of any one national state. This book acknowledges the particularly German blurriness of the categories *national identity* and *citizenship*, while illustrating at the same time the importance of the distinction between them. This book enables the identification of different registers of citizenship—of national belonging and claims making—and also delivers ample evidence of the significance of a participatory citizenship that is not subsumed by national identity.

Rather than reviving or rewriting the dichotomies in which citizenship is too often cast, this volume considers citizenship across a continuum stretching from instances of governmentality and legal concepts that "define the terms for political action" on the one end to the positioning and self-fashioning of subjects in relation to these terms on the other.[53] Across such a continuum are many possible sites or constellations of citizenship: individual and collective, political and cultural, local, national or—given the importance of empire and postwar international relations—global. The disparate citizenships analyzed here are not arbitrarily exchangeable; they do not substitute easily or stand in for one another; nor are they necessarily parts of a more comprehensive whole. In offering thick and contextualized historical analysis that attaches space, place, time, and actors to citizenship laws, claims, contests, and practices, the case studies featured here render German citizenships contingent and variable, yet not indeterminate or arbitrary. Given these disparate sites and scenarios of citizenship in the history of Germany's twentieth century, is it possible to discern parameters for citizenship that are relevant for most cases? One is perhaps that citizenship is a *relational* category that generally involves the positioning of citizens and would-be citizens to one another within a polity, or between themselves and the relevant instances of governmentality. Specific research projects also necessitate their own parameters of citizenship—the (passive) status it prescribes or the (active) engagement it engenders; its location in polities versus nation-states; its dissemination through texts versus its materialization in the practices of public order (police, courts, border or immigration authorities); citizenship interiorized versus citizenship performed.

At the same time, these articles make clear that citizenship, once defined and disseminated, can generate meanings and claims well outside of its legal or political bounds. A number of contributions to this volume consider citizenship from the standpoint of subjectivity—the articles by Jan Palmowski, Peter C. Caldwell, and Cornelie Usborne do so implicitly, while Geoff Eley takes up this challenge explicitly. Eley notes that under certain historical circumstances, the citizenship that mattered most was that which "grew from the individual and collective efforts of citizens and would-be citizens themselves." This citizenship, he argues, may have been "only unevenly ratified in national politics or institutionalized in law" or even "disobeyed" its prescribed legal or political definitions.[54] Indeed, as the historical examples contained in this volume show, the spaces for contests or claims were sometimes created by the contradictions between different catalogs of citizenship—racial and sexual in the case of German colonialism, local and national in the case of the German Democratic Republic. Another such space arose during the early years of the Weimar Republic, when the ascription of new political rights to women stood in stark contrast to their de facto loss of the right to work and their continued subordination in the realm of "private" civil law governing marriage and family.[55] Citizenship can be precarious in other ways as well: the articles by Dieter Gosewinkel, Annemarie Sammartino, and Geoff Eley point to instances of war, revolution, or prolonged crisis when the German state was unable to sustain its own boundaries of citizenship. This precariousness created spaces for new subjectivities of citizenship, both individual and collective. Positing citizenship as subjectivity means considering how its rules and norms were internalized, subverted, expanded, and/or publicly performed under these historical circumstances.

Finally, this book examines not only disparate spaces and sites of citizenship, but also its temporal framing in the history of Germany's twentieth century. The recurrent "indeterminacy" of Germany, the moments when nation and state came apart—1918–20, 1933–45, 1945–49, 1989–90—means that twentieth-century German citizenship was continually "under construction," in Eley's words. In fact, modern German citizenship was marked more often by ruptures than continuities, by the need to reorder state and civil society at crucial junctures and to envision a future in the aftermath of the catastrophes of the two world wars. The most profound rupture in German citizenship took place under Nazi rule, when entire registers of citizenship were reduced to a new "state of belonging" based on racial privilege.[56] The transformation of national to racial belonging in the Third Reich, juxtaposed with the Nazis' erasure of the rights and duties of participatory citizenship, underscores the importance of the distinction between the two kinds of belonging encompassed in the vocabulary of citizenship.

CHAPTER 14

Some General Thoughts on Citizenship in Germany

GEOFF ELEY

CURRENT DISCUSSION OF CITIZENSHIP among German historians began with the publication of Rogers Brubaker's *Citizenship and Nationhood in France and Germany* in 1992, which proposed a striking contrast between definitions of citizenship in those two countries.[1] The difference consisted not just in the respective juridical contexts, Brubaker argued, but in the political and broader public discourse surrounding nationhood, which was itself rooted in deeper histories of national self-understanding and their associated cultural idioms. If in both countries citizenship was transmitted generationally, this was regulated by two opposing principles of ascription, *ius sanguinis* (citizenship by descent) and *ius soli* (citizenship by place of birth). In the French case, the addition of a strong element of territoriality became decisive, opening citizenship to all those born within France, irrespective of descent; in Germany, by contrast, this territorial element was missing, while qualification by blood descent extended freely to ethnic Germans born and residing elsewhere. At the time Brubaker was writing, this seemed to translate into contrasting national responses to the consequences of immigration—expansiveness in France, where second-generation immigrants enjoyed access to citizenship rights, but restrictiveness in Germany, where such rights remained barred to the substantial resident immigrant population. Thus, in the 1980s, on average fewer than 5,000 foreign residents acquired German citizenship per year, whereas in France the figure was over 53,000. Meanwhile, more than one million ethnic Germans arrived in Germany from Eastern Europe and the Soviet Union between 1988 and 1991 to claim their citizenship by right, however tenuous their connections to any actually existing German society.

Given the convergence of economic and national-state interests, the two countries' common history as members of the European Community (EC), and the powerful late-twentieth-century logics of transnational integration, Brubaker asked, how do we explain this difference? That question became topically urgent during the 1980s as a result of two countervailing developments, which until the collapse of Communism in 1989 very much preoccupied the thinking of North American social scientists interested in Western European studies. On the one hand, national sovereignty was becoming renegotiated via the radical strengthening of the EC scheduled for 1992; on the other hand, a resurgence of aggressive far-right nationalism in most Western European societies was targeting "foreigners" or resident "immigrants" as alien intruders deemed not to belong to the nation. Indeed, demands were made for changing the national legislation: in 1986–87 in France by attempting to restrict immigrants' access to citizenship, and in Germany via an encroaching recognition that such access might need to be improved, each of which initially failed. As Brubaker published his book, however, such xenophobia further escalated—whether in the form of the continuing support raised in France by Jean-Marie Le Pen's National Front or in the antiforeigner violence erupting in Germany after unification.

Brubaker's own strategy for answering his question was a deep comparison of the two national histories going back to the French Revolution. This encompassed older arguments from the literature on national state formation, focused on territoriality and institutional development, as well as factors of demographic, economic, and military interest. But still more important, he argued, such interests were "mediated—indeed constituted—by a certain way of thinking and talking about membership" in each of the respective nation-states.[2] In his view, "existing definitions of the citizenry—expansively combining *jus soli* and *jus sanguinis* in France, restrictively reflecting pure *jus sanguinis* in Germany—embody and express deeply rooted national self-understanding, more state-centered and assimilationist in France, more ethnoculturally in Germany."[3] He called these contrasting definitions "particular cultural idioms," which became "reinforced and activated in specific historical and institutional settings." Once constituted, moreover, "these cultural idioms framed and shaped judgments of what was politically imperative, of what was in the interest of the state."[4]

What was most salient in Brubaker's approach in retrospect was exactly this recourse to *cultural* explanation: that is, the desire to base an argument about the contrasting juridical grounds for French and German citizenship—a topic that traditionally might have been addressed by extremely dry legal-historical and constitutionally focused institutional and political histories, after all—in a deep-historical claim about divergent cultural formations separating the two national histories across a period of two centuries. Yet in building that argument, Brubaker's approach was singularly lacking in the kind of microhistorical density of evidence, context, and close readings that in the meantime we have come to expect from the best achievements of the new cultural history. While he began with an elegant conceptual discussion of "citizenship as social closure," combined with accomplished analytical surveys of the French revolutionary and early nineteenth-century contexts of citizenship definitions in the two countries, the burden of history in his account was actually carried by a thin succession of paired analyses: two juxtaposed chapters on the Third Republic and Wilhelmine Germany, ordered around the laws of 1889 and 1913; and a similar pair of chapters on the politics of citizenship roughly a century later, in the 1980s. This stripped-down minimalist quality of his approach to political history failed to penetrate the evidentiary and interpretive complexities so familiar to specialists. On the one hand, the cultural difference held to explain the political divergence—the contrasting idioms of *civic* as against *ethnocultural* identification—was attached in overabstracted and overgeneralized fashion to the trajectory of the respective whole societies. On the other hand, the "ethnocultural" principle of coherence taken to characterize the specifically German pattern was ultimately derived from its extreme realization in the racialized definition of belonging in the nation imposed by the Nazis after 1933.[5]

For German historians, Brubaker's book is also notable for how rapidly it became superseded.[6] Both of the major intervening works on the subject of German citizenship law, those by Andreas Fahrmeir and Dieter Gosewinkel, each inspired partly by the terms and influence of Brubaker's comparative thesis, have exposed the detailed empirical weaknesses and larger-scale interpretive flaws in his account.[7] But the staying power of Brubaker's work has also suffered from a more general shifting of perspective inside the modern German field. As it happens, *Citizenship and Nationhood* appeared just on the cusp of what has since become an emerging trend of German historiography, whose terms now allow us to revisit the meanings of the 1913 law from a quite different standpoint from the one still occupied fairly naturally by a comparative historical sociologist in the later 1980s. By seeking to recontextualize our understanding of German modernities in a revised vision of the longer course of the nineteenth and twentieth centuries, this new work calls into question established readings of particular moments and motifs inside that overall time span. The impetus for this endeavor has two main sources. One comes from our lengthening distance on the mid-twentieth-century catastrophe of Nazism, which did so much to constrain and skew approaches to earlier periods of the German past. The other is the proximate reflection of the demise of the *Sonderweg* thesis, which for a long time formed the strongest interpretive framework for approaching Germany's supposed differences from "the West," that synthetic geohistorical and ideological construct that of course always included a particular image of France.

Thus during the 1990s, after the appearance of Brubaker's book, a series of works began reappraising facets of the pre-1914 era that previously had been coopted all too easily into linear arguments about continuity that emphasized the deep-seated "illiberalism" and proto-Nazi proclivities in German culture. Cumulatively, these works cast severe doubt on the dominance, pervasiveness, and cohesiveness of the "ethnocultural" idiom of national self-understanding Brubaker placed at the center of his German narrative.[8] Concurrently, other works sought to complicate the continuity argument from the opposite end of the chronology by acknowledging the unsettling modernity of many aspects of policy making under the Third Reich, particularly in areas of regional economic planning, welfare initiatives, popular leisure, and public health. Until then, any linking of National Socialism to arguments concerning "modernization" had remained controversial and usually tendentious, but this new work began breaking through the long-established generalizations about Nazism's "antimodernist" character. If reevaluating the valencies of social and cultural "reform" movements of the Wilhelmine period formed one key ground of historiographical revision, then reconceptualizing the meanings of Nazi antisemitism, the "racial state," and "the business of genocide" provided another. Each had enormous implications for how we understand the longer-term questions of continuity stretching before and beyond the Nazi years per se.[9]

In other words, whatever one thinks of the French half of Brubaker's argument, his reading of the German Citizenship Law for its enduring ethnocultural logic, which both descended from the early nineteenth century as part of a deep-cultural *Sonderweg* and reached down into the late twentieth century with "the inertial weight and normative dignity of tradition," now seems extremely problematic.[10] His German "ethno-cultural" thesis makes an extremely blunt instrument for interpreting the process that produced the 1913 law. Despite his careful disclaimer, it both elides the differences with the immeasurably more radical Nazi changes after 1933 and obscures what was distinctive about the generative dynamics inside the immediate late-Wilhelmine conjuncture itself.[11] In effect, Brubaker approaches the comparative history of citizenship through a symptomatic analysis conceived at the highest and most abstract level of societal generality in Germany and France, employing the twin criteria of "social closure" and "national belonging" to define inexorably path-dependent trajectories for the two societies from their beginnings in the era of the French Revolution.

If there is a strong argument to be taken away from this discussion of Brubaker's book and the intervening research for the purposes of our own proceedings, it concerns the importance of carefully historicizing the terms of German citizenship in any of the periods we are seeking to consider. That means getting inside the specificities and densities of any one of these particular times; it means foregrounding the dynamics of innovation entailed by any particular set of developments or departures; and it means emphasizing the priority of breaks and the distinctiveness of conjunctures as much as the longer-term continuities preferred by Brubaker and older exemplars of *Sonderweg* historiography. In that sense, the *most* salient starting point for considering questions of citizenship in German history is the extreme *indeterminacy* of "Germany" as a finished political term—that is, as any kind of stable and reliable territorial-political entity during that long epoch extending from the impact of Napoleon down to the present.

During that time, far more than for the old territorial states of western Europe and mainly in extreme contrast with France, the shape-shifting presence of "Germany" at Europe's center only ever approximated to the much-vaunted unity of land, language, institutions, high cultural traditions, and customary heritage that nationalist discourse liked to presume. Even after a single national German state was created for the first time during the unification of the 1860s, its official borders were frequently redrawn and its constitutional arrangements frequently overhauled. Within the general claims to German nationhood over this longer period, in other words, the gaps between territorial integrity and cultural formation have been variable and extreme. Within one and a half centuries, with special and almost continuous intensity during the "thirty years' war" of 1914–45, after all, *six major ruptures* occurred:

in 1864–71, in 1914–18, in 1918–23, in 1936–45, in 1945–49, and finally in 1989–90.[12] Given this radical indeterminacy, the possible meanings of German citizenship have been mobile, contingent, and highly contested. Quite aside from the other criteria that need to be applied, including those of gender and class, in other words, the claims and capacities of German citizens were situated from the very beginning within complex and uncertain fields of relations linking nationhood, cultural affiliations, and the state.

So far from being stable or transparent in meaning, or juridically fixed during the Wilhelmine and Weimar periods, as Brubaker implied, the meanings of German citizenship remained markedly under construction. In that sense, Brubaker's linkage of citizenship to *culture* might still be usefully explored, though for the purposes of a very different cultural history than the one he provided: if for *Citizenship and Nationhood* that meant an argument about the holistically understood and deeply formed characteristics of a national political culture shaped and then transmitted across the generations, for my own discussion I prefer the starting points of contingency, contestation, and indeterminacy. For as soon as we consider citizenship's *larger-than-juridical dimensions* as a body of thinking about *political identity*, it becomes clear that during the Wilhelmine era its terms were anything *but* fixed. They remained subject to complex languages and mechanisms of inclusion and exclusion, both explicit and subtle, blatant and disguised, that qualified Germans' ability to take their place in the nation. Those languages were subject to all manner of contestation—to disagreement and solidarity, conflict and consensus, interpretation and counterinterpretation. Beyond the main territories of the political system and the organized political rivalries among dominant and oppositional social forces and their parties, wider differences of meaning also circulated less visibly through the political culture. Some social groups and categories were privileged over others by the prevailing languages of legitimation and entitlement. Such differences among the national citizenry—or among those accorded the full faculties of citizenship and those who were not—were ordered around gender, class, race, religion, sexual orientation, and other logics of centeredness and marginalization. In exploring the meanings of citizenship in any of the periods we are dealing with, all these elements need to be in play.[13]

The paradox of Brubaker's approach was its combination of a "thin" account of citizenship as a status under law with an extremely grandiose and implicitly totalizing account of national cultural formation. In developing this book, in contrast, building on the extraordinary broadening of citizenship talk already under way as Brubaker published his account, we have sought not only to develop the "thickest" possible framework for considering citizenship's political dimensions but also to insist on the need for the most concrete of situated, microhistorical, and everyday perspectives, including studies of the languages of political subjectivity, in order to grasp the ways in which citizenship became socially and culturally grounded. If, as Brubaker argued, "Every state establishes a conceptual, legal, and ideological boundary between citizens and foreigners," then to understand the complex construction and workings of that boundary *inside* the ascribed solidarities of the particular society in question, we need a far more searching and creative kind of analysis.[14] *Citizenship* here not only signifies "nationality" qua belonging or affiliation to a particular state, together with the associated questions of the access to rights, but also points us to questions of identity, "voice," and subjectivity. As we put it, "citizenship is the central medium through which the collective experience of the nation is formed and sustained at the everyday level"; and in this expanded sense of the term, it suggests all the complicated ways in which the national becomes local and vice versa. If citizenship "enable[s] individual political agency," it does so in a context not only of law and the exercise of rights, but also of "continuous and open constructions of subjectivity."[15]

Once we begin thinking of citizenship in terms of *political agency* and *political subjectivity* in this way, rather than seeing it as merely or primarily a status under law, the widest field of analytical reference drawn from state, society, and the public sphere comes into play. In that sense, I would argue, claims to citizenship during the later nineteenth and early twentieth centuries implied or invoked a broadening range of entitlements and capacities. But if so, then the meanings of such claims cannot be grasped by looking only at the juridical frames of state-bounded duties and rights, because in Germany full citizenship in those terms was confined to adult men enfranchised under the 1871 constitution. As a more complex and inchoate ensemble of faculties, citizenship was being shaped by far more dynamic contexts of thought and practice, which require readings of Imperial Germany's political culture at large. *Those* contexts were defined by the organized social action of parties, clubs, committees, and associations, by the shifting boundaries of public and private, and by the exchange of ideas and images in an increasingly mass-mediated public sphere. Moreover, citizenship also grew from the individual and collective efforts of citizens and would-be citizens themselves. Seen dynamically in this way as a mobile aggregate of expanding or contracting political capacities, the claim to citizenship needs to be viewed on a wide and complex stage. The process of becoming a citizen might be only unevenly ratified in national politics or institutionalized into law. Further, the claims of citizenship might either stabilize an already constituted polity or unsettle it via pressure from below. The juridical nation could be constantly challenged by the uncompleted citizenship of those still placed or considered to be on the outside.

Approaching citizenship like this, as a "set of practices—juridical, political, economic, and cultural—which define a person or through which persons define themselves as competent members of society," opens the political history of the nineteenth and twentieth centuries for a more complex analysis than the older interpretive frameworks allowed.[16] In that sense, civil activism and civic agency were crucial for the reconfiguring of what it meant to be a member of the German nation—and therefore of what it meant to have a claim on citizenship—during the successive subperiods we are dealing with, from the wider mobilizations accompanying unification in the 1860s and proliferating during the new state's continuing construction, through Germany's accelerating transformation at the turn of the century and the more convulsive societal upheavals surrounding World War I and the Weimar Republic, to the subsequent periods beyond.

In each case, both *the scope for political self-fashioning* and the demands and pressures exerted on individuals by *the changing forms of governmentality* differed enormously. Assessing the complex intermeshing of those two logics, the ways they worked against each other or together, and the changing character of the resulting balance forms one of the biggest challenges for our discussions. During the succession of transformations between the 1860s and the end of the Weimar Republic, for example, we might argue that the meanings of *citizenship* were continually expanded, as ever more Germans made themselves into citizens by actively claiming a place in the nation. If for the *Kaiserreich* German historians have traditionally seen this process from above, as a state-driven stabilizing of traditional authority that concentrated popular identities around an unreformed political system, we can now see more clearly the possible "modernizing" or "progressivist" readings of the same histories, embracing both the evolving dynamism of the *Kaiserreich*'s governing system and its enabling consequences for society. But the one should not be considered without the other: if change was inciting new and more active ways of inhabiting the social, the state too was acquiring an ever-expanding presence in the lives of its populations. The tensions between those two logics became extreme in the course of World War I, before becoming wholly unmanageable during the political collapse and revolutionary upheaval accompanying the war's end. During the Weimar years, the consequent disordering was never surmounted. Under the Third Reich, arguably, the consequences of the coercive renormalizing of the relationship rendered the very category of citizenship questionable if not entirely nugatory. Despite the juridical restoration of citizenship rights after 1945–49, the wider meanings of citizenship in some ways contracted in each of the two Germanies, until a fresh period opened again during the 1960s and early 1970s.

At all events, we need a careful framework of periodization. For example, Fahrmeir's work has shown that in geographical Germany neomercantilist and bureaucratic preoccupations with managing populations, above all in relation to the convoluted and disorderly consequences of migration for conscription and poor relief, remained the primary context for considering questions of citizenship well into the middle of the nineteenth century. In light of those logics, accentuated by Germany's extreme pre-1871 fragmentation of jurisdictions and sovereignties, and meticulously illuminated by Fahrmeir's comparison with Britain, Brubaker's emphasis on some allegedly "ethnocultural" principle of belonging seems simply misconceived. In that case, the discursive coordinates of the 1913 law, which clearly *did* begin to incorporate such ethnocultural terms of justification, need to be seen as the emergent—and to a great extent *insurgent*—consequences of a set of developments that were specific to the Wilhelmine years themselves, especially to the heightening political conflicts of the immediate pre-1914 decade. Likewise, the persistence of the *ius sanguinis* principle down to the end of the twentieth century might be understood far more specifically in relation to the demographic disordering of "Germany" after 1945 and the associated problem of the expellees. *That*, rather than some deep-cultural reservoir of ethnocultural identification, was the more decisive generative peculiarity behind West German citizenship discourse in the 1980s.

Of course, many other conceptual issues might be raised in framing our general topic. The post-Foucauldian analytics of *governmentality* provide one obvious set, approaching the fixing of identities not from the perspective of emancipation, enablement, and the agency of citizens mainly employed above, but as a matter of surveillance, bureaucratic control, codification, identification, and other logics of the reasons of state. There is a growing reservoir of historiography of this kind by now, though mostly couched more generally or concentrated in other national fields than the German per se—including studies of statistics and the systematic gathering of information about society, of new patterns and practices of social administration and social work, of the elaboration of new languages and techniques for mapping the characteristics of "the social," of the growth of associated academic disciplines and new fields such as criminology, eugenics, and racial science, and of the general drive for ordering the social world's intelligibility.[17] As we all know, studies of medicalization, policing, and social discipline became especially fruitful for the German field under the early influence of Detlev Peukert and the feminist historians of social rationalization during the later 1980s.[18] The challenge here is that of resisting the seductively totalizing appeal of such post-Foucauldian analysis. Rather than simply explicating the new languages of power and objectification, we need to understand all the ways in which society—or the individuals and collectivities composing it—had the capacity for speaking back. Each new logic of governmentality, one might say, simultaneously entailed its new fronts of citizenship.

In that respect, a key focus of analysis will undoubtedly be that of gender. If, as Brubaker argued, citizenship as a legal status conferred by states is "bounded and exclusive," then it is rather the category's porousness that emerges once we move out from the juridical meanings to the other more elusive fields of relations joining the public to the self. There citizenship signifies that wider "ensemble of subject positions" available for enunciating claims and acting upon them politically, which frame "the ways people *see themselves as public, when they do.*"[19] Moreover, as Kathleen Canning points out, the concept of *social citizenship*, used so effectively by feminist historians for the comparative study of women's relationship to social policy, social work, and the growth of welfare states, can be expected for these purposes to do only limited service. Too often now, it closes off further questions rather than bringing them to the fore, allowing one genuinely crucial area of practice and legislation to subsume all the other possible claims to citizenship women might be able to make. Because social citizenship "most often refers to bundles of rights and duties for those who are deprived of political and civil citizenship rights," Canning observes, it engenders a kind of surrogate status, implying a subordinate and distinct domain counterposed *against* the political (or "real") forms of citizenship. Reinforced by other areas of policy, like protective labor law, child protection measures, and public health, it easily provides the license for what Teresa Kuwalik calls "an extreme masculinization of political identities."[20]

Part of the problem, Canning suggests, is a desire to integrate gender histories into established accounts in ways that will certainly reconstitute the latter, sometimes decisively, but without ultimately querying their overarching terms or indeed the whole feasible purpose of wanting such an integrative metanarrative to begin with. Rather than seeking to "mainstream" a gendered account of citizenship in that way, in fact, we might explore how "the new rhetorics or discourses of citizenship in early Weimar Germany" enabled forms of active recognition for women that precisely *transgressed* or *exceeded* the kinds of political agency made available by the conventional parliamentary and legislative arena. For the constitutional debates of 1918–19 and the revolution's wider upheaval left behind a mélange of contradictory outcomes affecting women's personhood or capacities, treating them as the bearers of political and civil rights to be sure, but also as the wives and widows of husbands, as the mothers of children, as the guardians of morality, as the recipients of welfare, as the consumers of commodities, and as the participants in a public sphere. If they acquired the vote and certain social rights, they also lost much of their access to labor markets and remained civilly dependent on husbands through marriage. Yet this discrepancy between the *promises* of citizenship and its *official ratifications* "designates the very space in which new subject positions were formed." On that basis, the experiential rhetorics of "political citizenship" could still remain "meaningful for women after 1918, even as they seemed to vanish from the arenas of formal politics." Through the dramatic opening-out of politics during the revolutionary crisis of 1918–19, women acquired "a new language for claims-making . . . with regard to matters well beyond the realms of party politics or the bounds of the welfare state, such as sexuality, reproduction, and consumption."[21]

If we force the gender analysis too ardently into converging with the familiar main accounts of Weimar history, we can easily miss this distinctive space of the aspirations and agency of German women, whom the upheavals of the war and the revolution had moved into thinking of themselves profoundly differently than before. The extent of that space, defined by the discourses, desires, and practices it enabled, spilled across the boundaries of the polity that the terms of the fragile and unfinished political settlement of 1918–19 had struggled to authorize. Political subjectivities—or *citizenship* in the difficult and extended sense proposed by this chapter, both for women and for men—disobeyed the definitions reached for during the constitutional debates and political maneuverings that established the Republic. The release of subjectivities surrounding the revolution, proceeding from the new mobility of expectations and the shaking up of previously reliable affiliations— Weimar's delirium of identity—cannot be assimilated to the familiar and necessary political narratives of the history of the 1920s. As Canning says, in these terms we might find "that 1918 forms a different kind of turning point for gender history than for political history," because those older "narratives, chronologies, and concepts that were conceived without the history of women or gender" cannot now be made very easily to accept these different forms of argumentation:

So the goal of historicizing citizenship for the Weimar period may not be exhausted by a close reading of constitutions and laws, but might productively turn to an analysis of women's novels, visual arts, theater, and popular culture, in order to gain a fuller sense of the arenas in which citizenship rights were made meaningful or were contested.[22]

The most fruitful treatments of citizenship during the past decade have taken some approach of this kind, emphasizing its larger-than-juridical meanings as a relationship "inflected by identity, social positioning, cultural assumptions, institutional practices, and a sense of belonging."[23] In some periods, one might argue—such as the 1860s or the years surrounding 1918–19, or perhaps again in the more recent conjuncture opened by 1989–92—the language of citizenship successfully condenses, or articulates together, the disparate range of subject positions encompassed in the relationship, whereas in other periods those positions circulate in ways that remain far more quiescent, fragmentary, and discrete. Thus in the 1920s, Canning argues:

citizenship may be seen as forming one thread that entwined the disparate subject positions of women in Weimar—as demobilized workers, widowed mothers, newly-endowed voters, consumers of popular culture, and sexually independent negotiators of their private lives.[24]

Analytically speaking, it allows us to appreciate how such variegated and dissimilar interests and standpoints might become politically centered for brief but powerful moments of change, and how at other times they might fly apart. Citizenship becomes best regarded as:

a multidimensional discursive framework encompassing the languages, rheto-rics, and the formal categories for claims-making, including those raised by those formally excluded from citizenship.[25]

A word of caution here: the thrust of my own argument in this chap-ter has been toward constructedness, contingency, and conjuncture, certainly attentive to the importance of structural forms of explanation, but building my discussion in the first instance from inside the im-mediate contexts and circumstances of each of the periods addressed rather than from the longer-run determinations and deeper historical continuities stressed by Brubaker on the model of the *Sonderweg* and other approaches that center on German differences from "the West."[26] Consistent with my thinking over a longer period, I prefer to under-stand the distinctiveness of the 1913 Citizenship Law in relation to the particular dynamics of the late Wilhelmine conjuncture rather than referring it back to some deeply embedded cultural pattern or inher-ited ideological formation. If there was a distinctive "ethnocultural" quality to the 1913 law, its genealogies are to be sought initially within the immediate Wilhelmine context itself rather than deeper in the nine-teenth century, whatever further illumination those earlier intellectual histories might then provide. At the same time, there is nothing *in prin-ciple* to preclude the cultural analysis of deeper patterns of nineteenth-century German life and thought. In the French context, for example, Leora Auslander has brilliantly shown the links between longstanding patterns of national state formation, the pedagogies informing national cultural policy, and the everyday aesthetics of consumption, taste, and design in order to make precisely such a case for the specificities of na-tional citizenship ideals and their cultural embeddedness, although her more recent comparative essays are flawed precisely by their reliance on Brubaker's notation of the German case.[27]

Finally, the growing importance of everything now conventionally summarized under the rubric of globalization—including the new supranational forms of law and jurisdiction, as well as the multi-form patterns of transnational migration—have encouraged attention among social scientists to new "postnational" forms of membership and identity.[28] In this notation, the access to civic protections, social entitlements, and "human" rights seems increasingly decoupled from the traditional field of citizenship claims based on nationality and state affiliation, becoming reattached instead to "the abstract quality of personhood."[29] Although it is easy enough to see this as a tenden-tially cosmopolitan advance over "the stuffy confines of the narcissistic nation," it has scarcely translated yet into any appreciable transnational gains for *political* citizenship in any of the senses expounded in this chapter.[30] On the contrary, under the current auspices of the "global war against terrorism," the simultaneous inducement and demonization of illegal labor migrations, and the vilification of asylum seekers, it more frequently means the circling of wagons around citizenship as an already constituted and beleaguered ground of privilege. Often the contemporary hopes of citizenship seem to entail not much more than the right to reside legally in a particular country of one's choice. For our own purposes, accordingly, the comparative arc linking that practical narrowing with the mid-nineteenth-century expansiveness of the perceived promise of citizenship—everything implied, for instance, in Lord Palmerston's ringing declaration of *Civis Romanus sum*—would be well worth pondering.[31]

REFERENCE MATTER

Notes

CHAPTER 1

1. See T. H. Marshall, *Citizenship and Social Class and Other Essays* (Cambridge: Cambridge University Press, 1950). The enormous body of work by British social historians on the growth of the welfare state was predicated upon the critique of Marshall's schema. For access to that literature, see J. R. Hay, *The Origins of the Liberal Welfare Reforms 1906–1914* (London: Macmillan, 1975). For an important early critique within sociology, see Nigel Young, "Prometheans or Troglodytes? The English Working Class and the Dialectics of Incorporation," *Berkeley Journal of Sociology* 12 (1967), 1–43.

2. T. H. Marshall, "Citizenship and Social Class," in *Citizenship and Social Class*, ed. T. H. Marshall and Tom Bottomore, 3–51 (London: Pluto Press, 1992).

3. Norman P. Barry, *Welfare* (Milton Keynes: Open University Press, 1990); Lawrence M. Mead, *Beyond Entitlement: The Social Obligations of Citizenship* (New York: Free Press, 1986).

4. Jürgen Habermas, *The Structural Transformation of the Public Sphere* (Cambridge: Polity Press, 1992). For an excellent introduction to the ideas of Habermas, see Chris Thornhill, *Political Theory in Modern Germany. An Introduction* (Cambridge: Polity Press, 2000), ch. 4.

5. Judith A. Vega, "Enlightenment's Differences, Today's Identities," in *States and Citizens: History, Theory, Prospects*, ed. Quentin Skinner and Bo Stråth, 116 (Cambridge: Cambridge University Press, 2003).

6. Geoff Eley, "Nations, Publics, and Political Culture: Placing Habermas in the Nineteenth Century," in *Habermas and the Public Sphere*, ed. C. Calhoun, 289–339 (Boston: MIT Press, 1992).

7. Joseph H. Carens, *Culture, Citizenship and Community: A Contextual Exploration of Justice as Evenhandedness* (Oxford: Oxford University Press, 2000).

8. Rogers Brubaker, *Citizenship and Nationhood in France and Germany* (Cambridge: Harvard University Press, 1992), 21–34.

250 Notes to Chapter 1

9. Hermann Kurthen, Jürgen Fijalkowski, and Gert G. Wagner, *Immigration, Citizenship, and the Welfare State in Germany and the United States: Welfare Policies and Immigrants' Citizenship* (Stamford, CT: JAI Press, 1998).

10. Antje Wiener, "From *Special* to *Specialized* Rights: The Politics of Citizenship and Identity in the European Union," in *Extending Citizenship, Reconfiguring States*, ed. M. Hanagan and C. Tilly, 195–227 (Lanham, MD: Rowman & Littlefield, 1999); Randall Hansen and Patrick Weil, eds., *Towards a European Nationality: Citizenship, Immigration and the Nationality Law in the EU* (Basingstoke, UK: Palgrave , 2001).

11. Charles Tilly, "Citizenship, Identity and Social History," in *Citizenship, Identity and Social History*, ed. C. Tilly, 6–8 (Cambridge: Cambridge University Press, 1996).

12. Will Kymlicka and Wayne Norman, "Return of the Citizen: A Survey of Recent Work on Citizenship Theory," *Ethics* 104 (1994): 354.

13. Ruth Rubio-Marín, *Immigration as a Democratic Challenge: Citizenship and Inclusion in Germany and the United States* (Cambridge: Cambridge University Press, 2000); William A. Barbieri, *Ethics of Citizenship. Immigration and Group Rights in Germany* (Durham, NC: Duke University Press, 1998).

14. Ruud Koopmans and Hanspeter Kriesi, *Citizenship, National Identity and the Mobilisation of the Extreme Right: A Comparison of France, Germany, the Netherlands, and Switzerland* (Berlin: Wissenschaftszentrum Berlin für Sozialforschung, 1997).

15. Margaret R. Somers, "Citizenship and the Place of the Public Sphere: Law, Community, and Political Culture in the Transition to Democracy," *American Sociological Review* 58 (1993): 587–620; Eley, "Nations," passim.

16. Michael Hanagan and Charles Tilly, eds., *Extending Citizenship, Reconfiguring States* (Lanham, MD: Rowman & Littlefield, 1999).

17. Tilly, "Citizenship," 5. See also Charles Tilly, *Contention and Democracy in Europe, 1650–2000* (Cambridge: Cambridge University Press, 2004). This book uses the historical dimension to construct a model for democratization whose parameters might be applied beyond the borders of Europe.

18. Andreas Fahrmeir, *Citizens and Aliens. Foreigners and the Law in Britain and the German States 1789–1870* (New York: Berghahn Books, 2000); Andreas Fahrmeir, "Nineteenth-Century German Citizenships: A Reconsideration," *Historical Journal* 40 (1997), 721–53.

19. Patrick Weil, *Qu'est-ce qu'un Français? Histoire de la nationalité française depuis la Révolution* (Paris: Bernard Grasset, 2002).

20. Dieter Gosewinkel, *Einbürgern und Ausschließen: Die Nationalisierung der Staatsangehörigkeit vom Deutschen Bund bis zur Bundesrepublik Deutschland* (Göttingen: Vandenhoeck & Ruprecht, 2001).

21. Eli Nathans, *The Politics of Citizenship in Germany: Ethnicity, Utility and Nationalism* (Oxford: Berg, 2004).

22. Kathleen Canning, "Class vs. Citizenship: Keywords in German Gender History," *Central European History* 37, no. 2 (2004): 225–44.

23. Kathleen Canning and Sonya O. Rose, "Introduction: Gender, Citizen-

ship, and Subjectivity: Some Historical and Theoretical Considerations," *Gender & History* 13, no. 3 (2001), 227–41.

24. Bryan Turner, "Contemporary Problems in the Theory of Citizenship," in *Citizenship and Social Theory*, ed. Bryan Turner, 1–18 (London: Sage Publications, 1993), quoted in Kathleen Canning, "Of Gender Stories and Master Narratives in the History of the Weimar Republic" (unpublished ms).

25. Geoff Eley, "Making a Place in the Nation: Meanings of 'Citizenship' in Wilhelmine Germany," in *Wilhelminism and Its Legacies: German Modernities, Imperialism, and the Meanings of Reform, 1890–1930*, ed. G. Eley and J. Retallack, 16–33 (New York: Berghahn Books, 2003).

26. Kate Lacey, *Feminine Frequencies: Gender, German Radio, and the Public Sphere 1923–45* (Ann Arbor: University of Michigan Press, 1996).

27. Madeleine Hurd, *Public Spheres, Public Mores, and Democracy: Hamburg and Stockholm, 1870–1914* (Ann Arbor: University of Michigan Press, 2000).

28. Thomas Lindenberger, *Straßenpolitik. Zur Sozialgeschichte der öffentlichen Ordnung in Berlin 1900 bis 1914* (Bonn: J. H. W. Dietz, 1995).

29. For an example of how this approach could work, see Dennis Sweeney, "Liberalism, the Worker and the Limits of Bourgeois *Öffentlichkeit* in Wilhelmine Germany," *German History* 22, no. 1 (2004): 36–75.

30. Andreas Fahrmeir, Olivier Faron, and Patrick Weil, eds., *Migration Control in the North Atlantic World: The Evolution of State Practices in Europe and the United States from the French Revolution to the Inter-War Period* (New York: Berghahn, 2003); see also Mark Roseman, Neil Gregor, and Nils Roemer, eds., *German History from the Margins* (Bloomington: Indiana University Press, 2006).

31. Karin Schönwälder, *Einwanderung und ethnische Pluralität. Politische Entscheidungen und öffentliche Debatten in Großbritannien und in der Bundesrepublik von den 1950er bis zu den 1970er Jahren* (Essen: Klartext, 2001).

32. Jan C. Behrends, Thomas Lindenberger, and Patrice Poutros, eds., *Fremde und Fremd-Sein in der DDR: Zu historischen Ursachen der Fremdenfeindlichkeit in Ostdeutschland* (Berlin: Metropol, 2003); see also Damian MacConUladh, "Foreigners in the GDR" (PhD diss., London University, 2005).

33. The following considerations build on the discussions at the conference "Citizenship and National Identity in Twentieth-Century Germany," which was held at Lady Margaret Hall, Oxford, on September 10–12, 2004. We are grateful to all the participants for some extremely stimulating debates, but should add that the views expressed here are entirely our own.

34. This point was forcefully made by Richard Bessel at the conference on which this book is based.

35. Chris Thornhill, "The Holy Roman Empire and the Law," *German History* 24, no. 1 (2006): 111–17.

36. Andreas Fahrmair, "National Colours and National Identity in Early Nineteenth-Century Germany," in *Napoleon's Legacy: Problems of Government in Restoration Europe*, ed. L. Riall and D. Laven, 199–216 (Oxford: Berg, 2000); Abigail Green, *Fatherlands* (Cambridge: Cambridge University Press, 2001).

37. For a critique of historicism's approach to the state from the perspective of citizenship, see Martin von Gelderen, "The State and Its Rivals in Early-Modern Europe," in Skinner and Stråth, *States and Citizens*, 63–78.

38. Canning, "Class vs. Citizenship," 237–38.

39. Nils Ole Oermann, "The Law and the Colonial State: Legal Codification Versus Practice in a German Colony," in *Wilhelminism and Its Legacies: German Modernities, Imperialism, and the Meanings of Reform, 1890–1930*, ed. G. Eley and J. Retallack, 171–84 (New York: Berghahn, 2003); see also Lora Wildenthal, "Race, Gender, and Citizenship in the German Colonial Empire," in *Tensions of Empire: Colonial Cultures in a Bourgeois World*, ed. Frederick Cooper and Ann Stoler, 263–83 (Berkeley: University of California Press, 1997).

40. Canning, "Class vs. Citizenship," 234.

41. Fahrmeir, *Citizens and Aliens*.

42. Michel Rowe, *From Reich to State: The Rhineland in the Revolutionary Age, 1780–1830* (Cambridge: Cambridge University Press, 2003).

43. James Retallack, *The German Right 1860–1920* (Toronto: University of Toronto Press, 2006), 137–67.

44. Bart van Steenbergen, "The Condition of Citizenship: An Introduction," in *The Condition of Citizenship*, ed. Bart van Steenbergen, 1–9 (London: Sage, 1994).

45. Jan Palmowski, *Urban Liberalism in Imperial Germany: Frankfurt am Main, 1866–1914* (Oxford: Oxford University Press, 1999), ch. 4.

46. For an analogous argument that predated the strong coalescence of "citizenship" talk in its contemporary form, see Geoff Eley, "State Formation, Nationalism, and Political Culture: Some Thoughts on the Unification of Germany," in Geoff Eley, *From Unification to Nazism: Reinterpreting the German Past*, 61–84 (London: Allen & Unwin, 1986).

47. Tilly, "Citizenship," 5–9.

48. Barbieri, "Ethics," viii, 1–37.

49. Shmuel N. Eisenstadt, Wolfgang Schluchter, and Björn Wittrock, "Introduction," in *Public Spheres and Collective Identities*, ed. S. N. Eisenstadt, W. Schluchter, and B. Wittrock, 10–14 (New Brunswick, NJ: Transaction Publishers, 2001).

50. Rogers Brubaker and Frederick Cooper, "Beyond Identity," in *Theory and Society* 29, no. 1 (2000), 1–47.

51. Lutz Niethammer, *Kollektive Identität: Heimliche Quellen einer unheimlichen Konjunktur* (Hamburg: Rohwolt, 2000).

52. This point is underlined further by Jan Palmowski's contribution to this volume.

53. Canning, "Class vs. Citizenship," 236.

CHAPTER 2

1. Rogers Brubaker, *Citizenship and Nationhood in France and Germany* (Cambridge: Harvard University Press, 1992).

2. See Geoff Eley, "Some General Thoughts on Citizenship in Germany," in this volume.

3. Eley, "Some General Thoughts."

4. Eli Nathans, *The Politics of Citizenship in Germany: Ethnicity, Utility and Nationalism* (Oxford: Berg, 2004), 9.

5. Bernhard Giesen, *Die Intellektuellen und die Nation* (Frankfurt am Main: Suhrkamp, 1993), 161.

6. Michael Jeismann, *Vaterland der Feinde* (Stuttgart: Klett-Cotta, 1992).

7. Dieter Gosewinkel, "Les historiens allemands," *Commentaire* 19 (1996): 320–26.

8. Dominique Schnapper, *La France de l'intégration* (Paris: Gallimard, 1991), 69.

9. See Eli Nathans, "Political Rights and Ethnic Duties: Citizenship Regimes and the Nationality of Married Women in Germany, France and the United States, 1900–1930" (paper submitted to the annual conference of the American Society for Legal History, San Diego, CA, November 7–9, 2002).

10. Patrick Weil, *Qu'est-ce qu'un Français? Histoire de la nationalité française depuis la Révolution* (Paris: Grasset, 2002), 50–53, 188–93.

11. Between 1876 and 1886, the absolute number of foreigners in France rose from 655,036 to 1,127,000; the percentage of foreigners in the population as a whole rose from 1.7% to 3.0%. Weil, *Qu'est-ce qu'un Français?* 53.

12. According to the "double *ius soli*," whoever was born in France and had parents who themselves were born in France became French. The grandchildren of a foreigner who immigrated to France thus became French. See Weil, *Qu'est-ce qu'un Français?* 50.

13. See, for example, Brubaker, *Citizenship*, 104ff.

14. According to the estimations by legislators, there were no more than 4,000 young men from foreign families in any one year, compared to 300,000 French men. Weil, *Qu'est-ce qu'un Français?* 55.

15. Patrick Weil, *La France et ses Étrangers* (Paris: Gallimard, 1995), 469–70; Weil, "Immigration, nation et nationalité: Regards comparatifs et croisés," *Revue française de science politique* 44 (1994): 308–26; Gérard Noiriel, *Le creuset français* (Paris: Seuil, 1988), 81ff; and Noiriel, *La tyrannie du national* (Paris: Seuil, 1991), 85ff.

16. Weil, *Qu'est-ce qu'un Français?* 61.

17. For an in-depth treatment, see Bernhard Giesen and Kay Junge, "Nationale Identität und Staatsbürgerschaft in Deutschland und Frankreich," *Berliner Journal für Soziologie* 8 (1998): 523–37, in which the authors introduce an additional "traditional element."

18. The term is taken from Pierre Nora, ed., *Lieux de mémoire*, 3 vols. (Paris: Gallimard, 1984–1994).

19. Dieter Gosewinkel, *Einbürgern und Ausschließen: Die Nationalisierung der Staatsangehörigkeit vom Deutschen Bund bis zur Bundesrepublik Deutschland* (Göttingen: Vandenhoeck & Ruprecht, 2001), 290.

20. Oberpräsident of Silesia to the Prussian Minister of the Interior, October 14, 1893, Preußisches Geheimes Staatsarchiv Dahlem, Rep. 77, Tit. 227, no. 53,

vol. 2. On the German side more generally, see Dieter Gosewinkel, *Einbürgern und Ausschließen: Die Nationalisierung der Staatsangehörigkeit vom Deutschen Bund bis zur Bundesrepublik Deutschland*, 2nd ed. (Göttingen: Vandenhoeck & Ruprecht, 2003), especially 286–94.

21. See Cécile Mondonico-Torri, "Aux origines du Code de la Nationalité en France," *Mouvement Social* 171 (1995): 31–46.

22. Pierre Milza, *Francais et Italiens à la fin du XIXe siècle* (Rome: École française de Rome, 1981), 172ff., 271.

23. They made up between 62% and 76% of immigrants, calculated according to the figures in Weil, *La France et ses Étrangers*, 356–57. To be sure, Polish immigrants, who represented the second largest group after the Italians from the 1930s on, faced increased reservations, but their Catholicism created a cultural bridge to French society. See Ralph Schor, *L'Opinion française et les Étrangers* (Paris: La Sorbonne, 1985), 143ff; and for a corrective view, Janine Ponty, *Les Polonais méconnus* (Paris: La Sorbonne, 1988), 152ff, 386. The Belgians were considered "good immigrants" or "northern Frenchmen" because of their geographical proximity and cultural kinship to France. Relatively, the most intense conflicts were with Italian immigrants, almost half of whom, however, were already integrated as French citizens on the eve of World War I. Secessionist tendencies in political organizations directed against France played no role to speak of in these conflicts, especially because there were strong tendencies toward fluctuation and return migration to Italy among Italian immigrants. See Marianne Amas and Pierre Milza, *L'immigration en France au XXe siècle* (Paris: Armand Colin, 1990), 64–65, 184–85.

24. This shifted after 1918 because of Germany's territorial cessions. In 1925, of 921,900 "foreigners" living within imperial Germany, 669,292 spoke German. See *Statistisches Jahrbuch für das Deutsche Reich* (Berlin: Puttkammer & Mühlbrecht, 1928).

25. Prussian Minister of the Interior to the Reich's Chancellor and Reich's Minister of the Interior, March 29, 1894, Preußisches Geheimes Staatsarchiv, Rep. 77, Tit. 227, no. 53, vol. 2.

26. Yves Lequin, *Histoire des français XIXe–XXe siècles*, vol. 1, *Un peuple et son pays* (Paris: Colin, 1984), 92.

27. Milza, *Français et Italiens*, 269.

28. Andreas Fahrmeir, "Paßwesen und Staatsbildung im Deutschland des 19. Jahrhunderts," *Historische Zeitschrift* 271 (2000): 57–91; more generally on federal German "citizenships" before 1870–71, see also Fahrmeir, *Citizens and Aliens: Foreigners and the Law in Britain and the German States 1789–1870* (New York: Berghahn, 2000).

29. See Eugen Weber, "L'Hexagone," in Nora, *Lieux de mémoire*, vol. 2, "La Nation," 97–116; and Daniel Nordmann, "Des limites d'etat aux frontières nationales," in Nora, *Lieux de mémoire*, vol. 2, "La nation," 35–61.

30. On the initial initiative of national associations and then, in 1913, with the agreement of all political parties in the Reichstag, Paragraph 17 of the Imperial and National Citizenship Law from July 22, 1913, repealed the regulation in

the Federal Law of 1870 according to which residence outside of Germany for more than ten years led in principle to the loss of German citizenship.

31. See Gosewinkel, *Einbürgern und Ausschließen*, 313, 319.

32. See Annemarie Sammartino, "Culture, Belonging, and the Law: Naturalization in the Weimar Republic," in this volume.

33. Nathans, *Politics of Citizenship*, 9.

CHAPTER 3

1. Walter Rathenau, *Der neue Staat* (Berlin: S. Fischer, 1919), 34.

2. See, for example, Oswald Spengler, "Prussianism and Socialism," in *Selected Essays*, 17–18 (Chicago: University of Chicago Press, 1967), in which active service to community takes on authoritarian forms; Rosa Luxemburg, "What Does the Spartacus League Want?" in *Selected Political Writings of Rosa Luxemburg*, 369 (New York: Monthly Review Press, 1974), on "socialist civic virtues." On whether socialist "civic virtues" can be incorporated in the socialist community, see Mark Roseman's interesting remarks in his paper "Opponents to Nazism and Conceptions of Citizenship" for this conference.

At issue in these discussions is, of course, the state as a "personality," a topic treated further by Chris Thornhill in his paper for this conference, "Citizenship and Legitimacy: Theoretical Transformations in Twentieth-Century Germany."

3. Georg Jellinek, *Das System der subjektiven öffentlichen Rechte*, 2nd ed. (Tübingen: Mohr/Siebeck, 1919), 117–18.

4. In general on the problem of citizenship and exclusion, see Dieter Gosewinkel, *Einbürgern und Ausschließen: Die Nationalisierung der Staatsangehörigkeit vom Deutschen Bund bis zur Bundesrepublik Deutschland* (Göttingen: Vandenhoeck & Ruprecht, 2001), especially p. 375 on "stateless" Jews under Nazism.

5. This list generally follows the famous threefold set of rights—civil, political, and social—outlined by Marshall. I use them here, though, in a static, descriptive sense rather than to imply any evolutionary development. There is no such necessary development. Social rights such as the right to an education did not appear first in 1945; social rights in Eastern Europe before 1989 were not connected with meaningful political rights.

6. Or, in Ulrich Preuss's terms, citizenship has two very different senses within the law: "as a status of political activity and participation and . . . as a basically apolitical legal status." "The Relevance of the Concept of Citizenship for the European Union," in *European Citizenship, Multiculturalism, and the State*, ed. U. Preuss and F. Requejo, 13–15 (Baden-Baden: Nomos, 1998).

7. See in particular Hans Kelsen's controversial discussion of the ideology of property rights in *Introduction to the Problems of Legal Theory*, trans. Bonnie Litschewski Paulson and Stanley L. Paulson (1934; repr., Oxford: Clarendon Press, 1992), 41–42.

8. For a good example, see Dieter Grimm, *Deutsche Verfassungsgeschichte*

1776–1866 (Frankfurt am Main: Suhrkamp, 1988). In private law (which, as noted above, also relates closely to the rights of the citizen), Franz Wieacker's classic *History of Private Law in Europe*, trans. Tony Weir (Oxford: Clarendon Press, 1995), presents a history of changing legal structures in social and intellectual context.

9. See especially Hans Kelsen, "Juristischer Formalismus und reine Rechtslehre," *Juristische Wochenschrift* 58 (1929): 1723–26.

10. Laying claim to such rights occurs within certain social contexts—and the question remains whether the development of rights claims is connected primarily to capitalism or to a combination of social contexts as well as traditions and practices of discussing the "public" and law. See, for example, Margaret R. Somers, "Citizenship and the Place of the Public Sphere: Law, Community, and Political Culture in the Transition to Democracy," *American Sociological Review* 58 (1993): 587–620.

11. For a contemporary example: a woman's right to have an abortion, based on her right to privacy, did not exist as objective fact in federal law before the 1970s, although it was claimed by citizens; after *Roe v. Wade*, that subjective sense of a right became objective law through judicial interpretation.

12. On the role of law and necessity of positivism in complex, modern societies, see Niklas Luhmann, "Positivität des Rechts als Voraussetzung einer modernen Gesellschaft," in *Ausdifferenzierung des Rechts*, 113–53 (Frankfurt am Main: Suhrkamp, 1981).

13. See the exemplary account of republican identity in Joan B. Landes's description of *The Oath of the Horatii*, in *Women and the Public Sphere in the Age of the French Revolution*, 152–68 (Ithaca, NY: Cornell University Press, 1988).

14. For example, Carola Lipp, "Liebe, Krieg und Revolution: Geschlechterbeziehung und Nationalismus," in *Schimpfende Weiber und patriotische Jungfrauen: Frauen im Vormärz und in der Revolution 1848/49*, ed. C. Lipp, 353–84 (Moos: Elster, 1986).

15. Kathleen Canning and Sonya O. Rose point to this as one of a variety of approaches to citizenship in "Gender, Citizenship, and Subjectivity: Some Historical and Theoretical Considerations," *Gender and History* 13 (2001): 427; as does Somers, "Citizenship," 589. Both, however, in their actual analyses point to specific kinds of relations that can develop into "rights."

16. "It is a matter of knowing what a nation, which has lost its traditions through the collapse of the old system of rule, actually wants." Friedrich Naumann's speech of July 31, 1919, in *Die Deutsche Nationalversammlung im Jahre 1919 in ihrer Arbeit für den Aufbau des neuen deutschen Volksstaates*, ed. E. Heilfron, VII:444 (Berlin: Norddeutsche Buchdruckerei, 1919–20).

17. Still useful background literature: Eberhard Kolb, *Die Arbeiterräte in der deutschen Innenpolitik 1918–1919* (Düsseldorf: Droste, 1962); and Peter von Oertzen, *Betriebsräte in der Novemberrevolution: Eine politikwissenschaftliche Untersuchung über Ideengehalt und Struktur der betrieblichen und wirtschaftlichen Arbeiterräte in der deutschen Revolution 1918–19* (Düsseldorf: Droste, 1963). On the People's Courts in Munich—and their unfortunate later history—see the re-

cent dissertation by Douglas Morris, "Politics, Law, and Miscarriages of Justice: The Criminal Defense Lawyer Max Hirschberg in the Weimar Republic" (PhD diss., University of Rochester, 2003).

18. See especially the introduction to *Der Zentralrat der deutschen sozialistischen Republik 19.12.1918–8.4.1919*, ed. E. Kolb and R. Rürup (Leiden: Brill, 1968), xiv–xxvii, on issues of sovereignty and Ebert's conceptualization of the transitional government; Hans Mommsen, *The Rise and Fall of Weimar Democracy*, trans. Elborg Forster and Larry Eugene Jones (Chapel Hill: University of North Carolina Press, 1996), 28–30.

19. Eberhard Kolb, "Rätewirklichkeit und Räteideologie in der deutschen Revolution von 1918/19," in *Vom Kaiserreich zur Weimarer Republik*, ed. E. Kolb, 165–84 (Cologne: Kiepenheuer & Witsch, 1972); Oertzen, *Betriebsräte*, 18–19, 84–87, 89–99.

20. Ernst Däumig, "Die Entstehung des Rätesystems," in *Arbeiterräte in der Weimarer Republik: Ideen-Wirkungen-Dokumente*, ed. D. Schneider and R. Kuda, 70 (1920; repr., Frankfurt am Main: Suhrkamp, 1968); and his speech of Dec. 19, 1918, at the General Congress of Councils, in *Die deutsche Revolution 1918–1919: Dokumente*, 2nd ed., ed. Gerhard A. Ritter and Susanne Miller, 380 (Hamburg: Hoffmann & Campe, 1975).

21. Ernst Däumig, *Das Rätesystem: Reden auf dem Parteitage der USPD am 4. und 5. Mai 1919* (Berlin: Arbeiter-Rat, 1919), 10.

22. Ibid., 14; "Entstehung des Rätesystems," 70. Note that this rejection of parties was not only directed against "bourgeois" parties but also against communist control: Däumig, "Partei und Rätesystem," *Arbeiterräte*, 105–8.

23. Däumig, *Das Rätesystem*, 5.

24. Ibid., 24–25.

25. Expressly including "spiritual labor": Wilhelm Koenen (USPD), speech of July 21, 1919, *Die Deutsche Nationalversammlung* VI:4369.

26. Especially Karl Korsch, "Fundamentals of Socialization," in *Karl Korsch: Revolutionary Theory*, ed. Douglas Kellner, 124–35 (Austin: University of Texas Press, 1977); Däumig, "Der Rätegedanke und seine Verwirklichung," *Arbeiterräte*, 69–70.

27. Däumig, *Arbeiterräte*, 86; dismissal of councils from the point of view of modernization theory in Hans-Ulrich Wehler, *Deutsche Gesellschaftsgeschichte, Vierter Band: Vom Beginn des Ersten Weltkriegs bis zur Gründung der beiden deutschen Staaten 1914–1949* (Munich: Beck, 2003), 211–13.

28. Indeed, the question of how white-collar employees (*Angestellten*) would be represented in factory councils became an important and controversial point in the debates of the National Assembly on factory councils: see *Die Deutsche Nationalversammlung* VI: 4348–80, passim. If they were integrated into the employees of a firm in general, they would stand in a clear minority in most cases; the "formal" principle of the head count would ensure that their proposals would rarely stand a chance of success. Once again, a parallel with the university is worth considering, where staff far outnumber professors.

29. In other words, the conflict over the secret ballot and economic power,

fought out over the decades before World War I, would necessarily arise again. In general, Margaret L. Anderson, *Practicing Democracy: Elections and Political Culture in Imperial Germany* (Princeton, NJ: Princeton University Press, 2000).

30. Max Cohen, *Der Aufbau Deutschlands und der Rätegedanke, Revolutions—Streitfragen Neue Folge 2* (Berlin: Verlag der Kulturliga, 1919).

31. Oertzen, *Betriebsräte*, 200–201, citing J. Kaliski, *Sozialistische Monatshefte*; see Cohen's comment in Cohen, *Aufbau*, 16–17.

32. Schneider and Kuda, *Arbeiterräte*, 28–29.

33. Willibalt Apelt, *Geschichte der Weimarer Verfassung*, 2nd ed. (Munich: Beck, 1964), 224–26; Gerhard Anschütz, *Die Verfassung des deutschen Reichs vom 11. August 1919*, 14th ed. (Berlin: Stilke, 1933), 743–50.

34. Cohen's proposals, however, constitute an important link between the two positions.

35. *Deutsche Nationalversammlung* III:1209–13.

36. Edgar Tatarin-Tarnheyden, "Die staatsrechtliche Entwicklung des Räte-gedankens in der russischen und deutschen Revolutionen," *Schmollers Jahr-buch* 49 (1925): 931–32; Frank Lechler, *Parlamentsherrschaft und Regierungsstabili-tät: Die Entstehung staatsorganischer Vorschriften in den Verfassungen von Baden, Mecklenburg-Strelitz, Oldenburg, Sachsen und Württemberg 1918–1920* (Frankfurt am Main: Peter Lang, 2002), 94–95, 124–25, 205; Christian F. Trippe, *Konserva-tive Verfassungspolitik 1918–1923: Die DNVP als Opposition in Reich und Ländern* (Düsseldorf: Droste, 1995), 139–42.

37. Edgar Tatarin-Tarnheyden, *Die Berufsstände, ihre Stellung im Staatsre-cht und die deutsche Wirtschaftsverfassung* (Berlin: Carl Heymann, 1922), 154–55; Düringer's comments on March 3, 1919, in *Deutsche Nationalversammlung* II:1171–72.

38. Clemens von Delbrück's comments at the first reading of the Weimar Constitution, July 21, 1919, *Deutsche Nationalversammlung* VI:4318–26.

39. Historical sketch in Tatarin-Tarnheyden, *Berufsstände*, 113–43; see also Heinrich Herrfahrdt, *Das Problem der berufsständischen Verfassung von der franzö-sischen Revolution bis zur Gegenwart* (Stuttgart: Deutsche Verlags-Anstalt, 1921).

40. Tatarin-Tarnheyden, *Berufsstände*, 106–9.

41. Ibid., 239.

42. Ibid., 233ff., noting that the citizens are not yet ready for this abandon-ment of formal democracy.

43. Ibid., 147.

44. Ibid., 41, 159.

45. Tatarin-Tarnheyden comments on all three thinkers in his work, citing Walther Rathenau, *Der Neue Staat*; Othmar Spann, *Der wahre Staat: Vorlesungen über Abbruch und Neubau der Gesellschaft*, 5th ed. (Graz: Akademische Druck-und Verlagsanstalt, 1972), from his lectures of 1920; and Rudolf Steiner, *The Threefold Commonwealth*, trans. E. Bowen-Wedgwood (1919; repr., London: The Threefold Commonwealth, 1922). The theoretical underpinnings of Steiner's reflections on the "post-Atlantean world" in his lectures from February and March 1919 are discussed in *The Esoteric Aspect of the Social Question: The Indi-vidual and Society* (London: Rudolf Steiner Press, 2001).

46. Hans Mommsen, *Rise and Fall*, 68; Kuno Graf von Westarp, *Konservative Politik im Übergang vom Kaiserreich zur Weimarer Republik*, ed. Friedrich Freiherr Hiller von Gaertringen, Karl J. Majer, and Reinhold Weber (Düsseldorf: Droste, 2001), 200–241. On the different conservative and authoritarian alternatives to parliamentary rule in the DNVP, see Trippe, *Konservative Verfassungspolitik*, 168–70.

47. Still valuable is Kurt Sontheimer, *Antidemokratisches Denken in der Weimarer Republik* (1962; repr., Munich: DTV, 1992). But, as the present discussion shows, the differences among those who rejected democracy are also significant—not all antidemocrats were opposed to popular participation, for example.

48. Carl Schmitt, *Verfassungslehre* (Berlin: Duncker & Humblot, 1928), 79; similar phrases occur throughout the book, as noted by Margrit Kraft-Fuchs, "Prinzipielle Bemerkungen zu Carl Schmitts Verfassungslehre," *Zeitschrift für öffentliches Recht* 11 (1930): 511–41.

49. Recent works reclaiming the *Verfassungslehre* include Jeffrey Seitzer, *Comparative History and Legal Theory: Carl Schmitt in the First German Democracy* (Westport, CT: Greenwood, 2001); and Renato Cristi, *Carl Schmitt and Authoritarian Liberalism: Strong State, Free Economy* (Cardiff: University of Wales, 1998). See my "Controversies over Carl Schmitt," *Journal of Modern History* 77 (June 2005): 357–87.

50. Schmitt, *Verfassungslehre*, 51.

51. Ibid., 84.

52. Ibid., 243.

53. Ibid., 245.

54. Ibid. Does Schmitt really believe that the People are able to speak with one voice? At another point in the *Verfassungslehre* (205–6), he asserts that representation is necessary in every system to provide coherence to the popular decision.

55. Ibid., 223.

56. Ibid., 224.

57. Ibid., 227.

58. Ibid., 233.

59. Ibid., 234.

60. For example, Carl Schmitt, *Staat, Bewegung, Volk: Die Dreigliederung der politischen Einheit*, 2nd ed. (Hamburg: Hanseatisch, 1934), 42. See a similar point in my *Popular Sovereignty and the Crisis of German Constitutional Law* (Durham, NC: Duke University Press, 1997), 102, 116–17.

61. Schmitt, *Verfassungslehre*, 253.

62. For example, ibid., 240, on proportional representation; 247.

63. Ibid., 277.

64. Schmitt's notion of the democratic citizen seems utterly incompatible with the idea of the citizen in the university or other corporate organization. The parallel I alluded to in the first two examples doesn't work in the case of Schmitt: how many of us have experienced faculty members who feel a sense

of identity with their colleagues and believe that the university president is *gleichartig*? Schmitt might explain the distinction as follows: the university, like the factory and the corporate estate (and the political party), is utterly unlike the realm of the truly political, where existential decisions on friend and enemy, state of exception and state of normality, are made. A counterargument would stress that the state is a large organization, and in this sense, like the university, consists of a variety of offices and opinions—and that Schmitt's notion of the political is too limited to describe reality.

65. See especially "Wesen und Werden des faschistischen Staates," in *Positionen und Begriffe im Kampf mit Weimar-Genf-Versailles 1923–1939*, 109–15 (Berlin: Duncker & Humblot, 1988).

66. See especially Hans Kelsen, "On the Essence and Value of Democracy" (1929), and Richard Thoma, "The Reich as a Democracy" (1930), both in *Weimar: A Jurisprudence of Crisis*, ed. Arthur J. Jacobson and Bernhard Schlink, trans. Belinda Cooper et al., 84–109, 157–70 (Berkeley: University of California Press, 2000).

67. Ian Shapiro, *The State of Democratic Theory* (Princeton, NJ: Princeton University Press, 2003), 146.

68. Especially Gosewinkel, *Einbürgern und Ausschließen*, 387–90.

69. Carl Schmitt, "Die Verfassung der Freiheit," *Deutsche Juristen-Zeitung* 40 (1935): 1133–35.

70. For a corporatist solution to the problems of governance at Rice University, see the recommendations at http://www.ruf.rice.edu/~faccoun/Task ForceRptSenate.htm (accessed June 2, 2005).

CHAPTER 4

1. Letter from the BMdI to the Thuringen Interior Ministry, February 7, 1923, BayHStA Ministerium des Äusseren [henceforth: MA] 100317 (emphasis in original). The first mention of Genkin's case is made in a letter from the RMdI to the Thüringisches Ministerium der Volksbildung from April 25, 1922, BayHStA MA 100317.

2. Letter from Maria Berenz to Ebert, March 9, 1923, BayHStA, MA 100317.

3. Letter from the Bavarian Representative to the *Reichsrat* to the Bavarian Justice Minister, May 12, 1923, BayHStA, MA 100317.

4. Letter from Maria Berenz to the Thuringian Representative to the *Reichsrat*, May 3, 1923, BayHStA, MA 100317.

5. Letter from the Bavarian Representative to the *Reichsrat* to the Bavarian Justice Minister, May 17, 1923, BayHStA, MA 100317.

6. If there was even the slightest suspicion that Genkin was a Communist, this certainly would have come up in the deliberations regarding his application, as it did for so many other citizenship applicants.

7. If Genkin had not spoken German, he could not have passed the medical licensing exam. According to the Thuringian Ministry for Education, Genkin had lived "at least ten years without pause" in Germany. Letter from the Thuringian Ministry of Education to the RMdI, June 14, 1922, BayHStA MA 100317.

8. This process was laid out in §9 of the *Reichs- und Staatsangehörigkeitsgesetz* from 1913 and was essentially left unchanged after World War I.

9. Dieter Gosewinkel, *Einbürgern und Ausschließen: die Nationalisierung der Staatsangehörigkeit vom Deutschen Bund bis zur Bundesrepublik Deutschland, Kritische Studien zur Geschichtswissenschaft; Bd. 150* (Göttingen: Vandenhoeck & Ruprecht, 2001), 359. As I will discuss, the relatively liberal policies of the first years after the war became stricter very quickly. Gosewinkel does not note what percentage of applications by *fremdstämmige Ostausländer* were approved and if (or how) that changed over this period.

10. Donald Niewyk writes that the obstacles eastern European Jews faced in gaining citizenship meant that only a small minority ever submitted naturalization applications. Donald L. Niewyk, *The Jews in Weimar Germany* (Baton Rouge: Louisiana State University Press, 1980), 16.

11. Guidelines sent from the RMdI to the Länder, BA R 1501/112384, 237 and 239.

12. Letter from the Bavarian Interior Minister to the Bavarian Representative to the *Reichsrat*, September 15, 1923, BayHStA, MA 100317.

13. Annemarie Sammartino, "Migration and Crisis in Germany, 1914–1922" (PhD diss., University of Michigan, 2004); see especially chapters 5 and 8.

14. There are a wide variety of approaches used by scholars interested in broadening the definitions of citizenship. See Ronald Beiner, ed., *Theorizing Citizenship* (Albany, NY: SUNY Press, 1995); Margaret Somers, "Citizenship and the Place of the Public Sphere: Law, Community, and Political Culture in the Transition to Democracy," *American Sociological Review* 58 (1993): 587–620; Craig Calhoun, ed., *Habermas and the Public Sphere* (Boston, MA: MIT Press, 1992); Lauren Berlant, *The Queen of America Goes to Washington City: Essays on Sex and Citizenship* (Durham, NC: Duke University Press, 1997). See also Noëlle McAfee's explication of political theory to explore how citizens' subjectivity and political agency are inextricably intertwined: Noëlle McAfee, *Habermas, Kristeva, and Citizenship* (Ithaca, NY: Cornell University Press, 2000). The issue of citizenship in Germany specifically has been most recently addressed by scholars of gender. On the Wilhelmine period, see Margaret Anderson, *Practicing Democracy: Elections and Political Culture in Imperial Germany* (Princeton, NJ: Princeton University Press, 2000). For the Weimar years, see Kathleen Canning, "Class vs. Citizenship: Keywords in German Gender History," *Central European History* 37, no. 2 (2004): 225–44; Kathleen Canning and Sonya O. Rose, "Gender, Citizenship and Subjectivity: Some Historical and Theoretical Considerations," *Gender and History* 13, no. 3 (2001): 427–43; Kathleen Canning, "Embodied Citizenships: Gender in the Aftermath of War and Revolution in Germany, 1917–30" (unpublished manuscript); Julia Sneeringer, *Winning Women's Votes: Propaganda and Politics in Weimar Germany* (Chapel Hill: University of North Carolina, 2002).

15. See Ruth Lister's point that citizenship needs to be seen as both practice and status. Ruth Lister, "Citizenship: Towards a Feminist Synthesis," *Feminist Review* 57 (1997): 25. Canning also makes this point in Canning, "Class vs. Citizenship," 242.

16. Timothy Mitchell, "The Limits of the State: Beyond Statist Approaches and Their Critics," *The American Political Science Review* 85, no. 1 (1991): 77–96.

17. For representatives of these two poles, see Rogers Brubaker, *Citizenship and Nationhood in France and Germany* (Cambridge, MA: Harvard University Press, 1992), in particular his explicit statement to this effect on p. 22; and Aihwa Ong, "Cultural Citizenship as Subject Making: Immigrants Negotiate Racial and Cultural Boundaries in the United States," in *Race, Identity and Citizenship: A Reader*, ed. Rodolfo D. Torres, Louis F. Mirón, and Jonathan Xavier Inda, 262 (Oxford: Oxford University Press, 1999).

18. See Benedict Anderson, *Imagined Communities: Reflections on the Origin and Spread of Nationalism* (London: Verso, 1991).

19. On tolerance in the Weimar Republic, see Sammartino, "Migration," chs. 8 and 9.

20. Letter from the Bavarian Interior Minister to the Mecklenburg Interior Minister, May 18, 1923, BayHStA, MA 100317.

21. Letter from the Bavarian Representative to the *Reichsrat* to the Bavarian Interior and Exterior Ministers, September 24, 1923, BayHStA, MA 100317.

22. Letter from Heine to the Staatsrat für Anhalt in Dessau, May 31, 1919, SächsHStA, Staatsministerium des Innern 9725, 14.

23. Ibid. See also Gosewinkel, *Einbürgern*, 353.

24. Ibid., 354.

25. Guidelines sent from the RMdI to the Länder, June 1, 1921, BA R 1501/112384, 237–40.

26. Ibid., 237.

27. Ibid., 239.

28. Ibid.

29. Ibid., 240.

30. Report on the results of a meeting at the RMdI about many questions regarding the law for citizenship in the Reich and the states, September 3, 1920, BayHStA, MA 100317.

31. Gosewinkel, *Einbürgern*, 356.

32. See the case of Frommert for an example of a situation where the *Fürsorgeverein für deutsche Rückwanderer* was called in to attest to an applicant's German descent: GStA PK, Rep. 77, Tit. 226b, no. 1F, vol. 2.

33. Letter from the Police President to the Oberpräsident zu Charlottenburg, February 28, 1919. GStA PK, Rep. 77, Tit. 226b, no. 1H, vol. 2. It appears that Halpern had married a German woman whose parents "would not have understood if he had been deported" and had to take their daughter along.

34. Letter from the Württemberg Ministry of the Interior to the Prussian Ministry of the Interior, September 20, 1920; letter from the Prussian Ministry of the Interior to the Württemberg Ministry of the Interior, November 9, 1920, GStA PK, I. HA., Rep. 77, Tit. 226b, no. 1B, vol. 3.

35. Application sent from the Polizeipräsident in Berlin to the Prussian Interior Ministry, February 17, 1919, GStA PK, 1. HA., Rep. 77, Tit. 226b, no. 1E, vol. 1. The Interior Ministry's response is not recorded.

36. These reasons were actually used to describe an application from Syllies, but the letter from the Regierungspräsident in Munster to the Prussian Interior Ministry from December 21, 1921, describing the case states that the same factors applied for the case of Müller. GStA PK, 1. HA, Rep. 77, Tit. 226b, no. 1, vol. 41.

37. See, for example, the case of Alfred Schoft, a Communist of German descent, who was denied citizenship by the Bavarians on the grounds that his citizenship would create a danger to public order: Letter from the Bavarian representative to the *Reichsrat* (Nüßlein) to the Bavarian Minister of Justice, October 22, 1922, BayHStA, MA 100317. See also: Letter from the PMI to the SMI, May 19, 1921 regarding the citizenship of Paul and Reinhard Richter, SächsHStA, MInnen, 9816, 20. The Saxons' response to this letter, specifically their contention that membership in the Communist party did not suffice as grounds for the denial of a citizenship application, is also interesting in this regard: Letter from the SMI to the PMI, June 6, 1921, SächsHStA, MInnen, 9816, 23. See also the multiple objections to the citizenship application of Johann Werner, who participated in the March 1921 Communist uprising: Letter from the PMI to the SMI, June 29, 1921, SächsHStA, MInnen, 9816, 39; Letter from the Württembergische Ministerium des Innern to the SMI, May 31, 1921, SächsHStA, MInnen, 9816, 40; Letter from the Lübeck Stadt und Landamt to the SMI, May 28, 1921, SächsHStA, MInnen, 9816, 41.

38. Letter from the Regierungspräsident in Cöpenick to the Prussian Ministry of the Interior, July 9, 1919, GStA PK, 1. HA., Rep. 77, Tit. 226b, no. 1B, vol. 3. According to a stamp, application was approved on August 22, 1919.

39. Letter from the Regierungspräsident in Potsdam to the Preussisches Ministerium des Innern, May 21, 1919, GStA PK, 1. HA., Rep. 77, Tit. 226b, no. 1D, vol. 2. According to a stamp, application was approved on August 16, 1919. It is unclear from this letter if Ms. Donat was married or single but, as special mention was made by the Potsdam Regierungspräsident of her lack of employment, I tend to think that she was single.

40. Letter from the Police President to the Prussian Ministry of the Interior, July 29, 1918, GStA PK, 1. HA., Rep. 77, Tit. 226b, no. 1M, vol. 3.

41. Letter from the Prussian Interior Ministry to the Regierungspräsident in Arnsberg, August 31, 1919, GStA PK, 1. HA., Rep. 77, Tit. 226b, no. 1E, vol. 1 (emphasis in the original).

42. Letter from the Mayor of Hagen to the Regierungspräsident in Arnsberg, October 6, 1919, GStA PK, 1. HA., Rep. 77, Tit. 226b, no. 1E, vol. 1.

43. See, for example, Letter from the Staatskommision für die öffentliche Ordnung to the Prussian Interior Ministry, September 28, 1920, GStA PK, 1. HA., Rep. 77, Tit. 226b, no. 1E, vol. 1.

44. Letter from Ellinghaus to the Prussian Interior Ministry, December 14, 1920, GStA PK, 1. HA., Rep. 77, Tit. 226b, no. 1E, vol. 1.

45. Estersohn's business success is not explicitly discussed, but I am assuming that he was at least relatively successful in order to be able to afford a lawyer, something that most applicants did not seem to have.

46. Letter from the Bavarian Interior Ministry to the Bavarian Foreign Min-

istry, December 9, 1921, BayHStA, MA 100317. In this letter, the official also writes that one needed to be careful because even some with German names were not necessarily Germans. Thus it was necessary to check what schools the applicant had gone to, whether he spoke German and "seemed German," etc. This official's own last name, by the way, was von Spreti.

47. Letter from the Mecklenburg-Strelitzisches Ministerium to the Bavarian Ministry of the Interior, BayHStA, MA 100317. The Mecklenburg-Strelitz minister acknowledged the Bavarian twenty-year requirement. This requirement was established by the Bavarians at least as early as 1922, as it was referenced by the Bavarian Interior Minister, von Spreti, in a letter from that year to the Badisches Staatsministerium, Ministerial Abteilung für Präsidiale, Reichs- und auswärtige Angelegenheiten, BA R 1501/108045, 12. The Prussians raised their minimum residency requirement in 1921 to fifteen years and in 1925 to twenty; see Gosewinkel, *Einbürgern*, 356.

48. See, for example, the heated debate between Saxony and Bavaria in 1922–23: BayHStA, MA 100317. This debate and others show how citizenship policy was not only a question of citizenship of foreigners per se but also of the rivalry between various German states. Württemberg's politics are discussed by Manfred Scheck, *Zwischen Weltkrieg und Revolution: Zur Geschichte der Arbeiterbewegung in Württemberg 1914–1920* (Köln: Böhlau, 1981). For more on Saxon politics during this period, see Karsten Rudolph, *Die sächsische Sozialdemokratie vom Kaiserreich zur Republik (1871–1923)* (Weimar: Böhlau, 1995); Benjamin Lapp, *Revolution from the Right: Politics, Class, and the Rise of Nazism in Saxony, 1919–1933* (Atlantic Highlands, NJ: Humanities Press, 1997); Sean Dobson, *Authority and Upheaval in Leipzig, 1910–1920: The Story of a Relationship* (New York: Columbia University Press, 2001). For the *longue durée* (or at least a longer *durée*) of Saxon history, see James Retallack, *Saxony in German History: Culture, Society, and Politics, 1830–1933* (Ann Arbor: University of Michigan Press, 2000).

49. Letter from the Prussian Minister of the Interior to the RMdI, February 17, 1923; Letter from the Saxon Minister of the Interior to the RMdI, May 17, 1922, BayHStA, MA 100317.

50. For the Dresden district office's position, see Letter from the Dresden Kreishauptmannschaft to the Ministerium des Innern, January 23, 1922, SächsHStA Ministerium des Innern 9725, 56; and Internal Memo, October 27, 1920, SächsHStA Ministerium des Innern 9710, 249.

51. Lipinski was a member of the USPD until that party disbanded in late 1920, after which he joined the SPD. Lipinski was Minister of the Interior for the first few months of the republic, and then again between July 1920 and February 1923: Sachsen.de, "Dynastien und Kabinette," http://www.sachsen .de/de/ll/geschichte/regenten/1918-1924/inhalt_re.html.

52. Kreishauptmannschaft Leipzig to Sächsisches Minister des Innern, November 28, 1919, SächsHStA Ministerium des Innern 9710, 255. The Kreishauptmannschaft Leipzig sent a later warning about Goluchowski, n.d. SächsHStA MdInnern 9710, 348.

53. Sächsisches Minister des Innern to the Kreishauptmannschaft Leipzig, May 17, 1922, SächsHStA MdInnern 9711, 19.

54. Lipinski's own skepticism regarding Goluchowski's chances of naturalization may be guessed at by the way that he ends his letter: "the Ministry of the Interior has no objections to including him in the monthly list [of people sent to the other Länder] for the goal of naturalization." Ibid. Lipinski surely had no illusions that Goluchowski would actually be granted citizenship, believing merely that he was worthy of inclusion on the monthly list. For other examples along the same lines, see the handling of the cases of Haber and Gewürz: Letter from the Sächsisches Innenministerium to the Kreishauptmannschaft Chemnitz, November 8, 1921, SächsHStA MdInnern, 9710, 356. See also the case of the widow Tumpowsky and her daughter. Tumpowsky had moved to Germany before 1870 and her daughter had been born in Germany. Tumpowsky's two sons had served in the military and been naturalized. Although the local authorities feared that both Tumpowsky and her daughter could become burdens on the state, the Ministry recommended their naturalization, claiming that this sort of potential burden was not sufficient grounds for denying their applications: Letter from the SächsMdI to the Kreishauptmannschaft Leipzig, January 17, 1923, SächsHStA MdI, 9711, 83.

55. Letter from the Bavarian Interior Minister to the Bavarian Representative to the *Reichsrat*, September 15, 1923, BayHStA, MA 100317.

56. After a letter from Baden describing the situation, the Bavarian Minister of the Interior relented in a letter dated May 4, 1921, BayHStA, MA 100317.

57. Letter from the Bavarian Minister of the Interior, June 24, 1921, BayHStA, MA 100317.

58. Gosewinkel, *Einbürgern*, 356.

59. Ibid., 361.

60. Ibid., 362.

CHAPTER 5

1. This final episode was broadcast on October 4, 1969.

2. Charles Tilly, "A Primer on Citizenship," *Theory and Society* 26 (1997): 599–603.

3. T. H. Marshall, *Citizenship and Social Class* (1950; repr., London: Pluto Press, 1992).

4. Marshall, *Citizenship*, 8.

5. Albert O. Hirschman, "Exit, Voice, and the Fate of the German Democratic Republic: An Essay in Conceptual History," *World Politics* 45 (1993): 173–202.

6. For thoughtful critiques of Habermas and Marshall, respectively, see, for instance, Geoff Eley, "Nations, Publics, and Political Culture: Placing Habermas in the Nineteenth Century," in *Habermas and the Public Sphere*, ed. Craig Calhoun, 289–339 (Boston, MA: MIT Press, 1992); Margaret R. Somers, "Citizenship and the Place of the Public Sphere: Law, Community and Political Culture in the Transition to Democracy," *American Sociological Review* 58 (1993): 587–620.

7. Charles Tilly, "Citizenship, Identity, and Social History," in *Citizenship,*

Identity, and Social History, ed. Charles Tilly, 1–18 (Cambridge: Cambridge University Press, 1996).

8. The perspective of citizenship does share many traits with that of "everyday history" and its concern with how power is transmitted. In practice, however, this has often led to a focus on different facets of everyday life that, for all its importance, often reads as though the GDR were an ideology-free sphere.

9. For an excellent overview of current research, see Günther Heydemann and Heinrich Oberreuter, eds., *Diktaturen in Deutschland: Vergleichsaspekte; Strukturen, Institutionen und Verhaltensweisen* (Bonn: Bundeszentrale für politische Bildung, 2003).

10. Patrice G. Poutrus, "Zuflucht im Ausreiseland: Zur Geschichte des politischen Asyls in der DDR," *Jahrbuch für Kommunismusforschung* 17 (2004): 255–57.

11. Hermann Klenner, *Studien über die Grundrechte: Mit Dokumentenanhang* (East Berlin: Staatsverlag der Deutschen Demokratischen Republik, 1964), 49–56. "In dem Maße, in dem der Einzelne seine persönlichen Kräfte bewußt in den geswellschaftlichen Strom zum Sozialismus einfließen läßt, in dem Maße wächst er und die Gesellschaft. Persönlichkeitsentwicklung und Volksherrschaft sind ihrem Wesen nach identisch" (56).

12. Uwe-Jens Heuer, *Marxismus und Demokratie*, 2nd ed. (Baden-Baden: Nomos, 1990), ii.

13. The textbook on *Staatsbürgerkunde* for teaching in schools was symptomatic in that it described the citizen through ideology, economics, and society while shying away from discussing the meaning of citizenship, and its relation to the state, explicitly. *Staatsbürgerkunde: Dokumente und Materialien*, 2nd ed. (East Berlin: Dietz Verlag, 1965). The first edition of this book was published in 1964.

14. Gerhard Riege, *Zwei Staaten, Zwei Staatsbürgerschaften* (East Berlin: Staatsverlag der Deutschen Demokratischen Republik, 1967), 6–7.

15. Riege, *Zwei Staaten*; see especially 1–92 and, for the conclusion, 92–96.

16. For a contrasting view asserting that a distinctive GDR citizenship developed in response to Willy Brandt's *Ostpolitik* (i.e., in the early to mid-1970s), see Mary Fulbrook, "Germany for the Germans? Citizenship and Nationality in a Divided Nation," in *Citizenship, Nationality and Migration in Europe*, ed. Mary Fulbrook and David Cesarini, 88–105 (London: Routledge, 1996).

17. Friedrich-Ebert-Stiftung, *Die Staatsbürgerschaft der DDR* (Bonn: Verlag Neue Gesellschaft, 1984), 11–12.

18. Gerhard Riege and Hans-Jürgen Kulke, *Nationalität: deutsch; Staatsbürgerschaft: DDR* (East Berlin: Staatsverlag der Deutschen Demokratischen Republik, 1979).

19. Riege, *Zwei Staaten*, 19–20.

20. *DDR: Gesellschaft, Staat, Bürger*, 3rd ed. (Berlin: Staatsverlag der Deutschen Demokratischen Republik, 1979), 85.

21. Hans-Jürgen Kulke, "Der Staatsbürger der DDR: Seine Stellung und sein Schutz in nichtsozialistischen Staaten" (PhD diss., Friedrich-Schiller-Universität Jena, 1977), 7–15.

22. Gerhard Riege, *Der Bürger im sozialistischen Staat* (Berlin: Staatsverlag der Deutschen Demokratischen Republik, 1973), 55–56.

23. Gerhard Schulze et al., *DDR: Bürgerinteressen als Staatspolitik*, ed. Akademie für Staats- und Rechtswissenschaft in der DDR Potsdam-Babelsberg (Berlin: Staatsverlag der Deutschen Demokratischen Republik, 1984).

24. On the difficult relationship between rights and duties, see Otto Luchterhand, *Der verstaatlichte Mensch: Grundpflichten des Bürgers in der DDR* (Cologne: Carl Heymanns Verlag, 1985), 39–106.

25. Gerhard Riege, *Die Staatsbürgerschaft der DDR*, 2nd ed. (East Berlin: Staatsverlag der Deutschen Demokratischen Republik, 1986), 74–79.

26. Riege, *Staatsbürgerschaft*, 73.

27. Karl A. Mollnau et al., *Rechtshandbuch für den Bürger*, 2nd ed., ed. Institut für Theorie des Staates und des Rechts der Akademie der Wissenschaften der DDR (East Berlin: Staatsverlag der Deutschen Demokratischen Republik, 1986), 49; Friedrich-Ebert-Stiftung, *Staatsbürgerschaft*, 17–19. According to GDR law, acquiring a foreign citizenship was only legal if the consent of the GDR authorities had been obtained previously. Riege, *Staatsbürgerschaft*, 320.

28. Kulke, "Der Staatsbürger der DDR," esp. 53–59.

29. Mollnau et al., *Rechtshandbuch*, 48.

30. Schulze, *DDR: Bürgerinteressen*, 101.

31. For an analogy with the practice of granting asylum, see Poutrus, "Zuflucht," 363–64.

32. Interestingly, the principle of revocation was enshrined in GDR law as early as 1964. Riege, *Staatsbürgerschaft*, 328–31.

33. K. Sorgenicht, "Vervollkommnung der sozialistischen Demokratie: Hauptrichtung der Entwicklung der sozialistischen Einheit," *Einheit* 31 (1976/77), 741–48; *DDR: Gesellschaft*, 74–76.

34. Mollnau et al., *Rechtshandbuch*, 56–57.

35. Inga Markovits, *Imperfect Justice: An East-West German Diary* (Oxford: Oxford University Press, 1995), 11.

36. Inga Markovits, "Civil Law in East Germany: Its Development and Relation to Soviet Legal History and Ideology," *Yale Law Journal* 78 (1968): 1–51.

37. Der Staatsrat der Deutschen Demokratischen Republik, *Schiedskommissionen: Organe der Erziehung und Selbsterziehung der Bürger* (Berlin: Schriftenreihe des Staatsrates der Deutschen Demokratischen Republik, 1964).

38. The aim of GDR law to be a "social lever" is a leitmotiv in the excellent Markovits, *Imperfect Justice*, especially 13–14, 34, and 45–46.

39. Wolfgang Bernet, "Verwaltungsrecht," in *Die Rechtsordnung der DDR: Anspruch und Wirklichkeit*, ed. Uwe Jens Heuer, 395–426 (Baden-Baden: Nomos, 1995); Peter Caldwell, *Dictatorship, State Planning, and Social Theory in the German Democratic Republic* (Cambridge: Cambridge University Press, 2003), 84–93; Markovits, *Imperfect Justice*, 104–10.

40. Erhard Poppe, *Der Bürger im Verwaltungsrecht der DDR*, Sitzungsberichte der Akademie der Wissenschaften der DDR, Gesellschaftswissenschaften, Jahrgang 1984, no. 6/G (Berlin: Akademie-Verlag der DDR, 1984).

41. Bernet, "Verwaltungrecht," 413.

42. Hermann Wentker, *Justiz in der SBZ/DDR: Transformation und Rolle ihrer zentralen Institutionen* (Munich: Oldenbourg, 2001). On Havemann, see the lively account of Katja Havemann and Joachim Widmann, *Robert Havemann oder Wie die DDR sich erledigte* (Berlin: Ullstein, 2003).

43. Markovits, *Imperfect Justice*, 12–13.

44. There is an excellent description of how the closeness between courts, the state attorneys, and political and social representatives led to the perversion of justice in Inga Markovits, "Rechts-Geschichte: Ein DDR-Zivilprozeß aus den 1980er Jahren," in *Akten; Eingaben; Schaufenster: Die DDR und ihre Texte; Erkundungen zu Herrschaft und Alltag*, ed. Alf Lüdtke and Peter Becker, 259–78 (Berlin: Akademie Verlag, 1997).

45. This corresponds to R. Bin Wong's point about the importance of a third-party adjudicator and enforcer in the state-citizenship relationship. What matters, according to Wong, is not the practical outcome of these adjudications, but that enforcement against the state is seen to be possible. R. Bin Wong, "Citizenship in Chinese History," in *Extending Citizenship, Reconfiguring States*, ed. Michael Hanagan and Charles Tilly, 97–122 (New York: Rowman & Littlefield, 1999).

46. Georg Brunner, "Rechtsschutz gegenüber der öffentlichen Gewalt," in *Menschenrechte in der DDR*, ed. Georg Brunner, 275–87 (Baden-Baden: Nomos, 1989).

47. Heidrun Pohl and Gerhard Schulze, *Anliegen der Bürger: Wie werden sie bearbeitet?* (Berlin: Staatsverlag der Deutschen Demokratischen Republik, 1984).

48. See the contributions by Manfred Gerlach and Hermann Kalb in *Eingaben der Bürger: Eine Form der Verwirklichung des Grundrechtes auf Mitbestimmung und Mitgestaltung, Materialien der 18; Sitzung des Staatsrates der DDR am 20 November 1969*, no. 10, ed. Abteilung Presse und Information des Staatsrates der Deutschen Demokratischen Republik (Berlin: Staatsverlag der Deutschen Demokratischen Republik, 1969).

49. Ina Merkel, ed., *Wir sind doch nicht die Meckerecke der Nation!: Briefe an das Fernsehen der DDR*, 2nd ed. (Berlin: Schwarzkopf & Schwarzkopf, 2000), 23–26.

50. See, for instance, the reports of the People's Chamber's petitions committee, which went on fact-finding missions to different electoral districts to report on the petitions there. Depending on the reporting deputy, the information that came to light on a range of economic and social problems was remarkable.

51. Pohl and Schulze, *Anliegen der Bürger*, 6.

52. Hence, petitions to the TV show *Prisma* constituted a way for citizens to vent their frustration or overcome their impotence vis-à-vis the state. Ina Merkel and Felix Mühlberg, "Eingaben und Öffentlichkeit" in Merkel, *Meckerecke*, 11–46.

53. A wealth of evidence in this respect is available in BArch SAPMO, DY 30/ IV B2/12. Zentralkomitee der Sozialistischen Einheitspartei Deutschlands, Abteilung Sicherheitsfragen 1972–1980.

54. In a different context, Ina Merkel has pointed to a precarious balance evident from the language of petitions between a tone signifying the petitioners' willingness to engage with the system on its own terms and a tone of frustration, which had an opposite, subversive effect. Ina Merkel, "'. . . in Hoyerswerda leben jedenfalls keine viereckigen Menschen.': Briefe an das Fernsehen der DDR," in Lüdtke and Becker, *Akten,* 279–310.

55. *DDR: Gesellschaft,* 75.

56. For the role of local party officials in integrating the population in accordance with the party ideals, see Detlef Schmiechen-Ackermann, "Die Staatsparteien NSDAP und SED als lokale Vermittlungsinstanzen der Diktatur," in Heydemann and Oberreuter, *Diktaturen,* 150–87.

57. On the responsibility of local state organs for the realization of policy, see *Die Versorgung der Bürger mit Wohnraum, Konsumgütern und Dienstleistungen—Rechtsfragen der Leitung,* Aktuelle Beiträge der Staats- und Rechtswissenschaft, 339 (Potsdam-Babelsberg: Akademie für Staats- und Rechtswissenschaft der DDR, 1987).

58. Fritz Ullmann, "Das A und O unserer Kommunalpolitik," in *Leiten zum Wohl der Bürger,* 8–43 (East Berlin: Staatsverlag der Deutschen Demokratischen Republik, 1986).

59. One former mayor stated at the end of an interview (after the tape recorder had been switched off!) that the more open level of discourse in the locality had been intentional, designed as a valve to let off steam. This is highly plausible, but I have not come across any archival evidence in support of this claim.

60. Adelheid von Saldern, ed., *Inszenierte Einigkeit: Herrschaftsrepräsentationen in DDR Städten* (Stuttgart: Franz Steiner Verlag, 2003).

61. Klenner, *Grundrechte,* 117.

62. Jan Palmowski, "Defining the East German Nation: The Construction of a Socialist Heimat, 1945–1962," *Central European History* 37, no. 3 (2004): 365–99.

63. Michael Benjamin, "Der Bürger und seine Heimatstadt im sozialistischen Vaterland," in *Der Bürger und seine Heimatstadt,* ed. Akademie für Staats- und Rechtswissenschaft der DDR Potsdam-Babelsberg, 11–23 (East Berlin: Staatsverlag der DDR, 1979); Erik Hühns, *Heimat; Vaterland; Nation* (Berlin: Verlag Tribüne and Deutscher Kulturbund, 1969), 96.

64. Klaus Lenk, "Die Nationale Front vertieft die Verbundenheit der Bürger mit ihrer sozialistischen Heimat," in Benjamin, *Bürger,* 44–47. Given the importance that the SED attached to reaching the individual at the workplace, it is most striking that the workplace took up a relatively minor position in contemporary publications on citizenship.

65. Adelheid von Saldern, "Öffentlichkeiten in Diktaturen," in Heydemann and Oberreuter, *Diktaturen,* 442–75.

66. "Der hatte was zu sagen."

67. "Der hat doch keine Chance gehabt. Hab ich gesagt, 'Junge, wenn Du keine Flocke machst, da gibt's 'nen grossen Schlag.'" Interview with Peter Apel, Eisenach, June 18, 2003.

68. "Ja, aber was wolln' se denn mit so einem Spinner in so'ner Gemein-schaft!" Interview with Peter Apel, Eisenach, June 18, 2003.

69. As Apel pointed out, you could not just say that you needed a pub to gulp down your beers; you needed to find the appropriate ways of expression.

70. ". . . der war 'n Arbeiter, der stand dazu." Interview with Peter Apel, Eisenach, June 18, 2003.

71. Bärbel Bohley, "Vierzig Jahre warten," in *40 Jahre DDR . . . und die Bürger melden sich zu Wort*, ed. Bärbel Bohley, et al., 5–11 (Frankfurt: Büchergilde Gutenberg, 1989).

72. This point echoes Sigrid Meuschel's argument that the state had to look for new areas of legitimacy due to the successive erosion of its political, economic, and ideological claims. However, citizenship provides a much more comprehensive framework of analysis than the concept of legitimacy, because citizenship is less biased toward an analysis of state and party, and considers equally the perspective of individual and communal relations at the everyday.

73. On the meanings of *Eigen-Sinn*, see Alf Lüdtke, *Eigen-Sinn: Fabrikalltag, Arbeitererfahrungen und Politik vom Kaiserreich bis in den Faschismus* (Hamburg: Ergebnisse Verlag, 1993).

74. Hermann Wentker, "Justiz in der SBZ/DDR und im 'Dritten Reich': Ein Vergleich aus der Perspektive der zentralen Institutionen," in Heydemann and Oberreuter, *Diktaturen*, 188–218.

75. Dieter Gosewinkel, *Einbürgern und Ausschließen: Die Nationalisierung der Staatsangehörigkeit vom Deutschen Bund bis zur Bundesrepublik Deutschland* (Göttingen: Vandenhoeck & Ruprecht, 2001).

76. In an interview, when talking about the problems of the Politburo and Honecker's leadership, Karl-Heinz Schulmeister referred explicitly to the Biermann case as something scandalous because "Germany had practiced the exclusion from citizenship before." Karl-Heinz Schulmeister was First Secretary of the Cultural League from 1959 to 1990 and the leader of the Cultural League's representation in the People's Assembly. Interview with Karl-Heinz Schulmeister, November 11, 2002.

77. See, for instance, Ernst Rudolf Huber, *Wesen und Inhalt der politischen Verfassung* (Hamburg: Hanseatische Verlagsanstalt, 1935), especially 16.

78. One striking feature that emerged from recent documentaries on the Stasi shown on German public television (ARD) is the repeated insistence of both Stasi officials and covert agents in the GDR and the FRG that their actions never led to the loss of life. *Verrat im Westen*, ARD, July 22, 2004; *Alltag einer Behörde*, ARD, July 28, 2004.

79. A good example of how sensitive the state was to public (and especially Western) criticism that it betrayed its own values can be gauged from Havemann and Widmann, *Robert Havemann*, passim.

80. Bohley, *40 Jahre DDR*, 7.

81. Charles Tilly, *Contention and Democracy in Europe, 1650–2000* (Cambridge: Cambridge University Press, 2004), 29–30.
82. Ibid., 31.
83. Ibid., 55–56.

CHAPTER 6

1. See the section "Louis-Philippe or the Interior," the fourth sketch in *Paris: The Capital of the Nineteenth Century*, in Walter Benjamin, *Charles Baudelaire: A Lyric Poet in the Era of High Capitalism*, 167 (London: Verso, 1983).

2. See, among others, Thomas Nipperdey, "War die Wilhelminische Gesell-schaft eine Untertanen-Gesellschaft?" *Nachdenken über die deutsche Geschichte* (Munich: Dt. Taschenbuch-Verlag, 1990), 208–24; Stanley Suval, *Electoral Politics in Wilhelmine Germany* (Chapel Hill: University of North Carolina Press, 1985); Kevin Repp, *Reformers, Critics and the Paths of German Modernity: Anti-Politics and the Search for Alternatives, 1890–1914* (Cambridge, MA: Harvard University Press, 2000); Margaret Lavinia Anderson, *Practicing Democracy: Elections and Political Culture in Imperial Germany* (Princeton, NJ: Princeton University Press, 2000); Geoff Eley and James Retallack, eds., *Wilhelminism and Its Legacies: German Modernities, Imperialism and the Meanings of Reform 1890–1930* (New York: Berghahn Books, 2003).

3. Kathleen Canning, "Class vs. Citizenship: Keywords in German Gender History," *Central European History* 37, no. 2 (June 2004): 225–44; Kathleen Canning and Sonya Rose, eds., *Gender, Citizenships and Subjectivities* (Oxford: Blackwell, 2002); Lauren Berlant, *The Queen of America Goes to Washington City: Essays on Sex and Citizenship* (Durham, NC: Duke University Press, 1997); Aihwa Ong, *Flexible Citizenship: The Cultural Logics of Transnationality* (Durham, NC: Duke University Press, 1999). Michel de Certeau's writings have been important to work in historical geography that conceptualizes "dominant discourses and practices of citizenship" as "techniques of spatial organization." For an example, see Anna Secor, "There Is an Istanbul That Belongs to Me: Citizenship, Space and Identity in the City," *Annals of the Association of American Geographers* 94, no. 2 (2004): 352–68. Such work also draws substantially on Ernesto Laclau and Chantal Mouffe, *Hegemony and Socialist Strategy* (London: Verso, 1985).

4. "Before 1914 the full-blown ideal of the nation-people-citizenry as the basis for state-political organization was still only in the process of being proposed." Geoff Eley, "Making a Place in the Nation: Meanings of 'Citizen-ship' in Wilhelmine Germany," in Eley and Retallack, *Wilhelminism and Its Legacies*; Geoff Eley, "State Formation, Nationalism and Political Culture: Some Thoughts on the Unification of Germany," in *From Unification to Nazism*, ed. G. Eley, 61–84 (Boston: Allen & Unwin, 1986); Andreas K. Fahrmeir, "Nineteenth-Century German Citizenships: A Reconsideration," *Historical Journal* 40, no. 3 (September 1997): 721–52. Rogers Brubaker [*Citizenship and Nation-*

hood in France and Germany (Cambridge, MA: Harvard University Press, 1992)], by contrast, emphasizes the constant of "descent" in the making of German citizenship law. For a useful specification of Brubaker's argument, see Dieter Gosewinkel, "Citizenship in Germany and France at the Turn of the Twentieth Century: Some New Observations on an Old Comparison," in this volume.

5. Berlant, *Queen of America*, 31.

6. Example given in Laurie Stein, "Germany: Design and National Identity, 1890–1918," in *Designing Modernity: The Arts of Reform and Persuasion, 1885–1945*, ed. Wendy Kaplan, 49–77 (London: Thames & Hudson, 1995).

7. Leora Auslander, "Citizenship Law, State Form and Everyday Aesthetics in Modern France and Germany, 1920–1940," in *The Politics of Consumption: Material Culture and Citizenship in Europe and America*, ed. Martin Daunton and Matthew Hilton, 109–28 (Oxford: Berg, 2001).

8. Eric Hobsbawm and Terence J. Ranger, eds., *The Invention of Tradition* (Cambridge: Cambridge University Press, 1983); Eugen Weber, *Peasants into Frenchmen: The Modernization of Rural France, 1870–1914* (Stanford, CA: Stanford University Press, 1976). As Edward Said pointed out, these strategies were aimed primarily at rural populations. See Said, "Invention, Memory and Place," *Critical Inquiry* 26, no. 2 (Winter 2000): 175–92. In contrast, the creation of the citizen consumer discussed in this article initially focused on urban areas and middle- and working-class populations.

9. Berlant, *Queen of America*, 30.

10. Stein, "Germany," 49.

11. See Auslander, "Citizenship Law," as well as her *Taste and Power: Furnishing Modern France* (Berkeley: University of California Press, 1996). I disagree with Auslander's reading of citizenship, consumption, and national culture in Germany in "Citizenship Law." Her assessment that German citizen consumers were "born" rather than "made" whereas French citizen consumers were "made" and not "born" comes too close to the essentialized conceptions that motivate Brubaker's work. This article, by contrast, picks up on her insights about France.

12. *Wohnkultur* is one way of thinking about the operation of what Eley, following Lauren Berlant, has called the "National Symbolic" and its connections to citizenship. Eley, "Making a Place," 18–19. For the term, see Lauren Berlant, *The Anatomy of National Fantasy: Hawthorne, Utopia and Everyday Life* (Chicago: University of Chicago Press, 1991), 20.

13. As Bruno Taut wrote to his brother Max, "[W]hat Alfred Messel has created here is more than a store—it is the archetype for all stores." Its function "exposed itself, so to speak, so nakedly to the observer." Quoted in Ian Boyd White, *Bruno Taut and the Architecture of Activism* (Cambridge: Cambridge University Press, 1982), 17.

14. Lux focused mainly on homes, but some of his works detail the proper furnishings for rented apartments. For the latter, see his *Die Stadtwohnung: Wie man sich praktisch, schön und preiswert einrichtet und gut erhält* (Berlin: Charlottenburg Schillerbuchhandlung, 1910).

15. Joseph August Lux, *Der Geschmack im Alltag*, 2nd ed. (Dresden: Kühtmann 1910), III.

16. Lux, *Geschmack*, 30.

17. On the *Werkbund*, see in particular Frederic J. Schwartz, *The Werkbund: Design Theory and Mass Culture Before the First World War* (New Haven, CT: Yale University Press, 1996); and John Maciuika, *Before the Bauhaus: Architecture, Politics and the German State, 1890–1920* (Cambridge: Cambridge University Press, 2005).

18. The literature on the *Werkbund* is extensive. See Joan Campbell, *The German Werkbund: The Politics of Reform in the Applied Arts* (Princeton, NJ: Princeton University Press, 1978); Staatliches Museum für angewandte Kunst München, *Zwischen Kunst und Industrie: Der deutsche Werkbund* (München: Dt. Verl.-Anst., 1975); Angelika Thiekötter and Eckhard Siepmann, *Packeis und Pressglas: Von der Kunstgewerbebewegung zum Deutschen Werkbund* (Giessen: Anabas-Verl., 1987); and Hans Eckstein, *50 Jahre Deutscher Werkbund* (Frankfurt: Metzner, 1958). The role played by architecture and design in addressing social and political issues is covered by Barbara Miller Lane, *Architecture and Politics in Germany 1918–1945* (Cambridge, MA: Harvard University Press, 1968); and Kathleen James-Chakraborty, *German Architecture for a Mass Audience* (London: Routledge, 2000).

19. On the nationalism and imperialism of the *Werkbund*, see Maciuika, *Before the Bauhaus*; Wolfgang Hardtwig, "Kunst, liberaler Nationalismus und Weltpolitik: Der Deutsche *Werkbund*, 1907–1914," in *Nationalismus und Bürgerkultur in Deutschland 1500–1914*, ed. Wolfgang Hardtwig (Göttingen: Vandenhoeck & Ruprecht, 1994); and Mark Jarzombek, "The Discourse of a Bourgeois Utopia, 1904–1908, and the Founding of the *Werkbund*," in *Imagining Modern German Culture 1889–1910*, ed. Francoise Forster-Hahn, 127–45 (Washington, DC: National Gallery of Art, 1996).

20. Schwartz's and Maciuika's excellent books thoroughly disabuse one or both of these assumptions.

21. See, above all, Maciuika, *Before the Bauhaus*.

22. Benedict Anderson, *Imagined Communities: Reflections on the Origin and Spread of Nationalism* (London: Verso, 1991).

23. Eley, "Making a Place," 17. Here Lux's discussion of taste and national character comes close to Eley's discussion of the "National Symbolic." This "politics of nationalist pedagogy" did depend, as Eley states, more on private than on official bodies in the Wilhelmine period, as in the 1860s, the period to which he attached the statement.

24. The "everyday" is used here to designate a space for organized intervention and rationalization, and not in the sense used by Michel de Certeau to point to a space of resistance. For the former, see Paul Rabinow, *French Modern: Norms and Forms of the Social Environment* (Cambridge, MA: MIT Press, 1989). For the latter, see Michel de Certeau, *The Practice of Everyday Life*, trans. Steven F. Rendall (Berkeley: University of California Press, 1984); and Alf Lüdtke, *Eigen-Sinn: Fabrikalltag, Arbeitererfahrungen und Politik vom Kaiserreich bis in den Faschismus* (Hamburg: Ergebnisse, 1993).

25. The quote is from Francesco Dal Co, *Figures of Architecture and Thought: German Architecture Culture 1880–1920* (New York: Rizzoli, 1990), 13.

26. See, among others, Sonja Günther, *Das deutsche Heim: Luxusinterieurs und Arbeitermöbel von der Gründerzeit bis zum Dritten Reich* (Giessen: Anabas-Verlag, 1984); and Daniel Rodgers, *Atlantic Crossings: Social Politics in a Progressive Age* (Cambridge, MA: Harvard University Press, 1998).

27. Werkbund Archiv Berlin (hereafter WBA Berlin) D24: Hermann Muthesius, "Wo stehen wir?" *Aus der Gründungszeit des Deutschen Werkbundes: "Die Durchgeistigung der deutschen Arbeit,"* 16.

28. Lux, *Geschmack*, vi–vii.

29. Ibid., vi.

30. Alexander Koch, "An die deutschen Künstler und Kunstfreunde!" *Deutsche Kunst und Dekoration* (October 1897), 1 (emphasis in original).

31. Koch, "An die deutschen."

32. See Alexander Koch, *Ein Dokument deutscher Kunst: Grossherzog Ernst Ludwig und die Ausstellung der Künstler-Kolonie in Darmstadt von Mai bis Oktober 1901* (Darmstadt: Koch, 1901).

33. Cited in Barbara Miller Lane, *National Romanticism and Modern Architecture in Germany and the Scandinavian Countries* (Cambridge: Cambridge University Press, 2000), 133.

34. Fritz Schumacher, "Zur Geschichte der Ausstellung," *Das deutsche Kunstgewerbe 1906: Die dritte deutsche Kunstgewerbe Ausstellung Dresden 1906,* ed. Direktorium der Ausstellung (Munich: Bruckmann, 1906), 11.

35. Schumacher, "Geschichte," 11.

36. Schumacher hoped to give a "systematic overview" of the national reach and importance of the arts and crafts movement with the exhibition "Sie will Klärung . . . Klärung für das Publikum und Klärung für den Schaffenden." Schumacher, "Geschichte," 11, 13.

37. Erich Haenel, "Raumkunst," *Das deutsche Kunstgewerbe 1906,* ed. Direktorium der Ausstellung, 27.

38. Ibid., 24–25.

39. The *Werkbund's* analysis of national *Stil* as opposed to foreign, or art nouveau, fashion was strongly gendered, an aspect that receives more attention in the longer version of this paper. The national consumer for the *Werkbund* before 1914 also was assumed to be male. Middle-class women were given subsidiary, and decorative, functions, but they were not given responsibility for aesthetically reforming the home. This situation began to change shortly before World War I.

40. Haenel, "Raumkunst," 25.

41. Muthesius, "Wo stehen wir?" 17.

42. Hermann Muthesius, "Die Bedeutung des Kunstgewerbes: Eröffnungsrede zu den Vorlesungen über modernes Kunstgewerbe und der Handelshochschule in Berlin," *Dekorative Kunst* 10 (1907): 177–92, under "Digital Archives of the Theory of Architecture," Brandenburgische Technische Universität Cottbus Department of Architecture, http://www.tu-cottbus.de/BTU/Fak2/Theo-

Arch/D_A_T_A/Architektur/20.Jhdt/MuthesiusHermann/DieBedeutung desKunstgewerbes.htm (accessed: May 15, 2007).

43. WBA Berlin D55: Hermann Muthesius, *Die Werkbund Arbeit der Zukunft* (Jena: Diederichs, 1914), 36.

44. The entries were published as *Hausgärten: Skizzen und Entwürfe aus dem Wettbewerb der "Woche"* (Berlin: Scherl, 1908).

45. As he wrote, "Von dem Publikum ist zu verlangen, daß es bei seinen Einkäufen vor allem die Gebote der höchsten Gediegenheit und eines veredelten Geschmackes anerkennt und höher stellt als die anrüchige Billigkeit." Lux, *Geschmack*, 43.

46. Willy Frank, "Warum neue Formen?" in *Das schöne Heim: Ratgeber für die Ausgestaltung und Einrichtung der Wohnung*, ed. Alexander Koch, 6–7 (emphasis in original) (Darmstadt: Koch, 1920).

47. Dipesh Chakrabarty, *Habitations of Modernity: Essays in the Wake of Subaltern Studies* (Chicago: University of Chicago Press, 2002), xix.

48. Eley, "Making a Place," 18.

49. Historians Harry Harootunian and Dipesh Chakrabarty make similar observations about the modern as a particular organization of the everyday in twentieth-century societies. As Harootunian writes, "This minimal unity of the present, however precarious, was increasingly seen by thinkers as the actual and unavoidable experience of everydayness that everywhere in the industrializing world—colonized and noncolonized—was identified as distinctively modern." *History's Disquiet: Modernity, Cultural Practice and the Question of Everyday Life* (New York: Columbia University Press, 2000), 4. Chakrabarty speaks of an everyday "language of modernity, of civic consciousness and public health, even of certain ideas of beauty related to the management of public space and interests, an order of aesthetics from which the ideals of public health and hygiene cannot be separated. It is the language of modern governments . . . and, for that reason, it is the language, not only of imperialist officials, but of modernist nationalists as well." See his "Of Garbage, Modernity and the Citizen's Gaze," in *Habitations*, 65–79.

50. For a summary of Vetter's lecture, see WBA Berlin D39: "Der Deutsche Werkbund," *Fachblatt für Holzarbeiter* (1910), 142. At the meeting, Wolf Dohrn spoke on the "Geschmacksbildung des deutschen Kaufmanns," Karl Ernst Osthaus on the "Deutsche Museum für Kunst in Handel und Gewerbe in Hagen," and Frau Else Oppler-Legband on the "Fachschule für höhere Dekorationskunst in Berlin." Other topics included the development of a standardized set of colors for use in products, *Heimatschutz*, and the business of faking antiquities. For a list, see WBA Berlin D39: "Aus der letzten Jahresversammlung des Deutschen *Werkbundes*," *Volkswirtschaftliche Blätter* 9, no. 15/16 (1910). The *Volkswirtschaftliche Blätter* gave no mention of Vetter's lecture. The *Fachblatt für Holzarbeiter*, by contrast, covered it in detail.

51. Schwartz, *Werkbund*, 6.

52. Georg Simmel saw this uniting of culture and power in the urban landscape of Florence.

CHAPTER 7

1. All translations are my own. Cited in Gustav Roscher, *Großstadtpolizei: Ein praktisches Handbuch der deutschen Polizei* (Hamburg: Otto Meißners Verlag, 1912), 2.

2. In Germany, the concept of citizenship recently has been considered in research on police and domestic security by the Institute for Citizenship Rights and Public Safety (*Institut für Bürgerrechte und öffentliche Sicherheit e. V*) at the Free University of Berlin, a project that has existed for two decades. See Zeitschrift des Instituts, *Bürgerrechte und Polizei/CILIP* (Verlag CILIP: Berlin, 1978–present). See also *Institut für Bürgerrechte und öffentliche Sicherheit e. V.,* "Bürgerrechte und Polizei. Cilip," www.cilip.de (accessed: June 4, 2007).

3. See Alan Silver, "The Demand of Order in Civil Society: A Review of Some Themes in the History of Urban Crime, Police and Riot," in *The Police,* ed. David Bordura, 1–24 (New York: Wiley, 1967); Albrecht Funk, *Polizei und Rechtsstaat: Die Entwicklung des staatlichen Gewaltmonopols in Preußen 1948–1914* (Frankfurt am Main: Campus, 1986).

4. The first section is based on my recent article "Vom Säbelhieb zum 'sanften Weg'? Lektüren physischer Gewalt zwischen Bürgern und Polizisten im 20. Jahrhundert," *Werkstatt Geschichte* vol. 12, no. 35 (2003): 7–22; see there for quotations from sources.

5. Erving Goffmann, *Relations in Public: Microstudies of the Public Order* (New York: Harper & Row, 1972).

6. For this part, see Michael Sturm, "'Der knackt jeden Schädel.' Überlegungen zur Vervendung des Polizeischlagstocks," in *Werkstatt Geschichte* 43 (2006): 96–108.

7. *Vossische Zeitung,* 16 July 1906, Nr. 327, 2nd supplement.

8. *Vossische Zeitung,* 20 July 1906, Nr. 334, 1st supplement.

9. *Berliner Lokalanzeiger,* 24 April 1907, Nr. 205.

10. *Vorwärts,* 17 July 1906, Nr. 163, 2nd supplement.

11. See my *Straßenpolitik: Zur Sozialgeschichte der öffentlichen Ordnung in Berlin, 1900–1914* (Bonn: Dietz, 1995).

12. Alf Lüdtke, "*Gemeinwohl," Polizei und "Festungspraxis': Staatliche Gewaltsamkeit und innere Verwaltung in Preußen, 1815–1850* (Göttingen: Vandenhoeck & Ruprecht, 1982).

13. See Christoph Gusy and Gerhard Nitz, "Vom Legitimationswandel staatlicher Sicherheitsfunktionen," in *Kontinuitäten und Brüche: Staat, Demokratie und Innere Sicherheit in Deutschland,* ed. Hans-Jürgen Lange, 335–54 (Leverkusen: Leske + Budrich, 1999).

14. *Landgericht Hamburg, Urteil in der Strafsache gegen O. H., O. A. wegen Körperverletzung im Amt pp,* am 26.6.1996 (Az 614 KLs 22/95; 830 Js 194/94), 26–28.

15. Ibid.

16. Sturm, "'Der knackt jeden Schädel,'" 102.

17. See the fundamental writings of Richard Bessel and Peter Leßmann; especially Peter Leßmann-Faust, "'Blood May': The Case of Berlin 1929," in *Patterns of Provocation: Police and Public Disorder,* ed. Richard Bessel and Clive Emsley, 11–27 (New York: Berghahn, 2000).

18. Sturm, "'Der knackt jeden Schädel,'" 98.

19. Michael Wildt, "Gewaltpolitik: Volksgemeinschaft und Judenverfolgung in der deutschen Provinz 1932 bis 1935," *Werkstatt Geschichte* 12, no. 35 (2003): 23–43; Klaus Hesse, "Sichtbarer Terror: Öffentliche Gewalt gegen deutsche Juden 1933–1936 im Spiegel fotografischer Quellen," *Werkstatt Geschichte* 12, no. 35 (2003): 44–56.

20. Quoted in Sturm, "'Der knackt jeden Schädel,'" 98.

21. Quoted in Sturm, "'Der knackt jeden Schädel,'" 98.

22. See Alf Lüdtke, "Gewalt und Alltag im 20. Jahrhundert," in *Gewalt und Terror: 11 Vorlesungen,* ed. Wolfgang Bergsdorf, Dietmar Herz, and Hans Hoffmeister, 35–52 (Weimar: Rhino, 2003).

23. See Klaus-Michael Mallmann, "Vom Fußvolk der 'Endlösung': Ordnungspolizei, Ostkrieg und Judenmord," in *Tel Aviver Jahrbuch für deutsche Geschichte* 26 (1997): 355–91.

24. Generally on the public police in East Germany, see my "Die Deutsche Volkspolizei (1945–1990)," in *Im Dienste der Partei: Handbuch der bewaffneten Organe der DDR,* ed. T. Diedrich, H. Ehlert, and R. Wenzke, 97–152 (Berlin: Ch. Links, Forschungen zur DDR-Gesellschaft, 1998); and my *Volkspolizei: Herrschaftspraxis und öffentliche Ordnung im SED-Staat, 1952–1968* (Cologne: Böhlau, 2003). For a very useful overview of the abundant scholarship on the June 17, 1953 uprising as well as on the event itself, see Ilko-Sascha Kowalczuk, "Die gescheiterte Revolution—'17. Juni 1953'; Forschungsstand, Forschungsgegenstand und Forschungsperspektiven," *Archiv für Sozialgeschichte* 44 (2004): 606–64.

25. See Thomas Lindenberger, "Diktatur der Grenze(n): Die eingemauerte Gesellschaft und ihre Feinde," in *Mauerbau und Mauerfall: Ursachen—Verlauf—Auswirkungen,* ed. Hans-Hermann Hertle, Konrad H. Jarausch, and Christoph Kleßmann, 203–13 (Berlin: Ch. Links, 2002).

26. See *Und diese verdammte Ohmacht: Report der unabhängigen Untersuchungskommission zu den Ereignissen vom 7./8. Oktober 1989 in Berlin* (Berlin: Basisdruck, 1991).

27. See the contributions in G. Fürmetz, H. Reinke, and K. Weinhauer, ed., *Nachkriegspolizei: Sicherheit und Ordnung in Ost- und Westdeutschland 1945–1989* (Hamburg: Ergebnisse, 2001).

28. On the "Cold Civil War," see Patrick Major, *The Death of the KPD: Communism and Anti-Communism in West-Germany, 1945–1956* (Oxford: Clarendon, 1997), conclusion.

29. Sturm, "'Der knackt jeden Schädel,'" 99.

30. See Gerhard Fürmetz, "'Kampf um den Straßenfrieden': Polizei und

Verkehrsdisziplin in Bayern zwischen Kriegsende und beginnender Massen-motorisierung," in Fürmetz et al., *Nachkriegspolizei*, 199–228.

31. For this complex transition phase in West German policing, see Klaus Weinhauer, *Schutzpolizei in der Bundesrepublik: Zwischen Bürgerkrieg und Innerer Sicherheit; Die turbulenten sechziger Jahre* (Paderborn: Schöningh, 2003).

32. See Martin Winter, "Polizeiphilosophie und Protest policing in der Bundesrepublik Deutschland: Von 1960 bis zur staatlichen Einheit," in *Kontinuitäten und Brüche: Staat, Demokratie und Innere Sicherheit in Deutschland*, ed. Hans-Jürgen Lange, 203–20 (Leverkusen: Leske + Budrich, 1999).

33. For the following, see Christoph Gusy and Gerhard Nitz, "Vom Legitimationswandel staatlicher Sicherheitsfunktionen," *Kontinuitäten*, 335–54.

34. See Rafael Behr, *Cop Culture: Der Alltag des Gewaltmonopols. Männlichkeit, Handlungsmuster und Kultur in der Polizei* (Opladen: Leske + Budrich, 2000).

35. Ute Frevert, *Men of Honor: A Social and Cultural History of the Duel*, trans. Anthony Williams (Cambridge, MA: Polity Press, 1995).

36. See Konrad Jarausch, *After Hitler: Recivilizing Germans*, trans. Brandon Hunziker (New York: Oxford University Press, 2006).

CHAPTER 8

1. The literature is too extensive to quote more than a few representative examples here: John E. Knodel, *The Decline of Fertility in Germany 1871–1939* (Princeton, NJ: Princeton University Press, 1974); Gerhard Kraiker, *§218: Zwei Schritte vorwärts, einen Schritt zurück* (Frankfurt a.M.: Fischer, 1983); James Woycke, *Birth Control in Germany 1871–1933* (London: Routledge, 1988); Susanne von Paczensky and Renate Sadronowski, eds., *Die Neuen Moralisten: §218—vom leichtfertigen Umgang mit einem Jahrhundertthema* (Reinbek b. Hamburg: Rowohlt, 1984); Cornelie Usborne, *The Politics of the Body in Weimar Germany: Women's Reproductive Rights and Duties* (London: Macmillan, 1992); Atina Grossmann, *Reforming Sex: The German Movement for Birth Control and Abortion Reform 1920–1950* (New York: Oxford University Press, 1995).

2. Usborne, *Politics of the Body*, 173ff.

3. See, for example, Regine Deutsch, "Der Schutz des keimenden Lebens," *Berliner Volkszeitung*, May 16, 1926 (Bundesarchiv Berlin Lichterfelde [BABL], Justice Min. 6235, Bl. 33); D. V. Glass, *Population Policies and Movement in Europe* (London: Cass, 1967), 281; Grossmann, *Reforming Sex*, 82–83.

4. See Usborne, *Politics of the Body*, 214ff.

5. Ibid., 214–15.

6. See Grossmann, *Reforming Sex*, 78ff.; Christine von Soden, "Verwünschungen und Prophezeiungen: Die Befürwortung des Paragraphen 218 in der Weimarer Republik" in *Wir sind keine Mörderinnen!*, ed. Susanne von Paczensky, 127–37 (Reinbek b. Hamburg: Rowohlt, 1984).

7. See, for example, Paul Weindling, *Health, Race and German Politics Between National Unification and Nazism 1870–1945* (Cambridge: Cambridge University

Press, 1989); James Woycke, *Birth Control in Germany 1871–1933* (London: Routledge, 1988).

8. See Cornelie Usborne, "The Christian Churches and the Regulation of Sexuality in Weimar Germany," in *Disciplines of Faith: Studies in Religion, Politics and Patriarchy*, ed. Jim Obelkevich, Lyndal Roper, and Raphael Samuel, 99–112 (London: Routledge, 1987).

9. Usborne, "The New Woman and Generational Conflict: Perceptions of Young Women's Sexual Mores in the Weimar Republic," in *Youth Rebellion, Generation Formation and Generation Conflict in Modern Germany*, ed. Mark Roseman, 37–163 (Cambridge: Cambridge University Press, 1995); for the meetings by the League during the war, see, for example, BAP RMindI 9353, *Der Tag*, Morgenblatt, October 30, 1915. Also see Kristin McGuire, "Citizenship and the Right to Sexual Subjectivity in Poland and Germany before World War I" (paper presented at the conference on Citizenship and National Identity in Twentieth-Century Germany, Oxford University, Oxford, September 10–12, 2004).

10. For example, Max Marcuse, *Der eheliche Präventivverkehr: Seine Verbreitung, Verursachung und Methodik; Dargestellt an 300 Ehen* (Stuttgart: Enke, 1917); Marcuse, "Zur Frage der Verbreitung und Methodik willkürlicher Geburtenbeschränkung in Berliner Proletarierkreisen," *Sexualprobleme* 9 (November 1913): 752–80.

11. Erin O'Connor, *Raw Material: Producing Pathology in Victorian Culture* (Durham, NC: Duke University Press, 2000), 215, quoted in Roger Cooter, "The Traffic in Victorian Bodies: Medicine, Literature, and History," *Victorian Studies* Spring (2003): 513–27.

12. BABL, Rmin.d.I. 9343, Bl. 235, November 2, 1916.

13. BABL, RMindI 9344, Bl. 110, April 13, 1917.

14. Geheimes Staatsarchiv Preussischer Kulturbesitz, Berlin Dahlem (GSABD), Kultusmin. 2013, Bl. 45, *Vorwärts*, April 18, 1918; ibid., 2017, *Münchener Post*, July 9, 1918.

15. Elisabeth Domansky, "Militarization and Reproduction in World War I Germany," in *Society, Culture, and the State in Germany 1870–1930*, ed. Geoff Eley, 427–64 (Ann Arbor: University of Michigan Press, 1997).

16. See Usborne, *Politics of the Body*, 8ff.

17. BABL, RMindI 9343, Bl. 146, *Vorwärts*, November 23, 1916.

18. Carole Pateman, "The Fraternal Social Contract," in *Civil Society and the State: New European Perspectives*, ed. John Keane, 101–27 (London: Verso, 1988).

19. BABL, RMindI. 9353, Bl. 5, *Vorwärts*, October 20, 1915.

20. BABL, RMindI, 9353, Bl. 5, *Vorwärts*, October 20, 1915.

21. BABL, RMindI, 9353, Bl. 5, *Vorwärts*, October 20, 1915; Cornelie Usborne, "'Pregnancy Is the Woman's Active Service': Pronatalism in Germany During the First World War," in *The Upheaval of War*, ed. Richard Wall and Jay Winter, 389–416 (Cambridge: Cambridge University Press, 1988).

22. BABL, RMindI, 9353, Bl. 5, *Vorwärts*, October 20, 1915.

23. Rosa Kempf, "Das weibliche Dienstjahr," *Archiv für Sozialwissenschaft und Sozialpolitik* 41 (1916): 424.

24. GSABD, MfHuG, BB.XV.65, vol. 3.

25. Usborne, *Politics of the Body*, 31–33, 182ff.

26. BABL, NL Schreiber, no. 60, n.d.

27. See Ute Daniel, *The War from Within: German Working-Class Women in the First World War* (Oxford: Berg, 1997), chs. 3 and 4.

28. See Usborne, *Politics of the Body*, 24.

29. Daniel, *War from Within*, 246–47.

30. See Domansky, "Militarization," 446.

31. See Usborne, "Wise Women, Wise Men and Abortion in the Weimar Republic: Gender, Class and Medicine," in *Gender Relations in German History*, ed. Lynn Abrams and Elizabeth Harvey, 143–76 (Durham, NC: Duke University Press, 1997).

32. BABL, RMindI, 9347, Bl. 45.

33. Ibid.

34. GSABL, Rep 84a, 8231, Bl. 84: petition Erfurt June 29, 1919, to the Prussian Justice Minister: "Möge doch jede Frau machen, mit ihrem Körper, was sie will."

35. *Die Internationale* 4, no. 20 (1922): 462.

36. BABL, JusMin., 30.03, Ora Referentenmaterial, B-761, 19131, 3; GSAD, R84a, 82321, Bl. 157.

37. GSABD, R83a, 82312, Bl. 151, *Die Rote Fahne*, 7, March 8, 1924.

38. GSABD, R83a, 82312, Bl. 152, *Die Welt am Montag*, 10, March 10, 1924.

39. *Die Internationale* 4, no. 20 (1922): 462; KPD party conference, 1924, *Protokolle*, 754.

40. See Usborne, *Politics of the Body*, 161.

41. Marie Juchacz, cited in Usborne, *Politics of the Body*, 159.

42. *Die Gleichh*eit, September, 15, 1922, 169.

43. GSABD, Rep 84a, 8231, Bl. 227.

44. BABL, RJusMin, 6232, Bl. 36.

45. For example, GSABD, Rep 84a, 8231, Bl. 98, 100.

46. GSABD, Rep 84a, 8232 Bl. 187 RS.

47. Usborne, *Politics of the Body*, 38; SPD women's conference, Weimar, 1919, *Protokolle*, 498–99.

48. See Usborne, "Abortion in Weimar Germany: The Debate amongst the Medical Profession," *Continuity & Change* 2 (1990): 199–224.

49. See Usborne, "Rebellious Girls and Pitiable Women: Abortion Narratives in Weimar Popular Culture," in *German History* 23, no. 3 (2005): 321–38.

50. Domansky argues that it entailed the "dissolution of the bourgeois family"; see Domansky "Militarization," 428.

51. Rosalind Pollack Petchesky, *Abortion and Woman's Choice: The State, Sexuality, and Reproductive Freedom* (London: Verso, 1986), 7.

52. Kathleen Canning and Sonya O. Rose, "Gender, Citizenship and Subjectivity: Some Historical and Theoretical Considerations," *Gender & History* 13, no. 3 (November 2001): 427–43.

53. See Peter C. Caldwell's contribution to this volume.

54. Canning and Rose, "Gender," 428.

CHAPTER 9

Many thanks to Corey Ross, Pamela Swett, and Wolfgang Bügel for their extremely helpful suggestions. I am also grateful for the comments I obtained at the conference Citizenship & National Identity in Twentieth-Century Germany and at Hartmut Berghoff's Colloquium for Wirtschafts- und Sozialgeschichte at Georg-August-Universität Göttingen.

1. Konrad H. Jarausch and Michael Geyer, *Shattered Past: Reconstructing German Histories* (Princeton, NJ: Princeton University Press, 2003), 270. For this idea of "getting and spending," see Susan Strasser, Charles McGovern, and Matthias Judt, *Getting and Spending: European and American Consumer Societies in the Twentieth Century* (Cambridge: Cambridge University Press, 1998).

2. On shifting meanings of citizenship, see Bryan Turner, "Outline of a Theory of Citizenship," *Sociology* 24, no. 2 (1990): 189–217. Turner discusses T. H. Marshall's classic notions of civil, political, and social citizenship. See also Kathleen Canning, "Class vs. Citizenship: Keywords in German Gender History," *Central European History* 37, no. 2 (2004): 225–44.

3. Lizabeth Cohen, *A Consumers' Republic: The Politics of Mass Consumption in Postwar America* (New York: Knopf, 2003); on the concept of the "citizen-consumer," see also Frank Trentmann, "Bread, Milk and Democracy: Consumption and Citizenship in Twentieth-Century Britain," in *The Politics of Consumption: Material Culture and Citizenship in Europe and America*, ed. Martin Daunton and Matthew Hilton, 129–63 (Oxford: Berg, 2001). On citizenship and consumption, see also Martin Daunton and Matthew Hilton, "Material Politics: An Introduction," in ibid., 1–32.

4. For introductions to consumerism in Germany, see Hartmut Berghoff, ed., *Konsumpolitik: Die Regulierung des privaten Verbrauchs im 20; Jahrhundert* (Göttingen: Vandenhoeck & Ruprecht, 1999); David F. Crew, ed., *Consuming Germany in the Cold War: Consumption and National Identity in East and West Germany, 1949–1989* (Oxford: Berg, 2003); and Alon Confino and Rudy Koshar, "Régimes of Consumer Culture: New Narratives in Twentieth-Century German History," *German History* 19, no. 2 (2001), 135–61. On consumerism more broadly, see Wolfgang König, *Geschichte der Konsumgesellschaft* (Stuttgart: Franz Steiner, 2000); Hannes Siegrist, Hartmut Kaelble, and Jürgen Kocka, eds., *Europäische Konsumgeschichte: Zur Gesellschafts- und Kulturgeschichte des Konsums (18 bis 20 Jahrhundert)* (Frankfurt am Main: Campus, 1997); and Frank Trentmann, "Beyond Consumerism: New Historical Perspectives on Consumption," *Journal of Contemporary History* 39, no. 3 (2004): 373–401.

5. On mass consumption in the FRG, see, for example, Michael Wildt, *Am Beginn der "Konsumgesellschaft": Mangelerfahrung, Lebenshaltung, Wohlstandshoffnung in Westdeutschland in den fünfziger Jahren* (Hamburg: Ergebnisse, 1994); and Erica Carter, *How German Is She? Postwar West German Reconstruction and the Consuming Woman* (Ann Arbor: University of Michigan Press, 1997).

6. See, for example, Jonathan R. Zatlin, "Consuming Ideology: Socialist Consumerism and the Intershops, 1970–1989," in *Arbeiter in der SBZ-DDR*

(Workers in the Soviet Occupation Zone-GDR), ed. Peter Hübner and Klaus Tenfelde, 555–72 (Essen: Klartext-Verlag, 1999).

7. On the ideological functions of the *Volksgemeinschaft* concept, see David Welch, "Nazi Propaganda and the *Volksgemeinschaft*: Construction of a People's Community," *Journal of Contemporary History* 39, no. 2 (2004): 213–38; and Norbert Frei, "People's Community and War: Hitler's Popular Support," in *The Third Reich Between Vision and Reality: New Perspectives on German History, 1918–1945*, ed. Hans Mommsen, 59–77 (Oxford: Berg, 2001).

8. There is a huge literature on the Third Reich's relationship to "modernity" and "modernization." For good overviews, see Riccardo Bavaj, *Die Ambivalenz der Moderne im Nationalsozialismus: Eine Bilanz der Forschung* (Munich: Oldenbourg, 2003), 50–81; and Paul Betts, "The New Fascination with Fascism: The Case of Nazi Modernism," *Journal of Contemporary History* 37, no. 4 (2002): 541–58; Mark Roseman, "National Socialism and Modernisation," in *Fascist Italy and Nazi Germany: Comparisons and Contrasts*, ed. Richard Bessel, 197–229 (Cambridge: Cambridge University Press, 1996); Norbert Frei, "Wie modern war der Nationalsozialismus," *Geschichte und Gesellschaft* 19 (1993): 367–87.

9. On KdF, see Shelley Baranowski, *Strength Through Joy: Consumerism and Mass Tourism in the Third Reich* (Cambridge: Cambridge University Press, 2004); and Matthias Frese, *Betriebspolitik im "Dritten Reich": Deutsche Arbeitsfront, Unternehmer und Staatsbürokratie in der westdeutschen Grossindustrie 1933–1939* (Paderborn: Ferdinand Schöningh, 1991). On "people's products," see Wolfgang König, *Volkswagen, Volksempfänger, Volksgemeinschaft: "Volksprodukte" im Dritten Reich; Vom Scheitern einer nationalsozialistischen Konsumgesellschaft* (Paderborn: Schöningh, 2004).

10. We have, to be sure, studies of the factory floor as the site of quality production, beauty in labor, and worker compliance and resistance: see Alf Lüdtke, *Eigen-Sinn: Fabrikalltag, Arbeitererfahrungen und Politik vom Kaiserreich bis in den Faschismus* (Hamburg: Ergebnisse, 1993).

11. Charles Tilly, "Citizenship, Identity and Social History," *International Review of Social History* 40, no. 3 (1995): 1–17. On the contested "rhetorics of citizenship," see also Canning, "Class vs. Citizenship," 241.

12. Studies of the German economy during the "peaceful years" include R. J. Overy, *The Nazi Economic Recovery, 1932–1938* (London: Macmillan, 1982); Frese, *Betriebspolitik*; and Michael von Prollius, *Das Wirtschaftssystem der Nationalsozialisten, 1933–1939: Steuerung durch emergent Organisation und politische Prozesse* (Paderborn: Federinand Schöningh, 2003).

13. Historians and scholars of mass communications have debated the theoretical distinctions between *publicity* and *public relations*. In this chapter, I will use both terms interchangeably. Importantly, too, while advertising and the ad industry have become a key focus for historians, I will treat advertising as one, albeit a central, component of public relations.

14. On the origins of public relations in the FRG, see S. Jonathan Wiesen, *West German Industry and the Challenge of the Nazi Past, 1945–1955* (Chapel Hill: University of North Carolina Press, 2001), 101–13; Elisabeth Binder, *Die Ent-*

stehung unternehmerischer Public Relations in der Bundesrepublik Deutschland
(Münster: Lit Verlag, 1983); and Christian Kleinschmidt, *Der Produktive Blick:
Wahrnehung amerikanischer und japanischer Management- und Produktionsmetho-
den durch deutsche Unternehmer, 1950–1985* (Berlin: Akademie, 2002), 204–21.

15. Barbara Wolbring, *Krupp und die Öffentlichkeit im 19 Jahrhundert: Selbst-
darstellung, öffentliche Wahrnehmung und gesellschaftliche Kommunikation* (Munich: Beck, 2000), 95–100. On the development of PR during this period, see
also Astrid Zipfel, *Public Relations in der Elektroindustrie: Die Firmen Siemens und
AEG, 1847 bis 1939* (Weimar: Böhlau, 1997).

16. Michael Kunczik, *Geschichte der Öffentlichkeitsarbeit in Deutschland* (Köln:
Böhlau, 1997), 193–95; on mid to late nineteenth-century developments, see Dirk
Reinhardt, *Von der Reklame zum Marketing: Geschichte der Wirtschaftswerbung in
Deutschland* (Berlin: Akademie, 1993), 429–41.

17. On the utility of the concept *die Öffentlichkeit* for historians, see Axel
Schildt, "Das Jahrhundert des Massenmedien: Ansichten zu einer künftigen
Geschichte der Öffentlichkeit," *Geschichte und Gesellschaft* 27 (2001): 177–206.
For a media studies perspective, see Peter Szyszka, ed., *Öffentlichkeit: Diskurs zu
einem Schlüsselbegriff der Organisationskommunikation* (Opladen: Westdeutscher
Verlag, 1999).

18. For two essential histories of public relations with focuses on the United
States, see Stuart Ewen, *PR! A Social History of Spin* (New York: Basic Books,
1996); and Roland Marchand, *Creating the Corporate Soul: The Rise of Public Relations and Corporate Imagery in American Big Business* (Berkeley and Los Angeles:
University of California Press, 1998). On the history of PR from the perspective
of mass communications, see Heinz D. Fischer and Ulrike G. Wahl, eds., *Public
Relations/Öffentlichkeitsarbeit: Geschicht—Grundlagen—Grenzziehungen* (Frankfurt am Main: Peter Lang, 1993). For a good volume that brings together the
insights of media studies and history, see Clemens Wischermann, Peter Bor-
scheid, and Karl-Peter Ellerbrock, eds., *Unternehmenskommunikation im 19 und
20 Jahrhundert: Neue Wege der Unternehmensgeschichte* (Dortmund: Gesellschaft
für Westfälische Wirtschaftsgeschichte, 2000).

19. Ewen, *PR!* 186.

20. Edward Bernays, *Propaganda* (New York: Liveright, 1928).

21. On the influence of Freud on advertising and PR, see Eli Zaretsky, *Secrets of the Soul: A Social and Cultural History of Psychoanalysis* (New York: Knopf,
2004), 144 and 237. On advertising, PR, and the shift from Freudian to Behavior-
ist understandings of consumer behavior, see Olivier Zunz, *Why the American
Century?* (Chicago: University of Chicago Press, 1998): 57–61.

22. Gustave Le Bon, *The Crowd: A Study of the Popular Mind* (1895; repr., At-
lanta, GA: Cherokee Publishing, 1982), xv.

23. See Gabriel Tarde, "The Public and the Crowd," in *On Communication and
Social Influence: Selected Papers*, ed. Terry N. Clark, 277–96 (Chicago: University
of Chicago Press, 1969). On the relationship between Le Bon's and Tarde's ideas,
see Ewen, *PR!* 64–70; Dominik Schrage, "Integration durch Attraktion: Kon-
sumismus als massenkulturelles Weltverhältnis," *Mittelweg* 36, no. 12 (2003):

57–86; Clark McPhail, *The Myth of the Maddening Crowd* (New York: Aldine de Gruyter, 1991), 2–9; and Rosalind H. Williams, *Dreamworlds: Mass Consumption in Late Nineteenth-Century France* (Berkeley and Los Angeles: University of California Press, 1982), ch. 8.

24. On the idea of the "virtuous" company, literally having a "soul," see Marchand, *Creating the Corporate Soul*, 7–26.

25. See Mary Nolan, *Visions of Modernity: American Business and the Modernization of Germany* (Oxford: Oxford University Press, 1994); on advertising psychology, see Reinhardt, *Von der Reklame*, 49–99. For a disapproving German appraisal of "mass persuasion" techniques, including commercial publicity, in the United States, see Friedrich Schönemann, *Die Kunst der Massenbeeinflussung in den Vereinigten Staaten von Amerika* (Stuttgart: Deutsche Verlags-Anstalt, 1924), especially 153–71.

26. On the links between personal gratification, political empowerment, and economic choice for Weimar women, see Julia Sneeringer, "The Shopper as Voter: Women, Advertising, and Politics in Post-Inflation Germany," *German Studies Review* 27, no. 3 (2004): 476–502.

27. Jörg Requate has called into question the extent to which "the public" is actually erased under dictatorships. For his focus on the GDR, see Requate, "Öffentlichkeit und Medien als Gegenstände historischer Analyse," *Geschichte und Gesellschaft* 25 (1999): 5–32. On concepts of "public" and "private" in Nazi Germany, see Kate Lacey, *Feminine Frequencies: German Radio and the Public Sphere, 1923–1945* (Ann Arbor: University of Michigan Press, 1996).

28. On Hitler's reading of Le Bon, see Ian Kershaw, *The Hitler Myth: Image and Reality in the Third Reich* (Oxford: Oxford University Press, 1987), 3. On the meeting between Ivy Lee and Goebbels, see Kunczik, *Geschichte*, 299. Ivy Lee also did PR work for I. G. Farben in 1933 and 1934: see Mira Wilkins, *The History of Foreign Investment in the United States, 1914–1945* (Cambridge, MA: Harvard University Press, 2004), ms p. 84. Many thanks to Mira Wilkins for a copy of her manuscript pages. Also see Scott M. Cutlip, *Public Relations: A History* (Hillsdale, NJ: L. Erlbaum Associates, 1995), 143–54.

29. On Hans Domizlaff's concept of "mental weapons," see Rainer Gries, Volker Ilgen, and Dirk Schindelbeck, *"Ins Gehirn der Masse kriechen!" Werbung und Mentalitätsgeschichte* (Darmstadt: Wissenschaftliche Buchgesellschaft, 1995), 45–73.

30. Already in 1939, Sergei Chakotin drew explicit connections between Pavlovian reflexes, autosuggestion, commercial publicity, and Hitlerian propaganda and symbolism: see Chakotin, *The Rape of the Masses: The Psychology of Totalitarian Political Propaganda* (London: Butler & Tanner, 1940). See also Gerhard Voigt, "Goebbels als Markentechniker," in *Warenästhetik: Beiträge zur Diskussion, Weiterentwicklung und Vermittlung ihrer Kritik*, ed. Wolfgang Fritz Haug, 231–60 (Frankfurt am Main: Suhrkamp, 1975).

31. On advertising under National Socialism, see Uwe Westphal, *Werbung im Dritten Reich* (Berlin: Transit, 1989); Reinhardt, *Von der Reklame*, passim;

Hartmut Berghoff, " 'Times Change and We Change with Them': The German Advertising Industry in the Third Reich—Between Professional Self-Interest and Political Repression," *Business History* 45, no. 1 (2003): 128–47.

32. On the Advertising Council, see Matthias Rücker, *Wirtschaftswerbung unter Nationalsozialismus: Rechtliche Ausgestaltung der Werbung und Tätigkeit des Werberats der deutschen Wirtschaft* (Frankfurt am Main: Peter Lang, 2000). On specific regulations, see Berghoff, " 'Times Change,' " 134.

33. "Jeder Deutschdenkende fährt X, deutsches Benzin," in "Unzulässige Werbung," *Blätter vom Hause* 15, no. 5 (1935): 212, Henkel Archive, Düssseldorf (hereafter "HA").

34. Peter Hayes, "Industry Under the Swastika," in *Enterprise in the Period of Fascism*, ed. Harold James and Jakob Tanner, 26–36 (Burlington, VT: Ashgate Publishers, 2002).

35. Mark Spoerer, "Demontage eines Mythos? Zu der Kontroverse über das nationalsozialistische 'Wirtschaftswunder,' *Geschichte und Gesellschaft* 31 (2005), ms p. 7. Many thanks to the author for an advanced copy of his article.

36. Avraham Barkai, *Nazi Economics: Ideology, Theory, and Policy* (New Haven, CT: Yale University Press, 1990), quoted in Pierre Aycoberry, *The Social History of the Third Reich, 1933–1945* (New York: New Press, 1999), 115.

37. Carl Hundhausen, "Public Relations," *Zeitschrift für Betriebswirtschaft* 15, no. 1 (1938): 48–61. On Hundhausen's career, see Eva-Maria Lehming, *Carl Hundhausen: Sein Leben, sein Werk, sein Lebenswerk, Public Relations in Deutschland* (Wiesbaden: Deutscher Universitäts-Verlag, 1997). For a critical study of West German PR pioneers, see Peer Heinelt, *PR-Päpste: Die kontinuierlichen Karrieren von Carl Hundhausen, Albert Oeckl und Franz Ronneberger* (Berlin: Karl Dietz, 2003). There was great disagreement during the Weimar and Nazi years about whether American advertising and PR methods were suitable for Germany. See Alexander Schug, "Wegbereiter der modernen Absatzwerbung in Deutschland: Advertising Agencies und die Amerikanisierung der deutschen Werbebranche in der Zwischenkriegszeit," *Werkstattgeschichte* 34 (2003): 29–52. On German perceptions of the United States during the Third Reich, see Phillip Gassert, *Amerika im Dritten Reich: Ideologie, Propaganda und Volksmeinung, 1933–1945* (Stuttgart: Steiner, 1997), 104–16; and Hans Dieter Schäfer, "Amerikanismus im Dritten Reich," in *Nationalsozialismus und Modernisierung*, ed. Michael Prinz and Rainer Zitelmann, 199–215 (Darmstadt: Wissenschaftliche Buchgesellschaft, 1991).

38. Hundhausen, "Public Relations," 49, 60.

39. Ibid., 49.

40. See Carl Hundhausen, *Werbung um öffentliches Vertrauen: "Public Relations"* (Essen: W. Girardet, 1951); and Hans Domizlaff, *Die Gewinnung des öffentlichen Vertrauens* (Berlin: Hanseatische Verlags-Anstalt, 1939). The latter book was reprinted in 1951 and has gone through numerous editions.

41. So-called *"Vertrauenswerbung"* was premised on the notion that faith in company merchandise would not only lead to healthy sales but also contribute to a greater social project of selflessness and honesty. A well-known slogan

in the 1930s for Bayer aspirin, *"Bayer—Zeichen des Vertrauen,"* took on added meaning in the context of these more ideological appeals. For the importance of trust to National Socialism, see, for example, Eugen Diesel, "Die Welt ohne Vertrauen," *Deutsche Rundschau* 64 (1937): 81–85; and Bruno Bauch, "Das Vertrauen als ethisches Problem," *Die Tatwelt* 14 (1938): 67–74.

42. For a discussion of the different publicity means available to companies, see Paul Mundhenke, "Wirkungsgrenzen der Markenartikel-Insertion und deren Beurteilung durch den Vertreter," *Blätter vom Hause* 18, no. 1 (1938): 7–13, HA.

43. See Georg Bergler, *Die Entwicklung der Verbrauchsforschung in Deutschland und die Gesellschaft für Konsumforschung bis zum Jahre 1945* (Nuremberg: Gesellschaft für Konsumforschung e.V., 1959/1960); and Christoph Conrad, "Observer les consommateurs: Études de marché et histoire de la consommation en Allemagne, des années 1930 aux années 1960," *Le Mouvement Social*, no. 206 (2004): 17–39. For a study from the period, see "Die 'Bayer'-Vertauenswerbung im Urteil des Laien: Eine Untersuchung, bearbeitet vom Institut für Wirtschaftsbeobachtung des Deutschen Fertigware" (1939), 167.9.10.1, Bayer Archiv, Leverkusen (hereafter, BAL). Also found as file S 1939 010-2, archives of the GfK, Nuremberg.

44. Gries, Ilgen, and Schindelbeck, *"Ins Gehirn,"* 45–73.

45. See "Olympide—*'Bayer'*-Tag: Programm für die Fabrikbesichtigung," 168.2.29, BAL.

46. Wilfried Feldenkirchen and Susanne Hilger, *Menschen und Marken: 125 Jahre Henkel, 1876–2001* (Düsseldorf: Henkel, 2001), 257. This book provides a valuable survey of Henkel's history of production, sales, and advertising.

47. See Elisabeth Schmidt, *Musterbetriebe Deutscher Wirtschaft: Henkel & Cie A.G. Chemische Produkte Düsseldorf,* vol. 30, *Die Waschmittel- und Seifen-Industrie* (Leipzig: Verlag Übersee-Post, 1934), 65.

48. See "Mütterschulungskursus," in *Henkel-Bote* 7, no. 4 (1938): 189, HA; and "Zur Eröffnung des Persil-Instituts in Zürich," *Blätter vom Hause* 19, no. 3 (1939): 131, HA. On state-sponsored household training for women, see Nancy Reagin, "*Marktordnung* and Autarkic Housekeeping: Housewives and Private Consumption Under the Four-Year Plan, 1936–1939," *German History* 19, no. 2 (2001): 162–83.

49. See, for example, *Blätter vom Hause* 20, no. 9 (1940): 224, HA.

50. Paul Mundhenke, "Der Begriff 'persil-gepflegt' als Bestandteil des hausfraulichen Sprachschatzes," *Blätter vom Hause* 17, no. 7 (1937): 274–75, HA.

51. This slogan was omnipresent; see, for example, "Brief aus Düsseldorf," *Blätter vom Hause* 15, no. 11 (1935): 423, HA.

52. For depictions of Jews, see the cartoons in Dr. Meyersahm, "Englische Gewaltpolitik: Der Raub der dänischen Flotte im Jahre 1807," *Blätter vom Hause* 20, no. 14 (1940): 341, HA. On African stereotypes, see also P. Maywald, "Mohrenwäsche: Eine Betrachtung über Reinlichkeit der Neger in den afrikanischen Kolonien Deutschlands," *Blätter vom Hause* 19, no. 5 (1939): 188–92, HA. See cartoon of a colonial explorer presenting Persil to a scantily clad Af-

rican carrying a tray of tropical fruit on his head. The caption reads: "Armer Mensch, so schwarz! Probieren Sie's doch mal damit!" in Mundhenke, "Wirkungsgrenzen," 12; also cartoon in "Frontmensch Vertreter," *Blätter vom Hause* 18, no. 9 (1938): 330–55, HA.

53. On the use of cheaper materials and ingredients in consumer goods and food production, see Reagin, "*Marktordnung*," 183.

54. "Ein aktuelles Zwiegespräch zwischen Hausfrau und Werbedame," *Blätter vom Hause* 15, no. 4 (1935): 169, HA.

55. Bernhard Menne, *Krupp: Deutschlands Kanonenkönige* (Zurich: Europa-Verlag, 1937). On Krupp's reaction to the Menne book, see files in WA 56/164, Krupp Archive, Essen. Menne was writing from abroad and was untouched by the Gestapo.

56. Reagin, "*Marktordnung*," 183.

57. On this exhibit, see file H480/229 (Ausstellungen—"Schaffendes Volk"), HA.

58. Hubert Werthenbach to "Meine lieben Arbeitskameraden!" undated, in H480/229, HA.

59. Ibid. For a study of *Schaffendes Volk* from a design historian's perspective, see Stefanie Schäfers, *Vom Werkbund zum Vierjahresplan: Die Ausstellung 'Schaffendes Volk' Düsseldorf 1937* (Düsseldorf: Droste, 2001).

60. Norbert Stern, "Über den persönlichen und geschäftlichen Takt," *Blätter vom Hause* 16, no. 9 (1936): 331–32, HA.

61. Mundhenke, "Wirkungsgrenzen," HA.

62. "Frontmensch Vertreter," HA.

63. Herbert N. Casson, "12 Winke für den reisenden Kaufmann," *ZP* [*Zentral-Nachrichtenblatt für die "Bayer" Werbung*] 1 (1937): 2–3, in 167.9.1, BAL. Excerpted from Casson, *Tips for Traveling Salesmen* (New York: B. C. Forbes, 1927). Casson was a British management expert whose works were widely read in Germany.

64. See feature called "Die Stimme des Publikums," *ZP*, heft 3 (1938): 11–14, BAL.

65. See, for example, Kurt Stern, *Masse: Persönlichkeit und Gemeinschaft; Ein Beitrag zur Frage der Auflösung der Masse* (Stuttgart: Verlag für Wirtschaft und Verkehr, 1938).

66. On the relationship between personal agency, individuality, and mass thinking, see, for example, G. A. Pfarrius, "Persönlichkeit," *Blätter vom Hause* 16, no. 10 (1936): 360–61, HA.

67. "Wir fangen an: Wieder: Henkel-Film-Matineen!" *Blätter vom Hause* 20, no. 1 (1940): 21, HA.

68. For images from the film, see E. Endress, "Henkel-Geist im Henkel Film: Ein Ufa Mitarbeiter berichtet über seine Eindrücke vom Henkel-Werk," *Blätter vom Hause* 19, no. 3 (1939): 120–25, HA. On the technical and aesthetic aspects of this film, see Jeanpaul Goergen, *Walter Ruttmann: Eine Dokumentation* (Berlin: Freunde der Deutschen Kinemathek: 1988), 154–55.

69. Werbeabteilung Henkel to Ufa, 25 January 1939, Zug-Nr. 438 (Akten-

Pressestelle), File 4 [Zensur des Films "Henkel—ein deutsches Werk in seiner Arbeit," 1938–39], HA.

70. For an introduction to advertising and industrial films in Germany, see Manfred Rasch, Karl-Peter Ellerbrock, Renate Köhne-Lindenlaub, and Horst A. Wessel, eds., *Industriefilm: Medium und Quelle; Beispiele aus der Eisen- und Stahlindustrie* (Essen: Klartext, 1997); also Reinhardt, *Von der Reklame*, 330–58; see also "Chronologische Darstellung der Entwicklung der BAYER-Filmstelle," n.d., BAL.

71. Paul Mundhenke, "Werbefilm-Erfahrung und Werbefilm-Erfolg," H430 (Filme—1927–39), HA.

72. On the Nazis' "Beauty of Labor" program, see Alf Lüdtke, "The 'Honor of Labor': Industrial Workers and the Power of Symbols Under National Socialism," in *Nazism and German Society, 1933–1945*, ed. David F. Crew, 67–109 (London: Routledge, 1994).

73. Loose page 2a, excerpted from a draft letter from the Henkel Werbeabteilung to the Firma Universum Film A.G. in Berlin (Ufa), December 31, 1938, Zug-Nr. 438 (Akten-Pressestelle), File 4 [Zensur des Films "Henkel—ein deutsches Werk in seiner Arbeit" 1938–39], HA.

74. President of *Werberat* to Henkel, January 16, 1939, in ibid.

75. Werbeleitung Henkel to Universum Film A.G., January 19, 1939, in ibid.

76. The correspondence in the Henkel archive ends before a final decision about whether to keep the film intact has been rendered. However, the film itself contains all of the controversial claims and images, with the apparent exception of crucifixes. Film available at the Bundesarchiv-Filmarchiv, Berlin. The actual details of the Werberat's decision require further exploration.

77. "Wir fangen an: Wieder," HA.

78. See Edward Bernays, *The Engineering of Consent* (Norman: University of Oklahoma Press, 1955).

79. Jürgen Habermas, *The Structural Transformation of the Public Sphere: An Inquiry into a Category of Bourgeois Society* (1962; repr., Cambridge, MA: MIT Press, 1991), 193–95. On Habermas and the concepts of *publicity* and *publicness*, see Geoff Eley, "Commentary: Politics, Culture, and the Public Sphere," *Positions* 10, no. 1 (Spring 2002): 219–36.

80. Cohen, *Consumers' Republic*, 62.

81. For a fascinating selection of consumer complaints about Persil, see the GfK report "Hausfrau und Waschmittel" (January 1939), GfK archives, file S 1939 007. On consumer complaints, see also Reagin, *"Marktordnung"*; Barkai, *Nazi Economics*, 232; and Hartmut Berghoff, "Enticement and Deprivation: The Regulation of Consumption in Pre-war Nazi Germany," in *Politics of Consumption*, 165–84.

82. Colin Crouch, Klaus Eder, and Damian Tambine, eds., *Citizens, Markets, and the State* (Oxford: Oxford University Press, 2001). See introduction.

83. Michael Mann has argued that in the absence of civil and political rights, Germans in the 1930s did witness advances in the realm of social citizenship.

Public works projects and full employment offered proof of how central the state (whether fascist or democratic) can be in creating social stability. I would argue that this social citizenship is itself predicated on the projection of economic, cultural, and psychological understandings of citizenship. Mann, "Ruling Class Strategies and Citizenship," *Sociology* 21 (1987): 339–54.

84. On notions of citizenship as intimately linked to ideas of individual entitlement on the one hand and attachment to a particular community on the other, see Will Kymlicka and Wayne Norman, "Return of the Citizen: A Survey of Recent Work on Citizenship Theory," *Ethics* 104, no. 2 (1994): 352–81.

85. While *"Wohlstand für Alle"* is associated with Economics Minister Ludwig Erhard's 1957 book of the same title and the national election of that year, the language of widespread prosperity predated its publication. Ludwig Erhard, *Wohlstand für alle* (Düsseldorf: Econ, 1957).

86. See Wolfgang König, "Adolf Hitler vs. Henry Ford: The *Volkswagen*, the Role of America as a Model, and the Failure of a Nazi Consumer Society," *German Studies Review* 27, no. 2 (2004): 249–68.

87. On the concept of "better living" during the years of the "Economic Miracle," see S. Jonathan Wiesen, "Miracles for Sale: Consumer Displays and Advertising in Postwar West Germany," in *Consuming Germany*, 151–78; and Arne Andersen, *Der Traum vom guten Leben: Alltags- und Konsumgeschichte vom Wirtschaftswunder bis heute* (Frankfurt: Campus, 1997). On how West Germans saw the Economic Miracle as a continuation of the "quiet," "good" times of economic recovery in the 1930s, see Ulrich Herbert, "Good Times, Bad Times, Memories of the Third Reich," in *Life in the Third Reich*, ed. Richard Besse, 197–210 (Oxford: Oxford University Press, 1987). On the arrival of widespread prosperity only in the late 1950s, see Michael Wildt, "Privater Konsum in Westdeutschland in den 50er Jahren," in *Modernisierung im Wiederaufbau: Die Westdeutsche Gesellschaft der 50er Jahre*, ed. Axel Schildt and Arnold Sywottek, 275–89 (Bonn: J. H. W. Dietz, 1993).

CHAPTER 10

1. Celia Applegate and Pamela Potter, eds., *Music and German National Identity* (Chicago: University of Chicago Press, 2002)

2. See Zentrum für Zeithistorische Forschung Potsdam, "Konf: Colloquium aus Anlass der Verabschiedung von Prof. Dr. Christoph Kleßmann," http://hsozkult.geschichte.hu-berlin.de/termine/id=2398 (accessed: July 27, 2004).

3. Albrecht Riethmüller, "'Is That Not Something for *Simplicissimus*?!' The Belief in Musical Superiority," in Applegate and Potter, *Music*, 288–304.

4. Eric Santner, *Stranded Objects: Mourning, Memory, and Film in Postwar Germany* (Ithaca, NY: Cornell University Press, 1990), 50.

5. Georg Steinhausen, "Die deutsche Kultur," in *Der Deutsche Genius*, ed. Deutsche Büchereigesellschaft, 5–20 (Falkenberg: Verlag der Deutschen Bücherei-Gesellschaft, 1921–22).

6. Alfred Heuss, "Die deutsche Musik," in ibid., 107–17.

7. Erich Müller, "Das Judentum in der Musik," in *Handbuch der Judenfrage: Die wichtigsten Tatsachen zur Beurteilung des jüdischen Volkes*, 31st ed., ed. Theodor Fritsch, 323–33 (Leipzig: Hammer Verlag, 1932).

8. Hans Günther, *The Racial Elements of European History*, trans. G. C. Wheeler (London: Methuen, 1927), 55. The lure is a long trumpet-like instrument.

9. *Meyers Lexikon*, vol. 2, *Deutsche Kultur* (Leipzig: Bibliographisches Institut AG, 1937), 1110–37.

10. See the reproduction in Irena Antonova and Jörn Merkert, eds., *Berlin-Moskau 1900–1950* (Munich: Prestel, 1995), 439. On the significance of the organ, and of organ music in the Third Reich, see Michael Kaufmann, *Orgel und Nationalsozialismus: Die ideologische Vereinnahmung des Instruments im "Dritten Reich"* (Kleinblittersdorf: Musikwissenschaftliche Verlags-Gesellschaft, 1997).

11. Hans-Joachim Moser, "Von der Steuerung des deutschen Musiklebens," in *Jahrbuch der deutschen Musik 1943*, ed. Hellmuth von Hase, 22–26 (Leipzig: Breitkopf & Härtel, 1943).

12. For a recent example, see Saul Friedländer, *Nazi Germany and the Jews*, vol. 1, *The Years of Persecution, 1933–1939* (London: Weidenfeld & Nicolson, 1997); for an earlier one, see I. A. Hirschmann, "The Degradation of Culture," in *Nazism: An Assault on Civilization*, ed. Pierre van Paassen and James Waterman Wise, 88–107 (New York: H. Smith and R. Haas, 1934).

13. Erich Müller, "Das Judentum," 324–34.

14. Helmut Siebert, "Der Weg zur Kunstmusik," *Musik und Volk* (1936/1937): 23.

15. See Michael Kater, *Different Drummers: Jazz in the Culture of Nazi Germany* (New York: Oxford University Press, 1992).

16. Hans Hinkel, ed., *Handbuch der Reichskulturkammer* (Berlin: Deutscher Verlag für Politik und Wirtschaft, 1937), 335.

17. Heinrich Strobel, "Sendboten deutschen Musik," *Pariser Zeitung*, June 14, 1944.

18. See Albert Speer, *Inside the Third Reich*, trans. Richard and Clara Winston (New York: Avon Books, 1971), 584–85.

19. See the account by Hannah Vogt, cited in *Ludwig Doorman: Ein Leben für die Kirchenmusik. Erinnerungen, Gespräche, Briefe, Berichte*, ed. Roderich Schmidt (Göttingen: Deuerlich'sche Buchhandlung, 1988), 28–29.

20. *La France en Allemagne, Numéro Special: Information et Action Culturelle* August (1947): 48.

21. "Rapport sur l'oeuvre de démilitarisation, dénazification et de démocratisation entreprise par la Direction de l'Information, January 8, 1947, 16–17," Centre des Archives de l'Occupation Française en Allemagne et en Autriche à Colmar, Affaires Culturelles 857/5. For a comparative survey of "music control" in all four zones of occupied Germany, see Toby Thacker, *Music After Hitler, 1945–1955* (Aldershot, UK: Ashgate, 2007).

22. See, for a thoughtful exposition of these ideas, Wolfgang Geiseler, "Zwischen Klassik und Moderne," in *So viel Anfang war nie: Deutsche Städte 1945–1949*, ed. Hermann Glaser, Lutz von Pufendorf, and Michael Schöneich, 244–49 (Berlin: Siedler, 1989).

23. Bayerisches Hauptstaatsarchiv, Munich, Office of Military Government, Bavaria, 10/48–1/5, Weekly Report to Chief, Film, Theater, and Music, July 6, 1946.

24. "Vorbericht für die gemeinsame Sitzung des Kunstausschusses der Kultusministerkonferenz und des Kulturausschusses des deutschen Städtetags am 7. 12. 1950 in Hannover, 15 November 1950," Nordrhein-Westphälisches Hauptstaatsarchiv, Düsseldorf, Bestand NW 60/861.

25. See, for example, the comments made in 1957 by Hermann Unger to Hans-Joachim Moser in a private letter, in Toby Thacker, "'Playing Beethoven like an Indian': American Music and Reorientation in Germany, 1945–1955," in *The Postwar Challenge: Cultural, Social, and Political Change in Western Europe, 1945–1958*, ed. Dominik Geppert, 365–86 (New York: Oxford University Press, 2003).

26. See the documents relating to this in the Bundesarchiv Koblenz, Kanzleramt 5815.

27. "Arbeitsgemeinschaft für Musikerziehung und Musikpflege," *Zur Notlage der Musikerziehung und Musikpflege* (Kassel: Arbeitsgemeinschaft für Musikerziehung und Musikpflege, 1953), 4.

28. Ernst H. Meyer, "Geleitwort," *Musik und Gesellschaft* 1, no. 1 (1951): 3.

29. See Konrad Niemann, *Ernst Hermann Meyer: Für Sie porträtiert*, 2nd ed. (Leipzig: Deutscher Verlag für Musik, 1989), 7–10.

30. This is above all evident in Meyer's writing on Handel and on the role of the choir in Handel's music. See, for example, "Einige Gedanken zu Händels Oratoriumswerk," in Ernst H. Meyer, *Musik der Renaissance—Aufklärung—Klassik*, 168–81 (Leipzig: Verlag Philipp Reclam jun., 1973).

31. Stiftung Archiv der Parteien und Massenorganisationen der DDR im Bundesarchiv, Berlin (hereafter SAPMO) DR 1/335, Bericht über die Situation auf dem Gebiet der Musik im Lande Mecklenburg [1952].

32. Stiftung Archiv der Akademie der Künste, Berlin, Ernst-Hermann-Meyer-Archiv 228, "Music life and musical composition in the G.D.R." [February 1965].

33. See Toby Thacker, "The Fifth Column: Dance Music in the Early GDR," in *The Workers' and Peasants' State: Communism and Society in East Germany Under Ulbricht 1945–71*, ed. Patrick Major and Jonathan Osmond, 227–43 (Manchester, UK: Manchester University Press, 2002).

34. See, for example, Peter Wicke, "Eine methodologische Versuch über musikalische Massenkultur," *Wissenschaftliche Zeitschrift der Humboldt Universität zu Berlin* 1 (1980): 95ff.

35. SAPMO DR 1/243, Meldung zur Teilnahme am Wettbewerb für Tanz- und Unterhaltungskapellen für die VI. Weltfestspiele in Moskau 1957.

36. SAPMO DR 1/243, Günter Dressel to Ministerium für Kultur, February 14, 1957.

37. SAPMO DR 1/243, Uszkoreit to Dressel, February 22, 1957.

38. See North American Hanns Eisler Forum, "Interview with Wolf Biermann," http://www.eislermusic.com/biermann.htm (accessed May 14, 2007).

39. I am grateful to Mark Fenemore for drawing this to my attention.

40. We should bear in mind that the infamous Nuremberg Laws of 1935 were accompanied by an explanatory rationale that included a section on "culture" and used racist understandings of the arts as one justification for the provisions of the new citizenship laws. See Wilhelm Stuckart and Hans Globke, *Kommentare zur deutschen Rassengesetzgebung* (Munich: Beck, 1936), especially "Rasse, Volk, und Kultur," vol. 1, 8–14.

41. Ernst H. Meyer, "Realismus: Die Lebensfrage der deutschen Musik," *Musik und Gesellschaft* 1, no. 2 (1951): 38–43.

42. Celia Applegate and Pamela Potter, "Germans as the 'People of Music': Genealogy of an Identity," in Applegate and Potter, *Music*, 1–35.

43. Hans-Hubert Schönzeler, ed., *Of German Music: A Symposium* (London: Oswald Wolff, 1976), 8.

44. See Amit Chaudhuri, "Provincialising Europe: Postcolonial Thought and Historical Difference," *London Review of Books* 27, no. 12 (June 2004): 3–8.

CHAPTER 11

1. For details see Pascal Grosse, *Kolonialismus, Eugenik und bürgerliche Gesellschaft* (Frankfurt am Main: Campus, 2000).

2. Michel Foucault, *Histoire de la sexualité,* vol. 1 (Paris: Gallimard, 1976); Giorgio Agamben, *Homo sacer: Sovereign Power and Bare Life* (Stanford, CA: Stanford University Press, 1998).

3. Michel Foucault, "Le sujet et le pouvoir," in Michel Foucault, *Dits et écrits 1954–1988* vol. 6, (Paris: Éditions Gallimard, 1994), 222–43.

4. Cathleen Canning and Sonya O. Rose, "Gender, Citizenship, and Subjectivity: Some Theoretical and Historical Considerations," *Gender and History* 13 (2001): 427–43; G. Bock and S. James, eds., *Beyond Equality and Difference: Citizenship, Feminist Politics and Female Subjectivity* (London: Routledge, 1992).

5. Ad hoc Committee of Harvard Medical School to Examine the Definition of Brain Death, "A Definition of Irreversible Coma," *Journal of the American Medical Association* 205 (1968): 337–40; on more recent debates regarding the concept of brain death, see S. Youngner, R. Arnold, and R. Schapiro, eds., *The Definition of Death: Contemporary Controversies* (Baltimore, MD: Johns Hopkins University Press, 1999).

6. Ursula Baumann, *Vom Recht auf den eigenen Tod: Die Geschichte des Suizids vom 18. bis zum 20. Jahrhundert* (Weimar: Verlag Hermann Böhlaus Nachfolge, 2001).

7. Of course, biological regulation has always taken place through marriage arrangements, abortion, infanticide, and so on, although these practices were not necessarily understood as biological.

8. Michael Hagner, *Homo cerebralis: Der Wandel vom Seelenorgan zum Gehirn* (Berlin: Berlin Verlag, 1997).

9. Franz Joseph Gall, *Sur les fonctions du cerveau et sur celles de chacune de ses parties* (Paris: Boucher, 1822–25).

10. Furthermore, he put forward the idea that the human faculties were

located in distinct regions of the brain, for which he used the term *organol-ogy*. Although none of these ideas were altogether new, it was Gall who syn-thesized them into a comprehensive research agenda and tried to demon-strate the evidence for them, starting in the early 1800s and continuing until his death in 1828. Gall is perhaps more famous for his constitution theory, known as *phrenology*, in which he asserted that the distinct parts of the brain imprint themselves on the surrounding skull and neck, which would allow an individual's qualities to be identified from the outside. It discredited his work for the next two hundred years to come and made him a figure of public mockery.

11. Virchow detailed his anthropology in his salient *Die Einheitsbestrebun-gen in der wissenschaftlichen Medicin* (Berlin: Reimer, 1849). This starts with a multilayered discussion of brain functions and their connection to conscious-ness, volition, and the essence of humankind.

12. Denis Diderot, *Oeuvres*, vol. 1, *Philosophie* (Paris: Éditions Robert Laffont, S.A., 1994), 1253–1317, esp. 1298ff.

13. Samuel Thomas Soemmering, *Ueber das Organ der Seele* (Königsberg: Nicolovius, 1796).

14. See, for example, Jean-Étienne Esquirol, *Des passions, considerées comme cause, symptomes et moyens curatifs de l'alienation mentale* (Paris: Didot Jeune, 1805); Pierre Cabanis, *Rapports du physique et du morale de l'homme* (Paris: Crape-let, 1802).

15. Wilhelm Griesinger, *Die Pathologie und Therapie der psychischen Krankhei-ten* (Stuttgart: Krabbe, 1845).

16. Ibid., 42.

17. Ibid., 44.

18. Fritz Lenz, "Menschliche Erblichkeitslehre," in Erwin Baur, Eugen Fischer, and Fritz Lenz, *Grundriß der menschlichen Erblichkeitslehre und Rassen-hygiene*, 407–8 (München: J. F. Lehmann, 1923).

19. Samuel Thomas Soemmering, *Ueber die körperliche Verschiedenheit des Mohren vom Europäer* (Mainz: n.p., 1784); Samuel Thomas Soemmering, *Ueber die körperliche Verschiedenheit des Negers vom Europäer* (Frankfurt am Main: Ver-rentrapp Sohn & Wenner, 1785).

20. Friedrich Tiedemann, "On the Brain of the Negro, Compared with That of the European and the Orang-Outang," *Philosophical Transactions of the Royal Society of London* 126 (1836): 497–527. Originally published as Friedrich Tiede-mann, *Das Hirn des Negers mit dem des Europäers und Orang-Outangs verglichen* (Heidelberg: K. Winter, 1837).

21. Ibid., 526–27.

22. Benjamin Gould, *Anthropological Investigations in the Military and Anthro-pological Statistics of American Soldiers* (New York: Riverside Press, 1869); San-ford B. Hunt, "The Negro as Soldier," *Anthropological Review* 7 (1869): 40–54.

23. Michael Stolberg, "A Woman Down to Her Bones: The Anatomy of Sex-ual Difference in the Sixteenth and Early Seventeenth Centuries," *Isis* 9 (2003): 274–99.

24. Emil Huschke, *Schädel, Hirn und Seele des Menschen und der Thiere nach Alter, Geschlecht und Race* (Jena: F. Mauke, 1854).

25. Jacob Fidelis Ackermann, *Über die körperliche Verschiedenheit des Mannes vom Weibe ausser Geschlechtstheilen* (Koblenz: Johann Kaspar Huber, 1788), 5.

26. Huschke, *Schädel*, 3.

27. Franz-Joseph Gall, *Sur les fonctions du cerveau et sur celles de chacun de ses parties* (Paris: A. Boucher, 1822).

28. Carl Westphal, "Die conträre Sexualempfindung, Symptom eines neuropathischen (psychopathischen) Zustandes," *Archiv für Psychiatrie* 2 (1870): 73–108.

29. Sigmund Freud, *Totem and Taboo: Some Points of Agreement Between the Mental Lives of Savages and Neurotics* (1913; repr., London: Routledge, 2003).

30. Paul Weindling, "Theories of the Cell State in Imperial Germany," in *Biology, Medicine and Society, 1840–1940*, ed. Charles Webster, 99–155 (Cambridge: Cambridge University Press, 1981).

31. Doris Kaufmann, *Aufklärung, bürgerliche Selbsterfahrung und die "Erfindung" der Psychiatrie in Deutschland, 1770–1850* (Göttingen: Vandenhoeck & Ruprecht, 1995), 32.

CHAPTER 12

1. For an introduction, see Christoph Conrad and Jürgen Kocka, eds., *Staatsbürgerschaft in Europa: Historische Erfahrungen und aktuelle Debatten* (Hamburg: Edition Körber-Stiftung, 2001); Manfred Hildermeier, Jürgen Kocka, and Christoph Conrad, eds., *Europäische Zivilgesellschaft in Ost und West: Begriff, Geschichte, Chancen* (Frankfurt: Campus, 2000).

2. See Klaus von Beyme, "Zivilgesellschaft—Karriere und Leistung eines Modebegriffs," in Hildemeier et al., *Europäische*, 41–56.

3. For the global dimension, see Stephen Castles and Alastair Davidson, *Citizenship and Migration: Globalization and the Politics of Belonging* (Basingstoke, UK: Macmillan, 2000).

4. In this respect, radical democratic projects like the Workers' Councils in the revolution of 1918–19 receive new attention, as Peter C. Caldwell's chapter in this volume demonstrates.

5. An intensively discussed problem is that of people's motivation for and disposition to civic commitment and activities. See, for example, part two of *The Demands of Citizenship*, ed. Catriona McKinnon and Iain Hampsher-Monk (London: Wellington House, 2000), 123–92.

6. Liberal theorists distinguish civic rights from welfare rights. See McKinnon and Hampsher-Monk, *Demands of Citizenship*, 1–12.

7. Margaret R. Somers, "Citizenship and the Place of the Public Sphere: Law, Community, and Political Culture in the Transition to Democracy," *American Sociological Review* 58, no. 1 (1993): 587–620.

8. Thomas H. Marshall, "Citizenship and Social Class," in *Citizenship, Social*

Class and Other Essays, ed. Thomas H. Marshall and Tom Bottomore, 3–51 (1950; repr., London: Pluto Press, 1992). Marshall belongs to the modernists who believed in continuing progress.

9. The role of the media in constructing citizenship cannot be overestimated. About the construction of *Volksgemeinschaft* by broadcast media, see Inge Marszolek and Adelheid von Saldern, eds., *Zuhören und Gehörtwerden,* vol. 1, *Radio im Nationalsozialismus: Zwischen Lenkung und Ablenkung* (Tübingen: Edition Discord, 1998).

10. S. Jonathan Wiesen's chapter in this volume stimulates one to find other inconsistencies of individuals, constructed by the media, and to determine the limits of the "permissible."

11. Paul Betts, *The Authority of Everyday Objects* (Berkeley and Los Angeles: University of California Press, 2004).

12. Tendencies of the decentralization of future democracy also determine the regional and the local level as pendants to transnational developments and globalization.

13. See, in general, David F. Crew, *Germans on Welfare: From Weimar to Hitler* (Oxford: Oxford University Press, 2001).

14. See *Informationen zur modernen Stadtgeschichte* 4 (2004), focusing on *Stadtraum und Geschlechterperspektiven.*

15. For the present time, see Roland Roth, "Auf dem Wege zur Bürgerkommune? Bürgerschaftliches Engagement und Kommunalpolitik in Deutschland zu Beginn des 21 Jahrhunderts," in *Die Bürgergesellschaft: Perspektiven für Bürgerbeteiligung und Bürgerkommunikation,* ed. Friedrich-Ebert Stiftung, Thomas Meyer, and Reinhard Weil, 163–84 (Bonn: Dietz, 2002).

16. With respect to migrants in Frankfurt, see Brett Klopp, *German Multiculturalism: Immigrant Integration and the Transformation of Citizenship* (Westport, CT: Praeger, 2002); and Adelheid von Saldern, ed., *Stadt und Kommunikation in bundesrepublikanischen Umbruchszeiten* (Stuttgart: Steiner, 2006).

17. Castles and Davidson, *Citizenship,* xi.

18. Dieter Gosewinkel, *Einbürgern und Ausschließen: Die Nationalisierung der Staatsangehörigkeit vom Deutschen Bund bis zur Bundesrepublik* (Göttingen: Vandenhoeck & Ruprecht, 2001), 427. Gosewinkel emphasizes the great break constituted by the Nuremberg law of 1935 in ibid., 369–420.

19. The restrictions on migration and migrants were, however, not a singularly German phenomenon. For similarities and differences, see Klaus Bade, *Europa in Bewegung: Migration vom späten 18. Jahrhundert bis zur Gegenwart* (Munich: Beck, 2000), 319–23; and Karen Schönwälder, *Einwanderung und ethnische Pluralität: Politische Entscheidungen und öffentliche Debatten in Großbritannien und der Bundesrepublik von den 1950er bis zu den 1970er Jahren* (Essen: Klartext, 2001).

20. Jan C. Behrends, Thomas Lindenberger, and Patrice G. Poutrus, eds., *Fremde und Fremd-Sein in der DDR: Zu historischen Ursachen der Fremdenfeindlichkeit in Ostdeutschland* (Berlin: Metropol, 2003).

21. David Cesarani and Mary Fulbrook, introduction to *Citizenship, Nation-*

ality and Migration in Europe, ed. David Cesarani and Mary Fulbrook, 1–17 (London: Routledge, 1996).

22. Equal rights, equal treatment, and equal chances for men and women in all segments of society are crucial features of the contemporary concept of citizenship as a matter of course. As long as they have not been achieved, women will be seen as disadvantaged citizens.

23. Foucault focuses on the close interrelationship between modern government and modern individuals, between power and subjectivity, and between education as a process "from above"—from society—and from oneself. For an introduction to governmentality studies, see Ulrich Bröckling, Susanne Krasmann, and Thomas Lemke, eds., *Gouvernementalität der Gegenwart: Studien zu Ökonomisierung des Sozialen* (Frankfurt a.M.: Suhrkamp, 2000).

24. Mitchell Dean, *Governmentality: Power and Rule in Modern Society* (London: Sage Publications, 1999), 209; Thomas Lemke, "Neoliberalismus, Staat und Selbsttechnologien: Ein kritischer Überblick über die *governmentality studies*," in *Politische Vierteljahresschrift* 41, no. 1 (2000): 31–47. This has included biopolitics, that is, modeling the body and modeling the brain. In his chapter on biopolitics in this volume, Pascal Grosse stresses the inner connection between different modes of coercion: against oneself as well as against others. In either case, people can be made responsible for their own fate. See Lemke, "Neoliberalismus," 38.

25. Dean, *Governmentality*, 57.

26. The problem for the *Werkbund* was that modernity in taste could not be nationalized, as was recognized later by the Bauhaus, which consequently acted in a spirit of transnationalism and universalism.

27. Zygmunt Bauman, *Moderne und Ambivalenz: Das Ende der Eindeutigkeit* (Hamburg: Europäische Verlagsanstalt, 1992); Zygmunt Bauman, *Dialektik der Ordnung: Die Moderne und der Holocaust* (Hamburg: Europäische Verlagsanstalt, 1992); see also, for example, Sven Reichardt, "Gewalt und Zivilität im Wandel: Konzeptionelle Überlegungen zur Zivilgesellschaft aus historischer Sicht," in *Zivilgesellschaft: National und transnational*, ed. Dieter Gosewinkel, Dieter Rucht, Wolfgang van den Daele, and Jürgen Kocka, 16–76 (Berlin: Edition Sigma, 2003). Reichardt also refers to Zygmunt Bauman.

28. See Michel de Certeau, *Kunst des Handelns* (Berlin: Merve-Verlag, 1988).

29. Dean, *Governmentality*, 97.

30. Compare Lemke, "Neoliberalismus," 41–43.

31. Michael Walzer, introduction to *Toward a Global Civil Society*, ed. Michael Walzer, 1–7 (Providence, RI: Berghahn Books, 1995).

32. This is a matter of concern in German universities, for example. In the pursuit of optimal effectiveness and global competition, the practices of self-administration and democratic decision making at a nonstate place, which were introduced in the aftermath of the 1968 student movement, have been radically curtailed in recent years.

33. Norbert Elias incorporates such procedures into a long-term process of civilization, through which, above all, violence is excluded from social life. Norbert Elias, *Über den Prozeß der Zivilisation: Soziogenetische und psychogenetische Untersuchungen* (Frankfurt a.M.: Suhrkamp, 1976). See also S. Jonathan Wiesen's example in this volume.

34. See, for example, the heavy, big *Gelsenkirchener Barock* furniture in working-class apartments of the 1950s.

35. This problem is discussed by John Schwarzmantel, *Citizenship and Identity: Toward a New Republic* (London: Routledge, 2003), 142–45.

36. Lesley Hodgson, "Manufactured Civil Society: Counting the Cost," in *Critical Social Policy* 24, no. 2 (2004): 139–64.

37. Ibid., 175.

38. Besides the already cited literature, on the concept of civil society see Gosewinkel et al., *Zivilgesellschaft*, 11–28.

39. See Jürgen Kocka, "Zivilgesellschaft als historisches Problem und Versprechen," in Hildemeier et al., *Europäische Zivilgesellschaft*, 13–41.

40. Arnd Bauerkämper, "Einleitung: Die Praxis der Zivilgesellschaft. Akteure und ihr Handeln in historisch-sozialwissenschaftlicher Perspektive," in *Die Praxis der Zivilgesellschaft: Akteure, Handeln und Strukturen im internationalen Vergleich*, ed. Arnd Bauerkämper, 7–30 (Frankfurt: Campus, 2003).

41. Markus Pins and Anthony Giddens, "Es wird ziemlich schwer, öffentlichen Raum zurück zu gewinnen," *Die Neue Gesellschaft/Frankfurter Hefte*, 47, no. 6 (2000): 335–40.

42. John Keane, *Civil Society: Old Images, New Visions* (Stanford, CA: Stanford University Press, 1998), 6.

43. Communitarians use the term *civil society* and focus on group activities in communities, especially on the local level. Charles Taylor, "Die Beschwörung der 'Civil Society,'" in *Europa und die Civil Society*, ed. Krzysztof Michalski, 52–81 (1989; repr., Stuttgart: Klett-Cotta, 1991); Michael Walzer, "The Concept of Civil Society," in *Toward a Global Civil Society*, ed. Michael Walzer (Providence, RI: Berghahn, 1995).

44. Walter Reese-Schäfer, *Was ist Kommunitarismus*, 2nd ed. (Frankfurt: Campus, 1995), 166; Nikolas Rose, "Tod des Sozialen? Eine Neubestimmung der Grenze des Regierens," in Bröckling et al., *Gouvernementalität*, 72–109.

45. In contrast to this assessment, Caldwell stresses in his chapter in this volume that people were forced to think in terms of homogeneity.

46. That means that the process of exclusion of Jews, for example, from provincial theaters, was already underway before Hitler came to power in 1933. See Lu Seegers, "Hansetradition, niederdeutsches Volkstum und moderne Industriestadt: Die Rostocker Kulturwochen (1934–1939)," in *Inszenierter Stolz: Stadtrepräsentationen in drei deutschen Gesellschaften (1935–1975)*, ed. Adelheid von Saldern, 147–81 (Stuttgart: Steiner, 2005).

47. The mixture of descriptive and normative elements in the common understanding of the two concepts is one of their most problematic aspects.

48. Bauerkämper, *Die Praxis*, 15. Usually, this is not the view of the communitarists.

49. Schwarzmantel, *Citizenship*, 157.

CHAPTER 13

1. Kathleen Canning, "Class vs. Citizenship: Keywords in German Gender History," *Central European History* 37, no. 2 (June 2004): 225–44.

2. Geoff Eley, "Making a Place in the Nation: The Meanings of 'Citizenship' in Wilhelmine Germany," in *Wilhelminism and Its Legacies: German Modernities, Imperialism and the Meanings of Reform, 1890–1930*, ed. Geoff Eley and James Retallack, 16–33 (New York: Berghahn, 2003).

3. A sample of this enormous body of literature includes: Lauren Berlant, *The Queen of America Goes to Washington City: Essays on Sex and Citizenship* (Durham, NC: Duke University Press, 1997); Evelyn Nakano Glenn, *Unequal Freedoms: How Race and Gender Shaped American Citizenship and Labor* (Cambridge, MA: Harvard University Press, 2004); Ruth Lister, *Citizenship: Feminist Perspectives* (New York: New York University Press, 1997); Mae Ngai, *Impossible Subjects: Illegal Aliens and the Making of American Politics* (Princeton, NJ: Princeton University Press, 2003); Aihwa Ong, *Flexible Citizenship: The Cultural Logics of Transnationality* (Durham, NC: Duke University Press, 1999); Iris Marion Young, "Polity and Group Difference: A Critique of the Ideal of Universal Citizenship," in *The Citizenship Debates: A Reader*, ed. Gershon Shafir, 263–90 (Minneapolis: University of Minnesota Press, 1998); Nira Yuval-Davis and Pnina Werbner, eds., *Women, Citizenship and Difference* (New York: St. Martin's Press, 1999); and Kathleen Canning and Sonya O. Rose, eds., *Gender, Citizenships, and Subjectivities* (London: Blackwell, 2002).

4. See the chapters by Pascal Grosse, Cornelie Usborne, and Annemarie Sammartino in this volume. See Lora Wildenthal's critique of Brubaker from the perspective of both gender and German colonialism: "Race, Gender, and Citizenship in the German Colonial Empire," in *Tensions of Empire: Colonial Cultures in a Bourgeois World*, ed. Frederick Cooper and Ann L. Stoler, 263–83 (Berkeley: University of California Press, 1997); and Julia Sneeringer's recent article, "The Shopper as Voter: Women, Advertising, and Politics in Post-Inflation Germany," *German Studies Review* 27, no. 3 (October 2004): 476–502.

5. See the chapter in this volume by Geoff Eley, "Some General Thoughts on Citizenship in Germany." These terms also surfaced frequently in discussions among the conference participants.

6. Adelheid von Saldern, "Citizenship in German Twentieth-Century History: Chances and Challenges of a Concept," in this volume.

7. Geoff Eley suggests approaching citizenship as "under construction" in the history of twentieth-century Germany in his chapter in this volume, whereas Adelheid von Saldern posits the notion of citizenship as process.

8. Kathleen Canning, "Claiming Citizenship: Suffrage and Subjectivity in

Germany after World War I," in Kathleen Canning, *Gender History in Practice: Historical Perspectives on Bodies, Class and Citizenship* (Ithaca, NY: Cornell University Press, 2006), 212–37.

9. Peter C. Caldwell, "The Citizen and the Republic in Germany, 1918–1935," in this volume.

10. von Saldern, "Citizenship."

11. See Eley, "Some General Thoughts."

12. Ibid.

13. Ibid.

14. Jan Palmowski, "Citizenship, Identity and Community in the GDR," in this volume.

15. This is elaborated in considerably more detail in his book, *Einbürgern und Ausschließen: Die Nationalisierung der Staatsangehörigkeit vom Deutschen Bund bis zur Bundesrepublik Deutschland* (Göttingen: Vandenhoeck & Ruprecht, 2001).

16. Ibid., 3–4.

17. Ibid., 7.

18. Gosewinkel, "Citizenship in Germany and France at the Turn of the Twentieth Century: Some New Observations on an Old Comparison," in this volume.

19. Here I rely on Gosewinkel, *Einbürgern und Ausschließen*.

20. Gosewinkel, "Citizenship in Germany and France."

21. Annemarie Sammartino, "Culture, Belonging, and the Law: Naturalization in the Weimar Republic," in this volume.

22. Jennifer Jenkins, "The Citizen at Home: *Wohnkultur* Before World War I," in this volume. Also see her book, *Provincial Modernity: Local Culture and Liberal Politics in Fin-de-Siècle Hamburg* (Ithaca, NY: Cornell University Press, 2003).

23. Toby Thacker, "'Gesungen oder musiziert wird in fast jedem Haus': Representing and Constructing Citizenship Through Music in Twentieth-Century Germany," in this volume.

24. Caldwell, "Citizen and Republic." In his schema, national belonging in the sense of *Staatsangehörigkeit* ("a subject's belonging to the state") constitutes the third frame for citizenship. The fourth—national identity ("the subjective feeling of identification with a certain state or community")—he associates with "a paucity of rights" and thus views it as distinct or separate from the other three.

25. Grosse, "Conceptualizing Citizenship as a Biopolitical Category from the Eighteenth to the Twentieth Centuries," in this volume.

26. Ibid.

27. Ibid.

28. Ibid.

29. Palmowski, "Citizenship."

30. Jonathan Wiesen, "Creating the Nazi Marketplace: Public Relations and Consumer Citizenship in the Third Reich," in this volume.

31. Lizabeth Cohen, *A Consumer's Republic: The Politics of Mass Consumption in Postwar America* (New York: Random House/Vintage, 2003).

32. Eley, "Some General Thoughts."

33. Thomas Lindenberger, "From the Chopped-off Hand to the Twisted Foot: Citizenship and Police Violence in Twentieth-Century Germany," in this volume.

34. Ibid.

35. Palmowski, "Citizenship."

36. Ibid.

37. Ibid.

38. Ibid.

39. Ibid.

40. Caldwell, "Citizen and Republic."

41. Ibid.

42. Ibid.

43. Ibid.

44. Ibid.

45. Ibid.

46. Ibid.

47. Ibid.

48. Ibid.

49. Peter Caldwell, *Popular Sovereignty and the Crisis of German Constitutional Law: The Theory and Practice of Weimar Constitutionalism* (Durham, NC: Duke University Press, 1997).

50. Cornelie Usborne, "Body Biological to Body Politic: Women's Demands for Reproductive Self-Determination in World War I and Early Weimar Germany," in this volume.

51. Ibid.

52. Lisa M. Todd, "War Wives and Sexual Treason: State Surveillance of Public and Private Morals in Germany During World War I" (PhD diss., University of Toronto, 2005); Ute Daniel, *The War from Within: German Working-Class Women in World War I* (Oxford: Berg, 1997); Elisabeth Domansky, "Militarization and Reproduction in World War I Germany," in *Society, Culture and the State in Germany, 1870–1930,* ed. Geoff Eley, 427–64 (Ann Arbor: University of Michigan Press, 1996).

53. Eley, "General Thoughts."

54. Ibid.

55. I investigate this contradictory space for citizenship in Canning, "Claiming Citizenship."

56. Caldwell, "Citizen and Republic."

CHAPTER 14

My thoughts in this chapter are hugely indebted to conversations with Kathleen Canning as well as to readings of her published and unpublished work.

1. Rogers Brubaker, *Citizenship and Nationhood in France and Germany* (Cambridge, MA: Harvard University Press, 1992).

2. Ibid., 15.

3. Ibid., 184.

4. Ibid., 16.

5. Here, the common ground linking Brubaker's approach to that of another work emphasizing deep cultural continuities as the key to the peculiarity of Germany's twentieth-century history might be noted; namely, Daniel Jonah Goldhagen, *Hitler's Willing Executioners: Ordinary Germans and the Holocaust* (New York: Knopf, 1996).

6. Here I am speaking specifically about its place in the German field. Among French historians this may be different. Within sociology, it certainly retains its influence.

7. See Andreas Fahrmeir, *Citizens and Aliens: Foreigners and the Law in Britain and the German States 1789–1870* (New York: Berghahn Books, 2000); Dieter Gosewinkel, *Einbürgern und Ausschließen: Die Nationalisierung der Staatsangehörigkeit vom Deutschen Bund bis zur Bundesrepublik Deutschland* (Göttingen: Vandenhoeck & Ruprecht, 2001). For Austria, see Hannelore Burger, "Passwesen und Staatsbürgerschaft," in *Grenze und Staat: Paßwesen, Staatsbürgerschaft, Heimatrecht und Fremdengesetzgebung in der österreichischen Monarchie 1750–1867,* ed. Waltraud Heindl and Edith Saurer, 3–173 (Vienna: Böhlau, 2000). See also Lora Wildenthal, "Race, Gender, and Citizenship in the German Colonial Empire," in *Tensions of Empire: Colonial Cultures in a Bourgeois World,* ed. Frederick Cooper and Ann Stoler, 263–83 (Berkeley: University of California Press, 1997).

8. See the following: Brian Ladd, *Urban Planning and Civic Order in Germany, 1860–1914* (Cambridge, MA: Harvard University Press, 1990); Matthew Jefferies, *Politics and Culture in Imperial Germany: The Case of Industrial Architecture* (Oxford: Berg, 1995); Kevin Repp, *Reformers, Critics, and the Paths of German Modernity: Anti-Politics and the Search for Alternatives, 1890–1914* (Cambridge, MA: Harvard University Press, 2000); Andrew Lees, *Cities, Sin, and Social Reform in Imperial Germany* (Ann Arbor: University of Michigan Press, 2002); Thomas M. Lekan, *Imagining the Nation in Nature: Landscape Preservation and German Identity 1885–1945* (Cambridge, MA: Harvard University Press, 2004); Geoff Eley and James Retallack, eds., *Wilhelminism and Its Legacies: German Modernities, Imperialism, and the Meanings of Reform, 1890–1930: Essays for Hartmut Pogge von Strandmann* (New York: Berghahn Books, 2003); and especially Jennifer Jenkins, *Provincial Modernity: Local Culture and Liberal Politics in Fin-de-Siècle Hamburg* (Ithaca, NY: Cornell University Press, 2003).

9. The quoted references are to Michael Burleigh and Wolfgang Wippermann, *The Racial State, 1933–1945* (Cambridge: Cambridge University Press, 1991); and Michael Thad Allen, *The Business of Genocide: The SS, Slave Labor, and the Concentration Camps* (Chapel Hill: University of North Carolina Press, 2002). More extensive citations cannot be provided here, but in retrospect the collection edited by Michael Prinz and Rainer Zitelmann, *Nationalsozialismus und Modernisierung* (Darmstadt: Wissenschaftliche Buchgesellschaft, 1991),

while certainly not free of the tendentiousness referred to above, was a key watershed.

10. Brubaker, *Citizenship*, 186.

11. On the one hand, Brubaker argues explicitly that the Wilhelmine "conceptions of nationhood and definitions of citizenship" were *not* "prefigurations of Nazi ideology and policy," insisting instead on "the radical novelty of Nazi citizenship policy, which differed not only in degree but in kind from Wilhelmine policy." Yet on the other hand, if "it is important to distinguish sharply between the ethnocultural aspect of the Wilhelmine citizenship law reform and the radical ethnoracial restructuring of citizenship under the Nazis," the "continuity of citizenship law from the Wilhelmine era to the present" remains nonetheless primary. In that sense, he is concerned "with continuity around the Third Reich, not continuity leading up to it." On that basis, "the broad patterns" separating German from French experience "have long been fixed," extending from the early nineteenth century right down to the present. See ibid., 165–66, 186.

12. I am defining these ruptures by simultaneous occurrence of territorial revision (loss or addition of new lands to the state) and upheaval in state forms and political arrangements. In contrast to their frequency in German history, there was only one clear instance of such a rupture in France—that of 1940–46—because the other major political and constitutional crises, with the possible exception of 1870–71, lacked territorial changes on anything like the German scale.

13. The best introduction to the more complex contexts of citizenship in Germany is through Andreas K. Fahrmeier, "Nineteenth-Century German Citizenships: A Reconsideration," *Historical Journal* 40, no. 3 (1997): 721–52. On the conceptual front, see especially the following: Margaret R. Somers, "Citizenship and the Place of the Public Sphere: Law, Community, and Political Culture in the Transition to Democracy," *American Sociological Review* 58, no. 5 (1993): 587–620; and Somers, "Narrating and Naturalizing Civil Society and Citizenship Theory: The Place of Political Culture and the Public Sphere," *Sociological Theory* 13 (1995): 229–74; Lauren Berlant, *The Queen of America Goes to Washington City: Essays on Sex and Citizenship* (Durham, NC: Duke University Press, 1997); Kathleen Canning and Sonya O. Rose, "Gender, Citizenship, and Subjectivity: Some Theoretical and Historical Considerations," *Gender and History* 13, no. 3 (2001): 427–43; Kathleen Canning, "Embodied Citizenships: Gender and the Crisis of Nation in Weimar Germany" (unpublished manuscript).

14. See Brubaker, *Citizenship*, x.

15. Geoff Eley and Jan Palmowski, "Citizenship and Identity in German History" (conference outline, "Citizenship and National Identity in Twentieth-Century Germany," Lady Margaret Hall, Oxford, UK, September 10–12, 2004).

16. Kathleen Canning, "Of Gender Stories and Master Narratives in the History of the Weimar Republic" (unpublished manuscript), quoting Bryan Turner, "Contemporary Problems in the Theory of Citizenship," in Bryan Turner, ed., *Citizenship and Social Theory* (London: Sage, 1993).

17. The possible citations are voluminous. The best introduction is now Jane Caplan and John Torpey, eds., *Documenting Individual Identity: The Development of State Practices in the Modern World* (Princeton, NJ: Princeton University Press, 2001). For a sampling of other works, see the following: John Torpey, *The Invention of the Passport: Surveillance, Citizenship and the State* (Cambridge: Cambridge University Press, 2000); Silvana Patriarca, *Numbers and Nationhood: Writing Statistics in Nineteenth-Century Italy* (Cambridge: Cambridge University Press, 1996); Joshua Cole, *The Power of Large Numbers: Population, Politics, and Gender in Nineteenth-Century France* (Ithaca, NY: Cornell University Press, 2000); J. Adam Tooze, *Statistics and the German State, 1900–1945: The Making of Modern Economic Knowledge* (Cambridge: Cambridge University Press, 2001); Richard F. Wetzell, *Inventing the Criminal: A History of German Criminology, 1880–1945* (Chapel Hill: University of North Carolina Press, 2000); Paul Lerner, *Hysterical Men: War, Psychiatry, and the Politics of Trauma in Germany, 1890–1930* (Ithaca, NY: Cornell University Press, 2003); Nikolas Rose, *Governing the Soul: The Shaping of the Private Self*, 2nd ed. (London: Free Association Books, 1999).

18. See Detlev Peukert, *Grenzen der Sozialdisziplinierung: Aufstieg und Krise der deutschen Jugendfürsorge von 1878 bis 1932* (Cologne: Bund-Verlag, 1986); and Peukert, "The Genesis of the 'Final Solution' from the Spirit of Science," in *Reevaluating the Third Reich*, ed. Thomas Childers and Jane Caplan, 234–52 (New York: Holmes and Meier, 1993); Renate Bridenthal, Atina Grossmann, and Marion Kaplan, eds., *When Biology Became Destiny: Women in Weimar and Nazi Germany* (New York: Monthly Review Press, 1984).

19. Brubaker, *Citizenship*, x; Lauren Berlant, *Queen of America*, 10.

20. Kathleen Canning, "Class vs. Citizenship: Keywords in German Gender History," *Central European History* 37 (2004): 240; Teresa Kuwalik, *Wohlfahrtsstaat und Mutterschaft: Schweden und Deutschland 1870–1912* (Frankfurt am Main: Campus, 1999). See also Geoff Eley and Atina Grossmann, "Maternalism and Citizenship in Weimar Germany: The Gendered Politics of Welfare," *Central European History* 30 (1997): 67–75.

21. Canning, "Class vs. Citizenship," 243.

22. Ibid., 244.

23. Pnina Werbner and Nira Yuval-Davis, eds., "Introduction: Women and the New Discourse of Citizenship," in *Women, Citizenship, and Difference*, 1–38 (London: Zed Books, 1999).

24. Canning, "Class vs. Citizenship," 242.

25. Ibid., 241.

26. Here I am very much following Kathleen Canning: "In proposing an understanding of citizenship as subjectivity, my intention is not to eschew the importance of the realms of law or the policies of states in designating the margins of inclusion and exclusion for specific communities or in defining the formal rights and obligations of their citizen-members. Rather my main interest is the process by which historical actors assigned meanings to the prescriptions and delineations of citizenship and hence became subjects in their encounters with citizenship laws, rhetorics, and practices." Ibid., 242.

27. In comparing German and French patterns of "national taste" during the 1920s in order to illuminate the respective coordinates of national citizenship thinking, Auslander seriously misconceives the pre-1914 German part of the story, underestimating the strength of the state-centered and broader drives for national cultural unification between the 1870s and 1914 while relying uncritically on Brubaker's "ethnocultural" thesis regarding German citizenship traditions. The novelty of the creation of a unitary German national state during the 1860s, in contrast with the longstanding existence of the French territorial state and its institutional infrastructure, is a better (and sufficient) starting point for considering Franco-German differences, in my view. See Leora Auslander, *Taste and Power: Furnishing Modern France* (Berkeley: University of California Press, 1996); Auslander, " 'National Taste?' Citizenship Law, State Form, and Everyday Aesthetics in Modern France and Germany, 1920–1940," in *The Politics of Consumption: Material Culture and Citizenship in Europe and America*, ed. Martin Daunton and Matthew Hilton, 109–28 (Oxford: Berg, 2001); Auslander, " 'Jewish Taste?' Jews and the Aesthetics of Everyday Life in Paris and Berlin, 1920–1942," in *Histories of Leisure*, ed. Rudy Koshar, 299–318 (Oxford: Berg, 2002). For a sampling of works that complicate the German picture, see note 8 above.

28. See especially Yasemin Soysal, *Limits of Citizenship: Migrants and Postnational Membership in Europe* (Chicago: University of Chicago Press, 1994).

29. See here John Torpey's very interesting extended review of Gosewinkel's *Einbürgern und Ausschließen*: John Torpey, "Review of Dieter Gosewinkel, *Einbürgern und Ausschließen: Die Nationalisierung der Staatsangehörigkeit vom Deutschen Bund bis zur Bundesrepublik Deutschland*," in *German Historical Institute London Bulletin* 24, no. 2 (2002), 87–93.

30. Ibid., 90.

31. See Palmerston's speech in parliament on the protection deserved by the Greek merchant David Pacifico, who had been born a British subject in Gibraltar on June 25, 1850, in Anthony Jay, ed., *The Oxford Dictionary of Political Quotations*, 2nd ed. (Oxford: Oxford University Press, 2001), 281: "I therefore fearlessly challenge the verdict which this House . . . is to give . . . whether, as the Roman, in days of old, held himself free from indignity, when he could say *Civis Romanus sum*; so also a British subject, in whatever land he may be, shall feel confident that the watchful eye and the strong arm of England will protect him against injustice and wrong."

Index